Laurence Oliphant, Rosamond Dale Owen, Haskett Smith

Scientific Religion

Higher Possibilities of Life And Practice Through the Operation of Natural Forces

Laurence Oliphant, Rosamond Dale Owen, Haskett Smith

Scientific Religion

Higher Possibilities of Life And Practice Through the Operation of Natural Forces

ISBN/EAN: 9783744753739

Printed in Europe, USA, Canada, Australia, Japan

Cover: Foto ©ninafisch / pixelio.de

More available books at **www.hansebooks.com**

SCIENTIFIC RELIGION

OR

HIGHER POSSIBILITIES OF LIFE AND PRACTICE
THROUGH THE OPERATION OF
NATURAL FORCES

BY

LAURENCE OLIPHANT

*WITH AN APPENDIX BY A CLERGYMAN OF
THE CHURCH OF ENGLAND*

Published for the Author by
WILLIAM BLACKWOOD AND SONS
EDINBURGH AND LONDON
MDCCCLXXXVIII

PREFACE.

In the last volume which I published, called 'Episodes in a Life of Adventure,' I said in the concluding chapter that the reason why I could not continue the records of my life beyond the year 1865, was because my attention, which had previously to that date been for some years directed to what is called "spiritualism," now became absorbed in a new and higher phase of investigation, which compelled me to abandon the pursuits and ambitions of the life I was leading, and retire from the world in order to surround myself by the most favourable conditions I could find under which to "prosecute my researches into the more hidden laws which govern human action and control events;" and I went on to say, that "although from time to time I have been suddenly forced from retirement into some of the most stirring scenes which have agitated Europe, the reasons which compelled me to participate in them were closely connected with the investigation in which I was engaged, the nature of which is so absorbing, and its results so encouraging, that it would not be possible for me now to abandon it, or to relinquish the hope which it has inspired, that a new moral future is dawning upon the human race—one, certainly, of which it stands much in need."

I did not then anticipate the possibility of my being

so soon called upon to publish my grounds for expressing this hope; but during a withdrawal of five months last summer, into the solitudes of Mount Carmel, I have felt myself irresistibly impelled to write the following pages, and they furnish the only answer I can give to my numerous critics who are kind enough to regret that I should have left the paths of diplomatic and political adventure "to wander amidst the phantoms and mirages of the occult science." Only those who have tried both are in a position to judge where the phantoms and mirages really are. As, however, access to books of reference, with which to support the conclusions at which I had arrived, was limited in so remote a spot, it was necessary for me to come to England, and my researches have more than fulfilled my expectations.

It has been impossible for me to do justice to the subject without intruding my own personality to an extent which would have been in the highest degree repellent to me, were it not that the results reached, seem to me of such general paramount importance as to supersede all other considerations, and that the experimental process by which they have been obtained, is a necessary prelude and explanation of them.

Excepting, however, where personal allusions are unavoidable, I have dispensed with them; while I earnestly trust that, in some minds at all events, the convictions which are here embodied as the result of long and arduous struggle and effort, may meet with a response.

LAURENCE OLIPHANT.

April 1888.

POSTSCRIPT TO THE PREFACE.

I FEEL impelled at the last moment to say one word with regard to the conditions under which this book was written. I had hesitated to do so until it was actually in the hands of the binder; but the problems of psychology are forcing themselves so strongly upon public attention, that I do not think that any experience which may throw light upon them should be withheld.

I became conscious on my arrival at Haifa last spring that a book, the plan of which I could not determine, was taking form in my mind, and pressing for external expression, and at once sat down to write it. I found the attempt to be vain; the ideas refused to arrange themselves, and I was strongly impressed that they could not do so, unless I went to a summer-house I have built in a remote part of Mount Carmel, and made the room from which the spirit of my wife had passed into the unseen, a little more than a year before, my private study, religiously preserving it from intrusion. I had no sooner taken my pen in hand under these circumstances, than the thoughts which find expression in the following pages were projected into my mind with the greatest rapidity, and irrespective of any mental study or prearrangement on my part, often overpowering my own preconceptions, and still more often presenting the subject treated of in an entirely new light to myself. On two or three occasions they ceased suddenly. I then found it was useless to try and formulate them by any effort of my brain, and at once abandoned the attempt to write for the day. The longest interval of this kind was three days. On the fourth I was again able to write with facility, and though always conscious of the effort of composition, it was never so severe as to cause me to pause for more than one or two minutes.

At the same time there was nothing, so far as I could judge, abnormal in my mental or physical condition. I was unaffected by trifling interruptions, and the ideas as they presented themselves seemed to be my own mingled with others projected from an unseen source, or new ideas struggling with and overpowering old ones with force that I could not resist. This must be my apology for a tone of authority which I should otherwise have been reluctant to impart to this book.

CONTENTS.

PART I.

INTRODUCTION.

Revolutionary tendency of modern thought—Its bearing upon theological dogma—Doubts and unsatisfied moral aspirations the result of spiritual quickening—The impending psychic crisis, and the moral and physical conflict which will result therefrom—Organic changes in man now in progress, . . 1

CHAPTER I.

Uncertainty attending all revelation purporting to be divine—Causes of this uncertainty—The responsibility of every man as the final judge of revelation—None of the most ancient revelations attempted to grapple with social and economic problems—Substitution almost immediately after Christ's death of a desire for personal salvation, in lieu of the practice of daily life inculcated by him—Theosophy, occultism, and mysticism, offer no remedy for the world's malady—Nature of Biblical inspiration examined—Later inspirational writings, . . 10

CHAPTER II.

Recent examination into the nature of the forces latent in the human organism—Hypnotic experiments in France, and the Psychical Research Society in England, familiarising the scientific mind with forces formerly ignored—Their origin in the unseen universe—Former conception of matter modified by recent discoveries—Sir Henry Roscoe on atoms—Inseparability of matter and force—Dynaspheric force—Scientific facts valuable, conclusions misleading—Hypnotic experiments witnessed by me in Paris—Hypnotism recognised by the medical faculty in France as dangerous—Spiritual insight necessary to discover the nature and origin of these forces, and to qualify the operator to deal with them, ... 28

CHAPTER III.

The interlocking of the invisible atoms of the seen and unseen worlds form a single system of animate nature—Glimpses into the invisible, conditioned on the moral state of the observer—Death a liberation of grosser atoms from those more sublimated—Material particles, the vehicles of force, constantly assuming new phases—*Anima mundi*—Interdependence of all created nature—Psychical experience attending the composition of "Sympneumata"—Duplex cerebral action—Vital atomic interaction between the living and the dead—Method of cerebral impregnation—Inspirations which do not grapple with the earth-malady, worthless—Christ, a radiative centre of healing force—The discipline of absolute self-sacrifice essential as a preparation to the highest inspiration—Defect in the Eastern systems of asceticism, ... 49

CHAPTER IV.

Introduction to the House-book; a treatise on domestic living, by the late Mrs Oliphant—Reasons why households should be formed to secure the advent of ideal good—Manner of life to be neither lavish nor parsimonious—Reasons for this—Religion now to be the possession of each man—All born to enact, what was formerly taught—Family groups, a machinery for social service—Necessity for the protection and nourishment of a home—All artificial distinctions of rank, occupations, and creeds abolished—Makers and maintainers of the family responsible for its development—The qualities required for social redemption—All to stand in sympathy with the laws of society, but not to be subjugated by them—Angelic co-operation with men—Division of responsibilities—Assistance in labour—Subordination to authority—Notes of expenditure, . . 64

CHAPTER V.

Insufficiency of the natural reason as a guide to divine truth, because it cannot divest itself of the ideas of time and space—

Hence theology and science both blind guides—Man the arena of conflicting atomic forces—Transmutation of material forces by conversion of moral particles—Methods and manifestations of infestation—Atomic constitution of moral atmosphere—Phenomena of heredity—Astrology—Will-force under specific influence—Faith-healing—Elixir of life—Radiation of divine life depends on magnetic conditions—Suffering involved thereby—Religion useless as a means to a personal end—World-regeneration to be accomplished by a radiation of divinely inspired human affection—Inspiration threefold: through union with God, man, and nature—Pollution of its current threefold: by pride, by selfishness, by apathy—Its force depends upon its concentration upon groups animated by the same motive, ... 84

CHAPTER VI.

History of the early Christian Church, a record of swift demoralisation; partly owing to desire to make converts, and partly to the substitution of a future life for present practice—Conflict between Rome and the East—Extinction of Gnostic sects destructive of much of the deeper truth—Compilation of the present canon of Scripture untrustworthy—Apocryphal gospels and epistles—"The teaching of the Twelve Apostles"—The Book of Enoch—The Church of England on the verge of a great moral revolution—The confessions of a parish priest—Need of a reformed Christianity, ... 102

CHAPTER VII.

Moral pall which shrouds earth's surface—Deterioration of moral atmosphere under invasion of Western civilisation—Christ's Christianity diametrically opposed to that of the Churches—False system of religious and secular education—Christendom: its politics, commerce, and finance, all on an infernal basis—Corruption of its Churches—Blindness and indifference of so-called Christians to the inconsistencies of their lives—Christian ethics buried under anti-Christian dogmas—A quickening of conscience taking place among the clergy—Canon Fremantle on the "New Reformation," 117

CHAPTER VIII.

The effect of dogmatic theology upon modern thought—The prejudices which it excites—The conflict between science and religion to which it has given rise—Intolerance both of theologians and men of science—Bigotry of the latter—Contradictions in which they have become involved—Facts of nature, discovered by superficial investigations, valuable—Empirical science incompetent to arrive at the divine truths in nature—This can only be achieved by development of inner faculties in man—Hence all scientific conjectures and hypotheses worthless—Conflicting utterances and conclusions of Professors Huxley and Tyndall illustrate this, ... 131

CHAPTER IX.

Religious systems: their uses and abuses—Aspiration demands inspiration—Religions extracted from the husk, instead of the kernel of revelation—Impossibility of demonstrating to the superficial reason, truths discovered by the inner faculties—Various channels and methods of inspiration—Development of subsurface consciousness—Magnetic condition of unseen world as related to ours—Attraction and repulsion depends on moral atomic affinities—Groups in the unseen with which every individual in the visible world is affiliated—So also with all Churches, religions, and sects—Christian, Buddhist, Moslem, and other religious organisations exist in the unseen, and inspire those here—Hence divergency of inspiration and religious intolerance, ... 143

CHAPTER X.

Force inconceivable except in connection with matter as a transmitting medium—The psyche or "spiritual body," the abode of the pneuma or "spirit"—Christ's birth and death established a new atomic relation between the seen and the unseen—The organisms of the seen and the unseen man described—Their relation to each other, and the methods of their interaction—The phenomena of spiritualism, occultism, hypnotism, telepathy, faith-healing, and thought-reading accounted for and explained under the operation of natural law—Phenomena unreliable as a guide to truth—Craving for it unwholesome and attended with danger—Insanity explained—Philosophy of death—Disease not an unmixed evil—Popular ideas of heaven, hell, purgatory, erroneous—Magnetic contact established between Christ and the world, the channel of a new moral reconstructive potency—The human and spiritual magnetic batteries now charged, and the consummation at hand—Qualities required in those who would co-operate in bringing it about, ... 159

CHAPTER XI.

The relation of man towards God, Christ, and the unseen world, here set forth, confirmed by the inner sense of the Bible—All sacred books have their hidden sense—Teaching of the Kabbalah and of the Fathers on this point—Inner sense of Christ's teaching has been lost, and the symbols and externals alone remain; hence superstition, bigotry, and hypocrisy — Frequent allusions to the "mystery" in the New Testament—St Paul's apprehension of it—The most ancient religions contain it in their universal conception of God, as an infinite paternal and maternal principle, pervading, animating, and sustaining all things by the "Word"—Judaism, which was an improved rendering of the Egyptian and Chaldean religions, contained it concealed in the Mosaic law, of which Christ was the fulfilment—Genesis composed and compiled under a most powerful inspiration—Mysticism: its uses and abuses, . . . 184

CHAPTER XII.

Masculine and feminine atomic elements—Sentient and non-sentient atoms—The Deity of the Bible, as well as of former sacred records, masculine and feminine—Effect of the divine maternity on man—Revelation by the Spirit, which is feminine, a personal one—This mystery contained in the hidden sense of both Old and New Testaments, ... 201

PART II.

CHAPTER XIII.

The generation of universes—First chapter of Genesis describes the creation by emanation of a previous universe—Analysis of its hidden meaning—The rebellion of Lucifer—Archangels or Seraphim, and arch-demons or Siddim—The first Adam, or Adam Cadmon, ... 219

CHAPTER XIV.

Second chapter of Genesis describes creation by emanation of our world — Analysis of its hidden meaning — The birth of bisexual man—Ancient beliefs in his androgynous nature—Story of his fall—And separation into two distinct sexes—Structural changes consequent thereon, ... 229

CHAPTER XV.

The origin of evil—Mixed conditions in the genesis of earth—Evolution of the first forms of life, under the opposing influences of Seraphim and Siddim—The Garden of Eden—Man's mission—Method of its accomplishment—The earth-malady caused by the pollution of its sex-life—Its purification possible—Nature of the struggle for purity thus involved, . . 243

CHAPTER XVI.

The first period of the race—Esoteric sense of the conflict between Cain and Abel—The mark of Cain—The introduction of physiological birth—Of polygamy—The fate of the Lamech races—Invasion of the planet by the Siddim—Their mixed progeny—The Book of Enoch—The deluge—Earliest cosmogonic traditions—The golden age, ... 256

CHAPTER XVII.

The Noachic race—The guardians of the mystery—Transmitted to the Abramic—Magnetic conditions of the Holy Land—The Divine Trinity of the early religions—Analogy of the religion of Accad with that of the Jews—The secret contained in the law of Moses—The fulfilment of the law—Effect of modern criticism on Judaism, ... 271

CHAPTER XVIII.

The mission of the Jews—The mystery of the Divine Feminine confided to them—The vision of Isaiah—The Divine Feminine enfolded in Christ—The method of His birth—Jewish belief in the Messiah—The Virgin Mary—Nature of the descent of the feminine principle—Covenants with the Jews—Reasons why they should recognise in this principle their Messiah, . . 290

CHAPTER XIX.

The true position of woman—The false position assigned her by civilisation—Her new functions in life—The descent of the Divine Feminine through her—The co-operative struggle of the sexes for purity—Woman's rights—The true higher education of woman, ... 314

CONTENTS. xiii

CHAPTER XX.

Method of the descent of the Divine Feminine—And of its reception by woman—The Sympneuma—Introduction of the Divine Feminine into the world, through the birth, life, death, resurrection, and ascension of Christ—The outpouring on the disciples on the Day of Pentecost—The sympneumatic consciousness, ... 326

CHAPTER XXI.

The sympneumatic descent—Its infernal simulation—The function of bisexual atoms—Contact with pneumatic centres—Social conventionalities impede male and female co-operation—Insane delusions—The relation of Christ to man through woman illustrated by St Paul—Kabbalistic interpretations, . . 340

CHAPTER XXII.

The twelfth and thirteenth chapters of the Book of Revelation interpreted—The effect of Christ's mission to earth upon the upper invisible region of our world—Concealment of the Divine Feminine—The two witnesses—The functions of John the Baptist—His relation to Christ—Temporary triumph of the Infernal Feminine—The Beast, Anti-Christendom, or the Gentile Church—The mark of the Beast, the false cross—Man's present relation to Christ, ... 362

CHAPTER XXIII.

The fourteenth and following chapters of Revelation interpreted—Collision on earth between the sympneumatic and anti-sympneumatic forces—Catastrophic changes in consequence—The fate of the Siddim—The triumph of the saints—The Second Advent, and the descent of the Bride—Recapitulation, . . 379

APPENDIX I., extracts from the Kabbalah, . . . 391
APPENDIX II., by a Clergyman of the Church of England, . 401

ERRATA.

Page 165, line 2 from top, *for* "dialectric" *read* "dielectric."
" 235, line 2 from foot, *for* "Salvine" *read* "Salome."

PART I.

SCIENTIFIC RELIGION;

OR,

HIGHER POSSIBILITIES OF LIFE AND PRACTICE

THROUGH THE

OPERATION OF NATURAL FORCES.

INTRODUCTION.

REVOLUTIONARY TENDENCY OF MODERN THOUGHT—ITS BEARING UPON THEOLOGICAL DOGMA—DOUBTS AND UNSATISFIED MORAL ASPIRATIONS THE RESULT OF SPIRITUAL QUICKENING—THE IMPENDING PSYCHIC CRISIS, AND THE MORAL AND PHYSICAL CONFLICT WHICH WILL RESULT THEREFROM—ORGANIC CHANGES IN MAN NOW IN PROGRESS.

It would be superfluous here to do more than cursorily allude to the remarkable moral and intellectual movement which has characterised the last half-century; it has been resumed in the literature of the jubilee year. The great problems of life are assuming a new form, as the theological landmarks are gradually fading away beneath the flood of light which has been let into them by theological research, antiquarian discovery, scientific investigation, and psychical phenomena; and men in their trouble are peering earnestly into the new region which is being thus illuminated, for a new order which they may substitute for the old—some vital truth-principle which shall conduce to a purer and nobler social life; for, though the dogmas crumble away one after the other, and the dry-rot of ecclesiasticism becomes daily more apparent, the religious instinct is more quickened than ever, and in proportion as men under its influence emancipate themselves from what they now perceive to be the ignorance, prejudice, or superstition of a dark age, do their aspirations strain after something higher and better, while their belief in the possible realisation of ideals, hitherto deemed unattainable, grows stronger. Nevertheless, this yearning for, and searching after, higher truth by the more advanced minds of the age, is attended by a consciousness of unrest and anxiety, often almost amounting to a vague feeling of alarm. There is a sense of chaotic surroundings, of unstable footing, of shrinking from the plunge into the unknown; and many of the weaker sort, after going a little way, become troubled as to their own future, and—deficient in such a love for humanity as should induce them to dare all for its sake, and in such a faith in God as should lift them out of all personal anxieties—they scramble back into what they were brought up to believe was an ark of personal safety. There they find comparative rest among those whose consciences have not yet been stirred to any perception of the fearful inconsistencies of their conduct; who distinguish between things religious and things secular; who are content to profess in pulpit and in pew on Sunday, moral axioms which they openly violate in almost every act of their daily lives, and who do this in all good faith, in the sincere belief that they are pleasing God, and following the example of their Lord and Master Jesus Christ, and will win for themselves heaven thereby. It is because they are in this morally darkened condition—the result mainly of fear of punishment and hope of reward—that they shrink appalled from the conclusions of modern investigations, and refuse to receive any light which should pierce into the gloomy nooks and musty corners of their most unchristian creed, and which should force upon them an investigation into the errors of their present faith, and into the reasons why they are utterly unable to carry out in their daily conduct, and not merely to pronounce with their lips, the moral teachings of their nominal Master.

In strong contrast with these is the class who live under the full blaze of the light to which I have alluded, but who are morally unaffected by it. "It is a useful light," they say, "for looking into the past,—it has even some interest materially with regard to the present,—but it is useless so far as the future is concerned. It has been valuable as showing us the extent of our ignorance, and in revealing to us the many delusions in which we have been living, but it conveys no other truth to us; on the contrary, it presents to us insoluble problems with more distinctness than before, and it has no power of penetrating these for others, further than it penetrates them for us. The limit of our range of vision under its influence must necessarily be the limit of theirs, and inasmuch as all that it shows us is that we don't know more than it shows us, (which is very little, because it does not penetrate below the surface of things, or beyond what we call the 'material'), therefore, what is impenetrable surface for us must be impenetrable surface for everybody else, and what we call the material must be material for everybody else, and we refuse to admit that anybody can see further or have more light than we have." The analogy does not seem to occur to such persons, that some people are naturally more short-sighted than others, and are obliged to wear spectacles; did they not refuse to admit that spectacles exist for facilitating such internal vision as I am about to describe, they might possibly be furnished with them. In the meantime, there is far more hope for this class than for the one with which I have contrasted it, for though "the light that is in them is darkness," they have the honesty to say so,—moreover, the light is in them unconsciously to themselves, and may burst out at any moment; but the others, more especially in the countries where the Greek or Roman Catholic religions prevail, have created their own darkness out of the bigotries, the superstitions, ignorance, and cruelty of ages, and they wrap it round them and call it light.

There is another class, again, who are not troubled by the problems of life; who consider that the pursuit of pleasure, fame, or wealth is the sane, laudable, and reasonable occupation of a human being, inasmuch as, for aught they know, they may have no continuity of existence beyond this life. They ordinarily profess so-called Christianity, nevertheless, as a matter of convenience, but differ from the ardent votaries of that cult, in that they are governed by an enlightened selfishness as to the present, instead of as to the hereafter. They also are in a more hopeful condition than these latter; for their consciences are torpid, not perverted, and are therefore more susceptible to the electric shock of the divine touch.

Far be it from me to say, however, that there are not thousands still embedded in existing forms of ecclesiasticism, who are daily becoming more highly sensitised morally; whose aspirations are as noble, whose loves are as pure, whose motives are as disinterested, as those of any of the earnest and devout truth-seekers and unbelievers in the popular theology; but this is in spite of its dogmas, not in consequence of them. Such men have always existed in the period immediately preceding reform in any religion, but they have always had the masses of their co-religionists against them; and indications of an approaching schism of a far more profound character than any of which we have any historical record since the disciples were first called Christians at Antioch, are apparent to those who watch the spiritual horizon. To them a cloud bigger than a man's hand is visible above it.

For the processes of the divine quickening are moving steadily forward, generating vital impulses which will prove uncontrollable to those who come under their influence, and suggesting an irresistible instinct for aggregation. Upon all classes, and in diverse countries, taking no account of race, or creed, or colour, does this new life descend; and as those who are stirred by it move, do they recognise their affinity to others similarly affected, and the magnetic attraction which is inherent in the vivifying principle, draws them together, at present slowly and athwart obstacles that would seem insurmountable—for in the early stages the recipients of this life feel weak and bewildered. Crushed by the weight of dry bones around them and above them, their first struggles are feeble and misdirected; they know not in which direction to look for help; the old deadness seems still to chain them to the spot where they first felt the vital touch, and yet they long above all things to leave it. Progress they feel is impossible in the midst of the old surroundings. The atmosphere feels charged with mephitic vapour, which sometimes appears even to interfere with the ordinary respiration. There is a sensation of struggle between the new life and the old, and the potency of the descending vigours seems at times as though it would destroy the outer bodily frame. It is the putting "the new wine into the old bottles," but the new wine takes no account of the condition of the bottle. Often it bursts it, and the spirit, vitalised and released, leaves its earthly shell, to carry on, from another vantage-point, the same work for humanity on this globe, which would have been allotted to it in its fleshly tabernacle.

It would be hopeless, however, to attempt to give any complete description of the mode of operation of this new life-principle, for in no two cases are the phenomena which attend its descent into the human organism similar in their manifestation, while each who has been conscious of its influence has a varied experience to recount.

With some, as I have said, it produces what may be called a life-and-death struggle; with others the physical organism does not suffer, while the moral anguish is acute; with some it is sudden, and seems to overwhelm and paralyse by the intensity of the shock; with others, it steals over them so slowly and so gradually—the preparation for its reception has been spread over so long a period of time—that there is comparatively little suffering, as the first perception of the change which is being operated dawns upon the consciousness. Sooner or later, however, spiritual suffering must ensue, though this varies much in degree, depending on moral conditions which it is not necessary now to enter upon. The main point upon which I wish to insist is the fact, with regard to which I have had abundant evidence during the last quarter of a century —and not I alone—that a spiritual wave is at present rolling in upon the world of a character unprecedented in its past history; that it is daily gathering force, and is already crest high. Before very long it will break; and the object of this book is to prepare men's minds for a crisis in the history of the planet which cannot, I think, be very long deferred, but which will take a very different form from that which is usually anticipated; for it *is* anticipated—anticipated in all the existing forms of religion, down to those which may almost be called heathen superstitions — anticipated by a dumb instinct in the minds of men who cannot be said to have any religion. It is in the air; and only those of a peculiarly dense and unsusceptible temperament are absolutely without consciousness of it. It will be a moral rather than a physical crisis; and its tendency will be (to use a Scriptural expression) to separate the sheep from the goats, and to bind together, in a way which no Churches have ever succeeded in doing, those who fight for the Powers of Light against those who fight for the Powers of Darkness. It will sweep away the present ecclesiasticisms, and substitute for them a religion in which there shall be "one body that hath many 'members, and all the members of that one body, being many, 'shall be one body. So also is Christ. For by one spirit we 'shall all be baptised into one body, whether we be Jews or 'Gentiles, whether we be bond or free; and we shall all be 'made to drink into one Spirit."[1] Now this one body can only be created, under the influence of that one vitalising principle to which I have already referred, by the strenuous co-operation and ardent effort of those who are conscious that they have received it, and the effort to create it will entail a struggle of stupendous proportions with the corrupt principle to which the misery and degradation of the world has been due. It is this struggle which will be so critical for the human race, for it involves an issue of inconceivable magnitude, and must be carried on under conditions which will develop many new and terrible experiences, and call into operation laws which have been more or less hidden from scientific investigation, though of late years these have been dimly perceived, and in a superficial manner experimented upon by some of the first scientific men in Europe. In a word, it will be a psychical rather than a physical conflict, though I do not mean to say that the ordinary weapons of so-called "civilised warfare" will not be called into requisition.

Now many have received, and are receiving, accessions of the special potency which shall enable them to engage in this

[1] Romans xii. 4, 5; 1 Corinthians xii. 12, 13.

warfare, without any due conception of its nature. They are conscious of a moral disturbance within them, of new experiences which they shrink from alluding to, and of which in some instances they even entertain a certain feeling of dread. Sometimes new light dawns upon them, relieving them of moral perplexity—at others, new sensations stir their nervous centres; they rise at times to conditions of exaltation which fill them with joy for which there is no adequate external cause, or sink into profound depths of despondency equally unaccountable. They may even be treated for hysteria by their doctors, who are none the less profoundly puzzled to know what hysteria is, and totally in the dark on the subject. All these are indications that they are being subject to the influences which are about to make war against each other in human organisms, and that the moment has come when those who know, or think they know, what these signs of the times mean, should not be deterred from throwing whatever light may have been vouchsafed upon it, by the hostile criticism of the majority—whose intelligence, by reason of their organic denseness, is still beclouded upon the subject. But before attempting to do this, it is expedient that I should explain how this light may be gained; for rays are shot athwart the spiritual firmament from opposing directions—lurid rays from below, flickering rays of many colours and from many diverse quarters. To no human being has it ever been given to transmit untainted the white ray that issues from the throne of the Most High, for our world could not bear the fierceness of its splendour. All revelation which proceeds from the invisible must be relative in its value, all inspiration imperfect. It behoves us, therefore, to consider, in our search after divine truth, how we are to judge of the value of revelation, and to arrive in our minds at a definite idea of what we mean by "inspiration."

I shall endeavour in the following pages to discuss the functions and characteristics of those subtle atomic forces in nature, which are now attracting increased attention on the part of the learned and the thoughtful,—show how they act upon man morally, intellectually, and physically; or, in other words, in what sense they stimulate his aspirations, control his inspirations, and affect his bodily health,—and consider further their practical bearing upon those biological and theological theories and problems which tend at present to confuse his religious instinct, and cloud his perceptions of the beautiful, the good, and the true.

Finally, I will offer the solution of those problems and theories which, under the operation of these forces, has been revealed to me.

I would only say in conclusion, that it would not be right for any man, desiring to know whether this inspiration is true or not, to begin by believing it after the manner of the Churches: no belief can stand in these days that is not based upon the evidence of personal experience. These are not things that one man can prove to another; all he can do is to say, that in all cases where certain experiments have been faithfully made, they have been attended with the same results. It is left to each to make them or not, as he chooses; but I should be highly culpable,—having tested them in my own person, having seen them tested in the persons of others, and having received what I feel to be a strong internal direction to place before others the conclusion at which I have arrived,—to allow myself to be deterred from doing so by any sense of my own incapacity to do justice to so great a theme—which is profound—by any fear of the hostility or ridicule which it may excite, or by any anticipation of failure to reach the hearts of those to whom it is addressed. The issues are with God, and His servants know not the word disappointment, for they are incapable of reading His designs. Only this they know, that the slightest hesitation in obeying what they believe to be a divine impulse, produces a suffering more intense than any consequences which may accrue to them from the world. If, in my attempt to exhibit the dangers to which moral progress is exposed by the present methods of theology and science, and their antagonism to each other, I have spoken more hardly of the two classes engaged in these pursuits than the circumstances seem to warrant, it has not been from any want of the deepest respect for good men wherever they are to be found, or however much in error they may appear to me to be.

Error is only dangerous when it is aggressive—and to

meet error of this description, when one is convinced by one's own personal experience that it is error, a certain attitude of aggression seems to be imposed upon one; but it is consistent with an entire tolerance and charity for individuals, and is, in fact, only applicable to those who are thoroughly honest and in earnest, even if their earnestness be misdirected.

CHAPTER 1.

UNCERTAINTY ATTENDING ALL REVELATION PURPORTING TO BE DIVINE—CAUSES OF THIS UNCERTAINTY—THE RESPONSIBILITY OF EVERY MAN AS THE FINAL JUDGE OF REVELATION—NONE OF THE MOST ANCIENT REVELATIONS ATTEMPTED TO GRAPPLE WITH SOCIAL AND ECONOMIC PROBLEMS—SUBSTITUTION ALMOST IMMEDIATELY AFTER CHRIST'S DEATH OF A DESIRE FOR PERSONAL SALVATION IN LIEU OF THE PRACTICE OF DAILY LIFE INCULCATED BY HIM—THEOSOPHY, OCCULTISM, AND MYSTICISM, OFFER NO REMEDY FOR THE WORLD'S MALADY—NATURE OF BIBLICAL INSPIRATION EXAMINED—LATER INSPIRATIONAL WRITINGS.

THE main cause of religious difference at all times has arisen from the attempt to define the indefinable, and this has necessarily involved the use of terms either not susceptible of accurate definition, or for which none could be found by common consent.

By the use of precise terms, on the exact meaning of which everybody was agreed, angry theologians would have often been saved the disagreeable duty—imposed upon them, as they believed, by their consciences and their love for God and their fellows—of flying at each other's throats, and many stumbling-blocks would have been removed from the path of earnest truth-seekers. This latter daily increasing class refuse to be satisfied with ancient theological formulæ and unproven hypotheses. The fact that they happen to be born in a country in which a certain form of faith has prevailed for a certain number of centuries, is no longer a convincing reason that that form of faith must be the right one. They have gone back in their investigations, behind what has been considered the only sacred record of divine truth, to see what the most ancient peoples believed before that record was compiled; for they remember that it is written therein, "In the beginning was the Word," and that the great Teacher said, "Before Abraham was, I am;" and they know that before Abraham was, mighty nations existed, with their aspirations after God and their worship of Him, and that He must therefore have revealed Himself to them in some form or other long before the law was given to the Jews. They have gone forward in their investigations into the domain of psychical science, and have encountered phenomena which throw new light upon the faith of their childhood, and which force upon them considerations which seem to increase their responsibilities to a degree unknown to a previous generation. When so much doubt is cast upon the old belief, when so many new possibilities for belief of another kind are springing into existence, it becomes a matter of supreme importance to consider the processes by which God has revealed Himself to man, and to estimate the values which are to be attached to those processes.

Revelation purporting to be divine has always come through human instrumentality, and it has differed according to the race, country, moral condition, and temperament of the transmitting medium, and the people to whom it was addressed. Whatever may subsequently have been the view of the disciples concerning the greatest teachers that the world has seen, as to their superhuman natures, there was nothing to distinguish them, as far as we know, in outward appearance, from other men. They depended for their authority on their words and on their acts; so their words were considered inspired, their acts miraculous. The disciples of the founders of all the principal religions of the world, have appealed to the wonders that their masters could perform, as an evidence of the truth of their teaching; and it is only since modern investigation has ventured into the regions of the psychical and the occult, that men are beginning to perceive that thaumaturgy possesses no value as an evidence for or against moral truth, and that the word "miracle" is misleading, if by that term is implied a violation of the laws of nature; as is also the term "inspiration," if by that word is implied an infallible communication to man from God.

It does not follow from this, however, that God does not

communicate with man, and that the communications do not receive strong confirmation, to the recipient of them, through the operation of laws which have hitherto been concealed from the ordinary man, of a nature which he, ignorant of these laws, might term miraculous. It was not to be wondered at that in an age when the intellect had not been divorced from the affections to the extent that it is now, and when the emotional and intuitive faculties were more highly developed, the tendency was towards superstition, and towards the recognition, in the exercise of occult powers, of the direct intervention of a Divine Being, and in the utterances of men thus gifted, of the voice of God.

The tendency of modern philosophy is to react to the exactly opposite extreme; to deny the existence of occult powers altogether, and to consider the most lofty utterances of men nothing more than the result of chemical changes in their brains, which thus inspire the ideas which they put into words.

The truth will be found to be between these two extremes; and this imposes upon us the consideration, which is vital to those engaged in the pursuit of divine knowledge, of the real meaning of inspiration.

No attempt, so far as I am aware, has ever been made by theologians to analyse the process by which the will of God is conveyed to the mind of man with such certainty that the human recipient shall not be mistaken as to the divine source, and that his fellow-men should not be mistaken as to the claims of the human recipient. It always resolves itself into this—that each man must himself be the supreme judge and arbiter of whether what is so conveyed, is, or is not, a communication from God. This is a fearful responsibility laid upon every man; and yet how few realise that there can be no higher test of inspiration for any man than he is himself: from this position there is no escape. If he attempts to shirk the responsibility by saying, "I will accept in this matter the teaching of the Church in which I was born," he only increases it; for he then becomes the final judge of the claims of the Church in which he was born to decide upon what is and what is not divine inspiration; and in determining to abdicate his own right to judge, in favour of another authority, upon him alone rests the responsibility of deciding upon the competence of that authority. It is thus that God lays upon each one of us the obligation of finding out truth for ourselves.

It will probably be urged that this obligation is incompatible with the multifarious duties of daily life—that it would be unreasonable to expect that the masses in their ignorance, in their struggle for existence, and the absorbing cares which it involves, should devote themselves to theological research, should study the sacred records of all religions, and that each unit should decide for himself or herself, upon the respective claims of revelations professing to be divinely inspired. If divine truth were to be discovered by a study of "divinity," in the sense in which that term is used among Christian theologians, or by contemplation, as enjoined by the religions of the East, the task would indeed be hopeless, and the objection would be unanswerable; but I propose to show that it is not a question of judging of rival existing inspirations, but of every man receiving his own message for himself in a fuller manner than he can obtain it from any book or from any pulpit; and that in proportion as he is prepared to make every sacrifice in order to receive it, will he gain strength to fulfil his daily round of duties even to their most minute details. The days of bibliolatry and of priestcraft are drawing to an end; for with the descent of the divine vital principle to which I have alluded in the last chapter—and which the Churches call the Messiah—into every man's organism who opens himself to receive it, will he rise out of ecclesiasticisms, with their forms and ceremonies, into "the liberty wherewith Christ has made him free."

It must not be concluded from this, however, that the Bible and the Churches have not been of inestimable value to humanity, while they have no less been the cause of sanguinary wars and bitter persecutions. Without venturing to question the divine methods of operation with man, or to enter upon any attempt of an exposition of the laws by which those methods are governed, we can recognise in the sacred literature which has inspired the world with its religious sentiment, however crude or distorted, the divine afflatus; and in its varied forms of worship, the most powerful restraining influence which their adherents were capable of obeying in their daily lives. In all cases the sacred record and the sacred rites, with the functions of the ministry, were adapted to the moral and intellectual condition of those for whom they were intended. It is because these moral and intellectual conditions have undergone such vast changes during this century, that the book and the Churches which have guided and controlled the nations of the West so long, must be interpreted and renewed by the light of fresh revelations, and by a more direct outpouring of the divine vitality upon human organisms than they have been heretofore prepared for,—revelations, the truth of which each man can test for himself, and which will rest on the experiences which he himself must make in his search after them; for the time has arrived when he refuses any longer to put his conscience in the hands of a priest, or unintelligently to accept dogmas because he was taught them in his childhood, or to blind himself to the anomalies and inconsistencies which certain doctrines involve, and which are so faithfully reflected in the daily lives of those who profess them.

The reason why the inspirations upon which the most ancient religions were founded, so often contradicted themselves and each other, and why their prophets so often prophesied falsely, was because they had lost sight of the great truth, that the highest inspiration comes through physical as well as intellectual service for the race; for the laws which govern the transmission of moral potency into man, are so interwoven with those which control the development of his physical energies, and the purest life influxes are so conditioned on the equal distribution of its currents through the physical, affectional, and intellectual human systems, that the undue expansion of any one of these at the expense of the others, must of necessity distort the ultimate manifestation, whether in word or deed. Hence we find that with all the beauties of the earliest religious expressions, there is the fatal defect of unpracticality. Not one of them attempts a radical, political, social, and industrial reform with the hope of striking at the root of the world's evil.

The most ancient religious records which exist are the Egyptian hieroglyphics and the Accadian and earliest Vedantic hymns, which contain mythical accounts of the struggles of divinely inspired heroes with the Powers of Darkness; symbolising in mystical language the cosmogony of the world and the progress of the human soul towards perfection; concealing, in images incomprehensible to the people, many truths of deep spiritual import, the true meaning of which have only been partially retained by the initiated. In them may be traced analogies to the mysteries concealed in the Druid, Chaldean, Persian, Jewish, Greek, and other ancient minor religious communities; but while some of these inculcated morality of the highest character, and while even those among them which ultimately degenerated into the worship of many gods, retained in their essence the worship of the one true God, they did not grapple with the social and economic problems of life. They made no attempt to construct society upon a basis which should enable men to give practical effect to it in their daily lives. With the suppression of the mystical sects in the early Christian Church, and with the inauguration upon a substantial basis of the present system of Christian ecclesiasticism, about the close of the second century after Christ, the so-called "heresies," which were the legacy that oriental mysticism had bequeathed to the West, gradually faded; and with them some of the deep internal truths which they contained, notwithstanding their many errors and exaggerations, were lost. Henceforward religion in the West became, not the repository of occult knowledge of mysteries more or less divine, but a system by which men were assured of their escape from eternal torments, and their safe passage to endless joys. While incidentally pure life and right conduct were enjoined, it was only as a means to this end; and as it was evident that no man could by his own efforts win the immortal crown for which all were striving, they were consoled by the further assurance that this was already achieved for those who would believe that God had sacrificed Himself (or His Son who was Himself) on the cross for the purpose. The whole tendency of this teaching was to fix men's minds far more intensely upon the future than upon the present; and as its cardinal principle in regard to the future was the selfish attainment of everlasting bliss, it followed as a natural consequence in most cases, that their object in the present life was to secure to themselves earthly happiness, or, if they feared that this might injure their eternal wellbeing, to lead them into asceticism.

This religion of selfishness has practically stimulated competition for the acquisition of money, because it is considered the chief ingredient of that earthly happiness; and the result has been a steady progress in the arts both of peace and war, and that strange compound of vast accumulations of wealth, of hideous depths of misery, poverty, and degradation, of luxury and squalor, of gigantic industrial and commercial enterprise, of huge standing armies and most formidable inventions for the destruction of human life, of rapid means of communication, of extraordinary intellectual activity, of international rivalries, jealousies, and lust of territory, and of universal competition, inciting to new forms of dishonesty, and new impulsions to hate, which goes by the name of "Christian civilisation." So far from there being any tendency in this outcome of so-called Christianity to build up society, its whole scope is toward its disintegration, and we are at this day trembling on the verge of a social revolution, which even physically as well as morally threatens to explode it.

The consequence is that the increasing hold which their material interests have acquired over men's minds, combined with the progress which has been made in external science, to the utter exclusion of all knowledge except that based on what they can see and feel, has produced a materialistic movement, which the Churches—to which indirectly it was primarily due—are utterly unable to stem, except in those parts of Eastern Europe where the people are still immersed in the grossest ignorance and superstition; and here it is only a matter of time.

The result of nearly 1900 years of Christianity is, that if Christ were to appear in the flesh in Christendom He would be unable to find a follower; for His literal moral teaching is practically ignored, and He could certainly not call Himself a Christian. He would be more at home among the people of His own race, for they only crucified Him once, but the Christians crucify Him daily. As, however, no human invention could extinguish the vitality of the seed which He planted in the world during His short term of existence upon it, the nature of which will be discussed later, the civilisation which calls itself by His name has still more divine life in it than the relative barbarism of the East. Under its influence alone is woman seeking her true position, though she has not yet found it; and in Christendom alone is there a burning desire on the part of a growing class of men and women, to rise out of the sham into the realisation of the true Christianity, to embody the ideal life at any personal sacrifice, and to spare neither money nor energy, fame nor position, if so be that by their efforts they might contribute towards laying a single stone of the foundations of a social system in which the relations of man to woman, and of man to his fellow-man, should be divinely regulated, and which should be built upon the corner-stones of sex-purity and mutual co-operation.

Hence it is that the Eastern races, with their mystical religions which neither terrify nor bribe, have lagged behind so-called Christendom. They have neither risen so high nor fallen so low; they have not conceived of new virtues nor invented new vices, for they had no spurs to goad them in either direction; they continue to treat sacred things with a genuine reverence and respect, while hypocrisy may be considered a Christian speciality; and, excepting so far as they have been influenced by the education introduced by their conquerors, they live in the daily moral practice of their ancestors. At the same time it is probable, to judge from their sacred books, that the general standard was higher when they were written; for men in the ancient times were evidently more open to occult influences than they have been in these more recent centuries, and it was doubtless this fact which produced that tendency to mysticism which proved in the end highly detrimental to moral, intellectual, or material progress. For already in the Vedantic period we find the practice of asceticism enjoined as essential to the mystical union of man with God; while Buddha, despite his intense sympathy for the sufferings of humanity, can suggest nothing better to his disciples than to practise self-hypnotisation by sitting under a bo-tree, and induce pious contemplation by keeping their eyes fixed on the tips of their noses. So in the fifth century we hear of Christian mystics gazing at their stomachs until they saw the light of Tabor issuing. The consequence of the special diet and of the solitary practices thus enjoined, was naturally to lead to trance obsession, which resulted in an inspiration that has proved of no earthly benefit to the human race, and which finds expression among its votaries in England, in such specific directions for obtaining a knowledge of divine truth as these—

"Hold fast to that which has neither substance nor ex-'istence.

"Listen only to the voice which is soundless.

"Look only on that which is invisible alike to the inner and 'the outer sense."[1]

Doubtless a chief fascination of mysticism with a large class of minds was the phenomenal development of certain faculties which men acquired, in the degree in which they succeeded in overcoming all natural appetites, and divinely implanted human instincts: the power of levitation, of suppressed respiration for incredible periods, of control over material substances, and of performing many other wonders, was calculated to impress the ignorant, and invest them with supernatural attributes and authority, which, in spite of the unselfishness that they practised theoretically, was gratifying to the natural man.

Those who deny the possibility of such phenomena can satisfy themselves on the subject by personal experiment, provided always that they have faith. Let any English philosopher, who is ready to make the necessary sacrifice, begin by accepting the hypothesis as possible that he can upset the laws of gravitation and sit in the air, or otherwise perform so-called miracles; let him go to India and sit for ten or fifteen years under a bo-tree, staring most of the time at one object; let him live on nothing but lentils and water, with perhaps a little fruit, avoid all contact with his fellowman, practise constantly holding his breath, and sleep as little as possible; it will not be long before he will pass occasionally into states of semi-consciousness to external things, which he will plainly distinguish from sleep, and if he does not die

[1] Light on the Path, p. 22.

in the process (which he probably will not do if his faith is strong enough), he will find himself at last developing forces undreamed of in his philosophy. Until he has done so he is not in a position to deny the existence or the extent of potencies which are latent in the human organism, in the face of the testimony of those who have investigated these phenomena on the spot, and of such well-known instances as that of the "burying fakir"; upon whom the experiment was officially conducted with every possible precaution by the Government of India.

There has never been much difficulty in recruiting the ranks of ascetics in India; and in proportion as they pass beyond this life into the other, and increase in numbers there, does their action upon this world become more powerful. Hence it is that we have seen within the last few years a movement in the direction of ancient oriental mysticism, which would not have been possible did not a very powerful society exist in the invisible world, which has taken advantage of the increased attenuated condition of the odylic sphere of this one to make an inroad into it. At the same time, the revival of mysticism on its old lines, at this period of the world's history, is not possible. Had it nothing to contend against but materialism and ecclesiasticism, the struggle might not be unequal; but there is another spiritual descent taking place more powerful than that which has developed into theosophic, hermetic, spiritualistic, and occult societies, and which, though working silently and apparently slowly, is none the less surely gathering its forces, not merely in the unseen world, but in the organisms of men and women in this one.

As the heat which this new life generates, and the light which streams from it, warms and irradiates the world, the latest scientific theory will share the fate of the oldest theological superstition, or the newest fashion of mysticism and the evolution of man from amœbæ, his eternal punishment in torments, in spite of the attempt of God to save him from them by suffering death, and the journey yet in store for him through successive "rounds," before he can hope to reach Nirvana, will all alike be relegated to the limbo of exploded fallacies; for a divine science will be built upon the *débris* of that which is purely human and superficial, a divine religion replace that which has been degraded by man's inventions, and divine mysteries supersede those which have been derived from sources more or less impure. The reason why this will be so is, that the growing desire to find truth will lead men to seek from God their own inspirations, and in the degree in which that desire is sincere and absolutely disinterested, they will find themselves magnetically attracted to each other by an impulse of co-operation in its pursuit, and will discover that mutual unselfish service is the first condition of the highest internal illumination: provided always that the mind is kept entirely free from prejudice or preconceived opinions; that the affections are emancipated from the thraldom which is imposed by ties of race, country, or family, in order that they may be bestowed freely upon humanity; and that, while it may be necessary for them to live in the world, they have internally dissevered themselves from it so completely, that they are uninfluenced by its public opinion, totally unaffected by its censure, and absolutely indifferent to its praise, with which, indeed, it is extremely improbable that they would be favoured.

In order to make clear the nature of this new inspiration, it will be necessary to describe its mode of operation, and discuss and contrast it with the old. The reason why old inspirations were defective, and the religions founded upon them degenerated so rapidly into superstitions, was because an equilibrium was not maintained between the physical, intellectual, and emotional functions—in other words, between body, soul, and spirit. Prophets were generally poets, often dreamers, rarely thinkers, never workers. It was to intensify this faculty of peering into the future, or, in other words, of looking into the world of substance—of which, though invisible to us, this is merely the shadow—and, by perceiving what was happening there, foretelling what would happen here (time being merely relative to our shadowy present, and having no real existence in itself), that they developed exclusively one side of their nature. But inasmuch as when they saw visions and dreamed dreams, they were in special conditions differing from those of other men, partly the result of heredity or constitutional temperament, and partly induced by fasting and self-hypnotisation, it was impossible for them to know whether what they saw, or what was impressed upon them during these states, was real or phantasmagoric. The unseen world teems with intelligences, whose action upon this one is very direct, and is governed by laws, most of which are hidden from us, and those which are known, imperfectly known only to the few, and not yet comprehensible to the many. A man thus open to that world, becomes a point of attraction, round which invisible hosts cluster, some with the desire of infusing into his mind, or presenting to his internal vision fallacies, or pictorial representations of them, others with the desire of protecting him against these malignant attempts to deceive, and of conveying to him images of truth. In other words, the powers of light and the powers of darkness war over him. But inasmuch as the laws which govern the projection of these impressions or images upon the mind, mainly depend upon the condition of the recipient, just as the representation conveyed to a photograph-plate depends upon the method with which that plate has been prepared, as well as upon the conditions of light, exposure, and so forth, so it is evident that upon no two different people would it be possible for those in the invisible world to cast precisely the same impression, because no two people are precisely similar in constitution and temperament, nor could they possibly prepare themselves, as photographic plates are prepared, so as to be in exactly the same state of receptivity.

I am not now talking of apparitions and elemental forms, or of phenomena, such as that of the transfiguration on the mount, or the appearance of Christ to His disciples after the resurrection,—these belong to a class of manifestation which appeal to the external senses. The conditions incidental to deep insight and lofty inspirations are, moreover, totally different from those known to ordinary "spirit mediums," who, finding themselves appropriately constituted, use the faculty they possess, in the case of those who are unprincipled, either as a source of profit, a means of imposture or amusement, or, in the case of those who are honest and well-principled, as a means of conveying such imperfect impressions from the other world as they think may benefit this one; but during forty years of modern Western spiritualism these have rarely proved of any practical value, from the fact that those obtaining them hardly ever go through the long and painful ordeals which are a necessary preparation for the reception of the higher truths.

Thus all prophets and seers who have at any time given such spiritual light to the world that men have felt the divine element in it, and incorporated their teaching into their sacred books, have been almost invariably recluses and anchorites, and one may almost add, that in the degree in which they have been so, have their utterances been obscure and unintelligible to the common herd; on the other hand, those who have conveyed moral teaching in language which contained such an element of divine life in it, as to produce upon men the impression that they were inspired, have been, more or less, thinkers and workers—as, for instance, in the case of Christ the carpenter, and Paul the tent-maker. It is evident that the latter was conscious of different processes during composition—one in which he says, I speak this of myself; and the other, where the projection on his mind was so strong that he attributed it to the Lord. This was not to be wondered at, when we consider how pure and full of a lofty spiritual impulse his moral teaching often was. Not knowing the laws which govern inspiration, it was natural, when he felt a noble sentiment projected into his mind, which did not seem to emanate from it spontaneously, that he should attribute it directly to God—being ignorant of the fact that all divine perceptions are only allowed to reach us from the Infinite through the channels provided for it, and that these are angelic, and can only imperfectly convey to us conceptions which have to be tempered, as they descend, to meet the imperfect condition of the human instrument through which they are transmitted; this human instrument being tainted by all sorts of impurity, warped by all manner of prejudice, seeing them only as through a glass darkly, with all the original brightness of their lustre dimmed, and with the reflection of his own personality cast strongly upon them. In the case of Paul and the other apostles, many of their finest utterances were no doubt directly inspired by Christ, and to this was due the extraordinary effect that they produced.

The readiness of men open to these impressions to attribute them all to the one Divine Source, receives striking illustration from the dispute which took place between the prophets Hananiah and Jeremiah, in the 28th chapter of Jeremiah, in which they both prophesy "in the name of the Lord"; and Jeremiah charges Hananiah with prophesying falsely, predicting his death the same year as a punishment.[1] One denunciation of prophets who prophesied falsely is so remarkable[2] that I will quote it: "And the word of the Lord came unto me, 'saying, Son of man, prophesy against the prophets of Israel 'that prophesy, and say thou unto them that prophesy out of 'their own hearts, Hear ye the word of the Lord; thus saith 'the Lord God; Woe unto the foolish prophets, that follow 'their own spirit, and have seen nothing! O Israel, thy prophets are like the foxes in the deserts. Ye have not gone up 'into the gaps, neither made up the hedge for the house of 'Israel to stand in the battle in the day of the Lord. They 'have seen vanity and lying divination, saying, The Lord saith 'it; albeit I have not spoken. Therefore thus saith the Lord 'God; Because ye have spoken vanity, and seen lies, therefore, 'behold, I am against you, saith the Lord God."

One of the remarkable features of inspirational writings or utterances of this description is the absolute certainty of the medium that the divine authority of his message is indisputable.

In the case of the prophets of Israel, it is evident that the poor Jews must often have been in a serious dilemma to know which to believe between those who claimed to be the spokesmen of God, and, as such, denounced the others as liars; and this is rendered still more complicated by the fact that in some instances the Deity Himself is said to have lied through them—as in the scene witnessed by Micaiah, in the 22d chapter of 1st Kings, when the prophet says: "I saw 'the Lord sitting on His throne, and all the host of heaven 'standing by Him on His right hand and on His left. And 'the Lord said, Who shall persuade Ahab, that he may go up 'and fall at Ramoth-Gilead? And one said on this manner, 'and another said on that manner. And there came forth a 'spirit, and stood before the Lord, and said, I will persuade

[1] Jeremiah xxviii. [2] Ezekiel xiii.

'him. And the Lord said unto him, Wherewith? And he
'said, I will go forth, and I will be a lying spirit in the mouth
'of all his prophets. And He said, Thou shalt persuade him,
'and prevail also: go forth, and do so. Now therefore, be-
'hold, the Lord hath put a lying spirit in the mouth of all
'these thy prophets, and the Lord hath spoken evil concern-
'ing thee."

That Micaiah should in a trance, or even in a state of hypnotic consciousness, have had represented to him, by the spirits who had attached themselves to his organism, a scene such as the one above described, is perfectly possible,—that he should honestly believe that he had seen a vision of the Almighty sitting on His throne, discussing with attendant angels how He should lure to his destruction a king with whom He was displeased, and attain this object by commanding a spirit to infest and lie through His prophets, is an evidence of a very debased mediumistic condition. Such a representation of God's methods of dealing with man, could only have been conveyed to the consciousness of one whose own moral and intellectual condition was of a very low order, and by spirits who were themselves of a low order. It is a remarkable fact that the mass of professing Christians, even of the present day, will believe in the truth of this monstrous picture of the prophet's subsurface consciousness—which reflected the images appropriate to it, as projected through the agency of spirits also appropriate to it—and will believe, further, in the psychical invasion of the prophets of Ahab by spirits under superior direction, who ridicule the idea that direct action by similar spirits, not only upon the subsurface consciousness, but upon the external minds of men, is as possible now as it was three thousand years ago; for the laws which govern our relations with the unseen world are as immutable as the laws which operate in this one, and nothing can be more trivial or shallow than the contention that what is possible at one period of the world's history is impossible at another.

The presentation of the Deity by the Jewish prophets, is really constructed by spirits out of the prevailing human conception of Him at the time, and is utterly irreconcilable with the instincts of a more enlightened age. It has ever been the tendency of men in their different religions to reverse the situation, and create God after their own image. At the same time, their prophetic presentations are not to be cast aside as worthless, because in their literal and external meaning they are often revolting. Behind them there is generally an internal sense, which, owing to the crude and untutored moral condition of those through whom such communications came, and of those to whom they were addressed, it was not possible to convey in terms which the transmitter or receiver either could understand or appreciate. Hence the deepest religious truths have had to be conveyed through symbols and images, and this has given rise to mysticism, and to the existence of a class of men who were supposed to understand, and who doubtless often in some measure did understand, their inner meaning, and who were called "Initiates."

It is evident that as the rational faculties are developed and brought to bear upon impressions projected upon the subsurface consciousness in the manner above described, the question must always arise in the mind of their recipient, if he is thoroughly honest, as to their origin and trustworthiness; and in the degree in which his moral nature is purified and elevated, and his humility prominent, will he shrink from daring to assert that he can recognise them as the direct verbal utterances of the Great Almighty. Certainly others should shrink from asserting, as many do assert, not merely that these prophets and apostles speak with the divine voice, but that it has been personally revealed to them that they did so; for it must always come to this, either in the first or second degree, and that every word written was suggested literally by God. It is to be remarked that this claim was not made by the early Church. Indeed it would scarcely be credible that Philemon, for instance, when Paul returned his runaway slave Onesimus, with a note asking him to receive him back, and told him to make a memorandum of the amount of any money he might be indebted to him, put it down to his (Paul's) account, and get a lodging ready for him, should have imagined, as Christians do now, that this epistle was dictated by God.

What is true is, that the canon both of the Jewish and Christian Scripture is full of inspirational writing, and the same may be said of the sacred records upon which the other great religions of the world are founded; this inspirational writing goes back two thousand years before Moses, to the mythological literature of that most ancient people the Accadians, to the funereal ritual of the Egyptians, to the earliest Vedas, to the Buddhist Suttas, and the Zend-Avesta of the Persians, and the sacred books of other religions, and is strongly exhibited in the Jewish and early Christians' writings, some of which are called apocryphal, but which were rejected by those who met to decide by the light of their own private judgment, what was and what was not divine inspiration, because they conflicted with certain theological dogmas to which they were attached, and which were the cause of a good deal of hard fighting both before and since. It has continued from that time to the present, when an unprecedented development of this description of literature has taken place.

There is a sense in which all writing may be considered inspirational, and in ordinary parlance is said to indicate genius, as in the cases of such poets as Shakespeare, Milton, Goethe, and Dante: but I am alluding here rather to those who believed themselves to be channels of divine revelation, or at all events of ideas projected from supermundane source, sometimes by means of mere impressions, sometimes by words which were quite audible to their inner hearing, or by representations which were quite visible to their inner sight; or by phenomena which they recognised as abnormal, and which differed entirely from the effort of ordinary literary compositions. Among many such since the early Christian epoch may be mentioned Mohammed, Hamzé, Jacob Bœhmen, St Martin, George Fox, Ann Lee, and Swedenborg; and in our own time the works of T. L. Harris, Andrew Jackson Davis, Joseph Smith the prophet of the Mormons, Eliphaz Levy, the Marquis of St Yves, Madame Blavatsky, the authors of 'The Perfect Way,' 'Light on the Path,' 'The Mother, the Woman clothed with the Sun,' 'The Flying Roll,' 'The Book of Life,' 'Geometrical Psychology,' and sundry theosophical, spiritualistic, and other publications, which are daily becoming more numerous. Besides these, many persons are guided largely in their own lives by private writings, which they receive either automatically or under impression, and in which they place absolute confidence. It is this fact which renders it of such great importance that some method of testing the relative values of these productions should be arrived at, for already many trusting and earnest souls have been led by them into difficult and devious paths, in their desire to find some solid standing-ground amid the quicksands by which they are surrounded.

CHAPTER II.

RECENT EXAMINATION INTO THE NATURE OF THE FORCES LATENT IN THE HUMAN ORGANISM — HYPNOTIC EXPERIMENTS IN FRANCE, AND THE PSYCHICAL RESEARCH SOCIETY IN ENGLAND, FAMILIARISING THE SCIENTIFIC MIND WITH FORCES FORMERLY IGNORED — THEIR ORIGIN IN THE UNSEEN UNIVERSE — FORMER CONCEPTION OF MATTER MODIFIED BY RECENT DISCOVERIES — SIR HENRY ROSCOE ON ATOMS — INSEPARABILITY OF MATTER AND FORCE — DYNASPHERIC FORCE — SCIENTIFIC FACTS VALUABLE, CONCLUSIONS MISLEADING — HYPNOTIC EXPERIMENTS WITNESSED BY ME IN PARIS — HYPNOTISM RECOGNISED BY THE MEDICAL FACULTY IN FRANCE AS DANGEROUS — SPIRITUAL INSIGHT NECESSARY TO DISCOVER THE NATURE AND ORIGIN OF THESE FORCES, AND TO QUALIFY THE OPERATOR TO DEAL WITH THEM.

WITHIN the last few years an increasing amount of attention has been directed to an examination of those forces connected with the human organism, which for more than half a century have been vaguely known under the name of magnetic, whose existence even under this general term science has been reluctant to recognise; or, if unable altogether to deny the fact that such forces did exist, it has shrunk from investigating them, lest it should be seduced away from the ground which it terms positive, but which might perhaps be more appropriately styled negative. As, however, these forces gained power under the new conditions which are invading the race, they forced themselves upon the notice of the world in general with such persistence, that it was no longer possible for them to be excluded from the range of scientific research, and as an evidence of this we have experiments of the leading medical practitioners in France, recording the result of their observations, in a monthly periodical started for the purpose;[1] and of the two schools devoted to this subject, one, directed by Dr Charcot in Paris, and the other by Professor Bernheim at Nancy; while in London the Psychical Research Society has sprung into existence, which, though hesitating and timid in its conclusions so far, refusing to recognise these forces as conditioned by the unseen, is still too daring for the stolid and conservative instinct of British science in general. The result has been that both in France and England these investigations have led to wide divergences of opinion as to the mode of operation of these forces: in France, between the schools of Paris and Nancy; and in England, between the Psychical Research Society and the body of members who dissent from its conclusions. Nevertheless the phenomena which have resulted from all this inquiry and experiment have been of the utmost importance, as familiarising the scientific mind with the existence of forces which were formerly ignored, of compelling it to try and account for their modes of operation, and of becoming speedily aware in the attempt, of the exceeding shallowness of its own acquirements, and of its incapacity to deal systematically with vital energies, which are as capricious as they are inexplicable in their manifestations. As illustrations of organic human potency, however, they have proved invaluable. It is no longer possible to deny the fact of what is termed telepathy, or to refuse to admit that, when certain conditions have been established between two organisms, one can be made subject to the other in thought and act, notwithstanding the most powerful effort on the part of the subjected organism to resist the subtle influence projected upon it by the other. The patient is compelled to perform every act and to say every word that may have been either silently or orally suggested—in other words, becomes completely controlled by the operator. This is an instance of human psychical inspiration. The reason why there is no regularity in the manifestations, and why the form they will take can never be predicated—except where the conditions have long been established between the same two organisms

---

[1] Revue de l'Hypnotisme : expérimental et thérapeutique. Psychologie. Médecine Légale. Malades Mentales et Nerveuses. Rédacteur en chef Docteur Edgar Berillon.

—is because no two organisms are exactly alike, and therefore the vital energies which animate them, and are conditioned by them, must always differ; and as those vital energies do not originate in the organism, which is merely a transmitting medium through which they operate in nature, the original projecting influence is not the human operator acting from his own initiative, but acting in unconscious relations with an unseen operator.

To those who are sceptics, chiefly through their ignorance of these matters, I may point the analogy of the past, when electric forces, now even with their laws laid down with hard and fast lines, were fields of untrodden research, captivating to a few, the scorn of many, and a danger for all.

It may be said that it is begging the question to say that these forces originate outside of ourselves, or, in other words, that we are not our own source of life, and that outside of us there is an unseen world. There is no way of proving that this is so to those who reject, and in many instances reasonably reject, the ordinary phenomena of spiritualism, unless such persons are prepared to train the will and subject the whole nature, physical, moral, and intellectual, to the severe and painful discipline by which their subsurface consciousness may be opened, and their interior faculties developed. But those—and they are the majority—who have no difficulty in assenting to the proposition that the life-principle which sustains and animates the visible world, is derived from a source outside of it, which we call God, and that this life-principle animates other worlds beside ours, both visible and invisible, will have no difficulty in further perceiving the possibility which has been assumed in the most ancient religions of the world, and is a fundamental doctrine of Christianity. This invisible world, whether it be called heaven and hell, or goes by some other name, is peopled with intelligences, hosts of whom have formerly inhabited this one, and whose influence may still be felt here. This is a fact of my own personal experience, as palpable to me as my own existence and that of the human beings by whom I am surrounded in the flesh, and it is confirmed by thousands of others; still, by the majority it is as yet only believed in theoretically, if believed in at all.

But a belief in it is absolutely essential to the belief that inspiration of any kind is possible, unless we hold that there is only one kind of inspiration—that which comes from God direct—and then we are in the dilemma of having to account for the fact that those who claim to speak in His name often denounce each other as not speaking really in it—of having to accept as the divine voice that which falls so very far below our ideal of what the divine voice should be, and of having to find a source for the inspiration of false prophets.

But if, on the other hand, we accept the ordinary religious assumption, founded doubtless on more than mere theory, that we are in contact with invisible beings, whose existence is recognised in the Christian Scriptures, where they are called sometimes "ministering spirits," sometimes "angels," and sometimes "devils," we need have no difficulty in admitting the possibility, according to the Bible the certainty, of our being influenced by them for good or for evil, as easily as by the people by whom we are surrounded; and this will be still further simplified when we come to consider what the substance we call matter really is, and what spirit is, and how they are allied with those forces which are put into operation through suggestion. Here modern scientific research is beginning, in spite of itself, to cut adrift from its old moorings, and to come to our aid, for it has arrived at the conclusion that "impenetrability" in a sense formerly employed, cannot now be properly applied to any form or condition of matter with which we are familiar; all bodies being made up of molecules separated from each other by distances greater than their supposed dimensions,—a mass of iron, for instance, is not the solid impenetrable thing it was thought to be, but an aggregation of particles that are not in contact, but are free to move, and that are in unceasing motion. What would have happened to an unscientific man who should have ventured to state this years ago?

Professor Clerk thus enunciates his conception of the state of motion in which are the molecules of the most solid matter: "Visible bodies, apparently at rest, are made of parts, each of 'which is moving with the velocity of a cannon-ball, and yet 'never departing to a visible extent from its mean place."[1]

[1] Can Matter Think? a Problem in Psychics. Biogen Series.

In a recent paper on atoms, molecules, and ether waves, Professor Tyndall makes the following statement: "When 'water is converted into steam, the distances between the 'molecules are greatly augmented, but the molecules them-'selves continue intact. We must not, however, picture the 'constituent atoms of any molecules as held so rigidly as to 'render intestine motion impossible. The interlocked atoms 'have still liberty of vibration. The constituent atoms of 'molecules can vibrate to and fro millions of millions of 'times in a second. The atoms of different molecules are 'held together with varying degrees of tightness, they are 'tuned as it were to notes of a different pitch. The vibra-'tions of the constituent atoms of a molecule may under cer-'tain circumstances become so intense as to shake the mole-'cules asunder; most molecules, probably all, are wrecked 'by internal heat, or, in other words, by intense vibratory 'motions."

Electricity, for instance, will tear these molecules to pieces. This is not the case, however, with atoms, which science so far asserts to be indestructible. Upon them electricity has no effect; and Sir Henry Roscoe tells us that "a hydrogen 'atom can endure unscathed the inconceivably fierce tempera-'ture of stars presumably many times more fervent than our 'sun—as Sirius and Vega." Indeed the address of the president of the British Association at Manchester is full of most interesting facts, as bearing upon the atomic theory, at which I have arrived from a very different source than from any investigation into the researches of Dalton, Prout, Huggins, and others, but which those researches seem in a most remarkable manner to confirm. We are told that, "in the 'mind of the early Greek, the action of the atom as one sub-'stance, taking various forms by unlimited combinations, was 'sufficient to account for all the phenomena of the world." And this is true when we divest our minds of all idea of space, which only exists relatively to our senses, and which it is impossible to imagine limited. Our present experience has already got to the vanishing-point of size in so far as these atoms are concerned;[1] and I am quite ready to admit

---

[1] Professor Roscoe goes on to say that "modern research has accomplished, 'as regards the size of the atom, at any rate to a certain extent, what Dalton

that "it does seem miraculous that chemists should now be
'able to ascertain with certainty the relative position of atoms
'so minute that millions upon millions can stand upon a
'needle's point;" and, what is still more wonderful, that
they should have discovered that each element possesses
distinct capabilities of combination—some a single capacity,
some a double, some a triple, and others again a fourfold
capacity for combination.

The importance of this fact will appear in the remarks
I am about to make, and we are further told that "the
number of carbon compounds far exceeds that of all other
elements put together, for these combinations not only possess four means of grasping other atoms, but these four-handed
carbon atoms have a strong partiality for each other's company, and readily attach themselves hand in hand to form
open chains or closed rings, to which the atoms of other elements join, to grasp the unoccupied carbon hand, and thus to
yield a dancing company in which all hands are locked together. Such a group, each individual occupying a given
position with reference to the others, constitutes the organic
molecule. When in such a company the individual members
change hands, a new combination is formed." It must be remembered that, small though these atoms be, nature may
contain others as small again, for all science can know to

'regarded as impossible. Thus, in 1865, Loschmidt, of Vienna, by a train of
'reasoning which I cannot now stop to explain, came to the conclusion that the
'diameter of an atom of oxygen or nitrogen was 1-10,000,000th of a centimètre.
'With the highest known magnifying power we can distinguish the 1-40,000th
'part of a centimètre; if now we imagine a cubic box, each of whose sides has
'the above length, such a box when filled with air will contain from 60 to 100
'millions of atoms of oxygen and nitrogen. A few years later William Thomson extended the methods of atomic measurement, and came to the conclusion
'that the distance between the centres of contiguous molecules is less than
'1-5,000,000th and greater than 1-1,000,000,000th of a centimètre; or, to put
'it in language more suited to the ordinary mind, Thomson asks us to imagine
'a drop of water magnified up to the size of the earth, and then tells us that
'the coarseness of the graining of such a mass would be something between a
'heap of small shot and a heap of cricket-balls. Or, again, to take Clifford's
'illustration, you know that our best microscopes magnify from 6000 to 8000
'times; a microscope which would magnify that result as much again would
'show the molecular structure of water. Or again, to put it in another form,
'if we suppose that the minutest organism we can now see were provided with
'equally powerful microscopes, these beings would be able to see the atoms."

C

the contrary; and that, in fact, when once the principle is conceded of the important biological factor which these atoms represent, there is no limit to the solutions which they may offer of phenomena which are now repudiated as impossible, or are a cause of perplexity to those who credit them. We learn from the distinguished authority I have already quoted, "that the phenomena of vegetation, no less than those of the 'animal world, have during the last fifty years been placed by 'the chemist on an entirely new basis." Yet science was as full of prejudices then as it is now. It is safe to predict that before another fifty years have passed, another basis will be found, for no basis is sound which does not take into account the forces which are active in what is called the unorganised world; and to do this involves the passage of a chasm, which all but a few enthusiastic materialists of the grosser sort pronounce to be impassable. Sir H. Roscoe says: "It is true 'there are those who profess to foresee that the day will arrive 'when the chemist, by a series of constructive efforts, may 'pass beyond albumen, and gather the elements of lifeless 'matter into a living structure. Whatever may be said re-'garding this from other standpoints, the chemist can only 'say that at present no such problem lies within his province. 'Protoplasm, with which the simplest manifestations of life 'are associated, is not a compound, but a structure built up 'of compounds. The chemist may successfully synthetise any 'of its component molecules, but he has no more reason to 'look forward to the synthetic production of the structure 'than to imagine that the synthesis of gallic acid leads to the 'production of gall-nuts."

The advance of science during the last fifty years has at all events proved to us that our previous conception of matter was entirely erroneous, and must undergo a complete change; and that the further it attempts to follow up matter into the new region thus opened, the greater the difficulty becomes. Professor Helmholz tells us "that the elec-'tricity which permeates all matter, and is like an envelope 'to all its atoms, is itself apparently composed of atoms, only 'infinitely finer than any others;" and Professor Maxwell talks of particles of electricity, and says that an electric current consists "of files of particles,"—one theory being that the passage of a current of electricity is a vibration or revolution of particles, each particle being a group of particles revolving upon themselves.

There are many elements in nature which are called imponderable, simply because at present hydrogen is the lightest thing we can weigh—in other words, they are not really imponderable, but only imponderable as far as we have got. This is admitted, and is illustrated by Mr Crookes in what he calls "the fourth state of matter," a form and condition vastly more rarefied than the lightest substance known—so we pass from the solids, which were formerly called matter, to liquids, from liquids to gases, from gases to electricity and magnetism, from these to aeriform or radiant matter; for we learn from Ganot's 'Elements of Physics' that "that subtle, imponderable, and eminently elastic fluid 'called the ether, distributed through the entire universe, per- 'vading the mass of all bodies, the densest and most opaque 'as well as the lightest and most transparent, is composed of 'atoms, and not merely do the atoms of bodies communicate 'motion to the atoms of the ether, but the latter can impart 'it to the former. Thus the atoms of bodies are at once the 'sources and the recipients of motion. All physical pheno- 'mena referred thus to a single cause are but transformations 'of motion. . . .

"In the present state of science we cannot say whether the 'forces in nature are properties inherent in matter, or whether 'they result from movements impressed on the mass of subtle 'and imponderable forms of matter through the universe. 'The latter hypothesis is, however, generally admitted."

This and many other like points can never be settled until we realise that our external senses are not tests upon which we can rely for anything—being mere organs for the transmission of sensations, which are conditioned not upon what things really are, but upon what they appear to us to be.

Science, to be *true*, must not be human but divine, and those who would search into the secrets of nature, must begin by searching into the mysteries of God, from whom it emanated. "Seek ye first the kingdom of God and His righteousness, and all other things shall be added to you;" and this kingdom, we are told, is "within us." Men have begun at the wrong end to work up to the Unknowable through the external manifestations of its power, by the aid of their own limited faculties of reason and observation, while they have failed to enlist in the quest the most powerful faculty of all, an instinct directed by love for God and humanity.

I do not mean to imply that scientific men are surpassed by any other men in the pureness and nobleness of their aims and aspirations, but that few of them have perceived that there is no such thing as physical science apart from religion, and that external nature should be read as a sacred record of divine mysteries of which they would become the high priests. It would be necessary to assume the hypothesis of an intelligent Author in thus seeking to turn the pages of His book of nature, but scientists made a greater demand upon their imagination than that in their latest assumption as to the origin of man: it now behoves them to develop within themselves the faculty of understanding these pages of nature, by submitting to the ordeals of absolute self-sacrifice and personal discipline of the affections, which shall leave that love paramount which furnishes the key to all knowledge. It is this mistaken attitude of the scientific mind in general, which makes it necessarily blind to the perception of the highest truths, whether moral or physical. A highly eminent member of the scientific fraternity sounds no uncertain note on the subject. "Anatomically," he says, "we 'find no provision in the nervous system for the improvement 'of the moral, save indirectly—through the intellectual— 'the whole aim of development being for the sake of intel-'ligence. Historically, in the same manner, we find that the 'intellectual has always led the way in social advancement, 'the moral having been subordinate thereto. The former 'has been the mainspring of the movement, the latter pas-'sively affected. It is a mistake to make the progress of 'society depend on that which is itself controlled by a 'higher power."[1]

Is there no provision in the nervous system for the sentiment of love, except indirectly through the intellect? When, with its passionate longing, it sweeps through the human

[1] Draper's Intellectual Development of Europe, vol. ii. p. 360.

organism, does it not carry away any feeble barriers that the intellect may have erected to stay its course?—unless, indeed, some still stronger moral impulse restrains it, and then it is not intellect, but conscience, or the operation of a higher love. In point of fact, whatever it may be anatomically, intellect is the sport of the passions, their slave and obedient servant, to carry out their behests; but as it is impossible to anatomise either the emotions or the intellect, or to push research beyond the cerebrum, any attempt to formulate their relations to each other by an analysis of the nervous system of man, must inevitably at present lead to confusion and error. The best proof that this is so, is to be found in what Professor Draper calls the "social advancement" at which we have arrived. If inventions by which wars can be conducted on a scale of more wholesale slaughter than history records, and explosions can be effected which will cause greater destruction in a moment than could formerly be accomplished in a week; if frauds can be perpetrated by which more money can be legally acquired by a financial operation in a day, and more innocent victims ruined than was formerly possible in a lifetime; if science, to use his own words, has given rogues such discoveries as "would 'suggest to the evil-disposed the forging of bank-notes, the 'sophisticating of jewellery, and be invaluable in the utter- 'ing of false coinage;" if more squalor, poverty, misery, and seething vice is now collected on a given area than we have ever heard of in ancient times; if the grinding of labour by capital has so exasperated the working classes that the social fabric of what is called "Christian civilisation" is threatened from its basis; if the unparalleled ingenuity in crime, extravagance in luxury, and the deliberate repudiation in daily practice of the moral teaching of Christ, are an evidence of "social advancement" and of intellectual supremacy, —and if these are the conclusions to which a study of the anatomy of the human frame leads its students, then the sooner the science of physiology is swept off the face of the earth the better, and the cerebrum abandoned as furnishing the highest source of human inspiration.

But, indeed, it is not the fault of physiology that its professors go so wide of the mark, but of the prejudices and preconceptions with which they approach it. If scientific men would only confine themselves to recording facts, their researches would be in the highest degree valuable—as indeed they are—in the cause of divine truth. It is when they come to forming hypotheses, and arriving at conclusions, that they so terribly mislead those who are unable to discriminate between those facts, and the fallacies of their deductions from them, and they thus work irreparable injury to the cause they most wish to serve.

Modern science, then, having reached the vanishing-point of matter, and there stuck hopelessly befogged, and unable to decide whether it generates force, in which case it might be called ponderable force—or is only acted on by force, in which case the force that acts upon it must also be material, or it would have no transmitting medium; and having also decided that matter can never touch matter, every atom being prevented from doing so by its own "dynasphere" (nobody knows what a dynasphere is made of); and being further satisfied that "the atomic abyss is as unfathomable as the interstellar space is immeasurable,"—leaves us there to scramble out of it as best we may. But it has carried us along far enough for our purposes, for it has given us a new conception of matter, and one which, if we could divest our minds completely of the definition which we received of it from science before it knew better, we might still use. This, however, is scarcely possible, and would be too misleading. Though it is scientifically admitted that matter is in gases and ether, in light and heat, as well as in solids and liquids, and that it pervades all known forces—electric, magnetic, galvanic, odylic, or by whatever name they may be called—and that, in fact, nothing has yet been discovered of which we can assert that no matter is there, not even the interstellar spaces, or the atomic dynaspheres themselves, it is evident we can conceive of no limit to it, either in time or space, for it is indestructible as well as illimitable. In other words, it is infinite and eternal; and as we cannot conceive of the Deity being outside of what is infinite and eternal, He also must be in this sense material—an idea which seems to crop out, though perhaps not consciously to himself, in Mr Norman Lockyer's suggestion that the varied forms of matter, simple and complex, are but presentations of diversified properties, of temporary conditions of that which is essentially one and the same for ever. Another scientific writer remarks that "the 'physical thing which energises and does work in and upon 'ordinary matter, is a separate form of matter infinitely refined 'and infinitely rapid in its vibrations, and thus able to pene-'trate through all ordinary matter, and to make everywhere a 'fountain of motion, no less real because unseen. It is among 'the atoms of the crystal and the molecules of living matter; 'and whether producing locked effects or free, it is the same 'cosmic thing, matter in motion, which we conceive as mate-'rial energy, and with difficulty think of as only a peculiar 'form of matter in motion."

The physical thing which is here described as a separate form of matter, and as being "able to penetrate through all ordinary matter, and to make everywhere a fountain of motion, no less real because unseen," is nothing more nor less than what we have been in the habit of calling spirit, when we wished to separate it from what is termed above "ordinary matter": mind is also composed of this extraordinary matter, so is will, so is every emotion; but in order to avoid confusion, it would be well to find a specific designation for it. Jacob Bœhmen calls it "heavenly substantiality," and Swedenborg "natural and spiritual atmospheres composed of discrete substances of a very minute form."

Mr Crookes has invented the word protyle, which may possibly convey the desired idea; and Professor Coues calls it soul-stuff or biogen; while occultists call it astral fluid. The most remarkable illustration of the stupendous energy of atomic vibratory force is to be found in that singular apparatus in Philadelphia, which for the last fifteen years has excited in turn the amazement, the scepticism, the admiration, and the ridicule of those who have examined it — called "Keely's Motor." Already more than £50,000 have been expended upon it, and so far it has not been possible to render it commercially available. Hence, in the practical land of its origin, it has popularly been esteemed a fraud. I have not examined it personally, but I believe it to be based upon a sound principle of dynamics, and to be probably the first of a series of discoveries destined to revolutionise all existing mechanical theories, and many of the principles upon which they are founded. Mr Keely has discovered that such a change can be effected by vibration, in the atoms of which the atmosphere is composed, that what he terms "atmospheric disintegration" can be produced, which has the effect of liberating a subtle essence, the nature of which has still to be determined, and which he believes to be "inter-atomic." The energy it possesses is so great that it exercises a pressure of 25,000 lb. to the square inch, and in the engine which he has just constructed for traction purposes, develops a force of 250 horse-power. All this is achieved without the introduction of any extraneous motive power, the whole apparatus being so constructed that the liberation of this tremendous agency from its atmospheric prison-house can be effected by the vibrations produced by a tuning-fork.[1] Those who are sufficiently unprejudiced to connect the bearings of this discovery, of what must be dynaspheric force, with phenomena which have hitherto been regarded as supernatural by the ignorant, will perceive how rapidly we are bridging over the chasm which has always divided the seen from the unseen, and obliterating the distinction between what has erroneously been called matter, and what has no less erroneously been called spirit.

From this we may infer that the dynaspheres of the atoms cognisable by science themselves contain atoms, which are in their turn surrounded by dynaspheres, and so on *ad infinitum*, and that this dynaspheric force is the agent of those phenomena of hypnotism, spiritualism, telepathy, and occultism generally, which are now puzzling the more advanced students of philosophy, and inquirers of the type of the Psychical Research Society. This force it is which, passing through the organism of the operator into the hypnotised patient, controls his will, and inspires his words and acts ; and in order to do this, it has to penetrate the atoms of the ordinary matter which compose the fleshly particles of the visible frames of both. It can now easily be understood how, when another class of operators intervene, who have "shuffled off this mortal coil," but who none the less live in the so-called spiritual

[1] See the British Mercantile Gazette, 15th February 1887, and the Scientific Arena, Dr Wilford Hall.—Ed.

bodies composed of this supersensuous material force, which are still invisible to the great majority of people, though by no means so to all, their influence can be more powerfully exercised than if they still remained in the flesh; for the finer atoms of which they are composed, are not encrusted with those coarser particles which we see, and with which the finer particles are interlocked. It is the relationship which these two varieties of atoms bear to each other, which regulates and controls all organic phenomena, and which suggests the cause of effects that have been heretofore considered unaccountable. Here we have the secret of that magnetic attraction and repulsion which we call love or hate, sympathy or antipathy, and of all the varieties of sentiment which we produce upon our neighbours and they upon us. We express this truth unconsciously when we say of a man that he makes "a certain impression" upon us, the impression being literally produced by the impact of one variety of atoms upon another variety. So, in the emotions of anger, joy, sorrow, &c., the varieties and movements of atoms are as infinite which compose these emotions, as those are which go to compose our ideas, and which Mr Herbert Spencer defines as the result of "the liberation of certain forces produced by chemical action in the brain." As he admits that these forces have their origin in the unknowable, and are not generated in the brain itself, and as these cannot exist without atoms as a transmitting medium, he is not so far from the solution of the mystery of the metamorphosis which takes place between the forces which he calls physical, and those which he calls mental, as he himself supposes.

"How this metamorphosis takes place," he says, "how a 'force existing as motion, heat, or light can become a mode 'of consciousness; how it is possible for aerial vibrations to 'generate the sensations we call sound, or for the forces liber-'ated by chemical changes in the brain to give rise to emotions, '—these are mysteries which it is impossible to fathom." But when once we perceive that the aerial vibrations consist of movements of atoms which make the tune in the case of music, and the words in the case of speech, and that they in turn receive their impact from other atoms behind them which suggest the tune or the thought, which again receive theirs in like manner, and so on up the scale of the universal consciousness to the source of all consciousness; and that by their impact on the atoms of what we term "ordinary matter," they affect these atoms in our nerve-centres, and so convey sensation, emotion, and thought to the brain, there is bottom found to the unfathomable, so far as this particular mystery is concerned: we no longer make chemical changes in our brains responsible for the ideas which they give forth, but we open the avenues to inspiration, which would otherwise be closed to it, and in opening those avenues afford ourselves the possibility and the hope of fathoming other mysteries besides this one.

When once we have clearly grasped the idea that physical, mental, and emotional forces are all material, and that their varied manifestations are conditioned by the varieties of which they consist, and of endless combinations and permutations which may be produced by those atoms, resulting in effects as infinitely varying, and all correlated to each other, and possessing conserved energies of undreamt-of potency, science will have a field before it in which discoveries transcending human imagination lie buried; but the spots in which they are concealed are holy ground, upon which no profane foot dare tread—mysteries which the ancients protected from profanation by their mysticism, and to which the moderns have blinded themselves by their scepticism. Though from what has been said we may vaguely perceive where these treasures of divine knowledge lie hid, no man can furnish another with a sure key to them. That is to be found by each who would learn the secrets of wisdom, only in his own heart; and it is by an effort of his affections, and not by one of his brain, that he can fit this key to the lock of knowledge. So long as he stands perched on the intellectual pedestal upon which it is his ambition to tower, the admired of all beholders, so long will he search in vain for that hidden treasure which his soul longs after, and continue to cast reflections upon the intelligence of his predecessors, if not upon his own, by exhibiting to the world the shallowness of many of those scientific conclusions upon which their greatness at the time was founded. Let him then beware of intellectual effort in this direction, unprepared by the necessary preliminary moral training and discipline to make it.

Science is already responsible for having put dynamite, roburite, melanite, and other destructive explosives into the hands of the vicious and cruel; and its manifold inventions have facilitated the perpetration of various kinds of crime; while it has already, panic-stricken, begun to perceive that the therapeutic advantages which may accrue from hypnotism, are more than counterbalanced by the fearful dangers which it involves. M. Liegois [1] tells us that it would be difficult to find twenty persons among the patients of Dr Liebault who could resist a criminal assault. Ladame writes [2]: "Personne ne doute plus au-'jourd'hui de la possibilité pour une femme de subir les 'derniers outrages pendent le sommeil hypnotique; et le 'Docteur Cullerre dans son intéressant volume [3] écrit que 'c'est là une des hypothèses le moins susceptible d'objections 'sérieuses parmi toutes celles qui pourraient être présentées." In the 'Archives de l'Anthropologie Criminelle, et des Sciences Pénales' of March 1886, p. 188, is narrated the case of a girl in which the operator produced a blister upon her arm, as well as stigmata, by simple hypnotic suggestion; and by the same means Professors Beaumis and Bernheim retarded or accelerated the circulation of the blood, and the pulsations of the heart to suit themselves, the experiment being recorded on a sphygmograph, and the evidence remains in the traces still existing made by the instrument, the conclusion being finally arrived at that, as by an act of will the vital functions could be so powerfully acted upon, they might by the same act of will be arrested altogether, and death would ensue. In the case of a woman with child, abortion could be produced by the same means. "Je ne parle pas," continues Mons. Toureaux, who was a witness, and sometimes an actor in these experiments, " de l'idée du suicide qu'il 'serait facile d'infliger à quelque individu. L'obsession de

---

[1] Liegois, professeur à la faculté de droit de Nancy. De la suggestion hypnotique dans ces rapports avec le droit criminel et le droit civil. Nancy: 1885.

[2] L'Hypnotisme et la Médicine Légale. Dr Ladame.

[3] Culture Magnetism. Paris: 1886.

'la mort ne cesserait en ce cas qu'avec le dernier instant la victime. La justice n'a-t-elle donc point a se soucier de de tous ces mystères." A suggestion is, for instance, made to a subject, who is a perfectly honest, well-principled girl, to steal a jewel at the same hour on the following day, the method to avoid suspicion being also pointed out. This she does with great dexterity, following the instructions exactly. She first denies the theft, then is made to admit it, and finally to write to the judge of the district accusing a third person of the theft by naming him in a letter of her own composition, and signed by herself. When she was in her normal condition she was entirely unconscious of the whole episode; though while the patient is in this hypnotic state there is nothing usually to indicate to an ordinary observer anything abnormal. Experiments have also been made to discover how long hypnotic suggestion retains its influence over a patient, and Professor Beaunis has succeeded in having a suggestion realised 172 days after he had made it—from the 14th July 1884 to the 1st of January 1885.[1]

Instances of all kinds, some of them even more remarkable than the above, could be quoted, for new developments are every day occurring, all tending, however, in the same direction, and all going to show that there is no limit to the danger with which society is threatened from this source.

When I was in Paris in February 1887, I went to the Salpetrière, where some of the most remarkable of Dr Charcot's experiments have been made, and witnessed the stage through which they were passing, and the phenomena that were being exhibited, and which Dr Charcot classifies under the three heads, lethargic, cataleptic, and somnambulic, including them all in "Le grand Hypnotisme." The operator on the occasion of my visit was Dr Babinski, the patient a girl of about twenty, partially paralysed on one side. On being seated in a chair, and her elbow pressed for a few seconds by Dr Babinski, she passed at once into the lethargic state, and became insensible to all surrounding impressions of sight, sound, or touch, but not rigid. In fact she presented somewhat the appearance of a limp corpse, and on a limb being

[1] Beaunis. Le Somnambulisme Provoqué: Études Psychologiques, p. 233. Paris: 1886.

raised it fell immediately. By simply opening her eyes, she was thrown into a cataleptic state, and her limbs remained in any attitude in which they were placed. She continued perfectly deaf, and though her eyes were open, they apparently received no visual impression; she was not rigid, but on a muscle being touched it stiffened, while a pass immediately released it. Sensation could be transferred to the paralysed side from the other by closing the eye on that side; the side which was formerly sensitive now became perfectly insensible to pain, while the slightest prick of a pin could instantly be felt on the other. Sensation could thus be transferred from one side to the other by opening the right or left eyes; when both eyes were closed she fell back into the lethargic condition; when both were open, insensibility remained in the paralysed side; on the forehead being briskly rubbed for a few seconds, she passed into the somnambulic state. In this condition she could see and hear, and in fact seemed thoroughly herself, excepting that she had lost all power of will, and was open to suggestion. When told there was a potato on the end of the nose of a gentleman who was present, she was for a moment inclined to deny it, but gradually the expression of her face changed, and assumed one of mingled horror and amazement, and she finally burst into a fit of violent laughter, and admitted that she did see a potato there. She was then told that she had a glass of champagne in her hand, and ordered to drink it, on which she lifted her empty hand to her mouth, and went through all the action of swallowing a highly satisfactory liquid. She sneezed violently on being told that she was sniffing smelling-salts. Closing her eyes threw her instantly into the lethargic state, and opening them, into the cataleptic. On electricity being applied to the risible muscles, she expanded into a sweet smile; she clenched her fists, and her features were convulsed with rage when it was applied to her frontal muscles; and when it was applied to those on her chin, her lips and nostrils curled into an expression of profound contempt. On another patient being introduced and thrown into the somnambulic state, the two were placed back to back with a high screen between them, a large magnet being put on the table in close proximity. The actions performed by one were then exactly reproduced by the other, although they were quite invisible to one another. If the muscles of one were made rigid by a touch, the muscles of the other became rigid sympathetically. If the hands of one were raised, the other raised her hands. The action of the magnet and the electric battery on the patient was an interesting demonstration of the intimate relations which exist between the atoms of electric and magnetic forces outside the organism and those in it. Dr Babinski informed me that it was difficult to obtain the reproduction of each other's motions by patients in the absence of the magnet in close proximity. The effect upon me of being present while scientific men are exploring these forces in this reckless manner, is very much what it would be if I was hunting for something in a powder-magazine with a man who did not know there was any powder there, and held a naked candle in his hand. That they themselves, however, recognise how great is the danger, is proved by the efforts that are being made to bring it under the action of the law, and render it penal for anybody to grope into these mysteries in the dark, except those who are supposed to be professionally qualified to do so. In Denmark it has already been rendered penal.[1] The result of the dabbling by amateurs into these phenomena, and the fashion of making hypnotisation an after-dinner amusement, has been to increase the annual percentage of patients to the Salpetrière to a very great extent, which I was told at the time, but the amount of the percentage has slipped my memory. The defence of those

[1] Since the above was written, an article has appeared in the 'Evènement' of the 1st November 1887, upon hypnotic suggestion, narrating an interview between Dr Luys and Dr Wulffs, in which it remarks—"Our free will, our 'honour, our very existence, are menaced; and it is in the name of society and 'of morality that medical men implore justice to act implacably against those 'who speculate upon public curiosity, by making use of practices which to-day 'form part of medical study, and the usurpation of which should bring them 'under the arm of the law."

But the knowledge of these forces on the part of medical men is very much what it was with regard to electricity in its early days. Their ignorance of their real nature and proximate source is as great as that of the amateurs they denounce.

For a full account of the experiments and the conclusions so far arrived at by the medical profession in France, the reader is referred to a work recently published, called 'Animal Magnetism,' by Alfred Binet and Charles Féré: Kegan Paul, Trench, & Co.

who are using it as a therapeutic agent is, that in a certain class of diseases it is attended with very beneficial results; but we have no means of knowing how much injury it inflicts in other ways—how hypnotic suggestion charged with the moral or immoral magnetisms of the operator, may taint the purer magnetisms into which they are projected, and with which they commingle, or what subtle interchanges of the vital principle take place. Unless an operator be absolutely free from any physical or moral taint—and which of us can say that he is?—some of that taint must perforce exist in the material atoms which he projects into the organisms of the patients, even though he may cure them physically.

We are experimenting with a factor more powerful and dangerous than any explosive, of the nature and properties of which we know scarcely anything beyond the fact that with it we can destroy not only the physical bodies, but the moral natures of those accessible to its influence, by a mere act of volition.

Many instances are cited by the French doctors in which they have succeeded in changing the whole characters of their patients—some of them have been quoted by Mr Frederick Myers in a recent article,[1]—and converted degraded, vicious, and uncontrollable criminals into respectable members of society. The converse process is equally possible. Who is fit to be intrusted with such powers? and how can we prevent them from being universally practised? Therefore it is that I say we are on the threshold of a moral convulsion, the like of which the world has never seen, which it is too late now to attempt to avert, but which may be mitigated by the proper application of that science to which it will have been so largely due. But its professors must rise from being mere empirics to being seers; and this they can never do so long as they refuse to recognise the direct action upon every human being in the world, of influences emanating from one which is not cognisable to their most superficial and external senses. Once let them assume the hypothesis that a Deity may possibly exist—by no means a more strained one than the transmutation of species—and that they can arrive at such close internal union with Him,

---

[1] "Multiplex Personality"—'Nineteenth Century.'

as to receive interior illumination from Him, and the very effort to attain union will lead them into the channel provided for its communication, and unfold to them the phenomena of a world which no spectroscope can reveal. It is no longer a matter of dealing with rocks, or beetles, or gases, but with the whole moral life of men, who are leaving the superficial ground upon which they may possibly have done more good than harm, but are not permitted to rush in where angels fear to tread, without a warning voice being raised of the tremendous responsibility that they are incurring, and the fearful catastrophe they are precipitating.

This is no longer a question of what has been called physical science, but it is a question of moral science of the most profound importance; and he who would become a professor of moral science—with which physical science is inseparably interwoven, the two combined constituting divine science—must first reconcile himself with the Divinity, and make those experiments upon himself, under divine guidance, which are necessary to qualify him to experiment upon others.

CHAPTER III.

THE INTERLOCKING OF THE INVISIBLE ATOMS OF THE SEEN AND UNSEEN WORLDS FORM A SINGLE SYSTEM OF ANIMATE NATURE — GLIMPSES INTO THE INVISIBLE, CONDITIONED ON THE MORAL STATE OF THE OBSERVER — DEATH A LIBERATION OF GROSSER ATOMS FROM THOSE MORE SUBLIMATED — MATERIAL PARTICLES THE VEHICLES OF FORCE CONSTANTLY ASSUMING NEW PHASES — *ANIMA MUNDI* — INTERDEPENDENCE OF ALL CREATED NATURE — PSYCHICAL EXPERIENCE ATTENDING THE COMPOSITION OF SYMPNEUMATA — DUPLEX CEREBRAL ACTION — VITAL ATOMIC INTERACTION BETWEEN THE LIVING AND THE DEAD — METHOD OF CEREBRAL IMPREGNATION — INSPIRATIONS WHICH DO NOT GRAPPLE WITH THE EARTH MALADY WORTHLESS — CHRIST, A RADIATIVE CENTRE OF HEALING FORCE — THE DISCIPLINE OF ABSOLUTE SELF-SACRIFICE ESSENTIAL AS A PREPARATION TO THE HIGHEST INSPIRATION — DEFECT IN THE EASTERN SYSTEMS OF ASCETICISM.

INVESTIGATIONS of modern science into the nature and properties of what has heretofore been termed "matter," and the experiments which have been made with material physical forces upon the human organism, as illustrated by the phenomena of hypnotism, have afforded us a basis upon which to argue, that a world may exist composed of material forces which are of too subtle a nature for us to cognise with our present external senses; and that if that world is peopled with material beings appropriate to it, there may be such an affinity between the finer atoms of the seen and the unseen worlds, as to render possible the interlocking of their respective atoms, thus forming a single system of animate nature—for there is no such thing as inanimate nature—of which one part is visible and the other part invisible, and of which the visible may be a broken and distorted image of some portion of the other part,—broken and distorted, because the medium of our senses through which we can become conscious of it, is so limited and imperfect. These, however, in the case of certain persons, are still sufficiently developed to enable them to perceive, in a dim and obscure way, that the world in which they live, is a reflex of events which are transpiring in one which is unseen, and of the processes of nature there, and of the moral and intellectual activities which prevail in it. At the same time, the representation is imperfect and partial in the extreme; while in the case of no two observers does the image thus observed present the same aspect of character, because the glimpses which they catch of it are conditioned by the quality of their material atoms, which become the transmitting medium for their internal vision.

He, however, who has penetrated far enough into the mystery of the union of these two worlds into one system, soon begins clearly to perceive that it is through the interlocking of the atoms of the unseen world with those of our own, and of the people on it, that all natural life is maintained. When apparent suspension of animation occurs in nature, a certain dislocation of these atoms takes place, resulting in entirely new combinations of them, by means of which the grosser ones are liberated from those which are more sublimated; these latter remaining interlocked with those with which they have affinity, and being for the time inseparably attached to them, contribute the life they have, as it were, withdrawn from this world, to the world to which they now belong; from which they again discharge it into this one, as water is drawn from the seas and the streams of earth into the heavens, where it recondenses, and descends with its life-giving moisture again to the soil. Thus there is an endless vital circle radiating life, none of which is ever wasted, for it is part of an endless system of absorption and distribution, deriving its life in turn from another system revolving eternally round the centre of all life, which at the same time permeates to the circumference of all life, till, once more in contact with the infinite, human thought fails in its faculties of conception.

We have an exact counterpart of this process in the cycle or evolution through which material particles, suitable for organisation, incessantly run in the same portion of our uni-

verse. Science tells us that "at one moment they exist as
'inorganic combinations in the air or soil, then as portions
'of animals, then they return to the soil, again to renew their
'cycle of movement. . . . Material particles are thus the
'vehicles of force. They undergo no destruction. Chemically
'speaking, they are eternal. And so, likewise, force never
'deteriorates nor becomes lessened. It may assume new
'phases, but it is always intrinsically unimpaired. The only
'changes it can exhibit are those of aspect and distribution:
'of aspect, as electricity, affinity, light, heat; of distribution,
'as when the diffused aggregate of many substances is con-
'centrated in one animal form.

"It is but little that we know respecting the mutations
'and distributions of force in the universe. We cannot tell
'what becomes of that which has characterised animal life,
'though of its perpetuity we may be assured. It has no more
'been destroyed than the material particles of which such
'animals consist. They have been transmuted into new
'forms—it has taken on a new aspect. The sum-total of
'matter in the world is invariable, so likewise is the sum-
'total of force."[1]

Here, then, we have science admitting that it does not
know what becomes of the forces which have characterised
animal life, while it is assured of their perpetuity; and of
course the same must be said of the finer material particles
which are the transmitting media of that force. The two
together form the "matter in motion," the sum-total of which
is invariable, but which, none the less, forms the endless cycle
by which it re-enters that portion of our universe which is
invisible to us, recombines there according to the affinity of
its constituent atoms, and returns charged with new life-
potency, vitalised first by the divine solar ray, and afterwards
by the material solar ray, to impart its vigours to the visible
creation, in the form of heat, light, electricity, or gaseous compound, appropriate to the functions it is destined to fulfil.

Hence it follows that we can arrive at no just appreciation
of the nature we see, without taking into consideration the
nature we do not see, for the two combined form one indivisible universe. It is on that part which is invisible that we

[1] Draper's Intellectual Development of Europe, vol. ii. p. 342.

depend for existence, for it is by means of the forces projected thence, on our finest nerve-centres, that we are enabled to exercise all the faculties we possess, whether they be moral, intellectual, or physical. That this is so, I am aware that I have no means of proving to those who have not passed through like experiences with myself, but it does not involve a very strained or impossible assumption, and will be found to solve many problems hitherto deemed insolvable; it is, in fact, the true origin of the idea of the "world soul," or *anima mundi* of the ancient philosophers,—and if it is so, it follows that there is no such thing as initiative absolutely independent of influence on the part of any created thing in this world; but inasmuch as the whole of our world, seen and unseen, and every living thing upon it, is pervaded by the divine principle, of which the essence is freedom of will, this remains indestructible in spite of the influences brought to bear upon it from both worlds, and constitutes the sensation which resides in the faculty of choice. This choice can of course be exercised for good or for evil; and in the degree in which we set our wills to obey one impulse or the other, do we come under the influence of good or of evil men and women, both seen and unseen, and are controlled by them.

As this fact takes form in one's mind, does one begin to perceive its truth by experience, and, in the case of unseen personalities, to realise the operation of the interlocked atoms which act and react upon one another with a systolic and diastolic motion, sometimes apparently in the brain, and sometimes in the nerve-centres and solar plexus. I will venture to illustrate this by the influence under which I am at present writing, and which I am conscious to be that of my wife, who is no longer by my side in the flesh; but in order to do so it will be necessary to describe first the circumstances under which a book edited by me,[1] and which appeared not long since, was written. I had been conscious for some months in the summer of 1882 that a book was taking form within my brain, though I could obtain no clear idea of its nature,—and indeed the same experience has preceded the pages I am now penning,—when. I decided

[1] Sympneumata: or, Evolutionary Forces now Active in Man. William Blackwood & Sons, Edinburgh: 1885.

one day to attempt a beginning, and trust to the inspiration of the hour to carry me on, as I am doing now. I had scarcely written the first sentence and begun the second, when the ideas which had presented themselves on taking up my pen, suddenly left me, and my mind became a sheet of blank paper. I remarked upon this to my wife, who was sitting in the room, and reading what I had written, asked her if she could finish the sentence; this, without a moment's hesitation, she had no difficulty in doing. I now most laboriously began another, but soon the same difficulty presented itself, which was solved in the same way. I found it hopeless to try and write another word. I therefore said to my wife that it was she evidently who was intended to write the book, and begged her to continue to dictate to me. To this at first she objected, on the ground of a want of literary practice, of material, and of capacity to treat properly so profound a subject; but she finally consented to try, and for a couple of hours dictated to me slowly, but without hesitation or correction. She then became too exhausted to continue. On the following day I suggested that, as I had a good deal of literary work to do, she had better write the book herself, and I went to write a magazine article in another room. After the lapse of a few minutes she came to me saying that she had not been able to write a line, or to find an idea in her head of any sort, suggesting that I should come back and continue to be her amanuensis. I had no sooner taken up the pencil than she began to dictate, and continued for some moments with apparent ease, when she paused, and finally announced that again all her ideas had vanished, and asked me if I could suggest a cause. As a few moments previously a new idea had struck me with reference to the article I was writing on quite another subject, I remembered that perhaps it might be owing to my abstraction from the matter in hand. On my again directing my attention to it she continued without hesitation, and wishing to help her, I endeavoured to formulate some ideas. "Now," she said, "you are ' doing something that confuses me terribly. I have a whole ' mass of thoughts crowding on my brain, and I cannot feel ' which is the right one." I told her how my mind had been working, and suggested that I should try as much as possible to keep it an absolute blank. This I managed, with more or less success, to do, and in the degree in which I succeeded, did she dictate with freedom. We also found that if I had written anything on any subject previously, or been engaged in any matter of business the same day, it was useless for her to attempt to dictate. We were obliged to begin our writing the first thing in the morning, to allow of no interruptions, and to be in no way anxious or preoccupied with worldly matters till it was concluded. In this way the book was written, but the process was a slow one, owing to the many days lost by interruptions, which were unavoidable, and her own feeble health during a great part of the time. But there was nothing abnormal in her condition when dictating—no indication of the state popularly known as "mediumistic." Her mind was in full and active operation, and all her intellect, which was a very powerful one, was concentrated on the effort of expressing in appropriate terms the ideas which were suggested to her.

The book speaks for itself as a remarkable effort of composition, the only defect of which is the length of some of the sentences, which are sometimes too involved; but I found that any attempt on my part to correct or modify, immediately interrupted the flow of idea. From a psychical point of view, this experience is interesting, as illustrating a condition of moral and intellectual affinity which was the result of a long and arduous effort, extending over many years, and by processes to which I may briefly refer later. The effect of this internal connection was to mitigate to an inconceivable degree the sense of loss which at first threatened to overwhelm me when she passed into her present sphere of usefulness; for she was soon able to reach me through the internal tie which had been formed by this interlocking of our finer-grained material atoms while in the flesh, and it was only during the short interval consequent upon their dislocation from the atoms of ordinary matter that my suffering was acute. On the re-establishment of the vital connection between us under new and more powerful conditions, I was enabled to advance into the appreciation of knowledge which had been concealed from me; but this enlightenment never takes the form of being projected upon my brain from any outside source, but rather as a spontaneous idea suggested by my own consciousness, and yet accompanied by the peculiar internal sensation produced by this atomic interaction, which is sufficient to check me if, in writing, I am following a current of thought which is in opposition to hers, and to convey to me a sense of approval when I have succeeded in conveying the idea which, interweaving itself with mine in the atomic cerebral processes, she desires to have conveyed.

It will readily be understood that nothing but what I conceive the paramount importance of the subject I am here endeavouring to elucidate, and of the interest to humanity at large which it involves, would induce me to enter upon these details; but they were necessary as an illustration of a certain form of inspiration—the atomic combination having been formed on earth—which involved a duplex cerebral action in order to the composition and production of a book. That atomic combination, composed as it was of those finer particles of two separate organisms which do not corrupt with the flesh, although dislocated at the juncture of their withdrawal from the coarse atoms of the one organism at the moment of death, could soon recover the faculty of reforming a new and more effective combination with the corresponding atoms in the one still alive, with which they had formerly been associated; the very fact of such previous association rendering a union of atoms possible, which would otherwise have been impossible. In the case of 'Sympneumata,' the elements which I contributed could only be so contributed during a period of entire mental inactivity on my part; for if I allowed my mind to work, I withdrew them from my wife—in other words, she appropriated all the powers of my mind, whatever these may be, incorporated them with her own by a process of which she was entirely unconscious; and the result was a composition containing ideas which were, many of them, new to both of us until they appeared in manuscript. A somewhat similar process is taking place now, and the means whereby I can distinguish one influence from any other, arises out of the fact of this prior intimate atomic association, which has so interwoven the subtle elements of our organisms, that their separation could not take place without producing premature physical death in my case, and acute suffering in hers. It is therefore quite impossible for any other influence to hold the ground thus occupied without involving dire disaster. At the moment of my death, which may occur at any moment from natural causes, this union will still remain intact; but means have been provided, into which it is not necessary now to enter, which will enable me to leave behind organisms as internally atomically united with the joint organisms of my wife and myself, though both in another state of existence, as we are to each other; but this is not possible except in the cases of those who have succeeded in forming a pneumatic atomic union here. These, however, will constantly increase in number as these truths come to be understood and acted upon, under the direction of those who have become conversant with their laws, and as they augment will the force and grandeur of the inspirational descent increase. This is necessary, for were it otherwise, an infernal inspirational invasion would sweep through the world, without any counteracting agency to check the disastrous consequences which would result from it, and which, in spite of the divine antagonistic inspiration which is now gathering force to meet it, will still prove powerful enough to produce the moral convulsion to which I alluded in the introductory chapter. The reason why I venture to predict this is because this moral convulsion has already begun in the unseen world, and its influence on this one must sooner or later be felt here.

The test of the value and nature of an inspiration is to be found in the efficiency of the remedy it proposes to meet the pressing human needs. Inspirations that do not pretend to grapple with the earth malady, and attack it at its root, lack the essential quality which is contained in the divine love for humanity, and which, as I propose to show later, was the one supreme animating principle of Christ, who was such an incarnation of divine inspiration as was never manifested upon the earth either before or since, and who is now the radiative centre of the seen and unseen worlds, which, enfolded one within the other, compose one system for the radiative influence of the highest forms of inspiration; and it will be found that all inspirations which ignore Him as their source, through whatever channel they may come, degenerate into speculative theories as to the nature and composition of man, and the cosmogony of the universe, which have no direct bearing upon its present actual condition with a view to fundamentally changing it; but which attempt rather to solve, *ex cathedra,* such problems as the character of man's previous existence, his reincarnation, his progress through future conditions, and final fate, than how to feed the hungry, clothe the naked, heal the sick, and infuse moral vitality into those who are spiritually dead to their obligations to God and their fellows.

In order to prepare the will, the affections, and the intellect to be collectively the transmitting media of an inspiration, which shall have a minute and practical bearing in this sense, their training and discipline must have lain in the performance of minute and practical details, controlled the while by an absorbing desire to perform them as an act of worship to God, and of benefit to the race. In the degree in which this motive dominates all thought of self, whether in the most sacred family affections, or in the ambition for spiritual progress of a personal character, will the divine inspiration descend into these minute and practical details, and the human problem begin to find its solution in the small everyday cares of life. The light which shines in upon a man who is sitting under a bo-tree with his eyes on his nose, or in a cave tapping a gourd, is of a very different quality. It may unfold to him the views of those in another state of existence with whom he is in atomic *rapport,* about the seven principles of which he is composed, and of the various stages through which human beings, after leaving this world, may pass before they return to it again, and what they may have been in a previous state of existence, but it gives him no hints as to social reconstruction in this one.

By abstaining from eating meat, by always eating alone, in order to avoid contagious magnetism, and by various other corporal disciplines, he may attract from his invisible associates into his organism such powerful magnetic forces as to enable him to make converts by hypnotic suggestion, or raise his body in the air, or suspend his respiration for an indefinite time; but so far from feeding others, as a rule he makes them feed him, so far from bearing their burdens, they bear his—in spite of his powers of levitation; and the final result of more than three thousand years of this kind of inspiration has been to crowd a greater number of idle useless monks, of ragged religious mendicants, and of revolting fakirs, upon a given area of the world's surface, than can be found in the same space in any other part of the world.

The most ancient religions of the East, whilst, as I shall presently show, they contain most valuable fundamental truths, have thus degenerated into practices by their devotees productive of no good to the human race, and the effort to apprehend mysteries which will help to raise man to a higher moral level, by attempting to put any such practices into operation in crowded cities of the West, exposed at all points to a hurricane of conflicting magnetisms, and in the midst of perverted social conditions, can only result in disappointment, and in inspirations of a most turbid and fantastic order. Those who think they can obtain light by sitting round tables with their little fingers joined, through mediums, whether professional or otherwise, are indulging hopes no less futile, so far as the direct application of what they receive to the great human needs is concerned. As a rule such communications are given to satisfy a curiosity which, if not altogether idle, is at all events rarely the result of an absorbing desire to find out what God's will is, and at all costs to do it; and such is the only motive by which an inspiration worth anything can be invoked, but even then it will be found that it cannot be relied upon as a guide. There is absolutely no certainty as to the source from which it springs, or the channel through which it has reached the medium, who is in his turn the automatic mouthpiece of an unknown influence, who is by no means independent of the physical, moral, and psychical conditions of the medium. Whatever be the source, then, of the purest communication, it only finally reaches the recipient, charged with the taint of those lower influences who — except under very special circumstances—alone frequent spiritualistic *séances*, in spite of the surface beauty of utterance, and with the taint not only of the medium, but of many others who take part in the performance.

Those who are so constituted that they can receive their

own impressions privately, provided they do not allow themselves to be used automatically, are far more favourably circumstanced; but even then they are as a rule too full of preconceived theological, or other prejudices of their own, to receive anything which transcends the commonplace, though occasionally, as in the case of some of the inspirational works referred to in a former page, they do transcend it, and that in a very remarkable degree; but these instances are comparatively rare, and the effusions, though often containing hints of sublime truths side by side with most exaggerated statements,[1] are generally worded so obscurely as to be unintelligible to the general reader, and not unfrequently to the writers themselves. This arises largely from the fact that the difficulty of conveying ideas thus presented in simpler language is extreme, and depends mainly on the processes of discipline which have been previously gone through as a preparation for their reception. If these have involved much study of other mystical writers, or abstract contemplation, or bodily austerities, unaccompanied by active physical labour to maintain a general equilibrium of the faculties, the inspiration is apt to be abstruse, mystical, or fanciful; because it is impossible for an influence, however pure and powerful, to communicate in such a manner as to be independent of the psychical condition of the medium; and the spiritual projection always finds its way into ultimate expression heavily charged with the idiosyncrasies, modes of thought and of phrase, and hereditary or acquired prejudices and tendencies of the human author. There is no human being, whatever may have been his training, who can avoid this, and it applies to this, and to every book, prophecy, or teaching which has ever attempted to convey subsurface ideas to the surface consciousness. Still this is no reason why those who have cause to believe that they have been charged with messages pregnant with import to humanity, should

---

[1] In illustration of this I may mention that no less than four individuals have come under my own observation who were informed inspirationally that they were immortal and would never see death in this world—of these the two most notable were "Jezreel," the author of the 'Flying Roll,' and T. L. Harris, the author of the 'Arcana of Christianity.' Of these four Mr Harris alone survives.

not give them to the best of their ability: it is only a reason why each such message should be fully tested on its own merits, why none should be regarded as infallible, and why those who become conscious of an inward monition conveying to them the impression that they may be chosen as messengers, should shrink from no sacrifice in the effort to fit themselves for the fulfilment of their mission.

If, with a most profound sense of my utter unworthiness for the task, I now venture to think that the time has come when these lines may be written, it is because I can no longer resist the impulsion to put into words, the thoughts that imperatively demand expression. This impulse was felt after an unconscious incubation, lasting many years, and for which I was prepared, together with my wife, by a long period of suffering and privation, involving the abandonment of country, family, and human ambitions, and during which time I worked as a day-labourer under a broiling sun, teamed as a common teamster through the rigours of a Canadian winter, served as a common domestic servant and cook's assistant, peddled grapes and flowers in American villages, lived at one time a life of almost absolute solitude, cooking my own meals, and holding no intercourse with the outer world; during several years I even remained separated from my wife, who at the same time, but in another part of the country, was either performing domestic housework, or earning her daily bread as a seamstress, or by giving lessons in music and painting, or as an under-mistress in a school. All this we did under a direction for which I shall ever feel grateful, although it involved a loss of many thousands of pounds; but it would have been absolutely valueless, had not the contact into which we were thus thrown with persons of divers nationalities and degrees, brought us into an internal sympathy with them, the nature and efficacy of which depended in its turn upon the fact that the ruling motive of our action, which was steadily kept uppermost in our minds, was, that we submitted to it all in the one hope that we might thereby become the more available instruments in God's hands.

I have ventured thus briefly into my own experiences, not for the purpose of suggesting that exactly similar ones are necessary for others, but with the view of illustrating the different psychical effect which must result from discipline of this kind, as contrasted with that which ascetics impose upon themselves, and the different inspirations which must ensue therefrom. The object to be attained in both cases is, an entire change in the distribution of the atomic particles composing the animal magnetic force, so as to render them susceptible by magnetic contact to the highest order of beings in the unseen world, and impervious to the invasion of counter-currents, whether from persons in this world or the other.

The ascetic endeavours to arrive at this condition by austerities, dirt, contemplation, isolation, trances, and like abnormal, physical, moral, and psychical efforts. The result is, that he infallibly attracts to himself kindred unseen influences, and while his magnetic forces undergo the change he desires, he becomes confirmed in his belief in the value of the process by which it has been accomplished, and receives without question the gloomy impressions of this world and the other, and man's mission and destiny, which they convey to him, mingled at the same time with lofty elevation of thought, a high moral code, and motives which to some natures, though they are more or less vague and shadowy, are not without their fascination.

In the case of those seeking their inspirations through the labour of their hands, and the active development of their affections towards those who are animated by the same motives themselves, and co-operating with them, they also attract to themselves kindred influences who are engaged in the unseen world in active service for God and the neighbour, who are full of the potent energies of this service, which they communicate to those engaged in it here, thus interlocking their atoms with those of their mortal associates, and conveying to their minds the ideas which enable these latter to perform the unaccustomed details of manual labour, under an inspiration which compensates for the lack of previous training, and brings with it a sense of joy to which the artisan or peasant, working for his daily wage, is an absolute stranger. Why this must be so may easily be understood, by the experience familiar to those who have had anything to do with prison discipline. Men who are turning a treadmill-wheel, which they know is doing nothing but revolving uselessly, suffer far more than if they knew it was attached to mill-stones which were grinding the corn to make their bread. The notion that the painful effort they are making is going to result in something, produces quite a different atomic combination from that which is produced by the conviction that it will result in nothing. And in the same way, the efforts that are made by a man who is learning how to be a carpenter, in order to arrive at a point that will enable him to sympathise internally with the artisan class, and so carry out a divine purpose, are quite different in their effect upon the atoms of his whole moral and physical structure, from what they would be if he was learning the trade because he had no other way of making a living for himself. But his endeavours in this direction have a far wider purpose than merely the outpouring of sympathy and the corresponding moral change which results from it. They go to the root of the matter which vexes his heart, and suggest the only remedy possible for the world's malady. For as he labours thus side by side with his fellow-men, tilling, perhaps, the land, and ploughing deep furrows into his own soul, which are destined in good time to bring forth an abundant crop, he perceives that he is in fact laying the foundations of a reconstructed society; and a vista opens out to his charmed gaze of co-operative industries, harmonious communities, and a political system in which liberty, equality, and fraternity shall develop under the ægis of absolute authority, and in association with a hierarchy composed of such different degrees of rank as correspond to their fitness to enjoy it.

The form which inspirations take, derived under these influences, is eminently practical, and those who seek truth thus find in their hours of hardest labour, the solution of economic, social, and political problems suggested to them, sometimes with marvellous lucidity and clearness; but they find, moreover, that all inspiration of this sort depends upon a correspondence between the results which they are producing practically, with those that reach them theoretically, and that they can only propose them on a large scale, in the degree in which they have been found to work on a small one.

Just as the first investigator into electricity could not logically assert that it might some day be possible to send a message round the world, until he had experimentally proved that he could make a needle vibrate by the force of a current passed from one end of his laboratory to the other, so, though the mental vision may picture a society perfectly constituted, on certain given principles, by the proper application of certain forces, it is necessary to begin by the application of those forces to the home, and work out the conditions of their application there. If, under this practical inspiration, which does not confine itself to ideas, but penetrates into atoms of the physical organism, directing with its energies the very fibres and muscles of the frame, a satisfactory result is produced, there is no reason why it should not be extended to another home; as the instinct of people seeking the same inspiration is to aggregate together, a community harmonised by a common inspiration would thus be formed, later on growing into a town, then becoming the centre of a district, and so increasing into a province, which, in its turn, should expand into a country, and gradually extend its influence, in the degree in which its consolidated magnetisms, all bearing the same current, attracted those who felt the attraction of sympathy, and repelled those who felt the repulsion of antipathy; and as the laws which govern magnetism in the human organism, are more or less identical with those which govern it in other substances, the smallest home could thus radiate the divine magnetism which it had received to an infinite extent, with no sense of loss or waste.

In order to illustrate the difference between mystical and practical inspiration, and to convey some idea of the principles upon which an inspired home should be constructed, I will here introduce a paper, dictated to me by my wife soon after we made our home in Palestine, and which is called "The Introduction to the House-Book."

CHAPTER IV.

INTRODUCTION TO THE HOUSE-BOOK; A TREATISE ON DOMESTIC LIVING, BY THE LATE MRS OLIPHANT—REASONS WHY HOUSEHOLDS SHOULD BE FORMED TO SECURE THE ADVENT OF IDEAL GOOD—MANNER OF LIFE TO BE NEITHER LAVISH NOR PARSIMONIOUS — REASONS FOR THIS — RELIGION NOW TO BE THE POSSESSION OF EACH MAN — ALL BORN TO ENACT, WHAT WAS FORMERLY TAUGHT — FAMILY GROUPS A MACHINERY FOR SOCIAL SERVICE — NECESSITY FOR THE PROTECTION AND NOURISHMENT OF A HOME—ALL ARTIFICIAL DISTINCTIONS OF RANK, OCCUPATIONS, AND CREEDS ABOLISHED — MAKERS AND MAINTAINERS OF THE FAMILY RESPONSIBLE FOR ITS DEVELOPMENT — THE QUALITIES REQUIRED FOR SOCIAL REDEMPTION — ALL TO STAND IN SYMPATHY TO THE LAWS OF EARTH'S SOCIETY BUT NOT TO BE SUBJUGATED BY THEM—ANGELIC CO-OPERATION WITH MEN — DIVISION OF RESPONSIBILITIES—ASSISTANCE IN LABOUR—SUBORDINATION TO LAW—NOTES OF EXPENDITURE.

IT may at first sight seem superfluous, and almost absurd, to preface a mere series of memoranda about simple housekeeping, with any explanation of the grounds upon which that housekeeping is carried forward. But there are various reasons which excuse this ceremony on the present occasion. The people who will use the following memoranda to refresh their memories, or to suggest the simple methods of life, are the people who, above all other desires, cherish that of understanding fully each other's motives and methods of work even in the slightest details, in order that the work which they may share may rest upon a perfect unity of motive and of method, and so establishing this unity amid the multiform necessities of domestic life, that such an organisation may admit of any work being performed according to convenience, now by one person, now by two, or now by twenty, &c.;

whilst this power of contraction and expansion in different branches of necessary work, must be secured for a system of life in which the individual must not be sacrificed for the work, nor the work for the individual, but in which both the members and the versatility of faculty would suffice to meet the fluctuating demands of daily needs; the methods of training the co-operating units in any household into this facile, expansive, and contractive machinery will be discussed a little further on, it being here in place to refer first to the reasons for domestic living which bring together the children of the sympneumatic era.

Let it then at once be established that it can never be asserted that any special manner of co-operative living is *per se* better or worse than another; that families, large or small, households large or small, divisions into ones or twos, or agglomerations of the size of communities, are to be adjusted beforehand as necessarily superior or inferior forms for the interdisplay of human love and power. Men and women should at all times select and reject their ways and means of righteous action, unhampered by any fixed opinions as to the relative merits among the rich choice of manners which experience and possibilities present.

The little household in which these lines are penned, has constituted itself by virtue of the apparent accidents of the moral and physical necessities of its various members, numbers of whom are not even able to be continuously resident in it. Its members, therefore, set up no pretension to offer, either by their number or by their differences of nationality, of occupation, or of age, any special model of what any other household actuated by the same motives, and following the same fundamental methods should be; for the essential living in homes of one blood, of one country, of one generation, or of fewer or greater numbers, or with entirely different pursuits, would be identical with theirs, wherever the belief were alight that men and women work to secure the advent throughout all the earth of ideal good—work in the presence and with the powers of a loftier order of unseen human beings, and do this equally in the minute or in the magnificent actions which they may deem it proper to perform. This little household has selected, however, its present scale of style with a motive and a plan somewhat more important than the mere guidance of external possibilities or desirabilities alone,—that is to say, that in deciding whether to have paid servants, and what servants to have; how many meal-times to establish, and what to place upon the table; what branches of semi-domestic industry to associate with the housekeeping (such as farming, chicken-keeping, bee-keeping, gardening, &c.); on what scale to facilitate by comfortable provision of domestic articles the various works, or in what measure to sacrifice temporarily the facility of work for economy of utensils,—I repeat, in deciding these things, it is making an effort to do something more than live honourably and rationally: it is trying to find a manner of life that shall be neither lavish nor parsimonious, that shall differ alike from the habits of the self-indulgent and the depraved—a manner of living to which the luxurious classes would readily, and without loss of health or mental vigour, descend, did they see a reasonable purpose for so doing, and to which all who live coarsely or poorly could be expected to rise with the better distribution of society's resources, whenever their improved intellectual condition demands for them a richer stock of the elements of food, of comfort, and of ease, than the masses of working men have hitherto been able to control. This little household would be ready to reconcile some people with a relative simplicity of living, and to call up some into a relative affluence: it is groping for ways of drawing together the extremes of waste and of want, of superfluity and of insufficiency, of suggesting the creation of recruits for the most divergent classes of earth's civilisation; and of the new middle class, whose function will not be that of preying upon the classes on either side of it, while it transmits the means of life from one to the other, but that of feeding in such diverse forms the legitimate wants of men, that they will be drawn together in it away from all the antagonisms established by their present unsatisfied requirements.

This search for moderation in the demands of daily life should not at the present day be a mere accidental result of necessity. The middle line of conduct serves no high spiritual end, while it is simply the line into which individuals are forced by artificial influences. There is no merit and no use in being neither rich nor poor, but something between rich and poor, if we cannot help ourselves; and in point of fact, if there is to be no exercise of personal intention in the style of circumstance in which we live, the middle style of moderation is not the one which people of high aspiration would wish to have offered to them, for it is, of all styles of living, the least generative of spiritual vitality. Devotion to high thought, and reverence for what is pure and elevating throughout human life, springs up more readily among people who are rich enough to pay others for relieving them entirely of every acquaintance with the methods of material existence. The trials of real poverty protect and urge the spirit, so that many of its virtues spring up in that condition which are almost lost to any other; but life which is without physical privation, but in which sufficiency depends upon the personal effort to acquire and manage material resources, is neither high nor low enough for excellence to be easy. It neither helps men to suffer, nor places them so far beyond suffering that they are ashamed not to aspire; and it is inclined to breed in them a stupid satisfaction in the easy accomplishment of operations requiring a purely material order of faculty, and resulting in nothing higher than the comfort and satisfaction of a few individuals.

Nevertheless a wise mediocrity of circumstance will necessarily be adopted more and more by all people who seek the general good; for those who can command luxury and the displays required for the forwarding of private and family ambition, will more and more refrain from wasting upon these the superfluity which they will prefer to devote to the better regulation of general social necessities; and on the other hand, such efforts as the wealthiest are at this day more and more desirous to put forth, will enable the poor to tend more to comfort. A condition, therefore, of moderate ease, in spite of its tendency to deaden spiritual sensibility, is the only one fitted to a rational moral development; and the art must be discovered of utilising it without falling into moral sloth for lack of privation, and of maintaining a concentrated aspiration for mental and spiritual growth in spite of labours amidst the material bases of earthly existence. We must learn to seize all the more delicate elements that the human spirit is accustomed to develop in its extremes of suffering and of refinement, and bind them to the wheels of vulgar working-day machineries. We must do this to redeem these machineries from misapplication to ends of mere private gain. We must not forget that the risk of decaying spiritually is all the greater with all those people who are conscientiously unable any longer to recognise as duties the demands of ecclesiastical organisations: these, at the time of their vigour, have always imposed practices which reminded men, at recurring intervals of time, that they lived for something beyond material good. But a great number of those natures most deeply fraught at this day with the desire of obtaining and distributing all highest sorts of excellence, find in themselves no response whatever to the expectations of any Church, and these have to beware lest ease of life, and the withdrawal even from ignoble effort, do not obscure their sense of the inner personal sanctuary where the divine presence dictates in the still small voice.

For that which has been called religion, and which has rested on wide bases of popular assent, has grown to self-dependence among men, and is now, or must be made, the personal possession of each one. As it fades out of public institutions, or as its practical influence weakens there, as the most earnest, single-minded, and spiritual people require less and less the forms and formularies of Churches, or obey them merely by innocent acts of social custom, that condition of high spirituality and morality which these Churches fostered in their day, which has outgrown their comprehension now, but is itself religion, this must be held by each individual as the atmosphere in which to act daily and hourly in the whole effort of duty. Individuals now generate religion as of old, but not isolated individuals—for this has man "evolved." But as the responsibility lay heavy upon the souls who formerly were charged, rarely with great powers of mind and thought, to give them forth to mankind; as would have been the loss if mighty teachers turned aside from the effort to deliver their high instruction,—so now is the responsibility with each, when all are born to enact that which used to be taught—so now is the loss to the whole mass of men, if any one fails to live striving to enact it.

It is this maintenance of the highest possible level of religious vitality in practical life, that is the all-sufficient reason why people should associate in groups, why homes should exist, — whether the individuals which compose them are drawn together by the apparent accident of blood or of material necessity, or whether by any more conscious process of mutual selection, it matters not. The home, the place where a rich atmosphere of varying elements of mind and spirit can be generated, protected, consolidated, and set in activity, is a necessary integer of elevated social conditions. If family connections, and the repose of all familiar customs which grow up in them, are not a means of obtaining strength of united moral action, they miss the performance of their proper function, and generate, perforce, harm to the world's interests, instead of help. But because this may be, it does not disprove the fact that ties of blood, which are the soil of spontaneous loves and virtues, of honour, fortitude, patience, and self-control, should be the strength and background of world-service, as they are fraught with power, even in their lowest development, to reveal the innate altruism of the human being. When the true strength of family groups is better understood in the research that man begins to institute for material of beneficence, the social brigandage which they now exercise, by means of their relative unity of action, will be converted instead into a machinery for social service. But unity of action, whether among blood relations or among people drawn together by sympathy or mutual dependence of any kind, is the great social necessity of the hour. The statement is not new: co-operation, and moral as well as material co-operation, is a cry that recent generations have learnt to repeat, and co-operative action is no longer an unknown thing. But the full meaning and necessity of spiritual unity is not generally understood; and is least understood, as a rule, by those people who are the most generous of their time and service in seeking general reforms. For public services, social or industrial, it is not difficult at this day to find people who will act harmoniously to improve the outer forms of life; nor has it been at any time otherwise than easy for bodies of people with any distinct religious bias, to recruit members willing and anxious to distribute physical relief by common methods as an assistance to the persuasion of religious forms; but the natural order of spiritual and social development requires co-operative unity in private as well as in public life—nay, requires it in the minutiæ of the home circle, as the basis of all vaster co-operation.

Those who go forth out of divided and unsympathetic private atmospheres, to enforce propriety in the various branches of public life, carry with them a theory, an intellectual conception of things that should be, but carry no elements of moral life, to create growth of co-operative intelligence among those for whom they labour. There is no truly reproductive species of virtue or moral power but that with which men and women are elementally charged,—no virtue or power with which men or women can impregnate others, so that they in their turn produce them afresh, except what has developed in each one by solid growth of moral particles which pervade the being; and this growth in each person of a healthy and potent moral organisation, as well as its constant increase in maturity, requires, as imperatively as the wellbeing of the physical constitution, the repose, the protection, the nourishment, and the pleasure of familiar home surroundings. It requires the simple essences that are struck forth by simple acts. It requires primary examples of the great social needs. It must call its own a dwelling-place where direct ministrations of love are easy, to keep alive the absolute conviction that love exists. It requires home, as meat or raiment or sleep, for the maintenance of its growing condition. Thus the tone of the familiar life becomes a more and more important matter for consideration to those who contribute to it,—more and more important with the uprising throughout the social bosom of this true sense, that social purity and truth and energy must now be striven for, and that the power of close co-operation is necessary to this strife; for there is no perfect knowledge nor practice on a large scale, that has not first been learnt upon a small, and he cannot contribute to true unity in great and far-spreading services, who has not learnt to practise it in the minute things of home.

The value of these groupings of individuals in intimate juxtaposition is incalculable: there are no other circumstances which are capable of producing the same results; and these results in the individual are indispensable, at this period of high social effort, to the lofty character which society strains to embody.

Such convictions lying at the root of the action which drew together the little fraternity here alluded to, it is evident that each member of it must adopt, with a solemn sense of responsibility to the world at large, whatever occupation befits them within it, or whatever they befit.

It is this sense of responsibility, this solemnity, which attaches to the action of all members of such a household while they constitute it, which makes them, old or young, embrace life now, not less as a training process, than as a field for work.

Those who have begun, however totteringly, to "walk with angels"—those even who but begin to train their faculties unto this thought, lest perchance they miss its truth—begin also to measure themselves with the ideal, with the true facts of higher human nature, with personalities whose type has hitherto drawn all pure imaginings before towards itself in aspiration, but who now join hands with men and women on planes of growing consciousness. Yes; now we look on this image and on that—those of us who will—we compare what we are, with the perfect manhood with which we feel, with greater or lesser clearness, that we have companionship, and we work to change ourselves. The nearer that the far ideal draws to us, the more we see the differences between it and ourselves; and as we would grow like it for great services on earth, as we would work by power of better natures against the sufferings and the vices of earth's masses, we must first establish this bettering of ourselves in the humble sphere of home. Thus we are obliged to exercise a self-criticism which magnifies each slight defect into a subject of world importance, for slight defects jar on the harmony, the regularity, the calmness, and the whole beauty of the domestic circle— jarring, in fact, the actual spiritual organisation of each member of it, whose action then upon the outer world, whenever exercised, is by that jar impaired—and not only must the members of households watch inquisitorially against their personal imperfections, to restrain them ceaselessly, holding these imperfections as being each one injurious to universal interests; but for the development of a large and generous wisdom, for the preparation of vaster organisations in the future, they must question constantly of their habits and their methods, whether they are such as would conduce to every highest interest, if used by tens and hundreds of people as well as by two or three.

The effort, therefore, to formulate and to obey simple and broad rules in the conduct of daily life, is more than important, — it is indispensable to all servants of God's world. Being thus indispensable, the little bands of workers who are devoted to it have their necessary places in the social scheme; and having these, their duty to fit themselves for every detail of united labour, is as necessary to general progress, as either the wise means that they would use materially, or the high spiritual condition which they endeavour to establish.

The difficulty of distributing financial responsibility in a satisfactory manner has broken up many of the best attempts at societary co-operation. It is probable that this responsibility, in common with others, the discharge of which affects equally every member of a family or group, will have to rest with all its weight and all its freedom upon one person. As time goes on, people will not be found lacking, who, in the name of the divinest service, the free evolution of the purest faculties of existing man, will gather others around them—their children, or their brothers, or their friends—the name of that service will prohibit disagreement of creed,—creeds and denial of creeds being all too weakly human, and too partial for the new necessity. It will prohibit all differences of social rank—these having done their service and become superfluous. It will prohibit artificial distinctions in diverse dignity in pursuits—this being obstructive to pleasure in work, and to its right selection. It will prohibit every motive for personal effort, for personal virtue, for personal enjoyment, except that they are necessary to the general human interest. They will be brave men who will call others to follow under this banner, brave and bold, even though an inner light of strong perception, rational and instructive, guides them surely; even though they know the attainments of strong developed faculty and enlightenment and power, that will grow beneath its folds upon each soldier that they have called. They need their courage, although in clearest consciousness they call down, hold down, and irradiate heavenly forces in earth; for work, true work, is slow, continuous, and quiet; yet the root of social excellence must thus be set. But the order of the courage they require is moral—the courage to maintain the purity of moral perceptions—courage to enact spiritual convictions in the strained intervals of their fluctuation—courage to obey the voice within during the pleasure of its silences. The wear and tear of recklessness, of wilful improvidence, of disregard of the divine law throughout external nature, will not be incurred by those who are seeking to draw forth inner wisdom into outer things; they will not kick against the known limitations of industrial possibilities; they will not court privation or starvation in carelessness or wilfulness for those whom they would empower for all good work. If they invite co-operation, they must practise a keen and inspired discretion in recognising the signs of rational possibility of success. It is true that, being relieved of the desire to maintain all artificial standards of what constitutes success, financial competence will often prove a sufficient basis for useful activities, whether of an intellectual or of a muscular nature, while obviously no one will struggle for enrichment by any processes that of necessity impoverish their neighbours, nor hold riches as *per se* valuable, or as certainly to be sought—the evidence of their use for special purposes requiring to be corroborated by the deepest and most earnestly sought internal guidance.

We will assume, therefore, that a man, or, probably of necessity, a man and woman, have summoned together, under the clearly felt guidance of God, people whose harmony of feeling is absolute in respect of the principles just enumerated, whose motto is free evolution; we will also assume that the wisdom of that gathering, of which the responsibility necessarily rests with those who have formed the group, is justified by a rational probability of providing the things necessary for daily life. This provision may at once exist in the established possessions of this head of the family, or it may exist partly in income contributed as shares by different members of the household, or it may exist only in the produce of the industry of the head and members. This gathering, to be a home, to be the indispensable fulcrum for power in far-spread labours, to be the battery of a love-force which shall unceasingly empower those who take rest in it, must be constituted in the form of a family of children, whose parents provide and guide. At the limits of the home this form breaks up; the various members who are not required for devotion to the immediate necessities of the establishment, may be carrying on occupations single-handed, or in co-operation with others of every description; and in those occupations they will act as free individuals, or as members of associated bodies, in every diversity of manner. Professions and industries of home management, unless they distinctly form part of domestic economy, should remain free in their exercise—there should obviously be no limit to the variety of method under which industries or public services will be carried on, or to the different ways in which professions or other occupations will be pursued; but in the home, which may be regarded as an artificial extension or reproduction of the natural family, a hierarchical system of direction is necessary for the spontaneous action constantly required in all its departments.

Now it is evident from this, that people who would create domestic bodies as the kernels of a new and high social development, whether by the mere training of children of their own, dedicated by their very birth to this object, or by the moulding of people who join them in this plan, must do more than to foresee the spiritual ground solidified by a common aim, and the material ground made safe by a sufficient basis for the works proposed. They must be prepared themselves to regard each member of the group which becomes their family, as held by them in charge for the world's service. These parents must take upon themselves the collection of all home funds, from whatever source contributed, in order to redistribute them with free exercise of judgment and of love among the members, according to the requirements of their moral and physical condition. They must remember that from the moment they have made themselves responsible to God for creating a domestic body, they cannot shift the responsibility of any action of which the results will affect the body as a whole. The responsibilities which they delegate must be those connected with special branches of activity, in which mistakes or failure will affect principally the special individuals charged with the control of such departments, and will only indirectly, and in unimportant degrees, affect the whole. The heads, for example, while they may derive valuable assistance from the perceptions and experience of any member of the household, with whom they will freely consult, cannot divest themselves of the duty of acting freely for the immediate interests of the group, and for the greater interest of spiritual evolution in general society, by the choice they make of a general plan of life, of a locality to live in, of the people to draw into the sphere of their own ministrations, of those to be removed from it, of managers and assistants in each branch of help or service, of what advice to offer on moral questions affecting the action of individuals, on the little social body as a whole. In a word, the makers and maintainers of the family, whose existence they regard as fraught with infinite importance to the divine plan for earth, must freely make it in the best way that they can find. But they will institute a systematic attempt to develop in each individual the highest degree of responsibility in special functions that is compatible with their age, judgment, or faculty and moral condition.

In view of the serious aspect which such efforts as are being now discussed, bear to those who maintain them, it will be no easy and no simple work to guard hourly against the disintegration of such associations by individual lack of perceiving the interest of the mass, or by too great a concentration of the individual on the interests of the mass to the sacrifice of one another. Yet it is useless to embrace the leadership of any mass, unless it is possible to watch equally over the welfare of the whole, and the welfare of the parts. Neither will this leadership be successful, unless each member of the co-operative body that it associates shares with it, in the degree of his or her personal capacity, this sense of the serious and important nature of their work. This sense must be developed in the young and fed in the adult, as the very basis of a true moral atmosphere.

It is not possible to produce lives which will show in joint action the qualities required for social redemption, unless the knowledge among them is strong and clear that they stand in weighty responsibility towards one another as individuals, and towards humanity as a group. To regard their position lightly or indifferently, is to annihilate it.

Isolated lives have always shown, and show at this day, immeasurably the strongest and the purest material for humane action; but the work of the world has become gigantic at the period in which we live. Life in its modern aspect creates co-operation in error: the vices, the industrial or social tyrannies, political rivalries, the craze for wealth, the pursuit of pleasure, in one place, reinforce—by the sympathy established throughout the civilised world in its ready intercommunication—all these things in every other place. It is not enough now to aim individually at affecting righteously immediate surroundings. The immediate neighbours of any given person are a hundredfold more powerfully affected by the myriad influences that strike upon them from the vast social universe, than by any impulse which a mere individual could communicate. We must, if we aim at a universal good, or indeed at any good, work in the methods calculated to affect large masses. The youth of the time instruct themselves for good or for evil out of the general movement, unconfined to country or to continent, and cannot be content to accept knowledge merely at the hands of parents, pastors, or masters. The grandest work yet delegated to physical sciences is accomplished.

The life-appliances that they have produced, make each human being a child of the universe, and the ordinary associations of civilised life at this era, focalise upon each individual direct movement from every part of universal society.

But if the gain be great of a personal acquaintance with the truth that each one is affected by the many scattered throughout the world, the danger is great of misunderstanding the divine purport of new possibilities thus opened for the individual and for the masses.

It is well to stand in mental and emotional sympathy with the laws of earth's vast society; but it is ill to be personally subjugated by them, as ill as to be subjugated by any more local tyrannies. Yet this is a common fate. Victims of the confusion which reigns amid the raw processes of unification in world interests are countless—not less in retired domestic circles than in heaving political scenes. And for these reasons associations of life among individuals become a necessity. They are necessary to protect in individuals their individuality of power; they are necessary to produce a united individual power massive enough to affect society at large; and they are necessary, because, by their existence, they generate the only moral material which can be reasonably expected to hold a sufficient amount of force to influence the colossal development of modern life. Humanity has developed needs so poignant, and individuals have responded so loudly those needs, that machineries must be found that will aim, by the utilisation of the greatest individual force, at the widest social good. To aim at less is insult to the constitution of individuals of the species now produced; and the aim of vast social rectitude, as motive for all individual action, is the only protection to be found for each individual against suppression by the vastness of existing social error.

Thus a universal quality, so to speak, has to be introduced into the minutest efforts and actions of domestic life, consecrating domesticity to the only true and persistent instincts of modern man, establishing at every hour the identity of the reason for mundane existence, with the reason of every exercise of man's operative power during the course of it. If to live in order to induce co-operation with the divine activities throughout the world is good, it is not less good, as an indispensable part of such living, to stand in the very current of these divine activities. With every motion of the hand and every action of the mind operating in this spirit, and co-operating for this object, the order of the simplest labours becomes experimental science, and the fitness for such order of each labourer becomes to himself a subject of constant inquiry. Hence self-discipline and self-modification will become the constant habit of each. They will scrutinise themselves for those things which render them imperfect assistants of consolidated operativeness—knowing that the quality of this operativeness must affect with endless consequences the future of all society.

But it will suffice, without enlarging on the more purely ethical side of this subject, to mention that the most difficult part of this work of discipline and modification *does itself*, by the very fact of juxtaposition of natures according to laws —the laws of mutual relief of superfluous vitality by spiritual organisms, as elsewhere described; and that it is generally sufficient to seek and recognise frankly the imperfections in question, to guard against the mental inertia which would otherwise impede the spontaneous action of true law.

Each person will also work on all sides to perfect in the details of his duties what has been missing in his previous education; and while this will be the more difficult for those who embark in co-operative efforts late in life, it will be the more necessary for them to do it in the degree of their opportunity, because it is assumable that they may find themselves, by the very reason of age and general experience, called upon at any moment to act as leaders, and to infuse a varied quality of power into the direction of many lives. It is difficult to say which is the more needful to true service in works both small and great, the little sciences of practical life, or the high arts and knowledge that place us in communication with the minds charged at all times with those inspirations by which man has been raised out of his grovelling among the bare necessities of physical existence. The superior necessity of either will exist only to individuals who have been led by circumstances to a special neglect of one class of knowledge. Those persons who have been obliged to confine the application of their faculties more exclusively to the requirements of the body in domestic and industrial arts, will feel more and more the degradation of exclusive participation in material interests, and will seize every opportunity of entering the realms of intellectuality and spirituality, by acquainting themselves with the rich products of the human spirit, mind, and imagination; by opening their blunted sensibilities to joy in art and beauty; and by storing their memories both with the acts of men and nations in all times, and their thoughts and mode of feeling,—because these acts and thoughts and feelings record the march of a divine growth on earth. Those persons, on the other hand, who, by drift of circumstance or pursuit of inclination, have held aloof from the whole region of material and industrial ways and means of living, will condescend towards these in spite of personal disinclination, when they reflect that the higher qualities of spirit, developed by lives and generations among refined pursuits, must be infused for the unification of the social body into material labours, that the basis of earthly existence may not remain foul when its superstructure can be so fair, and when they reflect further that no one can make this infusion, but he whose good fortune has developed in him the refining quality. Therefore the necessities are broad and many for meeting together of high and low, rich and poor, one with another, when those come forth out of the ocean of vague social movement who see, or think they see, in the idea of angelic co-operation in men, an explanation of the pressure now straining and fevering society, and a ground of faith in the rapid advance of society towards a state which human hearts desire.

Even a few thus gathered together may be the central machinery of a mighty social engine, if they aim thus vastly and work thus minutely. There must be order in every work, —the order and discipline of responsibilities judiciously distributed, faithfully recognised, and clearly limited. It should be known to each and all, as much as possible, under whose eye each detail of work is performed. When the general organisers have distributed the various domestic operations into their classes, and have laid the charge of each class upon special persons, and have selected for each the necessary assistance, it will require care to avoid confusion, and for many reasons. Say, for instance, that while the group of those ready for responsible charge is still small, one person has charge of several departments of domestic operations, that person may have to instruct assistants, either co-operative volunteers or hired servants perhaps, in respect of these different branches; that person must be careful to give such instruction to each assistant only in respect of the particular work of the said charge, and must not slide into the habit of offering suggestions to an assistant in this charge, about work performed by him or her at other hours under different superintendence. Any one person, volunteer or paid—that is to say, a corporate member or an accidental member of the household—may be helper in one or more departments, and may have full charge at the same time in several others, so that the boundary-line of these departments must be very exactly defined, or it will not be possible to know on what points simply to perform work according to instructions, and on what points to exert authority over others, or individual freedom of idea. Again, any person may be invited to give help temporarily at any moment in departments under others' charge, and much of the charm and sweetness of united lives arises from these spontaneous appeals from one another; but the person thus called in must be careful not to pervert the circumstance of this call to an opportunity for interference with the individual responsibility of the one temporarily to be served. The most highly and extensively burdened with free responsibilities, must simply serve without criticism, mental or expressed, when asked for help for the simplest and most mechanical operation. If the distribution of responsibility is clear, and the respect for them perfect, exchanges of assistance can be infinite, and the painful monotony of unchanging labours will be pleasantly avoided; but until co-workers are skilled to discern disorder, it will easily occur, and the most easily through the most generous and devoted. A kind person will, for instance, be inclined by the first movement or impulse to obey at once any demand for help; yet to obey it will often disturb the order of work. He must therefore reflect if the call is legitimate or not, provided always that he has time and strength at his disposal for the purpose. It is a legitimate call if the person who makes it has had given to him free responsibility for the work in question; in that case his freedom extends to the calling in of volunteer labour. It is not a legitimate call if the person who makes it serves in the work in question under the responsibility of another. In this latter case, the assistant who requires help should only obtain it through the responsible director or with his sanction. To illustrate this—a little child asks for some help in the matter of its play. This is a just demand: it has been left free in that play, and is not responsible to any one for the manner of its performance. But suppose a person charged, we will say, on the one hand with the whole administration of the cooking department, and accustomed on the other to assist for one hour in making clothes, falls ill, she must act differently regarding the two labours. In seeking her substitute, she will select one for the cooking amongst her own subordinates, or, not finding one, will refer the matter to the head of the house, and will not, of course, feel free to exercise her right of claim to friendly help, even as head of a department, if this would absorb the time required for the other duties; but should the amount of help she wants, require only the leisure of her neighbour, reference to the general head would not be necessary. As regards, on the other hand, the hour of needlework, she will obviously leave the choice of her substitute to the manager in that department. It is not difficult to train the least gifted with intellectual conceptions into obedience of the laws of organisation; and it is not difficult to reconcile the most spirited to perfect subordination, when it is the subordination to useful and intelligible law. It is more difficult to distribute each detail of a varied labour on a distinct organic scale, and watch over preservation of the whole plan by delicate guidance of authorities and obediences along their appointed channels; and this is an operation which, though it be necessary to all great and effective social work, should not be attempted even on a little scale by any one not prepared to guide individuals in their little acts with tender love, and to guard organisation as a holy principle with earnest devotion.

On the other hand, so necessary is the preparation, obtained only through familiarity with details for correct and beneficent organisation, that scarcely any sacrifice of time or personal inclination is too great a price for making it; and to work in meekness, in order as rapidly as possible to be fitted to watch over the lives of many others, is an ambition which will not unworthily replace many which are not productive of high moral and social evolution.

The foregoing remarks were suggested by the simple necessity of having, even in a very small household, ample registries of possessions. On the grounds here stated, it will often be found necessary for people otherwise talented and capable of what might appear higher employments, to award some part of their lives to simple things, and to concentrate upon them earnest efforts for perfection. Thus the house-book, or books it may be, including lists, and rules, and recipes, and

F

accounts, is a collection worthy of good faculties in the making, and of respect in the keeping of it. Current records, in the shape of accounts, lists, &c., of all operations, are more than ever indispensable to people who direct such operations, with the desire of training all engaged in them into such clear understanding of their effect, as will enable each one safely and intelligently to direct them on a still larger and larger scale.

Now, to be ignorant of the amount of material invested in any given domestic work, of its changing market values, to fail in noticing the accustomed consumption and wear and tear of the material, and to make no record of these things, for the purpose of assisting memory, of clearing understanding, and of instructing others,—is to carry forward a result, whatever artistic substitutes one may have at the moment, almost sterile from a co-operative point of view. To do well is very little, and may be less. To do well so as to make it possible and easy for others to do well also, and to do better, is necessary to work that makes its horizon wide. The type of persons who can produce good performance in any mode of labour by concentrating upon it their faculties with the single view of performing it well, is a very ordinary one; but the procreative quality of generous faculty at this date, requires us to develop a type of workers who hold the drive of personal energy in perpetual check; who scatter it by the way, preparing paths of others' work; who inquire of their own performance constantly if it creates facilities for performance by others; who act in all things in reference to the acting power of others. He can no longer be esteemed an excellent workman who can only work excellently. For his work to prove that it is living, it must be generative; and it will not be generative unless the workman has his mind trained to a clear conception of his own methods, and their connection with the laws of nature; unless he can impart that understanding by word of mouth at any time or write it down; unless the sum of his experience, while he is constantly increasing it, is as constantly forced by him into mental shape easy of registration, and, whenever useful, registered, so that it may be at all moments ready of access to all his fellow-creatures, and so that he may be at all moments in a mental position to impart his methods to others. We will suppose a household where there is no record kept of what moneys go for the buying of food, and what for the buying of clothes—that is to say, what sum for a purpose indispensable to health, and what for a more elastic necessity, —how can such a household know absolutely if it can afford to burden itself or not with the cost of another member, to whose destitution it might wish to minister? It would answer the question at once if it had made note of such expenditures as could be reduced or postponed without danger to the general wellbeing, by deciding to moderate these; but it would not wisely add heavy burdens to itself if they necessitated infringing upon the sums devoted to absolute necessities. Still more important must it be to keep graduated accounts of funds embarked, say, in uncertain speculations, imperfectly tested industries, or fine arts, or things termed luxuries, which, rightly selected, develop the refinements that lurk within all natures, but which are all among the things which could be set aside for the sake of any more important duty. There should, properly speaking, be no haziness about the financial condition of any occupation. What it represents of material, of labour, should stand clearly at all moments before the mind and before the eye of some one, and all people should be either possessed of the capacity for formulating clear ideas and statements concerning the value of labours, or be in training for that purpose.

CHAPTER V.

INSUFFICIENCY OF THE NATURAL REASON AS A GUIDE TO DIVINE TRUTH, BECAUSE IT CANNOT DIVEST ITSELF OF THE IDEAS OF TIME AND SPACE—HENCE THEOLOGY AND SCIENCE BOTH BLIND GUIDES—MAN THE ARENA OF CONFLICTING ATOMIC FORCES—TRANSMUTATION OF MATERIAL FORCES BY CONVERSION OF MORAL PARTICLES—METHODS AND MANIFESTATIONS OF INFESTATION—ATOMIC CONSTITUTION OF MORAL ATMOSPHERE—PHENOMENA OF HEREDITY—ASTROLOGY—WILL-FORCE UNDER SPECIFIC INFLUENCE—FAITH-HEALING—ELIXIR OF LIFE—RADIATION OF DIVINE LIFE DEPENDS ON MAGNETIC CONDITIONS—SUFFERING INVOLVED THEREBY—RELIGION USELESS AS A MEANS TO A PERSONAL END—WORLD-REGENERATION TO BE ACCOMPLISHED BY A RADIATION OF DIVINELY INSPIRED HUMAN AFFECTION—INSPIRATION THREEFOLD: THROUGH UNION WITH GOD, MAN, AND NATURE—POLLUTION OF ITS CURRENT THREEFOLD: BY PRIDE, BY SELFISHNESS, BY APATHY—ITS FORCE DEPENDS UPON ITS CONCENTRATION UPON GROUPS ANIMATED BY THE SAME MOTIVE.

IT is my hope that among those who have had the patience to follow me thus far, there may be some who will be ready to admit that we have reached ground where the theologian and the man of science may meet, without doing violence to those conscientious convictions which have hitherto driven them into opposite extremes: these atoms, which form the essence, so to speak, of what has heretofore been considered "matter," and which are the transmitting media of procreation and sustaining life, are sufficiently substantial to satisfy the requirements of science, while, as they also compose the immortal part of us, and are the habitations of thought and emotion, they should be sufficiently spiritual to satisfy the requirements of theology for those that make them. "The existence of nothing" being a contradiction in terms, the thing which exists, whether it be called body or soul, matter or spirit, must consist of substantial force of some kind—indeed, it is stated of Christ in the Nicene Creed that He is of one substance with the Father. The reason why conclusions at which disputants have arrived are irreconcilable, is because they both persist in introducing into the consideration of the question the elements of time and space, which have no existence outside of the relation which they derive from that very limited class of faculties, which we call our senses.

The revelations which we receive, as another class of faculty connected with our subsurface consciousness develops within us, are incapable of being transferred into language, because all our methods of verbal expression are derived from the experiences of our senses, with all their present limitations, and rest upon the assumption that time and space are realities,—just as another language and an entirely new vocabulary would need to be invented, to enable people who live in the third dimension of space to understand those who live in the fourth. It would be useless, therefore, to attempt to describe many things which, if people were in a position to apprehend them, would render such differences as now exist between them impossible. That neither the men of science nor the men of theology struggle to develop these more interior faculties, is entirely their own fault, and I am afraid must, in some cases, be set down to the complacent self-satisfaction arising from a conviction on the part of both, that they know their own business too well to condescend to take a hint from anybody. But a blind belief in the superficial senses is as unsafe a guide to truth, as a blind belief in a book: science is as mole-eyed as theology, and yet to one or the other the whole civilised world trusts for enlightenment. No wonder that these two sets of blind guides, leading their blind followers, should stumble against each other in the dark, and fight furiously. The pity is, that one ray of light let in from the proper quarter would show that they were fighting over a shadow; but this ray each man must let in for himself, nobody can do it for him, and he must do it by getting rid of all his old preconceived notions and prejudices, and by opening the chambers of his affections, through incessant service for others, and arduous discipline and painful self-sacrifice. There is no royal road to the hidden knowledge which reveals the mystery of the action of the vital forces on nature. Each man must laboriously travel it alone; but he reaps a rich reward as the light dawns on his heretofore beclouded consciousness, and the problems which distracted it melt away before its heat, like ice under the rays of the sun. But the divine sun can alone perform this marvel, and it is only by inmost union with God that man can attain a perception of the wonders of divine science.

Let us then assume as a hypothesis that the invisible world, with all the beings in it, as well as this one,—the two, in fact, forming a single universe,—is sustained and animated by a material force, which emanates from the Great Source of Life who pervades all things; and that owing to a disturbance in that force—the nature of which will be alluded to later—its energies are displayed in a disorderly manner, and produce what we term physical disease and moral evil;—the question naturally arises in the minds of those who would fain see that force restored to its normal activities, How can this result be brought about? and how can we contribute to bring it about? Is there any process by which we can convert our organisms—each one of which is a battery of that force—into a distributing agent for a purer and more powerful current than any which now exist? Manifestly only by approaching nearer to its source, and receiving it as unpolluted as possible by its passage through other impure organisms. The first experience of which the man engaged in this attempt becomes conscious is, that he is the arena in which two strongly antagonistic currents come into collision, and that he is frustrated in his attempt to open himself only to that which is pure, by a flood of that which is impure, seeking ingress by the opening which his efforts to receive a greater measure of the pure effected in his organism. If he doubted it before, he now becomes conscious that this invasion of the force he has roused, and which, though constantly prompting him to evil formerly, did so insidiously, and through a subtle action on what seemed to him his own initiative, is distinctly personal and intelligent; in other words, he perceives that a malignant influence seeks to possess and dominate him, which he recognises to be outside of his own personality; while his perhaps unconscious cry for aid, in the heat of the combat is responded to by a beneficent influence which he also recognises as personal; in other words, no matter how scientific he may have been when he began his experiment, he will very soon, if he is persevering and sincere, come to recognise in one influence what in old parlance was called a "guardian angel," and in the other an infesting demon, and he will further learn that the degree in which he can attract the one and repel the other, depends upon the force of his will, and the promptitude with which he puts into operation his determination to obey the one and resist the other, at all cost and sacrifice. Thus he seeks, through constant and unremitting combat, to fit himself to become a medium for the transmission of the pure life-current, instead of being, as he was formerly, a medium of mixed and opposing currents. For it cannot be too strongly urged that we are all of us mediums of one kind or another, and that however much polluted the current may have become by the channels through which it passed before it reached us, it derived its origin in the first instance from God, and to stop the impulses of life which are thus projected into us, would be synonymous with cessation of life itself. This increases the difficulty, for it becomes a question of the transmutation, not of the expulsion, of the material force, the atoms of which, interlocked with our own, form the basis of all that is bad and impure, as well as of what is good, in our own moral nature. By the aid which we derive from our angelic allies we transmute and recombine these; but as some of them form part of the life of the infesting being, the latter is thus directly affected by this conversion of moral particles, and can only escape from the regenerating influence thus cast upon him, by a very powerful exercise of will in the opposite direction, involving a painful dislocation of atoms.

As a general rule, the earth-man who has fought the good fight, and vanquished his unseen enemies, has also the satisfaction of knowing that he has converted them, and that they pass, through his instrumentality, into the tutelage of those who have helped him to release them from the bondage to which they had been reduced by their own evil passions. It is thus that the visible reacts on the invisible, and that we are here unconsciously the guardian angels of those whose vices remained unsubdued in this life, but who can now be reached in a more effective manner than was formerly possible; because an angel can act far more powerfully on a disembodied organism through an embodied one, and by its assistance, where the atoms of the two are interlocked, than directly. This is borne out by the fact, well known to spiritualists, when "elementals," as they are termed by them, or unfortunate beings, usually of a very debased type, who are still chained to this earth magnetically, owing to the gross condition of their atomic particles, implore human beings to release them—a testimony I am aware that will not be regarded as worth much by the world at large; but those who can realise that men here, influence most materially by their lives, the lives and conditions of those who have passed into another state of existence, must feel that it adds most seriously to their responsibilities; while it should operate as a powerful stimulant to them to rise into new and higher conditions in this world, than they have hitherto deemed possible. It should also be remarked that men suffer much, not only morally but physically, from these invasions; for the lower class of infesting spirits obtain magnetic elements from human organisms by which they sustain their own, and urge them to vices which furnish them with the sustenance they desire.

Thus the first impulse of a man who dies of drink, on reaching the other world, is to infest the organism of a drunkard here, and urge him to saturate himself with alcohol, the essential quality of which he drains out of the subjected organism, thus intensifying the desire of the victim, to an uncontrollable degree, to satisfy a craving that can never be satisfied, till the external tissues of the organism are finally wasted. During his drunken bouts he becomes a medium, through whom his infesting demon often speaks and raves; while the latter foresees and shrinks from the prospect of the physical death of his victim, because he knows that it will involve a dislocation of atoms, which will convey the same sensation of decease as if he were himself passing through the death-agony. In like manner, a coquette, accustomed to live on the admiration of men while in this world, no sooner passes from it than she seeks the form of a beautiful woman in which to take up her abode, and there nourish herself on the male elements which she draws from the homage rendered to her victim, whose love of admiration she excites to the utmost possible degree in order to obtain them. If the beauties of society, who live on the devotions paid to their attractions by the opposite sex, only knew that they were feeding sirens, by no means beautiful, all the time, they would be less vain of themselves, and more chary of their charms. These are truths which have been stated in a different form by Swedenborg and other seers; if I restate them here, I do so because I believe the majority of people to be ignorant of them, and because it is of the highest importance that they should know the truth.

From this it is plain that what is generally termed "sin," is, in fact, the outward and visible sign of infestation, and the expression "forgiveness of sins," so often used in the New Testament, means, in reality, "expulsion of infestation"—the word ἀφίημι having been wrongly rendered "to forgive." This reading will throw new light on many passages, the true import of which is now totally misapprehended.

As in certain of the grossest organisms an affinity exists between the atomic particles of man, and those of the lower animal creation, suggesting vices of the most degrading description, so those who exhibited this tendency in earth-life, now draw the magnetic elements they require from the bodies of animals, which they more or less inhabit. This occupation of the organisms, both of men and animals, by those in another state of existence, is the origin of the idea of metempsychosis so prevalent in Eastern religions, while the intimate association of the atomic particles of this world and the other, forms a medium by which the memory of the invisible associates passes into those they haunt here, and results in what seem to them flashes of recollection of a former state of existence. This is the origin of the doctrine of reincarnation.

It is in the atomic constitution of the moral atmosphere by which a man surrounds himself by his own acts during life, that he creates for himself what the Buddhists call his Karma; and it is the interlocking of the atomic particles of parents with their offspring, during the process of procreation and parturition, which accounts for all the phenomena of heredity. The ancient science of astrology was based upon the same fact; for inasmuch as no atom of the universe is absolutely unaffected by the combinations of all the other atoms, but are ever presenting kaleidoscopic changes, by reason of which every minute particle occupies a different relation to all the other particles, and inasmuch as they are interlocked through all apparent space, visible and invisible, the movements of the heavenly bodies, and their constantly changing relations to each other, cannot be without their influence upon the atoms of this world, and of the human beings who inhabit it. An illustration of this atomic connection between the sun and the earth, occurs in the well-known fact that electrical disturbances and hurricanes are most numerous during the years of the maximum of sun-spots.

The power which the will-force exercises over the atoms of the constituent principles of the organism, has been already alluded to in the phenomena which have resulted from hypnotic experiments; it is this will-force, concentrated under a specific influence, which constitutes what is known as "faith"—the potency of which is alluded to by Christ when he says that by it we can remove mountains, and the exercise of which was an indispensable preliminary to the cures which He wrought, deemed at the time miraculous. It is by means of the projection of this faith-force into nature, that some of the more remarkable instances of answers to prayer have been obtained; and it is by the combined operation of the atoms of the faith-force in the operator—provided that the magnetism is of the right quality—and of the patient, that those cures, of which a good deal has been heard lately, of healing by faith have been accomplished. The oriental mystics, who have from the most ancient times been conversant to some extent with the correlation of atoms and the laws which govern it, positively assert that they have succeeded in prolonging life to an extent quite incredible to the Western mind, and in modifying the conditions of death, though this has only been in rare instances, which I have not had any means of authenticating, but I see nothing impossible in it; and if it be so, it would probably account for the fable of the "Elixir of

Life"—the elixir being nothing more than the concentration of the will, exercised in an almost superhuman degree for many years upon the one idea of prolonging existence, accompanied by an absolute certainty on the part of the devotee that it would be prolonged; the effect of this fixed idea, backed by a fixed will, upon the atoms of the constituent principles of the man, being finally to bring them under a certain control, and so to regulate that constant mutation of them, which, it is well known to medical science, is accomplished every few years in the outer human frame. This involves a knowledge of the different principles of which man is composed, and which is placed by oriental science at seven. The question whether this is so or not, is too abstruse to discuss here, the more especially as it has no practical bearing—length of days not being by any means an object worthy of ambition in itself. That the term of a man's life will be prolonged if the atomic disorder, which now produces physical decay and moral evil, can be overcome, is certain; but it is an incident in the great triumph of the race, not the triumph itself.

The tremendous dynamic potency which is stored in the human will, when it is thus reinforced by the wills of beings who are unseen, is only just beginning to dawn upon Western science, which does not yet admit the invisible agency. It is manifest that those who happen to be exceptionally endowed with this will-energy, should learn how to use it to the benefit, and not to the injury of mankind; and these especially should open themselves, by the moral discipline and ordeals to which I have alluded, to receive divine impression. This is especially true of those engaged in healing the sick. Unless there is a strong internal impression that this power should be put forth for this purpose, faith or will cures are not in the divine order; for a healing power can be put through a well-intentioned human instrument by malevolent influences, and a life may thus be prolonged to its own serious injury. This does not imply that medical remedies should not in all cases of illness be resorted to, because the malevolent influences on them can always be counteracted by beneficent influences; but where the human will comes into play for selfish purposes, an entirely new set of atomic combinations are introduced, which resist the operation of those wills in the unseen which are acting under divine impulse.

We are thus furnished with the key to many problems which have hitherto been deemed insolvable, the value of which, unfortunately, can only be appreciated by those whose faculties are to some extent internally developed. As, however, the system of the visible and invisible worlds forms one indivisible whole, pervaded throughout by the same material forces, in infinite permutations and combinations, and as every unit in it is inseparably bound with every other unit in it, it is evident that no one, whether a human being or an angel—and by this latter term I mean only those who at some epoch of our planet's history have inhabited it—can reach a state where they are unaffected by the suffering consequent upon the debased moral condition which reigns both here and in the unseen world. Nor is it possible for them to receive divine life without giving it forth to those who need it.

This is the first and fundamental law of life, that it cannot be passive: it is, in fact, "matter in motion." In like manner the evil ones are perpetually giving out the life which they have polluted, and which is so poisoned that it carries with it the seeds of death. The human recipients of these opposite qualities of life cannot help magnetically imparting them to others. Hence we feel the presence of one person vivifying, and of another exhausting. Those who come into atomic relations of a deeper kind—induced, for instance, by intense sympathy of labour for a common divine end—become incredibly sensible to the interchange of atomic particles, charged either with sympathy, or, in the case of an evil influence invading too powerfully, with antipathy. The result is not merely moral, but actual physical suffering. To such an extent is this sometimes the case, that the moral defects of others with whom one is in this close relation, are each characterised by a different physical sensation, so marked that it is possible to tell by the sensation from whom the magnetism is projected, even though the person may be distant. Under such circumstances, the thought of the person increases the pain, which is also caused by the projection of thought by the person. Hence circumstances often arise when two persons may be strongly attached to each other, but when, owing to their respective magnetic conditions, it is not possible for them to live together without severe suffering to both.

These are facts which cannot be denied,—at all events their denial can only be the result of ignorance, and cannot render them the less true. I have lived with many others in this internal relation, the sensitive condition being more or less developed in all of us; thus, for instance, I had a dear friend who had naturally a violent temper, which, nevertheless, he succeeded in keeping under control, but however he might conceal the impulse to anger, I was always instantly aware of its existence by a pain in my face. I have felt shooting pains in the head or chest, and many other sensations, all indicating certain moral conditions in others, while they were equally sensitive to moral changes in me. In fact we acted as moral barometers to each other. It was possible to modify these conditions by varied groupings of the individuals, so that the magnetisms of one should neutralise those of the other; magnetism was employed to a large extent amongst us, and many devices resorted to, often involving great suffering and discomfort, to induce harmonic action between the conflicting currents from above and below, to which we were especially open. In a word, the experiences which I then underwent, resulted often in phenomena which would be deemed incredible, and to which it is, therefore, not necessary to allude here.

I gathered from the criticisms which appeared on a novel[1] which I published not long since, in which I endeavoured to describe the organic effects which might thus be induced by moral sympathy or antipathy, how completely in the dark the general public still is in regard to this whole class of subjects.

These things being so, and the angelic ministrants being in the constant radiation of their affections to those they desire to serve, it is plain that they can only reach them by a contact of atoms which produces suffering,—suffering, it is true, which contains within it a boundless peace and happiness. Indeed the capacities of the good for joy, and

[1] Masollam: A Problem of the Period. W. Blackwood & Sons.

of the bad for suffering, are infinitely beyond anything we can conceive here, owing to the presence of that gross material husk which we call our bodies, and which deadens emotional sensation in either direction. But the idea that we can reach a condition in which we can individually free ourselves from the great human disease is utterly vain; if one member of the universal body suffers, all the members must suffer with it; and the great mistake which Buddha made, was in thinking that any amount of bodily mortification, or abstract contemplation, could emancipate him from the common lot of all mankind. At the same time, his instinct that rest could only be found by penetrating the surface of physical and material life, was a sound one, but it was the rest of torpor.

In the first reaction from the inversions which we find in nature, there is in humanity a disposition to cast away its idol, or crush it as an unworthy or useless thing beneath its feet. But when divine science and experience can prove that no being, whether in this world or the other, can exist without a body, or be reverenced except through contact with its outward as well as its inward forms, and that nature herself is a reflex, although a broken one, of all that is most divine, we must return to an elevated worship of nature, if we would drink at one of the purest springs of inspiration.

There are three modes by which divine life and inspiration are continually acting upon us. They relate to our union with God, with man, and with nature. From the deep inmost of our spirit there penetrates to outer consciousness the far-sounding but distinctly audible echo of the voice which proclaims the eternal inner union between the Creator and the created. From man and from our loving fellowship with him, and service for him, come to us the love-gifts which we both impart and receive. From nature, when we, with the labour of our own hands, the energy of our wills, and the exercise of our faculties, redistribute and reorganise the dislocated atoms, there returns to us a vibration of harmonic motion in the magnetic currents which react upon our frames, and bring God down through us to the soil of outer things, placed in our own especial charge; the whole forming a grand inspiring trinity of Wisdom, Love, and Operation.

Of these three modes, Buddha, and the religious teachers

who preceded him, sought only the first. There was an intense desire for union with God, and an earnest longing for absorption into Him, accompanied by a moral code inculcating a pure and noble system of ethics; but it was only as a means to this personal end: their teaching took no cognisance of the atomic chain which binds man and nature into one inseverable whole, and its application to the human need has been, in consequence, absolutely barren of results.

It is only through the radiation of our affections upon man, and of our energies upon nature, that we can aid in the regeneration of the one, and in the reconstruction of the other, and so by co-operating with the divine purpose, find that inner union with God which the ancient teachers so evidently yearned after; and to do this effectively, we must realise the power which the affections can exercise, through the magnetic currents, of sympathy over man, and that the will can exercise, through the intellect, over nature; for in the human will and rational faculty reside those potential atoms, which are derived from the infinite creative potency, and which enable man to fashion, and to some extent control, the material nature by which he is surrounded. In the degree in which we open ourselves to the channels of the divine love, and of the creative life, will man and nature respond to our touch, and shall we be partakers of the joy which is inseparable from that love, and that life. There is in reality no such thing as passivity towards God: we must move towards Him, or we in effect close the avenue of His approach; and we can only move thus towards Him in the degree that we realise that every faculty of our being is generative and reproductive, and that our capacity of receiving divine potency is conditioned upon our promptitude in imparting it. We are life-receivers, because we are life-givers. Stagnation is as impossible in us as it is in the atoms of which we are composed: we are all "matter in motion," moving upwards or downwards in the great whirl of cause and effect, with a velocity which would startle us if we could watch our progress, as those can who are themselves hidden from our gaze.

If then, as I have endeavoured to show, the most divine inspiration issues from the threefold fountain of Wisdom,

Love, and Operation, whose life-giving currents should impregnate human thought, sympathy, and deed, and will retain their purity just in the degree in which the receptacles which receive them are free from taint, it follows that the diversion of them into devious channels, their pollution, and their obstruction, must be attended with the most untoward consequences to the human race. Nevertheless these three currents are invariably so diverted, polluted, and obstructed, and this is due to the pride, the selfishness, and the apathy of man.

Firstly, the current of the divine wisdom is diverted by man into devious channels by his pride, when he creates his God after his own image, and attributes to Him the qualities of anger, jealousy, cruelty, injustice, and revenge. Such a God is the God of the Old Testament: "Thou thoughtest," says the Psalmist, "that I was altogether such an one as thyself." Nor is His nature much modified in the New, out of which a scheme for the salvation of man has been constructed by human invention, as opposed to the spirit of the divinely inspired life of the pure Being whose teaching it records, as it must be revolting to all who have ever felt, however faintly, the ineffable touch of the Great All Father and All Mother, thrilling the inner sense by contact with the Word made flesh. Doctrines which are alike insulting to the Almighty, and dishonouring to Him whose mission it was to impart to man a new and higher conception of the Deity—however earnestly and devoutly held—form one of the most potent barriers to the descent of an inspiration by divine wisdom; for it renders impossible that inner union with God, through Christ, who is its channel; and this union can only be obtained by a true conception of the relations which God, the Saviour, and man, bear to each other; to which I shall refer hereafter.

In default of a pure conception of the attributes of the Deity, man can no more be a reflex of the divine wisdom, however faint, than the rays of the sun can be reflected from the surface of a slough of mud.

Secondly, the inspiration of divine love is polluted by man's selfishness, when it paralyses his activities in the service of his fellows. When this current of the divine affections pours into a man who is cold, and hard, and cruel, and selfseeking, its atoms are transformed into the atoms of which the selfish instincts are composed, and become potent for hate, just as they would have been powerful for love, were the large capacity which he has for loving himself, converted into one for loving his neighbours.

But even those who desire most earnestly to receive this love-current in its purity, and to crush out all selfish instincts which may impede their free and absolute devotion to their fellows, find that the effort is one which taxes all their powers of endurance; for we often meet with the most determined resistance from those whom we are called upon to serve, in whom coldness finally gives place to ingratitude, and passive opposition is succeeded by active persecution. Unless under these trials we are able to stand firm and to endure, all the concessions we make, and the weakness we show, pollute the love-current, until our usefulness is finally destroyed. If, on the other hand, we maintain our attitude of forbearance and tenderness, the love-currents store themselves till the requisite force has accumulated, until at last, by the outpouring of its energies, the enemies' citadel is stormed, and the victory, which seemed hopeless, is finally won.

But the combatant thus fighting for humanity against the forces which obsess it, must be prepared for apparent defeat. The nobler the cause, the more heroic and selfsacrificing the character of those to whom it is intrusted, the greater is the risk and probability of their becoming the victims and martyrs to the world's unwillingness, and unreadiness to respond to these inspirations. It must too often be the destiny of such, not only to suffer constantly from the necessary suppression of the stores of life they would otherwise receive and impart, but to pass through inward if not outward martyrdom, in the painful doubt whether it may not have been due to some shortcoming of their own, that they fail to see as yet the accomplishment of their purest and highest aspirations. It was under such an agony that the highest teacher and profoundest lover of humanity, passed from earth with the despairing cry, "My God! my God! why hast Thou forsaken me?"

Thirdly, the inspiration of the divine operation is obstructed by the apathy of man, when he does not put physical energy forth into the external nature by which he is surrounded. He must organise the atoms of his material environment, so that they may correspond with the atoms of the other two currents, if he would effect a perfect synthesis of the three, and this can only be done by a certain amount of physical energy.

The man who seeks the highest inspiration, and who neglects this important factor in it, may receive an impulse of a very high and pure quality, but it will lack the essential element of the practical. He may form a far higher and truer conception of God than other men, he may exercise an abundant charity, and feel a tender sympathy for his fellows; but his life will be relatively barren of results, because he will have organised nothing. He will not have added a stone to the foundation of that new society which we are labouring to reconstruct: he cannot form part of a home thus engaged, because on the one point of daily labour in details as an act of worship, he will be out of sympathy, and the current of operation being obstructed in him, it will be obstructed in all; for the magnetism of apathy which will radiate from him will paralyse the atoms of energy in the organisms of the others, and a sense of discomfort will ensue, which will render companionship impossible. Though external harmony may be preserved, the sense will become general that progress is hopeless with such an influence permanently active, and his absence will be necessarily but reluctantly enforced.

For the measure of inspiration is enormously increased by the number of those engaged in seeking it in one group, and in the same way, and whose atoms have combined in such a manner as to form one wire, so to speak, which may transmit from the unseen, the electric inspirational current. The result then becomes the inspiration, not of any one of the number—though upon him may devolve the duty of putting it into words—but of the group.

Thus I am conscious, while writing this, of receiving internal assistance from others with whom I am in special atomic *rapport* for the purpose. In proportion as the group increases, does the value and trustworthiness of the inspiration increase, as there is less chance of its being charged with the personality of the writer; while in the event of a statement being made out of harmony with the general current of the inspiration, it would be checked.

In order to ensure a wholesome and effective co-operation in all the details which make for divine progress, it is necessary that all those engaged in the same effort—especially if they are living together, and their magnetic interchange is constant and active—should put forth the utmost energy of which they are severally capable. It is as though a group of persons all attached together, were swimming against the current of a powerful stream: any slackness on the part of one, impedes the progress of all the others; nor is it possible for any one to strike off in a direction of his own, without rendering an immediate severance necessary of the cord which attaches him to all the others. On the other hand, the more numerous the group engaged, the more easy in some ways does it become to attach new members to it, though few who desire to be thus attached, have any idea, till they try, of the tremendous struggle in store for them in the foaming torrent into which they are about to be launched; while those who thus take on an extra charge, know full well from experience the extra risk which is thus incurred, and the more arduous effort which it will involve.

They also know—and this is perhaps the hardest lesson of all to learn—how slow and toilsome the progress is, how little there is to show for all the sufferings borne and labour accomplished, what faith and patience are required, and how immeasurable the distance between the real that they are grappling with, and the glorious ideal dimly showing in the glow of the far-distant horizon. But in spite of it all they have had their victories; and when the stress is hardest it is wise to look back on these for encouragement, as songs of joy and triumph bring strength and support along a way beset with pain and sorrow and disappointments, which, when seen in their true proportions, are only as faint and fading specks showing in a universe of infinite light.

It is when the earnest and awakened man, who has become thoroughly alive to the truth of the foregoing observations, has entered with unflinching determination and set purpose of will upon the apparently hopeless task of making himself, in conjunction with others, a radiative centre for the recreative life-current into nature and into man, that he becomes aware of the painful effect that it produces on his own organism. He has, as it were, placed himself directly under the concentrated ray of the Divine Sun; and, tempered though it be by its passage through the appropriate intermediate channels, its ardours are to many wellnigh insupportable. This is not so in every case; it depends largely on organic conditions and previous experiences. Some may have been long gradually and unconsciously, and through much suffering, approaching the burning bush; while others, suddenly awakened, as it were by an electric shock, from the life of coldness and indifference in which they had been steeped, are almost immediately forced into sharp suffering. But this very fact is the strongest evidence they could desire of the reality of the effort in which they are engaged, and of the truth on which it is based. And herein does it differ from every other religious impulse which has since crystallised into a Church or a sect. It involves the profession of no creed, the observance of no ceremony, the celebration of no rites, the construction of no dogma; it relies upon no evidence, on nothing that has been written in this book, but on the individual experience of every man or woman who is ready, on the assumption of the possibility of what is here stated being true as a hypothesis, to take the great risk, and undergo the great sacrifices which it involves, of making the experiment, on the chance that it may be true; and it differs from all existing religious corporations, sects, ecclesiasticisms, in this, that it cannot possibly become a formalism, inasmuch as it demands no profession of faith, and is not possible to be held as a theory. It is either the life itself, with all the daily acts of sacrifice and service that it involves, or it is nothing. These acts and this self-sacrifice are as much within reach of the peasant as of the duke, who, if they are equally whole-hearted and sincere, will very soon find themselves working side by side; for between the top and the bottom of society, there is an immense reorganisation and redistribution of atoms necessary; and it will reach the extremes—as it has already done to some extent—not so much through written or spoken elaboration of the matter I have here endeavoured to set forth, as through internal preparation, which will render one here and one there sensible to the magnetic influence of those who have already begun to radiate this life, and who will thus be drawn to it often almost in spite of themselves. But inasmuch as they will very soon find their own efforts powerless to enable them to realise the expectations here held out, and become conscious of a feebleness of will, and a physical, as well as a moral incapacity to fight successfully against those powers of darkness to which I have already alluded, and who will concentrate all their infernal enginery upon the aspirant feebly struggling to evolve his dormant faculties, and rise into new and higher conditions, a divine potency, hitherto latent in nature, has been developing during these latter years, to which allusion is made in the first chapter, and without which the stupendous task of the regeneration of man and of nature, through the instrumentality of man, would be utterly hopeless.

I will presently endeavour to describe what this potency is; how the world has been prepared to receive it; how it has been dimly foreshadowed in the sacred books of all religions, of which it is the fulfilment; and how at the moment when society is most threatened with revolution by explosive elements from below, it will descend from above with a counter-energy of construction, even more powerful, to enable man to rear a new and perfected social fabric upon the *débris* of the one which its own vices had laid low.

Before, however, entering upon this subject, it will be necessary to expose the weakness of all social and ecclesiastical institutions, and the dangers which threaten them, in consequence of the vices inherent in their operation and constitution.

CHAPTER VI.

HISTORY OF THE EARLY CHRISTIAN CHURCH, A RECORD OF SWIFT DEMORALISATION; PARTLY OWING TO DESIRE TO MAKE CONVERTS, AND PARTLY TO THE SUBSTITUTION OF A FUTURE LIFE FOR PRESENT PRACTICE—CONFLICT BETWEEN ROME AND THE EAST—EXTINCTION OF GNOSTIC SECTS DESTRUCTIVE OF MUCH OF THE DEEPER TRUTH—COMPILATION OF THE PRESENT CANON OF SCRIPTURE UNTRUSTWORTHY—APOCRYPHAL GOSPELS AND EPISTLES—"THE TEACHING OF THE TWELVE APOSTLES"—THE BOOK OF ENOCH—THE CHURCH OF ENGLAND ON THE VERGE OF A GREAT MORAL REVOLUTION — THE CONFESSIONS OF A PARISH PRIEST—NEED OF A REFORMED CHRISTIANITY.

AN examination into the history of all existing religions will show us, either that the prophet or teacher himself adapted his morality to the conditions of the people he taught, as in the case of Moses and Mohammed—or that, if the teaching was too elevated for the masses, as in the case of Christ, and in a minor degree of Buddha, it was very soon reduced to their level by their followers.

The first instinct of the disciple is to deify the master; the second, to make concessions in order to gain converts. It never seems to have occurred to the disciples of those who enunciated the highest doctrine, that the ethics which it contained, should form the foundation upon which a new society should be reared, in which the moral standard thus suggested should be practicable. The desire of making converts invariably supersedes every other consideration. The history of the early Christian Church is a lamentable record of swift demoralisation, largely owing to this cause. In the abandonment of the practice of having all things in common, in the disputes which arose between the disciples, in the suppression of the writings which were deemed authoritative by the most spiritual and enlightened portion of the early Church, and the struggle between the worldly element—which founded a Church in the most dissolute capital in Europe, by reason of the concessions it made to the social conditions which prevailed in it—and the Gnostic sects, which, until extinguished, retained hold of the spiritual life which had been preserved in the Church of the brethren in Jerusalem, presided over by James, the brother of Christ,—we have the story of a spiritual *fiasco* unparalleled in the history of religious movements. No sooner was the great Personality removed from the midst of His followers, than those who had asked which should sit upon His right hand in heaven, began to struggle for the highest place here, and jealousies, rivalries, and bitternesses envenomed the infant communities,[1] which were finally to give birth to the ecclesiastical monstrosities represented at this day at Jerusalem in the different angles of the Church of the Holy Sepulchre, where, on the occasion of sacred Christian festivals, the worshippers over the tomb of the Lord of love, are only kept from flying at each other's throats by a strong guard of Moslem soldiery. The fact that the Church of the Holy Sepulchre is not over the tomb of Christ is a lie the more, but the desecration of His memory is none the less on that account. It has been reserved for the most sacred city in the world to represent the most degrading spectacle of human ignorance, superstition, and hypocrisy which exists anywhere in the nineteenth century; as it was reserved for those who call themselves the vicegerents of Christ on earth, to rival the wickedest sovereigns of their time in lust, cruelty, and the worst vices of the dark ages. These are they to whom Christ referred when He said, " Beware of false prophets, which come unto you in ' sheep's clothing, but inwardly they are ravening wolves. By ' their fruits ye shall know them."

Modern research is now happily enabling us to estimate at their true value the books which form what is called "the

---

[1] In illustration of this, see the first chapter of the 1st Epistle of Clement to the Corinthians, in which he denounces " that wicked and detestable sedi-
' tion, so unbecoming in the elect of God, which a few headstrong and self-
' willed men have fomented to such a degree of madness, that your venerable
' and renowned name, so worthy of all men to be beloved, is greatly blas-
' phemed thereby."

canon of Scripture." We find that, so far as the New Testament is concerned, it is not possible to disconnect it from the bitter feud which originated in the divergent views of Peter and Paul, and their violent hostility towards each other.

While the Christian Church at Pella, where it was established after the destruction of Jerusalem, retained to some extent the pure spirit of the teaching of Christ, its rival at Rome was adapting itself to its worldly surroundings, and had already inaugurated that policy of compromise and duplicity which soon enabled it to claim a universal supremacy. Meantime at Alexandria, and throughout most of the Eastern Churches, the internal sense was clung to, and they were thus enabled to invoke—as such of their writings as have been preserved, show—a far purer and truer inspiration. It was, in fact, a war at last between the spirit and the letter, between the East and the West; and it is scarcely to be wondered at that the inspirations which animated the former should have been the purest, when we consider the corrupt social and political conditions under which the Church of Rome had struggled into life, as compared with the purer influences which surrounded the Gnostic communities and the Ethnico Christians. The quarrel culminated in what was known as the Marcion heresy, towards the end of the second century, and the canon of Scripture clearly bears on its record the traces of the struggle which terminated in the triumph of Rome, and the suppression of all that militated against the doctrines it had espoused. Hence we find that the Gospels have been tampered with, especially Luke's; that the Acts of the Apostles are an incorrect narrative of events, in which few traces of any lofty inspiration are to be found; and that interpolations have occurred in the various writings which were then collected to form the text-book of the religion, though even its compilers did not assert that they were infallibly inspired—that was a dogma that was not invented until many hundreds of years after.

I am aware that this will be controverted, and the martyrdoms and persecutions of nearly four hundred years will be pointed to as an evidence of the staunchness of the early Christians in Rome to their principles. But men will die for what they believe to be fundamental dogmas of faith, while they will yield for the sake of expediency, details which they consider of less importance, in the presence of an overwhelming pressure. Our records of the history of the first four or five centuries after Christ are too meagre to enable us to assert that belief as well as practice did not undergo great changes during that period. Indeed we have every right to assume, from the controversies and disputations that we know occurred, that they did. Although it has now become necessary to consider the compilers of the canon of Scripture to have been as fully inspired as the books we owe to their selection, their authority was not universally considered infallible at the time. Indeed, the divisions and scandals which took place among them, the numerous so-called heresies and sundry patristic discussions, fully justified scepticism on this point then, as it does still.

Thus we have St Paul's epistle to the Laodiceans, which, in his Epistle to the Colossians, he expressly orders should be read in the Church, excluded from the canon of Scripture, with about twenty other books, which were deemed authoritative during the first four centuries in the Christian Churches, among them the epistles of Barnabas, Clement, and Ignatius, which contain many passages full of an inspiration as pure and lofty as are to be found in the canonical epistles.

When we investigate the constitution of the Council of Nice, convoked by the Emperor Constantine—himself not a Christian at the time, and a man of dissolute character—charged with the high function of providing Christendom with its Bible, we find that it was composed of 318 violent partisans, of whom Sabinus, the Bishop of Heraclea, affirms that, "excepting Constantine himself and Eusebius Pamphilus, they were a set of illiterate creatures that understood nothing;" but then he was of the opposite faction. They began by quarrelling among themselves, and libelling each other to the Emperor; but we learn from Mosheim's 'Ecclesiastical History' that the Emperor burnt all their libels, and exhorted them to peace and amity; while Pappus tells us in his Synodican to the Council, that the means employed for discovering what books should be selected as canonical, was promiscuously to put all the books referred to the Council for deliberation, under the Communion-table in a church, when they besought the Lord that the inspired writings might get on the table, while the spurious ones remained underneath, "and that it happened accordingly."[1]

Whatever may have been the method adopted to discover which books did, and which did not contain the mind of God, Archbishop Wake and other learned divines were not satisfied with it, and have translated all the rejected books into English from the original, professing at the same time their belief in their inspiration. Meantime, that portion of Christendom which especially resents the pretensions of the Church of Rome, cling with the most intense tenacity to the infallible inspiration of the letter of the books thus selected for them 400 years after Christ, out of a mass of sacred literature, by 318 Roman Catholic bishops.

It is remarkable that of the three writings which are generally supposed, and with reason, to have issued from the Church of Jerusalem, practically the first Christian Church, two have been excluded. These consist of the Epistle of St James, which Canon Spence says "possesses that indefinable '*something*—we call it inspiration—which distinguishes the 'writings, included by the general voice of the Church in the 'New Testament Scriptures, from all other writings in the 'world."[2] The other two are "The Teaching of the Twelve Apostles," and "The Testament of the Twelve Patriarchs," which all three dwell entirely on life and practice, and ignore the atonement and other dogmas. Many will feel the two last to contain more of the "indefinable *something*" called inspiration, than much that is written in the canonical Epistles, with some of which they are contemporaneous.

How early corruptions and interpolations began, may be gathered from the 2d chapter of Ignatius's Epistle to the Philadelphians, the 19th, 20th, and 21st verses, where he says: "Nevertheless I exhort you that you do nothing out of strife, 'but according to the instruction of Christ. Because I have 'heard some who say, unless I find it written in the originals (or 'archives), I will not believe it to be written in the Gospel. 'And when I said 'It is written,' they answered from what 'lay before them in their corrupted copies. But to me Jesus

[1] Mace's Com., N. 7, p. 875.
[2] The Teaching of the Twelve Apostles, by Canon Spence, p. 99

'Christ is instead of all the uncorrupted monuments in the 'world; together with those undefiled monuments, His cross 'and death and resurrection, and the faith which is by Him, 'by which I desire through your prayers to be justified." If corrupted copies existed in the Church in the time of Ignatius, a contemporary of St John, whose epistles are mentioned by Origen, Irenæus, Eusebius, Jerome, and others, what guarantee for their purity have we now? What other test of the value of writings purporting to be inspired can exist beyond each man's own inner consciousness? And of what avail can intellectual effort be in this direction? As Jesus Christ was to Ignatius, "instead of all the uncorrupted monuments in the world," so He must ever be to those who have found Him.

When these facts become understood and realised, it is impossible that history or prejudice can cling much longer to this compilation as an infallible guide to spiritual truth, excepting where that truth is confirmed by the spiritual insight which it is in each man's power to obtain for himself; he will then feel more than ever its transcendent value, and rejecting the dross, which, after all, is but a small proportion of the whole, rejoice in the evidence which its main body of testimony affords in its more interior sense, to the truths which have been personally revealed to him, but which take a totally different aspect from those which the Church has constructed out of the dross, or the external letter, as dogmas.

A better illustration of the lukewarmness of the Church in its search after divine truth, cannot be afforded than in the history of the Book of Enoch. This book is quoted by Jude: it was accepted as divine authority by many of the fathers of the Christian Church, and seems to have been in existence until about the year 800 A.D., when it is quoted at length by the Byzantine chronicler, George Syncellus. Then it disappears until 1773, when Bruce discovered it in Abyssinia and brought three manuscripts of it to Europe. It was translated into English by Laurence, but few have ever heard of it, and it would be considered as great a sacrilege to bind it up as an inspired book in the Old Testament, as to expunge Jude as an inspired book from the New, and yet it is evident that either one or other should be done. In the fourteenth

verse of his epistle, Jude says, "And Enoch also, the seventh
' from Adam, prophesied of these, saying, Behold, the Lord
' cometh with ten thousand of His saints, to execute judgment
' upon all, and to convince all that are ungodly among them
' of all their ungodly deeds which they have ungodly com-
' mitted, and of all their hard speeches which ungodly sinners
' have spoken against Him." Now it is very important to
know the end of this prophecy, and it is surely the business
of the Church to afford the earnest inquirer in search of truth,
the facility of finding it in the Bible, instead of having to go
for it to the British Museum. Otherwise Jude should be
expunged from the New Testament as uninspired and misleading. I do not offer any opinion as to the authorship of
the Book of Enoch, excepting in so far that it was certainly
not written by Enoch, any more than the Pentateuch was
written by Moses, or the Psalms, with very few exceptions,
by David, or all Isaiah by Isaiah, or Daniel by Daniel; but
it contains, nevertheless, inspired truth of the deepest import
to humanity, in regard to which I shall have more to say
presently.

Meantime men will not be contented with this lukewarmness on the part of their spiritual pastors or guides, and the
mutterings of the coming storm are already beginning to be
heard within the pale of the Church itself.

As men are conscientiously and impartially examining the
history of the birth and infancy of the Christian Church,
and as new documents are discovered which throw new
light upon it, those among them who are honest, whether in
the Church or out of it, are compelled to abandon the contention that the dogmas it most relies upon have a divine origin,
and to seek for some new basis for their theological superstructure. Thus the Hon. and Rev. Canon Fremantle remarks, in a striking article recently published, "The early
' history of the Church has likewise been subjected to a minute
' criticism, which has been stimulated of late by the discovery
' of 'The Teaching of the Twelve Apostles.' The result has
' been to give us a simpler view of the organisation of the
' Christian societies, and of their life and thoughts, to show
' the influence of various social circumstances working nat-
' urally upon them, and forming their institutions and their

'theology. It becomes less and less possible to attribute to 'the earliest period of the Church, as having been formally 'imposed, or exclusively admitted, any of the theories of 'Church government which we now know, whether Episcopal, 'Presbyterian, or Independent, or the formed doctrines of 'later times, whether relating to the plan of redemption, or 'to the incarnation, or the Trinity."[1]

It must, I think, be admitted, that when Anglican clergymen are permitted by their Church to publish their readiness to give up these cardinal doctrines, that Church itself must be on the verge of a great moral revolution. It has never been by the operation of the Spirit of God which was in the Church, that men—outraged by its profanities or its apathy —from time to time struggled to reform it, but by the Spirit of God working in them in spite of the Church; and this Spirit is at the present day more active than ever, and will, before long, accomplish the sacred work of its entire transformation. At the same time, I am willing to admit that even in its most corrupt form it has had its use, as the Levitical law had its use to those to whom it was given; but the religious instinct of man has outgrown its dogmas, and, revolted by its superstitions, demands a new departure. It would be in the highest degree ungrateful to deny that we owe this tendency to self-emancipation from the thraldom of priestcraft, in a large measure to science, and to the materialistic tendency of the day. If superstition is the bane, oldfashioned materialism is the antidote; they are both poisons, but they have a tendency to neutralise each other.

That the Church of England, though preserved from many of the more glaring vices of the Roman and Eastern Christian Churches, fails altogether to satisfy the consciences of a large class of those who nominally belong to it, must be generally admitted, and this uneasiness of spirit is not confined to the laity only. I will here introduce a document with which I have been favoured by a clergyman of the Established Church, and which, I am assured, is not without its echo in the breast of many of the clergy in England.

[1] Fortnightly Review, March 1887. "The New Reformation : Theology under its Changed Conditions."

THE CONFESSIONS OF A PARISH PRIEST.

"In my training for the priesthood, I was taught to accept implicitly all that is inculcated by the Church, without question or demur; and I was warned of the awful danger of schism and heresy which might happen to me, if I ventured to indulge in any private opinion, or, as it was called, free-thought, on the subject of religion.

"I was told that what the Church taught was identical with what Christ taught; that the doctrines of the Church were all derived from Him; that the outward government of the Church, and administration of the Church's offices, were all modelled on a plan laid down by Him; and, above all, that the whole Bible was directly inspired by God, or, as it were, written by God, using as a pen the human agent whose name is connected with the authorship of each book. I was told that I must hold and teach that salvation is to be found entirely, and found alone, in the Church, its ordinances, sacraments, functions, and devotions; and that all outside the pale of the Church, however pure and noble their daily lives and conduct, were in a hopeless miserable state of darkness and death, included under the category of unbelievers.

"So for several years I believed and taught; or rather I taught, and flattered myself that I believed. But by degrees some serious considerations forced themselves upon my mind, and set me thinking for myself.

"I. The first thing that I remarked was that all my preaching, all the services of my Church, all my religious functions and sacraments, had very little, or rather no, practical effect on the daily life and conduct, either of myself or of those to whom I ministered.

"I could not help feeling that salvation, if it was worth the name at all, must mean a transformation of daily life; and that if salvation were really the result of Church doctrine, ritual, and function, it would show itself in the disappearance from the Church's members of evil passions, worldly ambitions, lusts, envies, and all sinful thoughts, words, and actions—and the substitution for them of whatsoever is pure, holy, and of good report. That this was not the result of the Church's influence was very apparent, both in my own individual case, and in the case of all with whom I had to do.

"I tried to discover the point of weakness. I found in self-examination very many causes of failure, clearly to be attributed to my own lack of steadfastness of life, earnestness, diligence, care, and purity of intention and purpose; and these faults I tried hard to correct, with more or less success.

"But this was not sufficient to account for all the utter failures.

As I looked around on other parishes, I found it everywhere the same. Professing Churchmen were no better than those who belonged to other Christian sects—nor these in their turn than those who professed no religion at all, so far as their daily conduct, and the principles which guided their words and actions were concerned; and though there were to be found here and there bright and holy exceptions to the general rule, I found these exceptions also outside the Church, and was therefore forced to the conclusion that they were not the result of the work of the Church, but of some other independent cause. Religion and daily life were universally regarded in practice, if not in words, as two distinct matters; worship and work were placed on entirely different planes; and, in short, so far as regenerating human lives on earth was concerned, Christianity—*i.e.*, the Church's influence—must be pronounced a total failure.

"I began to question whether mankind, in its daily life, was better now than it was before the existence of Christianity, or than it would have been if Christianity had not been actively at work for 1900 years.

"II. The realisation of this fact set me thinking deeper. What is the cause of this failure? I asked myself. The answer came at once. Either what the Founder taught was wrong, or else His followers have departed from His teachings. This alternative I was obliged to face, painful and serious as the ordeal was. I read the life of Christ carefully as related in the Gospels; I studied His teaching, His principles of morality, His rules for daily conduct, and I saw that He at any rate had never been given a fair trial. What He taught was not taught by the Church; what He denounced was not denounced now; His rule of life was no one's practical standard now; and the worst of it was, I could not see how to set about making it so, either for myself or others.

"I went to consult a bishop; but he lived in a rich and luxurious mansion, waited on by servants in livery, 'clothed in purple and fine linen, and faring sumptuously every day;' and at the very beginning of our interview I had to disobey the teaching of Christ by addressing him as 'Rabbi,' 'my Lord.' I turned instinctively away from consulting him on the matter most deeply affecting me, and spoke to him instead of some minor subject quite foreign to my original purpose; and as I did so there passed in review before me all the pomp, wealth, pride, ambition, and self-satisfaction of Christian popes, cardinals, abbots, bishops, and priests, and I shuddered as I thought that I was one of those apostate followers of the meek and lowly Jesus, who preached the doctrine of self-abasement, purity, and humiliation.

"I unburdened my mind to some of my brethren, fellow-priests of the Church. I was met by them in various ways. Some I found who shared my disquiet feelings, and who were anxious to find a remedy if possible; but they did not see what to do. Others rather pooh-poohed the matter, as being of an unpleasant nature, calculated to disturb their equanimity and peace of mind—and these dwelt on the nature of unsettling faith; whilst others, again, sheltered themselves beneath the wing of the Church, and persuaded themselves that, notwithstanding outward appearances and inward misgivings to the contrary, it must be all right, because it was the practice of the Church. Lastly—and probably these were really the majority—there were those who did not dare to face the question, unconscious to themselves that they were living a perpetual lie, teaching what they did not believe in the depths of their souls, practising devotions, administering sacraments, and discharging functions, which, if honest in themselves, they would acknowledge to be as fruitless in remedying the human malady of sin and suffering as any fetich of the barbarian savage. Driven back upon myself and my own meditations, I resolved to try and get rid of all prejudice resulting from my education and training, and forget for the time that I belonged to any Church, or to any religious party, and from the standpoint of an unbiassed outsider, to examine the fundamental principles of the Christian faith, as it is held and taught by the Church of the present day.

"But this, again, I found that I could not do, until I had freed myself from the false position in which I was living. In my desire to keep up the position of a country parson, and owing to other causes to which I need not now refer, I had for several years been living beyond my income, and was heavily oppressed with debt. The burden of this debt had long weighed me down with the utmost anxiety and care, and, combined with my religious doubts and questionings, rendered my life almost intolerable to me. I did not at that time realise the actual wickedness of living beyond one's means, or the dishonesty of being in debt beyond one's power to discharge. My great aim was to keep up appearances, and to avoid bringing scandal on the Church, and I lived in a vague hope that sooner or later I should be in a position to pay all that I owed; nevertheless, though I did not realise the wickedness of my condition, I was fully alive to the unpleasantness of it, and the evil that would result from a crisis in my pecuniary affairs. Thus I was driven to adopt all kinds of schemes for tiding over my difficulties, and borrowed money from various friends without any reasonable prospect of paying them back. At the same time, as my living was a good one, and as my wife's relations were well to do, I justified myself by imagining that 'it would all come right' in the end.

"Thus distracted with worldly cares, and overwhelmed by religious doubts, I existed rather than lived, striving to satisfy the voice of conscience by a zealous discharge of the functions of the Church.

"During six years I preached 1800 sermons, and conducted special missions in numerous parishes all over England. My fame as a preacher became tolerably widespread; yet all the time I felt myself to be a living hypocrite. I longed most earnestly to see my way out of my false position. I prayed fervently and frequently for divine guidance and help. I sought light in the sacraments of the Church; I studied the Bible; I meditated and made resolutions without end;—and yet no practical benefit apparently ensued.

"At last, in the providence of God, I was aroused to the conviction that a decisive step must be taken without further delay, be the cost to me what it might, and even though it seemed certain to involve loss of home, position, and reputation. I therefore called my creditors together, and my living was placed under sequestration till all the debts which I owed should be discharged in full. I was then freed from the grinding distractions of care, and at the same time was enabled to seek the retirement which I needed for a candid and impartial inquiry into the truth of God.

"This blessed result I owed to a combination of circumstances which brought me into contact with one who pointed out to me the only course that I could pursue in honour to my neighbours, and in obedience to the dictates of my conscience. It was thus that Providence, in answer to my earnest longing, and at the moment of my sorest stress, opened the way to a retreat, far from the busy haunts of men, where the conditions were most favourable alike to the realisation of my highest aspirations, and to the development of those faculties which had been dormant during my ministry in the Church. The result has been what I can only describe as a personal revelation made to me by God, and as a living consciousness of a union through Him with Christ, so intense as to furnish me with a daily and hourly guide to my conduct in life. In the degree in which I submit myself to this guidance, do I receive light upon those divine mysteries which contain the essence of the truth that I have so long and earnestly sought, and which hold out to me the hope of the possibility of realising that ideal which will literally coincide with the teaching of Christ."

It is certain that many most devout and earnest men only remain within the pale of the Church because they cannot see what is to be put in its place. In the degree in which they can discard prejudices, which are the results of the accidents of birth and education, and narrowly and impartially investigate the history of the canon of Scripture, and of the spiritual chaos of conflicting thought and belief in which the existing Christian Churches had their origin, and in the degree in which they consider the full force and meaning of the word "inspiration," will their doubts increase as to the value of the authority to which they have hitherto yielded obedience, and will they dare to explore for themselves regions beyond the limits of what is considered orthodox. As ecclesiastically all Churches or sects form an integral part of that system of enlightened selfishness, upon which the whole system of society—from which it is not possible for the Church to disentangle itself—is based, they are bound by the very exigencies of their office, to preach that doctrine of compromise which is the chief corner-stone of all Churches; for they are well aware that any attempt to preach social reform upon the lines of Christ's moral teaching, literally applied and carried out to its logical consequences, would be to undermine the foundations of every existing ecclesiastical establishment, whatever its age, size, or form, and bury its hierarchy in its ruins. Therefore they are obliged to maintain that the moral teaching of Christ is not to be held literally, because it is utterly impracticable in society as at present constituted.

It is not possible to turn the other cheek when one is smitten; it is not possible to give the man who asks for your coat your cloak also; it is not possible to take no thought for the morrow, or to expect men to act practically upon the principle that the love of money is the root of all evil. All these words must be understood in such a qualified way as to allow men to act in direct opposition to their literal sense —and, indeed, they can only act up to their spirit, to the very limited extent that the constitution of society permits. The only persons who cannot be blamed for holding this attitude, whether in the Churches or out of them, are those— and they are probably the majority—who hold it conscientiously; but the minority, who do so as the result of a conscious compromise with their highest convictions, will not be held irresponsible for thus violating their purest and divinest instincts, even though they may not see clearly what practical step to take themselves. It implies a distinct want of faith, if a man's conscience clearly shows him that he is violating it, not to obey the impulse it suggests at all hazards. God does not act thus directly upon the inmost essence of man's nature, without having provided a satisfaction for the craving after truth, which the uneasiness thus engendered indicates. The conscience becomes restless when it desires to progress Godward; and to stifle it from fear of consequences, or lest some worse evil may befall by obeying it than by disobeying it, is not merely an act of weakness and of timidity, but it is a deliberate insult flung into the face of the Almighty.

Those who, perceiving the glaring evils attached to the ecclesiastical system with which they are connected, are impelled by their conscience to believe that they can best remedy those evils by remaining within its pale, and working for its reform from within, are bound to follow that guidance; and may rest satisfied that in doing so they are carrying out the will of God, as certainly as others to whom a different message is conveyed by the same still small voice: both may be the voice of God, though the message to each may be different—for abuses may be attacked from within as effectively as from without. But those who feel called to quit their present form of ministry, need not fear that another will not be provided for them, where each aspiration will be responded to by the inspiration appropriate to it, and every prayer for guidance be answered by the revelation of a duty, involving prompt and unhesitating performance. It is not the finding out what God desires to be done, which is difficult—it is the doing of it. If the path is rugged and narrow and dangerous, and beset with snares and pitfalls, there is never any lack of light upon it to him who knows in what quarter to look for it: for the light of the world is shining more gloriously than ever to those who wait for its appearing; and there is again a star shining in the East, to guide wise men to the cradle of a new birth of divine life into the world.

If the work to which such men find themselves called, is vast, it is eminently practical; for it consists, not in preaching against the views which they condemn, but in undermining them by means of the explosive energy of a spiritual dynamite, which will soon be recognised as a new and irresistible force in the world, and which will work its own social revolution; and this it will do at the critical juncture when the elements of socialism have culminated, and the triumph of anarchy seems to its promoters to be assured; for the flood of infidelity which is now gathering force, with spoliation in its train, to burst the social barriers, will rush in with such tumultous energy, that sovereigns, priests, and soldiers will be powerless to stem it. That can only be done by the divine reconstructive energy, operating through the willing organisms of those who, perceiving the fatal defects of society as at present constituted, have banded themselves in the sacred cause of divine order, and have freely offered themselves to be used as instruments by the hand of God for the purpose. They will accomplish this, in the words of Paul, so badly rendered in both versions of the New Testament, "Not 'in persuasive words of human wisdom, but in personal ex- 'perience of pneuma and force. In order that your faith might 'not depend upon man's wisdom, but upon God's force."[1]

That those who are ready to give themselves to this great work may the better realise its nature, I will endeavour, as concisely as possible, to point out the moral defects which render society so vulnerable, and to suggest the method by which alone it can be so reconstructed, as to be rendered impregnable to the fierce assaults with which it is menaced.

[1] 1 Corinthians ii. 4, 5.

CHAPTER VII.

MORAL PALL WHICH SHROUDS EARTH'S SURFACE—DETERIORATION OF MORAL ATMOSPHERE UNDER INVASION OF WESTERN CIVILISATION—CHRIST'S CHRISTIANITY DIAMETRICALLY OPPOSED TO THAT OF THE CHURCHES—FALSE SYSTEM OF RELIGIOUS AND SECULAR EDUCATION—CHRISTENDOM: ITS POLITICS, COMMERCE, AND FINANCE, ALL ON AN INFERNAL BASIS—CORRUPTION OF ITS CHURCHES—BLINDNESS AND INDIFFERENCE OF SO-CALLED CHRISTIANS TO THE INCONSISTENCIES OF THEIR LIVES—CHRISTIAN ETHICS BURIED UNDER ANTI-CHRISTIAN DOGMAS—A QUICKENING OF CONSCIENCE TAKING PLACE AMONG THE CLERGY—CANON FREMANTLE ON THE "NEW REFORMATION."

To any one who has caught a glimpse, however transient, of this world as it appears to those who are in the superior regions of the one which is interlocked with it, though invisible to us, it presents a most appalling spectacle. What we call the beauties of nature are more or less concealed by what I can only describe as clouds, composed of living, sentient, perpetually moving atoms. The thickness of these clouds corresponds in density to the moral condition of the invisible human beings whose atoms compose them. Intermingled with them are the atomic forces of the animal creation, and in a lower stratum those of nature, which reveal themselves in a more or less distorted aspect, according to the medium through which they are seen. There are still portions of the globe where nature does not appear altogether unlovely. These are the regions sparsely inhabited by savage tribes, where the population is extremely thin, and which, excepting in the case of some rare explorer, are unknown to, and untouched by, civilisation. Here the atmosphere is comparatively clear, and nature relatively undefiled.

There are other portions also to some extent free from taint: these are the regions from which an ancient civilisation has long since vanished, and which, having been left for many centuries undisturbed, have regained a comparative purity of atmosphere. This moral pall, which seems to shroud the earth's surface, is constantly spreading and increasing in denseness and darkness. From this point of view the dark continent *par excellence* is Europe. London is enveloped in a moral fog as black as the blackest it has ever known materially: on all the planet's superficies there is no blacker spot than this, though the other European capitals are as dark. But everywhere there are degrees of texture, of colouring, and of vivacity, on the part of the atomic particles, corresponding to the national character, and the prevailing moral quality. Thus visualised, the atoms take the form in the beholder's eyes of infusoria, and the whole of this material atmosphere seems a vast scene of the most ferocious animal life, where every unit is struggling in incessant and never-ending combat with those around. It is a field of predatory warfare of the most sanguinary description. It is "matter in motion" indeed, and very angry matter. Whole hordes of these militant atoms seem now and then to invade spaces where the texture of the atmosphere is finer, the colour lighter, and the atoms less voracious; then the nature which appeared beneath it becomes obscured, and a new region is more completely subjugated than it was before by the in-rolling volume of more dense and concentrated evil.

Japan is especially an illustration of an invasion of this description. Before the opening of this island to Western civilisation, "so called," there was no area, containing the same denseness of population, where the moral conditions of the enveloping cloud were so relatively pure. Alas! now it has altogether changed both texture, colour, and disposition of atoms, and though differing widely in all other respects from that of China, the process of deterioration is going on far more rapidly than in the latter empire.

I am aware that this picture will be considered fantastic in the highest degree,—the product of the inexplicable but convenient expression "a disordered imagination," or of that still more unknown quantity, "a slight tinge of insanity,"—so I present it to the incredulous and—if I may without offence call him so—dense reader, as an image, and not as a fact, if he cannot entertain the possibility of its being one. It will still enable him to form some vague idea of the horror and the darkness of the moral conditions by which he is surrounded, and in the midst of which he lives so cheerfully. Of this he may rest assured, whether he believes it or not, nothing that he can picture, at all approaches the reality. It is true there is to this black cloud a silver lining, of which I will speak later; were it not so, nothing would be left to humanity but utter despair.

In order to contrast the light with the darkness, let us compare Christ's Christianity with the world's.

Christ said, "Suffer little children to come unto me, and forbid them not;" and again, "If any man desire to be first, the same shall be last of all and servant of all." The Church says, "Little children, come regularly to the Sunday-school; try and get to the top of the class, and if you succeed in defeating your companions, you shall have a prize." Thus from its early infancy the child is taught the vice of competition, the door is opened by its spiritual pastors and masters to the evil spirits of envy, ambition, conceit, and egotism, who do not fail to rush in and lock it after them. When it is well barred against the entry of the angelic ministrants of love, meekness, and humility, and the child arrives at a certain age, under the stimulant of rivalry, jealousy, and emulation, the Church says, "Now you are old enough to eat some bread and drink some wine. This is the royal road to Christ's favour; now keep the interests of your own soul steadily in view—which you will find all the more easy after the training to keep yourself always at the top of the class at school—'communicate' regularly, and you are safe."

Meantime the religious teaching which the child received, began probably in its infancy with Bible anecdotes illustrated with pictures. First he is told the story of the Fall, and shown the serpent twisting round a tree, and Eve under it eating an apple. It is explained to him that in this way sin entered into the world. He now knows the reason why he sometimes feels naughty. Then he is shown God as a grey-bearded man walking in the Garden of Eden in the cool of the day, looking very angry, and searching for Adam and Eve, who are hiding behind a bush; and the conversation which takes place is repeated to him. He now understands the nature, character, and appearance of the Deity, and of the relation he occupies towards Him. He is now told the story of Adam and Eve's expulsion from Eden, all because Eve was disobedient and ate an apple. When he reflects upon his tendency to fall into the same temptation, he feels very sad, has a lurking sympathy with Eve, and a slight sense of undue severity and injustice on the part of God. This is confirmed by the story of Cain and Abel, in which God disregards Cain's sacrifice without any apparent cause, and afterwards brands him with the mark of a curse for killing his brother; but what infuses the first slight distrust into his innocent confiding mind, is Cain's remark that every one who finds him will slay him, when, as Abel was dead, the only man alive on earth was his own father Adam. Then he is told the story of the Flood, when all the world was drowned except eight persons, which he also thinks was a very terrible thing for God to do; and to impress it upon him, he is given an ark with a great number of little wooden animals in pairs. If he is a child of a thoughtful turn, this gives him much food for reflection, more especially as they are the only toys he is allowed to play with on a Sunday; and he asks why these are holier toys than other toys, and speculates how the animals could all get into the ark, and on what they were fed, and how only four men could take care of them all, and which was the smallest that it was worth while to save;—and so on through the whole Bible, till his religious conceptions are reduced to the level of those of a savage on the Congo, and are stamped upon his tender imagination with an indelible impress which carries its hateful mark upon him far into life, and either develops into an ignorant and superstitious fanaticism, or crystallises into an apathetic conformity, or, by the force of reaction, impels him to break out into open unbelief.

Under the combined influence of an imagination thus excited, and a temper thus roused to emulation, the child enters upon life. At school and at college his worst passions are stimulated, that personal success may be achieved at the cost of his fellows. He is punished if he helps them; every triumph that he gains, every prize that he wins, is purchased at the price of a humiliation upon some of those brethren whom he is told by Christ to love better than himself.

This desire to be first, which is actually denounced in so many words by the great Teacher as fatal to moral progress, is the one which so-called Christian teachers insist upon most earnestly, because it is essential to worldly progress; and men strive to be senior wranglers, in the hope that it may be a stepping-stone to what is called "ecclesiastical preferment," and ultimately possibly to rich bishoprics.

These be thy teachers, O Israel!

Nor is the educational system all over the world fundamentally wrong only in the principle of competition which it excites, but all intellectual development as at present practised in all Christian countries is anti-Christian, in the sense that it is not preceded by a corresponding moral development. To force intelligence alone, before the affections have been trained to steer the human will Godward, is like crowding sail upon a ship, and exposing her to the tempests of the ocean without a rudder. This is especially true of state-aided education. Inasmuch as the popular idea of religion is, that it consists of dogmas, about which people differ, and that moral training is inseparable from these dogmas, moral training is left to depend upon the accident of the home, and the acquisition of secular knowledge is forced upon children, who thus grow up into educated devils, instead of into uneducated ones. Unless there be an inherent instinct of rectitude, or the family training happens to be good, the development of the intelligence and the acquisition of knowledge, means simply the development of the capacity for crime, and the acquisition of means for committing it. At this moment many governments—the British among the number—are actually contributing large sums from the pockets of the tax-payers, for the manufacture and education of socialists, nihilists, internationalists, and the whole party of anarchy in Europe, which are a speciality of Christendom. So are hypocrites. Secular teaching produces the one, and religious teaching the other. In Moslem countries, where there are no schools in which the Koran is not taught, neither class exists. Society is nevertheless infected in other and not less fatal ways. The nature of the moral training to be given to the young, does not consist in instructing them by word of mouth as to what is right and what is wrong, and as to the difference between what we call good and evil, that standard being at present a purely arbitrary one, based not upon the divine law, but the law which enlightened selfishness has suggested, as being the most expedient in the interests of society. The process by which a child can be brought into internal union with the Deity, is one of those mysteries which may have been known to the mystics, and the sages of the most early religions; but those of their interpreters who have attempted to unravel them for us in these latter days, are silent upon the point: it nevertheless exists, though I am not able to do more than allude to it here, because it can only be apprehended as it is unfolded in practice. There is much hidden knowledge of this description, which can only be mentioned as existing at present, because it is by experiment and illustration alone that it can be understood. It will be readily admitted by any lecturer on chemistry or electricity, for instance, that if he could not illustrate his lecture as he went along by experiment, he could not convey his meaning to his audience, and indeed many of his facts would excite their incredulity if they rested upon his *ipse dixit* alone. It is the same thing with the divine science which governs the chemical changes, the magnetic affinities, and the atomic combinations of human organisms. Suffice it to say that in them, when their laws come to be understood, will be found to reside the potencies by which the pure life-current may be invoked, charged with divine wisdom; and that under its guidance those little children who are not now suffered to come to Christ, will be no longer the victims of an educational system which forbids them to do so, but will be gently led to the loving arms which long to fold them now, as they did 1900 years ago, to the infinitely tender bosom.

It is no wonder that the man who has been thus educated, enters keenly into the competitive system, which gives its infernal life and energy to civilisation, "so called." In commerce he struggles to enrich himself at the expense of his fellows, and inasmuch as the commercial code is elastic, and it is impossible even for the most cunningly devised laws to anticipate the ingenuity of pirates, who could not live at all if they did not prey upon each other, there are hundreds of ways by which even the relative honesty which these laws seek to impose may be evaded, so that men's consciences are often practically regulated by the dangers they may incur of being sent to prison. Here, again, the Church affords no assistance: it does not consider it to be its province to interfere in the practical details of finance; but, on the contrary, as it forms part of a great financial system, and is bound up with the economic interests of the country, it thrives in proportion as the country is rich—in other words, in the degree in which other countries are *exploités* for its own benefit—and fattens on the prosperity of rich bankers, brokers, merchants, tradesmen, and so forth, who in turn find that the ostentatious profession of religion gains them confidence, and consequently facilities for their financial combinations; the most pious men, therefore, not unfrequently figure in the list of the most fraudulent of bankrupts.

The whole system of commerce and finance is as rotten to the core, as fundamentally anti-Christian, as the system of education. That love of money, that taking thought for the morrow, that hasting to be rich, which is denounced in the most unequivocal terms by Christ, who told His disciples that it was easier for a camel to pass through the eye of a needle, than for a rich man to enter into the kingdom of heaven, flourishes under the ægis of the Christian Church, which makes its own rich livings an article of commerce, which traffics in the cure of souls, and instead of claiming for its head the lowest station in society, claims for it the highest, utterly denying that there is any truth in the divine saying, "He that abaseth himself shall be exalted, and he ' that exalteth himself shall be abased." So Christ says now, as He said then, "Beware of the scribes, which love to go ' in long clothing, and love salutations in the market-places, ' and the chief seats in the synagogues, and the uppermost ' rooms at feasts; which devour widows' houses, and for a ' pretence make long prayers: these shall receive greater ' damnation." Indeed there is not a denunciation which He hurled at the Pharisees, which does not apply with equal force to the Christian priesthood of the present day all over the world. There is not a Church called by His name, which is not full of money-changers, or one to which the scourge and the epithets which He employed, are not as appropriate as they were then. The "dens of thieves," and the "serpents," and the "generation of vipers," the "blind guides," the "fools," and the "hypocrites," are all here awaiting their judgment, "straining at the gnat and swallowing the camel," with this difference, however, that while they also omit "the weightier matters of the law, judgment, mercy, and faith," instead of paying tithes of mint, anise, and cumin, they insist upon receiving them. This is the Church which awaits, decked with bridal attire, the approach of the Bridegroom. Those "long robes" which distinguish the spiritual from the temporal peer, are perchance "his wedding garment," and the electric light which illumines his palace, the "lamp kept trimmed and burning."

Under the auspices of these spiritual lords does the State make wars, annex territory, break treaties when necessary, and perform all and sundry acts of statecraft, in its struggle for supremacy with other Christian States, each engaged in one perpetual effort to suppress the others, and aggrandise itself at their expense, by force or fraud.

In co-operation with these Church dignitaries does each political party in the State intrigue for place and power, too often sacrificing what they know to be the interests of the country to party supremacy, and always sacrificing the interests of true religion, as embodied in the teaching of Christ.

I do not mean to imply that they can help doing this. As society is at present constituted, it is practically impossible for any class of men, in whatever profession they are engaged, to fulfil the law of Christ.

Soldiers and sailors must murder; statesmen must rob, since it is always a question of robbing or being robbed. lawyers must lie; parsons must compromise, and so violate their consciences, if they have got any; merchants and tradesmen must cheat if they expect to live,—and so on. There is not a man from the top of society to the bottom, who is not compelled to live a life of crime, regarded from the standpoint of divine morality, and the essential spirit of

Christ's teaching and example. That it was impracticable in His day, is proved by the fact that He was not allowed to preach it and live more than three years. But it has become practicable now, and though those who combine to prove it to be so may suffer a moral martyrdom in the attempt, their success sooner or later is assured. It was for this Christ was born into the world, and He accentuated it when He said, "Blessed are the meek: for they shall inherit the earth." For as St Ignatius says in the third chapter of his Epistle to the Ephesians,—"Christianity is not the work 'of an outward profession, but shows itself in the power of 'faith, if a man be found faithful unto the end. It is better 'for a man to hold his peace, and be, than to say he is a 'Christian, and not to be. It is good to teach, if what he 'says he does likewise."

So long as men persist in considering that secular life is one kind of life, which is to be followed during six days of the week, and that the one remaining day is to be devoted to another kind of life altogether, which they miscall religious, so long will the anomalies which characterise Christendom continue; because it implies that a wide distinction must be maintained between the service of God and the service of self —and that the latter is legitimate apart from the former. Whereas, there is only one service for man on earth, and that is the service of God and the fellow-man.

Unfortunately many of those who will admit the fearful inconsistencies by which their consciences are grieved, are reconciled to them by the fixed belief that they are irremediable in this world, owing to the evil inherent in the nature of man. They console themselves by the consideration that his heart is deceitful above all things and desperately wicked, and must always remain so; that man is the victim of a moral malady, which they call "original sin," which is incurable because it was born in him; that because we are suffering from the fault of our first parents, therefore our redemption does not lie in any effort that we can make ourselves, but that we have been bought with a price, and our salvation in another world has been secured by the blood of Christ, who is the propitiation for our sins; that to think that we can overcome or expel the evil taint in us, is in fact an outrage upon the majesty of God, and a denial of the efficacy of His scheme for our salvation; that it is not the function of religion to do this—which would be to try and achieve the impossible—but to prepare us for another world, and imbue us with a belief in the efficacy of the sacraments, and the means appointed by Providence for reaching it; that the contrast between the luxury of the rich, and the squalor and misery of the poor, is included in the divine social order, because it is said, "The poor ye shall have always with you," unmindful of the divine method ordered for the relief of these same poor, "Sell all that thou hast, and give to the poor;" that a human effort to change all this would be futile as well as presumptuous, because it would strike at the basis of the whole social fabric—the defects of which are freely admitted—and would, if it were persisted in, excite a number of visionary enthusiasts to engage in an attempt at what might appear reform, but which would have the practical result of bringing down both Church and State, and producing a condition of chaos, the evils of which latter state would be worse than the first,—for there would be nothing to put up in the place of that which had been pulled down. While, therefore, not attempting to deny that these evils exist, they maintain that it is better to bear the ills we have, than to fly to others that we know not of, more especially as these last but a short time; while we have the promise of God that, if we believe in the merits of His Son, we have a future of eternal bliss secured to us in spite of our manifold shortcomings.

It will be observed that the whole of this line of argument is based on doctrines which have been constructed out of the Bible, on the hypothesis that it is literally, or at all events, in a spiritual sense, infallibly inspired. Happily I am relieved from entering upon any discussion on these points, for evidences are every day multiplying that, in the Church itself, many eminent divines are rapidly abandoning them one after another, and I will allow some of them to speak for themselves. Thus, a professor of divinity, preaching in the University of Oxford not long since, said: "The field of speculative 'theology may be regarded as almost exhausted,—we must be 'content henceforward to be Christian agnostics." The rector of the City Church, at Oxford, Mr Cartaret Fletcher, preached

a sermon before the University recently, in which the following passage occurred: "Not long since it was the general
'belief that man had been created perfect, and that he had
'fallen from perfection into an abyss of doom, whence only
'an elect fragment of the race would emerge; but it is now
'dawning on us that man was created in an undeveloped state,
'with a splendid potential wealth of faculty, and that he had
'advanced through long ages to his present stage, whence he is
'destined to rise higher than imagination can follow him. In
'him we see a rough-hewn block being moulded into perfect
'shape, and not the reconstruction of the shattered pieces of
'a faultless image." This may not be orthodox according to
the majority, but it is consolatory to know that there are men
in the Church, who dare to preach their belief in the possibility of moulding the rough-hewn human block into perfect
shape. Canon Fremantle, in the remarkable article already
quoted, writes: "As regards the Scriptures, the theologian of
'our epoch will start without any theory of inspiration. He
'will be ready to admit that God has revealed Himself in part
'in other systems, ancient and modern. He will not pretend
'that the Scriptures are absolutely perfect in any part, but
'will take them for what they are really worth, and as consti-
'tuting a history and a literature in which the development
'of a religion is to be studied." "The theology of sin and
redemption" is treated in an equally broad and enlightened
spirit. "This," says the writer, "is the department of the-
'ology in which a kind of ideal dogmatism has most interfered
'with truth. The ideal characters of the wicked and the
'just, as they are described in Scripture, have been taken as
'literally existing; and since men cannot be ranked with the
'ideally righteous, they have been taken in the mass as belong-
'ing to the ideally wicked. Each atom has been regarded as a
'conscious and open-eyed contradiction of a revealed standard
'of right—a contradiction which is described in the Gospel
'as a sin against the Holy Ghost. The false judgments, the
'mutual condemnations, the hypocrisy, the strange theories
'of redemption, the readiness to believe in eternal torments,
'the ascetic practices and unreal life which have resulted
'from this, could hardly be traced out in a lifetime. The re-
'construction which will be required will need great labour.

'But in no department will the results be more fruitful. They
'will bring theological ethics into closer alliance with general
'science and practice. They will enable Christian teachers to
'treat all men as brothers, and make Christianity the means
'by which the state of men generally may be ameliorated."

Here, then, we have the popular idea of inspiration abandoned, the theological dogmas concerning sin and redemption repudiated, and the Church arraigned for "the false judg-
'ments, the mutual condemnations, the hypocrisy, the strange
'theories of redemption, the belief in eternal punishments,
'the ascetic practices and unreal life which have resulted from
'those doctrines,"—in a popular review by a clergyman of the Church of England, without official protest by the authorities.

Nay, more, the existing state of the Church being utterly unsatisfactory, he proposes to "reconstruct it upon altogether new lines." "The theologian of our epoch," he says, "will
'take care not to represent God as a demiurge standing outside
'His work, and putting His hand in here and there. . . . He
'will probably be little concerned with miracles. It is evident
'that the arguments relied on in the last century do not help
'us now, . . . so little stress will be laid on the accounts
'of the infancy of Christ, since they are mentioned nowhere in
'the New Testament outside the first chapters of the first and
'third gospel."[1]

The conclusions at which the writer arrives, after a careful study of early Church history, and the accretions which have buried Christian ethics under anti-Christian dogmas and formularies, is one which commends itself to the religious instinct of all earnest and thinking men. "The notion of the
'Church," he says, "the study of Church history, the practice
'of Church life, will be profoundly modified when once men
'realise that the Church is not necessarily a society held apart
'from the rest of mankind by having different pursuits as its
'object, and a peculiar form of government enjoined upon
'it. The Church will be simply that section of society in
'which the Christian spirit reigns; its history will be the his-
'tory of the working out of the divine principle in human
'society, with all its blessed results. The Church of the
'future will make its worship bear upon the higher end of life,

[1] Fortnightly Review, March 1887.

THE CHURCH OF THE FUTURE.

'or rather it will teach that the true ritual is a holy life in
'all its departments, and thus it will merge itself more and
'more into the general society, being ready, in the true spirit
'of the Lord, to lose itself that it may save mankind."

That an Anglican divine should have discovered that the
true mission of the Church is to lose itself that it may save
mankind, and that he should be able to write that his views
"are not opposed by any solid array of party opinion, but
rather find men in all parties who admit them," is in itself
a justification for this attempt to point out the way by which
the Church may "lose itself" with the greatest advantage to
the humanity it professes to desire to benefit.

I have quoted Canon Fremantle's article freely, because
it is always more desirable that corrupt institutions should
be assailed by those who are within their pale, than by those
who, being without it, may be supposed to be swayed by
undue prejudice; but I venture to differ widely from him as
to the quarter to which we must look to find foundation-
stones on which to rear that Church of the future, to which
he has so eloquently alluded. "The ground," he says, "has
been cleared and the building has to be erected. The chief
point on which our energies must be expended is"—not,
as one might suppose, the search after divine truth where
alone it is to be found; not the withdrawal with bent head
and uncovered feet into the Holy of Holies, into that inward
sanctuary where God dwells in each of us, into which, when
we have prepared it by lives of self-abnegation and self-
purification, His own glory shines, and the light of inspiration penetrates, to show us how we may be builded up as
living stones into His temple,—it is not in that "kingdom of
God which is within us" that we are to seek for guidance
at this supreme moment, when all that we have heretofore
believed in is so rapidly slipping away from us. No; the
chief point on which our energies must be expended is—
"Church history"! Oh, most lame and impotent conclusion!
What shall we get out of it, except wrangling in these days,
over the wranglings men had in those? Renewed strife over
dogmas and doctrines which no man can settle, because the
disputations to which they will give rise will be intellectual
disputations; and it is not upon the intellect that the Church

of the future must be founded, but upon the affections. Men fought over the letter then, for the spirit had soon vanished out of it, and the concentration of our attention on the quarrels of the first Christians, beginning with the apostles, will only increase our conviction that the divine life by which alone the world can be redeemed, cannot be extracted from so impure a source. This study will be most useful in stimulating us to pull down: it will help us in no wise to build up.

If all impartial, laborious, and conscientious research hitherto, has only revealed the essential rottenness of that foundation which is causing the whole fabric to totter, why imagine that a further investigation into musty parchments, or long-buried scripts, will afford more solid building-ground? If they contain most brilliant flashes of inspiration, as undoubtedly they do, it is only he who has the faculty of detecting inspiration when he sees it, who can discriminate between the true and the false. To begin by grubbing into these records is to put the cart before the horse. "Seek ye first the kingdom of Heaven and His righteousness, and all other things shall be added unto you," even these gems of early inspiration; but they will come as confirmations of truth already discovered by quite another process than that of the antiquary, and herein they possess a great value to those who need such confirmation, as I shall presently proceed to show. Meantime there is another class, for whom such records will have a very slight value indeed; and as no Church of the future can stand, of which they do not form the living stones, as well as the theologians, and as they are quite as sincere in their search after divine truth, as those whose profession it is to teach it, it is time to see how this new structure, which is to be at once social, scientific, and religious, can be adapted so as to meet their requirements.

CHAPTER VIII.

THE EFFECT OF DOGMATIC THEOLOGY UPON MODERN THOUGHT—THE PREJUDICES WHICH IT EXCITES—THE CONFLICT BETWEEN SCIENCE AND RELIGION TO WHICH IT HAS GIVEN RISE—INTOLERANCE BOTH OF THEOLOGIANS AND MEN OF SCIENCE—BIGOTRY OF THE LATTER—CONTRADICTIONS IN WHICH THEY HAVE BECOME INVOLVED—FACTS OF NATURE, DISCOVERED BY SUPERFICIAL INVESTIGATIONS, VALUABLE—EMPIRICAL SCIENCE INCOMPETENT TO ARRIVE AT THE DIVINE TRUTHS IN NATURE—THIS CAN ONLY BE ACHIEVED BY DEVELOPMENT OF INNER FACULTIES IN MAN—HENCE ALL SCIENTIFIC CONJECTURES AND HYPOTHESES WORTHLESS—CONFLICTING UTTERANCES AND CONCLUSIONS OF PROFESSORS HUXLEY AND TYNDALL ILLUSTRATE THIS.

No one who has watched the signs of the times can doubt that the Church has exercised a very disastrous influence, during the last few years, upon the more intelligent part of the community; and upon no section has it operated more detrimentally than upon men of science, and the youth who are developing under the impulse which science has given to independence of thought. It has acted disastrously in this way, that the tendency of those who are reverting to the autocratic pretensions of Rome, is to invest the priestly body with a monopoly of knowledge of spiritual things as an inherent attribute of their sacred office, a sort of third-hand inspiration derived from the Church. In these days a claim of this sort is a barbarism, which will no more be tolerated than that of a Red Indian "medicine-man." The only monopoly any Church has a right to claim, is a monopoly of the errors which are peculiar to it—what truth it has, is generally common to all. The arrogance of this assumption is especially galling to scientific men and philosophers—who are, as a rule, equally arrogant in their own way—for it implies that those who make a business of science, are morally inferior to those who make a business of religion, and are excluded from any knowledge of it by reason of their rejection of clerical authority. Hence arises a prejudice against truths, which, if they were not so inseparably linked with error and authority, might appeal to their purer and nobler instincts. In throwing the dirty water out of the theological tub, they throw the child out with it, and the emotional part of their natures is apt to wither under the constant exercise of that rational faculty, which they insist is the only guide to truth. Looked at from the angelic standpoint, these two classes present a very painful and startling spectacle. Inasmuch as religion deals entirely with the affectional side of nature, when this is perverted, it takes, in the eyes of those who regard it with the tender gaze of pure love, the form of lunacy; and inasmuch as science, as at present pursued, exercises only the intelligence, when this is perverted, it takes, under the clear eye of perfect reason, the form of imbecility. Looked down upon from the lofty summit of pure love and perfect wisdom, the contest which rages here between philosophers and theologians, seems to be one between idiots and maniacs.

Swedenborg, who was one of the most learned men of science which the last century produced, and whose opinion, therefore, is entitled to some weight, insists very strongly on this point. "The insanity of science," he says, "is likened in
'the Bible to drunkenness. Those are called drunkards who
'believe nothing but what they comprehend, and therefore
'investigate the mysteries of faith; in consequence of which
'they necessarily fall into errors, since they are under the
'guidance of sensual, scientific, or philosophic knowledge only.
'The thinking principle in man is merely terrestrial, corporeal,
'and material objects, and in which the ideas of his thought
'are founded and terminated. Now to think and reason from
'those ideas concerning things divine, is to plunge into erron-
'eous and perverse opinions. . . . The errors and insanity thus
'derived are called in the Word drunkenness. Thus Isaiah
'says: 'How say ye unto Pharaoh, I am the son of the wise,
'the son of ancient kings? Where are thy wise men? and let
'them tell thee now. Jehovah hath mingled a spirit of per-

'versities in the midst thereof; and they have caused Egypt
' to err in every work thereof, as a drunken man staggereth in
' his vomit.'[1] A drunken man here denotes those who desire
' to investigate spiritual and celestial things by the light of
' science; and Egypt signifies the scientific principle, and hence
' calls himself the son of the wise. They who believe nothing
' but what they comprehend by the evidence of the senses, and
' the light of science, were also called 'mighty to drink.' As
' in Isaiah, 'Woe unto them that are wise in their own eyes,
' and intelligent in their own sight! Woe unto them that are
' mighty to drink wine, and men of strength to mingle strong
' drink!'"[2] Again the Swedish seer remarks: "A desire to
' investigate the mysteries of faith, by means of the senses and
' of science, was not only the cause of the decline of the most
' ancient Church, but it is also the cause of the fall or decline
' of every Church, for hence come not only false opinions, but
' also evils of life. The worldly or corporeal man says in his
' heart, if I am not instructed concerning faith and everything
' relating to it by the senses, so that I may see them, or by
' science, so that I may understand them, I will not believe;
' and he confirms himself in his incredulity by this fact that
' natural things cannot be contrary to spiritual. Thus he is
' desirous of being instructed in celestial and divine subjects
' by the experience of his senses, which is as impossible as for
' a camel to go through the eye of a needle—for the more he
' desires to grow wise by such a process, the more he blinds
' himself, till at length he comes to believe nothing, not even
' the reality of spiritual experiences or of eternal life."[3]

When we reflect upon the bigotries, the hatred, the persecution, and the intolerance which have characterised all Churches that have taken as their chief corner-stone the teaching of Christ, which was pure love and nothing else, we can only account for the people who profess to be animated by this love, and who manifest it by a hate which has provoked bloody wars, as having become insane; while those who maintain that the laws which govern the world are the result of a fortuitous concourse of atoms, and that man derived his origin from the amœba, and his intelligence from

[1] Isaiah, xix. 11, 12, 14.   [2] A. C. 1072.
[3] A. C. 126, 128.

the monkey, propound theories which suggest a feeble and distorted condition of the rational faculty. It is a somewhat melancholy reflection, that as ancient superstitions lose their hold upon religious devotees, men of science should pander to their credulity with scientific superstitions of another kind, concerning the physical basis of life, the evolution of man from protoplasm, and so forth, in which the public are exhibiting extraordinary readiness to believe. If the effort of imagination which the Biblical narrative calls upon them to make, in supposing man to have stepped full-fledged on earth from the hands of his Creator, is too great for the modern mind, that which the popular theory of evolution involves is no less violent. It does not seem to have occurred to searchers after truth on this subject, that the resources of the Deity are not so easily exhausted, and that there may have been a third way; but this is not to be found in the superficial letter of the Bible, nor in the superficial observations of science. Both classes of truth-seekers must learn to dive deeper, for there is a spirit within the letter, as there is a soul in nature, and it is in their concealed arcana that the book of nature, and the most divinely inspired passages in the books of God, find their synthesis. It is there that the theologian who has found the key to the inner meaning of what is now obscure, unintelligible, and even often obscene, in what is called Holy Writ, will arrive at the same truth with the philosopher who has found the key to the mysteries of the book of nature, by probing into them by the light of his own intelligence, when this has become divinely illuminated by the development of his purest affections. It is not in the outer material sense of words, nor in the outer material aspect of things, that divine truth is to be found: they are merely the caskets in which it is hidden. Both sets of investigators must develop the inner material sense; and with that—enlightened by the spirit of God, which pervades both—they may each continue their respective methods of research: but they must begin by admitting that this inner material or subsurface sense exists, as contradistinguished from the outer material or literal sense, which is surface, and, turning away from the husk, must go in search of the kernel. This can only be accomplished in one way, and that is the same for both. It involves a special effort of self-sacrifice and self-purification, which would be impossible of human attainment, had God not provided the special potency to which I have so often alluded, but the nature of which it is not possible to describe without entering upon these preliminary remarks, which have extended over a greater number of pages than I anticipated when I first took up my pen.

From passages which I have already quoted, it has been made clear that there are men in the clerical profession who are ready to abandon their old dogmas; who, conscious of the defects in the Church, are ready to see it lose itself for the sake of humanity; and who are anxious to co-operate in building up a Church for the future, which shall "teach that the true ritual is a holy life in all its departments." Here is a basis for reconstruction, upon which the man of science cannot refuse to build; once let it be clearly understood that the Church of the future does not demand a belief in any special dogma, that it imposes no ceremonial observances, and demands no subjection of the reason, no violation of the conscience, and the man of science will be the first to join hands in the good work of rearing such an edifice. If we are to judge from a recent utterance by Professor Huxley, he is already far on the road towards such a consummation. In an article entitled "Science and Morals,"[1] he writes:—

"The student of nature, who starts from the axiom of the
'universality of the law of causation, cannot refuse to admit
'an external existence; if he admits the conservation of energy,
'he cannot deny the possibility of an eternal energy; if he
'admits the existence of immaterial phenomena in the form
'of consciousness, he must admit the possibility, at any rate,
'of an eternal series of such phenomena; and if his studies
'have not been barren of the best fruits of the investigation
'of nature, he will have sense enough to see that, when Spinoza
'says, 'Per Deum intelligo ens absolute infinitum, hoc est sub-
'stantiam constantem infinitis attributio,' the God so conceived
'is one that only a very great fool indeed would deny, even
'in his heart. Physical science is as little atheistic as it is
'materialistic."

The importance of this passage is that it is written from

[1] Fortnightly Review, December 1886.

the heart and not from the intellect, for it is in indirect contradiction with the logical deductions of Professor Huxley's scientific conclusions. In the same article he remarks, "That it would be quite correct to say that material changes are the causes of psychical phenomena." And again, he talks of the "phenomena of consciousness as such, and apart from the physical process by which they are called into existence." These phenomena he has already described as being immaterial phenomena, and these, he says, are *called into existence*, not by God, but by a physical process, a conception as unthinkable as any ever propounded by theologians, and irreconcilable with the statement that physical science is not materialistic. The words "psychical phenomena," are a little vague; and Professor Huxley would probably include affection, volition, and reason under this head, and he makes them have their origin in "material changes." But his nature is too noble, and the affectional side of him too highly developed, to allow him to be dragged by his rational faculty down to the atheism and surface materialism, which have reduced some philosophers to the condition of imbecility I have already alluded to, and which, he admits, makes a man "a fool indeed"; so he clings to his God, and to immaterialism, in spite of the logical dilemma in which he is landed thereby, and which forces from him some curious and contradictory utterances.

Thus he says at one moment that "consciousness is a function of the brain," and as it certainly cannot be of a brain which has undergone the chemical change called death, he goes on to explain that by function he means "that effect or series of effects which result from the activity of an organ." This implies that the brain is made active by a force acting on it, otherwise it would keep itself alive by its own generative energy, and contradicts his previous statement that "material changes are the causes of psychical phenomena." It is evident they are only the transmitting media for them. In discoursing to the Christian young men of Cambridge, he tells them that "it is an indisputable truth that what we 'call the material world is only known to us under the forms 'of the ideal world; and, as Descartes tells us, our knowledge 'of the soul is more intimate and certain than our knowledge 'of the body."[1] If our knowledge of the soul is so intimate and certain, is it identical with that consciousness which is a function of the brain? or is the brain the organ which it renders active? If the soul is not material, of what does it consist? On these and many other questions regarding the soul we should have been glad of some light from Professor Huxley, more especially as he tells us that, "If there is one 'thing clear about the progress of modern science, it is the 'tendency to reduce all scientific problems, except those which 'are purely mathematical, to questions of molecular physics '—that is to say, to the attractions, repulsions, motions, and 'co-ordination of the ultimate particles of matter." Is the composition of the soul a scientific problem? and if not, why not? If it is not, because it is beyond the region of scientific investigation, and cannot be reduced to a question of molecular physics, why venture to say that our knowledge of it is more intimate and certain than that of our body; or to include in that investigation consciousness, and dare to tell us what it is or is not a product of, and that it is immaterial, and therefore "devoid of the ultimate particles of matter"?

In a word, why trespass upon the regions of subsurface matter with the processes of surface observation, and presume to tell us anything about them? Science plumes itself upon refusing to investigate anything outside the region it calls positive—but to this region it fixes no limits; and no medium at a spiritual circle makes greater claims upon our credulity than when it tries to tell us how we are made, and what part of us is material, and what immaterial.

The professor of biology, discoursing upon the origin and nature of human life as an authority, is as arrogant and presumptuous as the professor of theology who assumes to himself the right to dictate on matters of divine truth. It is difficult to say which set of guides is the blindest.

"The phenomena of matter and force," says Professor Tyndall, "lie within our intellectual range, and, so far as 'they reach, we will at all hazards push our inquiries; but 'behind, and above, and around all, the vast mystery of this 'universe lies unsolved, and, so far as we are concerned, is

[1] Lay Sermons, p. 340.

'incapable of solution."[1] Then why go beyond it? Unfortunately that intellectual range is so excessively limited, that it just perceives the few surface croppings up of the laws which govern the phenomena of matter and force; but the data which they furnish are not only totally inadequate for the construction of any sound theory of the universe, but are highly misleading. This is because all attempt to solve the vast mystery of this universe, under the limitations imposed by our external senses and our intellectual faculties, must prove abortive, because it necessarily involves the ideas of space subject to those limitations, and dependent upon measurements which they afford, but which do not exist in fact.

This is illustrated by the statement of Professor Tyndall, "that the idea of distance between the attractive atoms is of 'the highest importance in our conception of the system of 'this world; for the matter of the world may be classified 'under two distinct heads,—atoms and molecules which have 'already combined, and thus satisfied their mutual attractions '—and atoms and molecules which have not yet combined, and 'whose mutual attractions are therefore unsatisfied." But inasmuch as there is no limit to atoms, which are as eternal, infinite, and indestructible as the forces of which they are the transmitting media, it is evident that we shall soon reach a region which transcends the range of intellectual speculation, and to which the idea of distance is absolutely inapplicable, because it implies the existence of space, which is merely a creation of our limited faculties. It never seems to enter the head of any man of science that faculties may exist within us, which would enable us to extend our range of vision. "Granted," says the same distinguished man, "that a definite thought and a definite molecular 'action in the brain occur simultaneously; we do not pos- 'sess the intellectual organ, nor apparently any rudiment of 'the organ, which would enable us to pass by a process of 'reasoning from the one to the other: the chasm between 'the two classes of phenomena would still remain intellec- 'tually impassable." Intellectually impassable — yes; but morally passable by those organs of which we all possess the rudiments, if they were developed by processes of discipline

[1] Fragments of Science, vol. ii. p. 95.

which it is the province of those engaged in the "New Reformation" to discover and apply. These have no limitations, either of time or space, for they are evolved by love of God, who is infinite, and by service of the neighbour, whose collective life is eternal. It is satisfactory to have Professor Tyndall's own statement of a belief in the existence and efficacy of spiritual insight which can grapple with problems beyond the scope of superficial observation, for in describing the ultimate problem of physics, he says that it is "to reduce matter
' by analysis to its lowest condition of divisibility, and force
' to its simplest manifestation, and then by synthesis to con-
' struct from these elements the world as it stands. We are
' still a long way from the final solution of this problem, and
' when the solution comes, it will be more one of spiritual
' insight, than of actual observation."[1]

He, too, like his distinguished colleague, becomes involved in contradictions by the conflict which takes place between the forces of his spiritual and intellectual nature. For elsewhere he says that "the aim and effort of science is to explain the unknown in terms of the known;" so he proceeds to describe an "entity," and tells us that it is not necessarily "a free human soul." This is a definition of one unknown as being not necessarily another unknown. Again he remarks, "All our philosophy, all our science, and all our art —all are the potential fires of the sun." And again: "What
' are the core and essence of this hypothesis (physical evolu-
' tion)? Strip it naked, and you stand face to face with the
' notion that, not alone the more ignoble forms of animalcular
' or animal life, not alone the exquisite and wonderful mechan-
' ism of the human body, but that the human mind itself,
' emotion, intellect, will, and all their phenomena were once
' latent in a fiery cloud."

Professor Huxley differs from him here, for in an attempted definition of vitality he compares it with "aquosity." After referring to some of the well-known properties of water, he remarks: "Nevertheless, we call these and many other
' strange phenomena, the properties of water, and we do not
' hesitate to believe that in some way or other they result
' from the component elements of water.

[1] Fragments of Science, vol. ii. p. 94.

"We do not assume that something called 'aquosity' 'entered into and took possession of the oxide of hydrogen as 'soon as it was formed. What justification is there then for 'the assumption of the existence in the living matter, which 'has no representative or correlation in the not-living matter 'which gave rise to it? What better philosophical status has 'vitality than 'aquosity?'"

Those who have begun to bridge, however imperfectly, Professor Tyndall's impassable chasm, know that all the properties of water contain life, and what Professor Huxley calls aquosity is the result of vitality in its constituent elements; that there is no such thing as "not-living matter," and that the only difference between it and so-called living matter consists in a chemical transformation of the atomic life-particles; that matter without life is a contradiction in terms; that death is merely an appearance which is conditioned by our senses, and that it is in reality only another form of life, the one set of non-sentient interlocked atoms continuing to act vitally, though unconsciously, in surface nature, and the other set of sentient atoms, which have been set free, acting vitally and more or less consciously in sub-surface nature; and that a theory on "the practical basis of life," based on the hypothesis that the phenomenon we call death implies an actual extinction of the vital principle, must be from first to last a contradiction in terms. What is energy but another name for life? and what is the "conservation of energy" but the conservation of life? Of the two great scientific discoveries of the day—the origin of species, and the conservation of energy—the one involves a great fallacy, though there is a reflection of truth in it; and the other, if by energy is understood life, is the most fundamental truth that science has ever discovered.

Professor Tyndall says: "Believing as I do in the continuity 'of nature, I cannot stop abruptly where our microscope ceases 'to be of use. Here the vision of the mind supplements 'authoritatively the 'vision of the eye.' By an intellectual 'necessity I cross the boundary of the experimental evidence, 'and discover in matter . . . the promise and potency of all 'terrestrial life." There is a stronger indication of Professor Tyndall's "rudimentary organ" in this than in anything he has ever written. It is this potency which resides in the matter of all terrestrial life, which vivifies aquosity, and "dead" as well as living protoplasm, and soul, and consciousness, and physical phenomena, and all the other products of the universe, visible or invisible, surface material or subsurface material; and this potency we call God. Once admit that, and surface materialism, with atheism in its train, disappears from the region of philosophy; and scientific men, and professors of biology, will no longer find themselves dragged in opposite directions by their higher moral and lower intellectual natures. The sayings of these distinguished men and their colleagues all over Europe might be quoted *ad infinitum*, to prove that the more they seek to probe the secrets of nature, the more vague, contradictory, and shallow are the deductions which they extract from those secrets.

If I have felt impelled to write strongly on this subject, it is because, while their discoveries are most valuable, the conclusions drawn from them are becoming daily more dangerous to the higher moral development of man. Their names carry great weight, their singleness of purpose, their devotion, indefatigable industry, and earnestness cannot fail to inspire the highest respect; but so long as each conclusion at which they arrive tends more and more to make surface nature its own first cause, and relegates the creative agency into an idealism which many of them only cling to because they are afraid to abandon it in the face of a world not yet prepared to lose its God,—so long will they continue unwittingly but insidiously to undermine the moral fabric of society, in the hope of rearing in its place an intellectual phantasy, which, while it tortures good men with doubt, will open wide the doors to social disintegration and increasing moral depravity.

In saying this, however, I must make many exceptions. I am merely alluding to the general tendency of scientific research. In 'The Unseen Universe,' by Professors Balfour Stewart and Tait; in 'Life after Death,' by Fechner, formerly Professor of Physics at Leipzig; in a work called 'Extra Physics,' and in the writings of several men of science in America,—we have indications of that spiritual insight, without which all scientific investigation must be vain indeed.

Professor Huxley says that "in whichever way we look at the matter, morality is based on feeling, not on religion;"[1] but he also tells us, in the article above quoted, that "the safety of morality is in science." From the present standpoint of religion and science, these utterances directly contradict one another; but they would not if science, like morality, was looked at through the burning-glass of divinely illuminated feeling or affection. Religion could then be made rational enough to satisfy science, and science divine enough to be incorporated into religion. So soon as scientific men have laboured as energetically and as conscientiously with themselves morally, as they have intellectually; and have flooded those mental expanses, which their studies have rendered receptive, with that divine scientific illumination,—so soon as, by arduous effort and ordeal, they shall have placed themselves upon that moral eminence, where atomic contact can be established with appropriate divine force, will they solve their doubts as to God's existence, His overruling providence, His surpassing love, and His infinite attributes. They will not understand Him—for who by searching can find out God? —but they will feel Him, and receive revelations in regard to Him adapted to their own condition, but often incommunicable to others. They will know more. They will understand what that latent potency in matter is, by means of which the world is to be lifted by their efforts, combined with those of others, of all countries, ranks, and races, out of the slough of selfishness in which it is wallowing, and placed on that solid foundation of love; the first stone of which was laid on earth by Christ, acting under the direct operation of the divine affection, as never man did before or since, and especially adapted for this great work in a manner to which I shall presently allude.

[1] Huxley's Hume, p. 207.

CHAPTER IX.

RELIGIOUS SYSTEMS: THEIR USES AND ABUSES—ASPIRATION DEMANDS INSPIRATION—RELIGIONS EXTRACTED FROM HUSK, INSTEAD OF KERNEL OF REVELATION—IMPOSSIBILITY OF DEMONSTRATING TO THE SUPERFICIAL REASON, TRUTHS DISCOVERED BY THE INNER FACULTIES—VARIOUS CHANNELS AND METHODS OF INSPIRATION—DEVELOPMENT OF SUBSURFACE CONSCIOUSNESS—MAGNETIC CONDITION OF UNSEEN WORLD AS RELATED TO OURS—ATTRACTION AND REPULSION DEPENDS ON MORAL ATOMIC AFFINITIES—GROUPS IN THE UNSEEN WITH WHICH EVERY INDIVIDUAL IN THE VISIBLE WORLD IS AFFILIATED—SO ALSO WITH ALL CHURCHES, RELIGIONS, AND SECTS—CHRISTIAN, BUDDHIST, MOSLEM, AND OTHER RELIGIOUS ORGANISATIONS EXIST IN THE UNSEEN, AND INSPIRE THOSE HERE—HENCE DIVERGENCY OF INSPIRATION AND RELIGIOUS INTOLERANCE.

IN the foregoing pages I have endeavoured to analyse the nature of what is called "inspiration"; to apply that analysis to the sacred books upon which religions have been founded from the earliest times, and especially to the Bible; and to show that the systems of theology which have resulted from them, while they have no doubt served as a valuable moral agent, and were adapted to the moral and intellectual condition of the races, and the epochs at the time of the delivery of the ethical teaching and ceremonial observances which they enjoined, were also a fruitful source of evil, giving rise to a peculiar class of violent passions, and engendering among men bigotry and hypocrisy, spiritual pride, intolerance, and infidelity, by reason of the arrogance with which they claimed a monopoly of truth; by the bitterness with which they denounced unbelievers; by the narrow and human view which they took of the divine attributes; by the mystical, vague, and contradictory character of their utterances; by the terrors which they flaunted before evildoers, and the bribes they held out to the good,—thus causing bloody wars and relentless persecutions, and barring all progress towards a better knowledge of divine truth than that which they presented—excepting at the cost of martyrdom to those who dared to attempt to advance Godward.

It was not possible that this should be otherwise. It is a condition of man's existence, that he should be engaged in a perpetual struggle after a knowledge of God; and he is thereto impelled, in pursuance of an instinct as firmly implanted in him as that which causes an infant to seek for its nourishment at its mother's breast. This craving after the Deity is universal, excepting in the still happily very small class, which is confined to Christendom, which is suffering from mental indigestion, and in which exclusively intellectual development is rapidly crushing out all moral aspiration, and committing suicide by the unwholesome strain. For, though science may not yet realise it, the negation of the Deity, and the adoption by man of surface matter as his origin, would inevitably, sooner or later, destroy his sympathy for his fellows, were it not that no amount of metaphysical rigmarole—though it may do much harm to the few—will ever extinguish the yearning after God of the many. Men may crave after matter, and even go so far as to eat the clay of which they think they are made, like some South American tribes, but they will never instil this unnatural appetite into the world at large.

It is, then, to this insatiable longing, that the world owes its blind attachment to its religions; but inasmuch as the men who thus crave are nevertheless full of imperfection, and of evil passions of all sorts, as well as of aspiration after God, and of an instinct of brotherly love, their inspirations partake of the prevalent character of the period and of the race, and although more or less charged with divine truth, are also heavily charged with moral imperfection. For the inspired teacher, though in advance of his time, was nevertheless a reflection of it. The misfortune has always been that he could not convey to his followers the divine life which had charged him with the message he delivered, and which had raised him to his high office, without tincturing it with his personal imperfections.

While the religious aspiration was powerful enough to demand a revelation with such persistence that it was obtained, it was not powerful enough to keep men up to the spirit of it. They treasured the husk and worshipped it, principally quarrelled over it, and appropriated it from each other, because they considered it a sort of talisman to avert danger, and ensure safety; but with the exception of those who are called "mystics," they never tried to get at the kernel; and even these, as I shall presently show, only partially succeeded, and kept what they knew so buried in secrecy, that the world was none the wiser for it. For this, however, the mystics are not to be blamed; for in its then condition the world was not ready for it, and now humanity has passed into a new phase, to which mysticism is not appropriate. It is from this husk instead of from the kernel, then, that religious systems have been extracted—upon it the Churches have been built, and with it society has been fed. No wonder that the results have been what we have shown them to be! But the time has come for the prodigal to turn away from this unwholesome diet, for the husk has ceased to satisfy his awakened religious instinct, and he craves food more suited to his spiritual digestion—food not administered to him, in the first instance, by inspired prophet or seer, in the second by inspired Church, and in the third by semi-inspired priest, but drawn from the richer storehouse of his own inspiration, and his deep inner experience and consciousness. The day of exclusively inspired men, and exclusively inspired Churches has passed away. The universal inspiration is about to descend upon all who earnestly seek for it; the day of that 'Comforter'—or, more literally, 'Helper'—which was promised, and which will guide those who receive it into all truth.

If, therefore, I am about to enter upon a series of what may appear dogmatic statements, as being the result of what I believe this 'Helper' has taught me, I shall endeavour to do so in all humility — conscious that they must be very imperfect; for, as I have already said, knowledge thus derived, must always partake of the taint of the individual through whom it comes — it being morally as well as physically impossible for any human being to purge himself from it;

K

and for this very simple reason—that he forms an integral part of a great diseased whole.

The popular theological idea, that by the action of the Spirit of God a man can become actually dissevered spiritually from his fellows, and elevated above them by a "discrete degree"—to use Swedenborgian phraseology—on to another moral platform, is a stupendous fallacy, the nature of which none knew better than Christ, when He was incorporated into the earth-malady. Therefore He said, "How am I straitened until these things be accomplished!" If a man is full of scrofula, there is not a speck of his organism which is free from taint; and so it is with the world, and all that is in it—if one member suffers, all the members must suffer with it. Moreover, any attempt of a man to disconnect himself from his fellows in the hour of their need, by rising higher, would be so selfish, that the very effort would cause him to sink, instead of to rise. It is not, therefore, because I imagine myself to be any better than others, or more favoured than others, or expect to be saved more than others, or, so far as I am aware, have any personal feeling in the matter, that I enter upon this task, but simply because I feel it to be imposed upon me as a sacred duty, from which I dare not shrink.

If I am obliged to make statements dogmatically, which are incapable of proof by a process of reasoning, it is because, when one is absolutely certain of a fact, it is difficult to speak of it otherwise than dogmatically, even if it is not susceptible of proof. Thus I may be conscious of having pain in some part of my body in consequence of a remedy which I had applied, and state it as an absolute fact; though it may be quite impossible for me to prove it except by saying to those who doubt me, "Apply the same remedy, and you will feel the same pain." And as a certain class of spiritual experiences are either emotional, psychical, or physical, and not intellectual, they are not susceptible of intellectual demonstration, and, in fact, may not be demonstrable by emotional, psychical, or physical evidence—much depending in that case on temperament or organic conditions. Thus one person is a powerful magnetiser and another incapable of magnetising, but very susceptible to magnetic influence.

Scientific men who are now dealing with forces which are

inexplicable to them, in consequence of their capricious character and irregular manifestation—should have no difficulty in admitting that when one is dealing with these same, or analogous forces, in a far more subtle region of nature, one is neither bound to explain their action, nor to guarantee any similarity of result in every case. The most one can do is to give the conclusions at which he has arrived, as the outcome of experience; and having put others on the same track, leave them to work out their own results. The great difficulty which presents itself in the endeavour to describe these experiences, is the poorness of the language, which does not provide terms for the elucidation of them. Any attempt to convey the nature of the conclusions arrived at, must suffer from this cause. Moreover, as comparatively few persons have entered into conditions where their subsurface consciousness has been at all developed, many statements which are made, must necessarily appear fantastic and scarcely comprehensible.

I have already used the illustration of Keely's Motor to show how dynaspheric force can operate on external substance, and the tremendous potentiality which it possesses. It is this same interatomic energy — of which science has now discovered the existence, but which is itself transmitted by means of atoms—that produces the phenomena of hypnotism, telepathy, mediumship, and the abnormal manifestations which characterise occultism and oriental magic, and which is called, in the language of the Esoterists, "astral fluid." It is this same force, in a still higher development, which is projected from invisible beings into the organisms of persons still in the flesh, by various processes which I shall presently describe, and which enables them, under certain conditions, to interweave their organisms with ours in a manner inconceivably intimate, and by acting directly on our nerve-centres, to affect us sensationally in a manner indescribable to those who have not undergone the experience, but unmistakable to those who have. It is to this dynaspheric contact that the hysteria and convulsions that so often attend religious exaltation and revivals are due, which are generally supposed by the enthusiasts who witness them, to be the operation of the Holy Ghost.

Assuming, then, that conditions can be reached by the

interlocking of the dynaspheric atoms of those who are invisible, with those of persons still in this life, especially in the case where pneumatic as well as psychic interlocking has preceded the decease of one of the parties; and that it is possible for a commingling of ideas to take place, in which those of the invisible partner shall largely predominate, though they will have to take form through the channel provided for it in the moral expanses and mental processes of the living partner; and assuming, further, that the invisible partner was possessed of a powerful and well-trained intellect, and was developed morally to a very exceptional degree,—it is evident that, being released from the trammels of the flesh, the faculty of insight and observation into natural phenomena of such a person would result in knowledge of a deeply interesting and valuable kind. It would not be infallible, for the highest angels of which we have any knowledge are progressing, and progress implies imperfection; but it might contain certain truths which are absolutely vital to our own progress, and warnings by which terrible and unknown disasters may be averted. So far as we know, no prophets or seers have had any other channels of inspiration than those thus provided by the invisibles of our own universe, who are in immediate *rapport* with those above them, and so on up the series; and any claim to a higher inspiration is the result of ignorance or conceit on the part of those claiming to be inspired. The value of the inspiration must always be conditioned on the moral status of the recipient here, and of the recipient in the unseen part of our world; and as there are those who have risen to very lofty and pure states, what they transmit cannot be other than lofty and pure—indeed the difficulty they feel is to reduce their inspiration to the level of our faculty of reception and apprehension; the visible side of the world not being in a condition to receive any inspiration higher than it can obtain from the invisible side of it. Why, in ninety-nine cases out of a hundred, these are either so mystical, or so unpractical, or so vague, or so vulgar as to be of very little use, I have explained in an earlier chapter.

In order, however, to understand what follows, it is necessary again to revert to the moral, social, and intellectual composition of that subsurface or supersensuous world which forms part of our own. The magnetic conditions there being altogether different from what they are here, in consequence of the absence of any of those gross molecules, which we call 'material,' the functions of the supersensuous physical bodies of those there can scarcely be conceived of by us; and any attempt to describe the relation they bear to intellect and emotion, would be like trying to describe red to a man who is colour-blind. Suffice it to say, that both the physical and mental systems are, far more than they are here, absolutely dominated and controlled by the emotional, which, operating through the will, projects the powerful forces which are stored in it. The result is, that attraction and repulsion, as between individuals, act infinitely more powerfully there than they do here; and as locality there is the result of the moral conditions which create it, the place where people are, means the moral state or condition in which they are. Time in the same way is calculated by the progression of states, neither time nor space having any existence as we understand them here. It results from this, that people are all either irresistibly attracted or repelled according to their moral affinities; but these in turn depend upon the moral and intellectual condition in which they were at the time of leaving this earth, with reference to the societies in the other, through which, by atomic correlation, they derived their life.

To these on leaving this world they are at once and irresistibly drawn. As, however, impermanency is, as Buddha so strenuously and earnestly insisted, the law of the universe, it is not to remain with them always, for the individuals of which these societies are composed, in obedience to the powerful magnetic conditions which prevail, are constantly changing, and passing into higher or lower conditions, as the case may be. It follows from this that every individual here is affiliated, so to speak, with a group who correspond to his moral and rational condition, and from whom he draws his life. It is a curious reflection that materialists here derive their inspiration that there is nothing beyond the matter of which their senses are cognisant, from the materialists who hold the same view there, and who consider that there is no matter outside of that of which their bodies are composed, and which they hold to be the origin of life. This view having once impregnated the minds of those who are affiliated to them here, the latter are also unable to conceive of any matter outside of them, and which is not sensuous.

In the same way, all races and religions have their corresponding races and religions from which they draw their life. Thus the very lowest types—such, for instance, as the Bosjesmen of South Africa, or the Vedas of Ceylon, or the aborigines of Australia—are physically sustained through, and morally inspired by, those who have passed from this world, and who belong to the same races; for their atomic condition would render it impossible for them to draw life, intelligence, or moral consciousness from the highest earthly human types, with whom their atomic elements have no affinity. Thus there are races in the unseen world who have not yet developed there, as there are races in the natural world who have not yet developed here, according to our notions of development. This is due to the fact of the time not having yet come for the efflorescence of the peculiar spiritual type which they represent, in which the intellectual side of their nature is subordinate to the emotional; as, for instance, in the case of the African races, whose moral evolution, when it once begins, will progress with vast rapidity. These races will not suffer in the evolutionary process from having lived so long in a state of barbarism, and from having been preserved until now from the blighting influence of what we call "civilisation."

The law of the affinity of atoms governs the relations of the two sections of the universe, and the transmission and interchange of life between them. Thus, the good of each race, according to their quality of moral consciousness and intelligence, act upon their own race on earth to enlighten them, while the bad endeavour to influence them for evil, all being atomically interlocked together psychically, and thus possessed by good and evil people, who, to distinguish them from those in the flesh, we call "spirits."

It is the same with the religions, Churches, and sects. Their influence is very powerful, because it is always more or less organised. The most powerful organisations of this kind are the Buddhist, the Moslem, and the Romanist. Of these the Buddhist is the most powerful. It owes its strength to its antiquity, to its numbers, and to the mighty stores of force it has garnered up, by the practice of religious asceticism during 2500 years—to its profound knowledge of the laws of that force, and the methods of its conservation and application—and to the potency of its spirit of self-sacrifice, which, although misdirected, renders it by far the most powerful spiritual agency which now exists of a special kind; the best evidence of which is, that it has but to put forth a little of its long-latent energy, and it can affect the most mighty, educated, and civilised community in Christendom, far more powerfully than that society, with all its missionary enterprise, can affect it. I do not mean in the number of so-called converts, but in their quality.

The Moslem is the next most powerful society, because there is far more faith in its adherents than there is among the Romanists, the large proportion of whom, who believe, are women or peasants. It is also far more in sympathy with savage tribes; and the religion itself being of a debased, and, at the same time, fanatical type, can more rapidly come into atomic relation with them than Christians can. It therefore makes more converts annually than any other religion of the present day; though, as these are among the Central African tribes, its operations in this direction are little known.[1]

The Romanist society derives its strength from its admirable organisation, its unscrupulous methods, and its immense prestige. The internal corruption of the Greek Church, the degradation of its priesthood, its race limitations, and the social and political elements which are combining against it, render its invisible organisation much less powerful than that of Rome.

It is the most encouraging sign of the times, that there is no religious society in the unseen part of our universe which is weakening with the same rapidity as the Anglican. This arises from the fact of its defective organisation, of the wide differences of opinion which obtain within its pale, and which prevent all cohesion of the numbers who profess to belong

---

[1] Since the above was written, attention has been called to this fact by Canon Taylor and Mr Bosworth Smith.

to it here, but who abandon it immediately they leave earth-life—for the same reasons for external conformity do not exist in the unseen which do here—and also from the defection of that immense class of truth-seekers who desert it here, because they are in atomic relation with many who have abandoned it there, and whose reasons for having done so, are so forcibly projected into the minds of their earthly friends, that these latter at once follow their example.

At the same time, the identical differences continue to prevail among those who cling to it in the invisible world, which do here. There are those who, not having found the bliss they anticipated by an act of faith here, still trust to the merits of the blood of Christ to procure it for them there; and others who, for the same reason, rely on the promise made to Peter, as to the rock upon which the Church was to be built, and on the efficacy of the Eucharist; and so with every sect, down to that small and worthy body the Christadelphians, they all draw their life and inspiration from the group that belongs to them, and that to which they belong. A special peculiarity attaches to the latter sect alluded to, because they derive their inspiration from a class of persons in the unseen, who imagine themselves to be dead. This is not an uncommon form of hallucination; and Swedenborg gives some singular instances of persons who were convinced that they would not live again until the resurrection, and refused to rise from their beds, which they believed to be their graves. The delusion common to some people that death is tantamount to annihilation, and that which possesses others, that there is no life after death until the judgment-day, is one which those who have died under its spell, and therefore continue to cherish in the unseen, project unconsciously to themselves into the minds of mortals here, because they remain fixed in it. Those who arrive at this conclusion from their interpretation of certain texts in the Bible, do so from a mistaken conception of the event which is called the resurrection, the nature of which the apostles themselves did not clearly understand, or they would have stated it in terms which would have avoided the divergencies of opinion which exist among Christians on the subject. The "resurrection" does, in fact, express in one word that recombination of atoms, which will be rendered

THE RESURRECTION. 153

possible as the result of the new development of dynaspheric force now beginning to operate in the surface world, and which certainly could not operate were it not for the existence and active labours of those very beings who are to rise again. By these labours, they will, with the co-operation of human beings here, so assimilate the conditions of the visible with the invisible, that the moment will finally arrive —it may be more or less catastrophically—when we shall once again see those who have been laid in their graves, living and moving amongst us as human beings, while our own organisms will have undergone such a mighty change that they will partake of the same nature, and death will have been swallowed up in victory. This is the dawn of the restitution of all things, a certainty in the dim future, but of the times and the seasons knoweth no man.

It should always be remembered that those from whom this inspiration comes are, as a rule, those who have most recently "joined the majority," because of course they are in the most intimate atomic *rapport* with those they left behind; in fact, except in the case of a direct blood-tie, which creates a special atomic relation, it is impossible for those who have long since passed away, to establish atomic relations with a person on this earth, excepting through the channel of an organism which had established such atomic relations with that person previous to external dissolution.

The Hindoo, Jewish, and Parsee religions deserve a word of notice; the first, because it is the only religion now extant which has existed since prehistoric times—a fact which bears sufficient testimony to the extraordinary spiritual energy which must have launched it into the world, through the personalities of Rama and Khrishna, who, although they have come to be regarded as mythical personages, were none the less men, and the recipients of a divine wisdom superior to anything that has existed since, with one exception, and whose work remains the most stupendous religious monument of which we have any record, debased, degraded, and fragmentary though it be now, and though the subsurface Hindooism which has sustained it through so many thousands of years, has long been undergoing a process of gradual but sure disintegration and decay.

The Jewish and Parsee societies have many points in common. Among the great teachers of the world, none have had more marked personalities than Moses and Zoroaster. The religious life which they infused into the societies they taught, has resisted in a remarkable way attack both from within and from without. It has survived spiritual treachery and worldly persecution, and has been powerful enough to bind and hold together, by its internal atomic tie, each of these two sets of wanderers over the earth's surface. They have had a peculiar and trying ordeal to pass through, because a peculiar destiny awaits them. The special characteristic of the unseen societies of which they form the visible portion, is toughness combined with flexibility. It is this pliable obstinacy which has enabled them to weather the storms through which they have passed, and which is now beginning to take an altered shape in the unseen societies preparatory to a new development, which need not involve their destruction, but which must involve their transformation. In this they will differ from all the other religions to which I have alluded. The reason of this is that with them alone to name the race is to name the religion. This tribal characteristic, which is identified with their respective religions, operates in a special manner in the relations which the Jewish and Parsee communities in the invisible part of the universe occupy towards the rest of its inhabitants; and when the religious and social cataclysm which is now beginning there, culminates, they will not be affected by it in the same way as the other races and religions; but it is not given to me to know any details in regard to this. All that is certain is, that as religions have waxed and waned in times of yore, until nothing was left of them but inscribed monuments, or engraved tablets, or mythological legends and poems, so all existing religions are doomed again to wane, and indeed are waning now, and from their *débris* the quickened life of humanity will burst forth, to the realisation of a new and higher ideal than the most ardent disciples of the greatest teachers ever deemed possible.

As to the rapidity of the growth of this new development, no one can predict; for that depends upon man's exercise of his own free will, in fostering and co-operating with the forces that must use him as their channel of operation; but it will aid him immensely to give his will an impetus in the right direction, if he is made aware of some of the laws that govern that force. The most important of these is that it can only act through a chain of atomic particles specially adapted for it. This law was apparently unknown to seers, who have imagined themselves in direct communication with the prophets and sages of a bygone period, and notably with Christ. This was the case with Swedenborg, whose splendid intromissions into the unseen, equal, if they do not surpass, those of any other seer, and palpitate with divine truth, and who was doubtless convinced that he conversed face to face with Christ; but this was not possible, and for this reason.

It is well known to science that in the natural body all the atomic particles undergo periodical change in the course of a certain number of years. The same holds good with the spiritual body, only there is not the same periodicity as in natural time; but the atoms of a person who has passed into the inner world are perpetually changing, as the person rises or falls morally, and so at last lose all direct affinity with persons still in the flesh. In the case of those whose moral condition here is very advanced, they can still remain attached atomically to those who are rising upward, for a longer period than persons of a lower type; but sooner or later their hold becomes attenuated, and they either follow them, or are attached to a more recently deceased organism in the unseen, suited to their moral condition. In any case, it would be impossible for a person here to be so attached to one who had passed away—say, more than a hundred years ago—or beyond the extreme limit of natural old age; but it would be perfectly possible to be indirectly attached to such a one through an intermediary who had passed away more recently, and thus could form the link between the two. In that case the contact would seem direct, though in point of fact it would not be; and whatever apparent communication took place between the two, would be heavily charged with the individuality of the intermediary.

When it comes to a question of contact between a human personality and the personality of Christ, the intermediaries would be more numerous, though the effect upon the human being here would still be that of direct contact with Christ.

Were the communications not so tempered, the potency of them would be such that no man could receive them and live, —even if he could survive, he possesses no faculties which would enable him to comprehend them. They therefore reach him exactly adapted to his moral state, and the quality of his internal faculty; transforming their character by new atomic combinations with the atomic elements of each intermediary on the downward scale; and in each case taking up some of the quality of those atoms, and finally reaching the human being in a form which his own idiosyncrasies enable him to assimilate. Had Swedenborg, for instance, been born and bred a Jew, he might have equally supposed he saw and talked with Moses. His "memorable relations," which were representations projected on his mind by those with whom he was in sympathy and atomic attachment, would in that case all have been adapted to the Jewish instead of the Christian theology; he might have been perfectly honest, and yet have conveyed a totally erroneous impression of the relations which actually subsist now between Moses and Christ. For the same reason, it would be almost impossible now for a strong believer in Swedenborg, whose internal faculties were thus opened, to see anything but a Swedenborgian view of things.

When, at spiritual *séances*, Newton, Kepler, Aristotle, and other ancient sages profess to appear, and write their names as an evidence of their identity, it is absolutely certain that it is not Newton, Kepler, or Aristotle at all, but a lately deceased individual, probably of a very low type, or the medium himself, if he happens to be a dishonest man.

As human relations with the unseen have become much closer during the last half-century, in consequence of a certain alteration which has taken place in the gross external molecules of the human organism, groups have been formed in the unseen which concentrate their energies upon individuals selected here, whose organic conditions render them appropriate to psychic or pneumatic-psychic impact or impression, as the case may be. Hence, we have mediumistic centres of various groups of spiritualists, with varying forms of communication, directing or misdirecting their votaries, according to the fancy or belief of their unseen dominating group; and we have impressional writers controlled or inspired by such groups, and endeavouring to form societies, which are daily increasing in number, with more or less occult or mystic pretensions, all of whom, no doubt, sincerely believe that they have been furnished with a key to the mysteries, and all of whom are conscious of very distinct guiding and direction, which the more orthodox and devout naturally ascribe to Providence. In regard to the group under whose inspiration I am writing this, I only offer the impression which they have conveyed to me in the pages of this book, as the purest and loftiest revelation which it has been in my power to obtain, the value of which can only be estimated by those whose inner perceptions have been opened by such a long moral disciplinary process as may constitute them judges on such an important question.

It is not to be wondered at that persons whose internal faculties are open—and these are increasing every day—and who imagine themselves to be in direct personal communication with Christ, should ultimately arrive at very exalted ideas of their own spiritual function and general moral condition—though this cannot in any manner be said of Swedenborg. Herein lies the terrible danger of an opening of the supersensuous faculty, beyond the stage where the moral nature is able to bear the strain. The man who thus finds himself lifted, as he supposes, to the highest regions of our unseen world, and made a companion on equal terms with its denizens, soon imagines himself to be one of them, and their vicegerent on earth. He becomes in his own eyes infallible, and incapable of sin, and invested with supreme dominion; his "proprium," to use a Swedenborgian term, becomes inflated, and consequently a magnet which attracts a very powerful class of influences, in whom pride, tyranny, ambition, hypocrisy, and deceit, the lust of money and the lusts of the flesh, rule supreme—and who in turn use their intermediaries to take possession of their victim, until he finally becomes spiritually insane,—of such a one it may be truly said, that his last state is worse than his first. Nor is the danger to himself alone, for he becomes a channel of enormously potential magnetism of a virulently poisonous kind, which enables him to control hypnotically those who may have unwarily come under his influence, attracted by the beauty of many of his utterances, which may often still continue full of the majesty and force of inspiration. To such he still appears an angel of light—the only chosen medium for divine truth on earth to men, and the pivotal centre of all humanity.

There is no doctrine attended with greater danger than this one, which involves the necessity of a pivotal man, through whom alone God can act upon the human race. It was invented by the early Church, is illustrated in Rome, and has since been acted upon by others. It is a doctrine which casts its magnetic fetters round the affections, the will, and the understanding, and makes abject slaves of those who yield themselves to it. The whole tendency of the divinely vital descent now occurring, is to develop the entire nature of man, morally, rationally, and physically; to emancipate him from the bondage of Churches and of men; to make him his own pivot, standing erect in the light of his own divine illumination, and lifting his arms Godward, inspired by the dignity of his own aspiration—neither borne into the unseen in the swaddling-clothes of a sect, nor driven thither in a chain-gang under the cruel lash of a slave-driver, nor projected into it upon the fagot of an *auto da fé*.

CHAPTER X.

FORCE INCONCEIVABLE EXCEPT IN CONNECTION WITH MATTER AS A TRANSMITTING MEDIUM—THE PSYCHE OR "SPIRITUAL BODY," THE ABODE OF THE PNEUMA OR "SPIRIT"—CHRIST'S BIRTH AND DEATH ESTABLISHED A NEW ATOMIC RELATION BETWEEN THE SEEN AND THE UNSEEN—THE ORGANISMS OF THE SEEN AND THE UNSEEN MAN DESCRIBED—THEIR RELATION TO EACH OTHER, AND THE METHODS OF THEIR INTERACTION—THE PHENOMENA OF SPIRITUALISM, OCCULTISM, HYPNOTISM, TELEPATHY, FAITH-HEALING, AND THOUGHT-READING ACCOUNTED FOR AND EXPLAINED UNDER THE OPERATION OF NATURAL LAW—PHENOMENA UNRELIABLE AS A GUIDE TO TRUTH—CRAVING FOR IT UNWHOLESOME AND ATTENDED WITH DANGER—INSANITY EXPLAINED — PHILOSOPHY OF DEATH — DISEASE NOT AN UNMIXED EVIL — POPULAR IDEAS OF HEAVEN, HELL, PURGATORY, ERRONEOUS — MAGNETIC CONTACT ESTABLISHED BETWEEN CHRIST AND THE WORLD, THE CHANNEL OF A NEW MORAL RECONSTRUCTIVE POTENCY—THE HUMAN AND SPIRITUAL MAGNETIC BATTERIES NOW CHARGED, AND THE CONSUMMATION AT HAND—QUALITIES REQUIRED IN THOSE WHO WOULD CO-OPERATE IN BRINGING IT ABOUT.

FROM the foregoing remarks it will be seen that, as it is impossible to conceive of force as disconnected from matter, and that as all matter of which science is surfacely cognisant is in motion, dynaspheric force—which is the transmitting energy of the will, the emotions, and the intellect—must also be in motion, and must differ in quality, as light, heat, electricity, and other forces, of which we are sensuously cognisant, differ from each other; and this brings us to a consideration of the nature of the bodies which people inhabit after they have shuffled off the gross external covering which formed their fleshly tabernacle. St Paul calls these "spiritual bodies,"[1] and in fact that is the name generally given to them by

---
[1] 1 Corinthians xv. 44.

non-materialists; but few Biblical students form any definite idea of the terms "soul" and "spirit," or "psyche" and "pneuma," which are so constantly employed in the New Testament, and of the wide distinction which exists between them, or they would have clearer notions than seem to obtain at present, of the condition of those who have passed through the phase of their earthly existence. The masses who derive their ideas on these subjects from pictorial representations, believe in an unknown cloudy region, inhabited by sexless diaphanous beings, with wings and harps, whom they call angels, and whom they do not connect directly with this world; but beyond that, their minds are a blank upon the subject.

Now, in order to have definite ideas, we must begin by attaching definite meanings to words, and understand the precise signification we connect with the terms soul and spirit. The expression "spiritual body" is an accurate definition of soul, only so far as it conveys the idea that the psyche or soul is the abode of the pneuma or spirit—in other words, the psyche is composed of those atomic particles which form the outer covering or body of the pneuma, and without which the transmission of pneumatic force would be impossible, though they may transmit it in very different ways.

The word pneuma is used in several separate senses in the Bible. In one of these it means the human spirit of man, whether embodied or disembodied. In another, the divine influx or afflatus—it is then called "a spirit," or "the spirit of God." In another signification, it applies to the divine feminine, when it is called "a holy spirit," or "the spirit which is holy."[1]

The translators not having recognised any such difference, and having utterly ignored the particles, and made an arbitrary and capricious use of capitals, the only way of appreciating the full force of the distinction is by reading the original Greek text.

At present we are considering the pneuma only as applied to man. Thus an intimate fusion or interlocking of pneumatic atoms between a person here, and one who has lately passed from this earth, has only quite recently become pos-

[1] See Note in Appendix to Chapter xxi.

sible. The potency thus derived does, in fact, furnish man with the moral energy which he has lacked hitherto, and which will enable him to give practical effect to his highest aspirations, until now impossible; to overturn the false systems of science, religion, and society which prevail, and to build upon their ruins a fabric patterned after a divine model.

It is an event more pregnant with consequences of the deepest import to humanity, than anything that has happened on earth since the appearance of Christ upon it, for it alone renders His coming a second time possible; and it was to establish this new link between the visible and the invisible regions of our universe that He was born into the world, and suffered death by violence.

It is to indicate how this was rendered possible for man by that event, and by what process it can be achieved, that this book has been written.

Hitherto the loftiest communications, and the most powerful displays of celestial spiritual energy which the world has seen, have resulted, not from identic pneumatic vibration of atoms, but from pneumatic vibratory combinations of these atoms of an irregular kind. These have been exhibited in the prophecies and visions of seers in old time, in a few rare instances up to the present day, and in a very special and orderly manner on the occasion of the phenomenon which occurred shortly after Christ's departure from earth, when, as the result of the close atomic affinity which He had established with His disciples, the great outpouring of spiritual energy, known as the descent of the Holy Ghost, took place. This divine force is constantly alluded to in the New Testament; but the word δυναμις is usually rendered "power" by the translators, and its real meaning, which is "force," is thus weakened.

In order to make this clear, the reader must bear in mind that the psyche is, in fact, a body, differing only from ours in the composition of the atoms of which it consists, but otherwise exactly resembling ours in its physical construction. We call it the soul, but it is not the less a body, of which our outer body is the outer shell or covering. It is separated from the spirit, or pneuma, which resides within it, by a medium or substance in the nature of an insulator or dielectric, which is nevertheless capable of transmitting the vibrations of the pneumatic atoms within to the psychic atoms without, and, combining with these, to radiate upon human beings. In the case of the earth-man there is a human body outside his psychic dielectric, encompassed by a third dielectric, which Reichenbach called his odylic sphere—the functions of which I shall explain presently. I will endeavour to make my meaning more clear by a diagram.

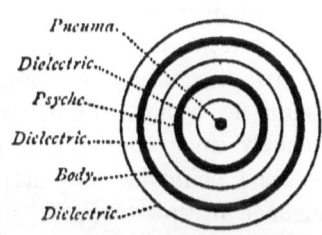

The three human dielectrics are all permeable to the atomic forces which radiate from spiritual beings, in varying degrees. In the case of the highest inspiration formerly known, and to which we owe sacred writings, the human dielectrics not only almost lost their insulating properties, but became powerful conductors of atomic vibration from the spiritual pneuma to the human pneuma, but this was unaccompanied by any interlocking of the respective pneumatic atoms.

By the absence of interlocking, I mean that no such harmony was established between the two as to render the atomic vibration identical. It is from contact of this sort that we obtain impressional writing and preaching that is not purely automatic. Its character and value must always depend upon the harmony which exists between the vibration of the pneumatic atoms, as well as upon the purity and elevation of the inspiring pneuma. What is called "genius" is the result of pneumatic contact of this sort; and poets and artists in particular must be conscious of the inspirations that proceed from it, and of times when ideas suddenly present themselves, projected from some invisible source into the brain.

As both the human and the spiritual dielectrics differ infinitely in their capacity of conductivity, there is an infinite variety in the intellectual and moral characteristics of every human being, the great majority of whom are unconscious of any radiation of spiritual influence upon them, and find it exceedingly difficult to believe that contact of this sort is possible. Where there is cerebral disturbance, the external or body dielectric is violently ruptured, and insanity or mania of some sort results—its nature depending upon the nature of the disturbance, and of the infesting influence which takes advantage of it, and other causes.

In the case of the grosser forms of spiritualistic manifestation and mediumship, the two outer dielectrics are powerful conductors, while the pneumatic or inner one generally, but not always, retains its insularity. In this case the spiritual pneumatic atoms, taking up the psychic atoms, impinge violently upon the human psyche of the medium, who for the time being is completely dominated by them, or, in the language of spiritualists, "under control." In proportion as the two outer dielectrics are permeable to this impact, is he what is called "a powerful medium for physical manifestations;" and in proportion as his pneumatic dielectric is permeable, are the results of value. The reason why they scarcely ever are of value, is because the control of his psyche by the spiritual influence, destroys all rational balance between it and his pneuma, which thus becomes open to fantastic impressions, often leading to insanity; while this control of both body and psyche, being utterly disorderly, sooner or later depletes the organism of vitality, destroys the nerves, and results in many painful forms of mental and bodily malady. The cultivation, therefore, of the mediumistic faculty is in the highest degree to be deprecated. It is of little practical use, and involves bodily and spiritual danger of the most serious kind.

The function of the external human dielectric, or odylic sphere, is the transmission between human beings of the sentiments of sympathy, antipathy, and other emotions depending on the affinity of the atoms, or the reverse, and on the accord with which they vibrate. In some cases they are peculiarly subject to spiritual agency, as, for instance, when they are projected in the human form of their living owner before the gaze of another living man, forming, with the atoms of his dielectric, a presentation visible to him alone, sometimes in dreams, sometimes in waking states. In the same way apparitions of persons who have passed into the other world are formed out of their psychic dielectrics, and are presented visually to persons in the flesh who happen to be in appropriate dielectric conditions.

The reason why phenomena of this kind, as well as those called spiritualistic, are so capricious and irregular in their manifestation, is because they depend entirely on the quality of the human dielectric. Where there is scepticism in the human pneuma or inmost thought of the man, antipathetic atomic combinations are formed in his two external dielectrics, and interpose a hostile atomic element which encompasses the medium, and forms a barrier that the psychic force of the spiritual agent cannot penetrate. It is for this reason that physical manifestations are successful just in proportion as there is a strong faith-sentiment in the spectators, whose external dielectrics are then co-operating with the spiritual agent. It constantly happens, however, that some may be present whose external dielectrics oppose an insurmountable obstacle from other causes, too varied to enter upon here, which prevent visible results from being obtained.

It is by this abnormal vibration of psychic atoms that most of the phenomena known as "telepathic" or psychic are produced — that wills are dominated, suggestions obeyed, trances induced, automatic writing and speaking are propelled through the medium, materialisation and all the grosser exhibitions of a physical character are displayed, which have for the last forty years or more excited the incredulity of one class of mind, while they have exercised a powerful fascination over another class. There has never been a period of the world's history, nor a country, in which phenomena due to this cause have not exhibited themselves in some form or other, and they form the basis of savage superstitions, and of their barbarous and often cruel rites and customs. They depend entirely for their character and value on the force of the pneumatic battery, and the quality of the dielectric of the medium—whether he be a Cingalese devil-dancer or an American "sensitive."

Another class of phenomena depends chiefly upon the affinity which exists between the atomic elements of two human beings and their dialectric conditions. Thus there are those whose atomic elements have a powerful capacity for psychic vibration, or, in other words, of domination; while others again are exceptionally receptive of psychic influence. These two classes, in cases of hypnotic experiments, healing by faith, and kindred phenomena, become operator and patient respectively. The operator is always—often unconsciously to himself—in close psychic *rapport* with the influence in the unseen, which is sometimes a beneficent and sometimes a maleficent one, who projects, by pneumatic impulsion, his or her atomic psychic force into the operator, where, becoming reinforced by the magnetic elements of the latter, it passes on into the patient with whom atomic affinity has been established; and the results are rapid, powerful, and direct, just in the degree in which, by constant exercise, the magnetic influence has been rendered dominant. As the relations of the operator with the invisible influence are subject to constant variations, arising from the fact that their atomic affinity is liable to change—and the same holds good as between operator and patient—and as there is an infinite variety of operators and patients, it is no wonder that the results are capricious and irregular, and that all attempts to classify or reduce them to sharply defined categories must end in failure, and in such disputations as have already occurred between the hypnotic schools of Paris and Nancy, who are only agreed to deny the operation of any invisible agency whatever.

This is merely a rough sketch of the processes by which seen and unseen beings act upon each other, and does not profess to classify, after the manner of oriental philosophy, the series of vital principles of which the invisible human organism is composed—a subject so complex, that it would only tend to confuse the reader. It would also be impossible to put into language, the process which distinguishes the orderly method of acting through spirit agency upon the pneuma of the natural man in its centres, from the disorderly method of reaching it through the circumferences. Suffice it to say, that all divine action proceeds from centres outwards to circumferences, and all infernal action from circumferences inwards upon centres.

Until this whole class of considerations is recognised as existing, and worthy of investigation, science will continue to flounder in a very dangerous quagmire indeed; and although much good may be done by conscientious practitioners, the dangers, as I pointed out in a previous chapter, are of a fatal character.

From which it will appear that the lowest order of contact with the invisible world—so far as the attainment of divine truth is concerned—is that which usually, though not necessarily in every instance, accompanies spiritualistic phenomena—which is only psychico-pneumatic impulsion; that the phenomena of hypnotism, and those ordinarily termed psychic, are due to this method; that a higher order exists, to which we owe what is called divine inspiration, and impressional communications of the more elevated kind, which is due to pneumatic-atomic combinations and psychic interlocking; but that a higher still has now become possible, by means of pneumatic as well as psychic interlocking, when the atoms of the pneumas vibrate in exact accord, the nature of which will be more precisely defined presently, as well as the difference which exists between that and what I have called vibratory combination.

It must be observed here, that there is a projection of ideas into the mind open to this highest order of inspiration, accompanied by an internal visualisation, altogether different from clairvoyance, in that the latter is objective to the internal senses, while the former is subjective to them. The difference is not to be described in language, because so few have undergone any experiences which would render it intelligible to them; but this should be understood in estimating the value of any inspiration, that inaccuracy with regard to the external facts of history, science, and so forth, does not affect its possible accuracy with regard to the deeper matters affecting the progress and destiny of the human soul. The reason of this is, that it is not possible, even for an angel, to put into the mind of a human being knowledge for the reception of which no mental expanses exist in his brain—except automatically. Then the inspiration loses all its value, because the human instrument has no means of judging of its origin by his own internal consciousness. The more he can retain the full control of all his faculties, the more the inspiration seems to come spontaneously from himself, the keener does his internal perception become as to its true source. Then it seems to flood the centre of his consciousness, and to allow the circumference to take care of itself. But as external facts are on the circumference, the accuracy with which these are presented by him must always depend upon his own faculties, his training and education, and the amount of everyday information which has previously been stored in his mind, and which he can use to illustrate the ideas pictured in his deep internal consciousness.

The inspiring genius cannot, therefore, be held responsible for historical or scientific errors any more than for grammatical ones. The external presentation of the inspiration must ever depend upon the man's own surface education and surroundings. Hence the numerous astronomic and other errors contained in the Bible, which, however, do not affect the transcendent value of its inspiration, in some places where these errors are most apparent.

This is the reason why, as inspiration becomes fuller and deeper, and therefore more divine, it will lose its phenomenal character. It is a great mistake to suppose that occurrences termed "miraculous" or "supernatural" are any evidence of a divine origin. It is true that most religions are based on such occurrences; but that was because the human mind at that time was more open to a due discrimination of their nature and value — because the rational faculty had not swollen to the undue proportion it has now, at the expense of the emotional.

It was, in fact, in an unduly suppressed condition, and few divine truths were appreciated intellectually; but in these days we must have a reason for the faith that is in us beyond phenomena, which are quite as likely to be infernal as divine.

There is no more unwholesome craving than that after phenomena, none more weakening to the reason, more unbalancing to the judgment, or more fruitful in misleading those who indulge it, from the truth of which they are in quest; and there is no statement in this book which will be more vehemently denied by spirits through the mediums under their control, than the above explanation of their methods of action. For if spiritualists acted upon it, their occupation and their amusement would be gone; it will be confirmed by some, however.

Above all are those in danger who seek to open themselves to the operation of this psychic force from motives of curiosity, gain, or the mere desire to exhibit phenomena which may gratify their vanity. They are playing with fire, and I would earnestly warn all those before whose eyes these lines may fall, on no account to take part in any of those after-dinner experiments in which telepathy, thought-reading, and hypnotism are trifled with as a more lively amusement than a round game. They may be unconsciously opening themselves to influences, and establishing connections with agencies in the unseen, from which they may find it almost impossible to free themselves, and which may possess a power of torturing them, both here and hereafter, in ways very little dreamt of; nor will they ever be able to trace the source of their misery to the fatal evening when, unconsciously, they let the poison into their systems. All superficial dabbling in the occult, or in spiritualism, or in hypnotism, should be carefully avoided. God is not approached by these methods—they lead, as a rule, in quite the opposite direction. Many sad cases of illness from these causes, which have terminated fatally, have come under my notice.

On the other hand, it is of the highest importance that all should remember that they are in intimate connection with the unseen part of the universe, from which they draw their life, and from which it is impossible that they can disentangle themselves; and that in the degree in which they rise morally here, will they unconsciously to themselves become associated with high moral intelligences there, and create, as it were, for themselves the home and the society which they will find waiting to receive them.

Let those who have sown in tears here know that, if they have learned the lesson their grief was intended to teach them, the harvest will be found on the other side. There is not an atom of suffering—and suffering, like everything else, is composed of atoms—which they have endured here which has been wasted, for it is a peculiarity of the atoms of the emotions, that they become transmuted by the amount of divine vitality which can be projected into them during their earthly passage. The suffering, and the pain, and the misery of the world, are its dross, but they are all capable of being transformed in the crucible of life into pure gold. Every pain-atom, whether it be moral or physical pain, becomes a joy-atom when it has done its work of purification here, and passes upwards, like incense, to that bright atmosphere, where it condenses into a joy-atom, and forms a piece of substantial happiness, waiting to be entered into by the one who felt the agony of it on earth, and who, instead of rebelling then, cherished it as a priceless gift from God. This is the true Karma.

And let those who have lost loved ones here know that they are not lost, but only gone before, if, while on earth, all were struggling to fulfil the divine behest, and that it is possible to be more deeply and interiorly united with them after their departure, than could ever have been possible through the medium of their fleshly atoms; and let them realise further, that death is indeed a new birth, and necessary to the soul's progress. If this were properly understood, partings would lose half their sting, and it would no longer be incomprehensible why so many bright examples and useful lives were nipped in the bud, at the moment when the example was most bright, and the life most useful. The influence which seemed so powerful for good here was removed, because it could be more powerful for good there in its operation upon those who are left behind, and because in many cases the finer moral atoms had developed so rapidly, that they could no longer be compressed by those which were more material, but burst their fleshly bonds because they needed expansion, and that freedom to rise which was denied them on earth. Their work now consists in lifting those they left on earth to higher moral conditions, and this they can accomplish just in the degree that the latter deny themselves the luxury of selfish grief, and throw themselves with redoubled energy into their daily duties—recognising in the apparent loss they have sustained, a new evidence of their Father's love—and invoke by constant and cheerful recollection of the loved one, who is no longer outwardly visible to them, the potency of the inward presence to guide, aid, and sustain them in the service of the neighbour. It is not by visiting the carved tablet that marks the resting-place of a few bones, or decorating it with *immortelles*, that this presence can be enjoyed; but in co-operating with it in the daily activities of life, in the consciousness of its inspiring affection for others, of its faculty of illuminating the understanding, nerving the will, and stimulating the energy,—in the conscious sensation of thrills of vital force pulsating through the organism, in the delight of the well-known moral and mental touch spurring to new endeavour, lifting to new contact with beings ineffable, and so lightening the burden of the remaining days of the earthly pilgrimage, by an earnest of bliss to come, and the promise of a meeting under conditions which shall more than compensate for all pains endured, and all worldly hopes extinguished.

At present, through the universal ignorance which prevails of the relations which the seen bears to the unseen, these experiences are vouchsafed to few, but they are within the grasp of all; nevertheless they will not be accorded to those who shape their lives on earth with a view to attaining them, for in that case the selfishness of the motive would vitiate the endeavour. The effort for union with God, through service for the neighbour, must be solely based upon the idea that the neighbour cannot be saved except by virtue of this union—because it is this union alone which can render man a fitting instrument in divine hands to aid his fellows; and as no human being should be dearer to one than God and humanity at large, therefore to try and serve God and humanity, in order to retain an internal union with any one human being, is to degrade the celestial principle of love of God and the neighbour, by making it the means to a selfish end.

What we call death, however, is not generally caused by the development or growth of spiritual life, but is more often due to various other causes, of which the principal is the decay of spiritual life, owing to the invasion of infernal energy, which poisons the celestial vitality, until the outer frame sinks under the mephitic influences thus brought to bear. This is the case where the man gives way to the uncontrolled indulgence of his evil passions, and allows himself to become the habitation of unclean spirits, who feed on the atomic elements of the vices in which they indulged during earth-life. Another cause of death is the draining of the elements of the vital atoms by human vampire organisms; for many persons are so constituted that they have, unconsciously to themselves, an extraordinary faculty of sucking the life-principle from others, who are constitutionally incapable of retaining their vitality.

Thus, it is well known that old people can derive physical life from fresh young organisms by sleeping beside them, and the experience is common among invalids, whose organisms have been rendered sensitive by illness, that the presence of certain people is exhaustive, and of others life-giving. It is rare for married people to exchange the elements of vital atoms in equal proportions, one of the partners nearly always gives more than the other receives; nevertheless, this constant change of vitality is a necessary condition of our existence as we are at present constituted; but as the laws by which it is governed are absolutely unknown to the medical profession, which does not treat patients except on their surfaces, an appalling amount of wholesale mutual slaughter now goes on unchecked. This might be very much diminished if doctors would open themselves to divine illumination, and not relegate to the Church that part of the human organism, which, if they knew a little more about it, they would perceive comes directly within the sphere of their operations.

All these three causes of death exhibit themselves externally in various forms of malady known to the profession, and which are treated by them irrespective of their origin, which is further complicated by heredity. Hereditary taint is in itself another cause of death, and diseases which spring from it are so intimately connected with the human source from which they were derived—whether the patient be alive or dead—that any treatment, to be thoroughly successful, involves considerations connected with the invisible world which would entail ruin of the professional reputation of any medical man who should dare to entertain, much less act upon, them.

When death ensues from old age, it is because the psychic

atoms have burst the physical atoms which contain them—in other words, the physical frame dissolves from excess of internal vitality, which it is not capable any longer of assimilating, and therefore slowly decays. Death is also the result of violence and other causes not necessary to specify here; but in all cases, our relation with those who have passed away is retained in one form or other, and we are able to influence their lives where they are, as they are able to influence our lives here. It is of the utmost importance that this should be thoroughly understood and appreciated, as it is calculated powerfully to affect our conduct in this life. Few realise how much they can often help those who have preceded them, and how much they can be helped by them. When, however, it is clearly apprehended that visible matter is purely relative to our senses, and that the matter which is invisible to us bears the same relation to the senses of invisible beings that surface-matter does to our senses, we shall have less difficulty in imagining a condition of things in some respects analogous to the nature with which we are familiar. It differs in this, however, that its aspect to its inhabitants is conditioned upon their moral vision: thus, the same scenery in the invisible world will present a totally different appearance to two persons in opposite moral states—the one esteeming divinely beautiful what seems to the other infernal and altogether unlovely. In the same way, their modes of life and personal appearance present the most violent contrasts, while their external bodies are totally dissimilar from each other—those of the lowest order appearing to those of the highest as gross, and often, indeed, far grosser than our own; and increasing in repulsiveness in the degree in which they sink into depths of moral depravity, and their atomic vices take expression in their outward forms. We can form some idea of this from the face of a man in the flesh, in whom the furrows ploughed by vice and dissipation are strongly marked, and betray the character within.

It is to this low and debased creature in the invisible, that we owe the phenomenon of insanity. When, through heredity, accident by violence, sudden shock, nervous overstrain, or any other cause, a cerebral disorder takes place, depriving the victim of that control which, in the normal condition of his faculties, he retains over his brain-power, he instantly becomes a field for invasion of influences in whom the indulgence of especial vices, pushed to their extreme, become insanities. For in the eyes of beings in the upper invisible world, the lower presents the appearance of a vast lunatic asylum; its inhabitants literally take possession of human beings thus afflicted, and melancholia, religious frenzy, inordinate vanity, and all sorts of infernal delusions are thus represented before our eyes. As, however, the derangement is caused by a disturbance in the most exterior cerebral structure, new atomic combinations take place during the process of transition into the invisible world, and the sufferer is placed in conditions where his cure can be speedily effected. When, therefore, we read in the Gospels of the cures by Christ of men possessed by devils, the expression is literally accurate: they would have been styled by us lunatics; but, in some respects, knowledge in those days was more accurate than it is now.

We read every day, in our law courts, of the abortive attempts of medical men of the present day to define insanity; it is, in fact, undefinable—for no such thing as a perfectly sane human being exists, or he would be sinless, and the patients are often more sane than their doctors. It being perfectly impossible, so long as our earth is atomically interlocked with its own lower region, to impede infernal cerebral invasion, it is all a question of degree, and it is not possible to draw a hard and fast line between sanity and insanity. All we can do is to put under treatment those who develop tendencies dangerous to life or property; and this might be done far more effectually, and with far happier results, if medical men would look beyond the actual brain-cells for the cause of the malady, for they are, in fact, only its habitation.

The same remark applies to all diseases—even the most trivial; a cold in the head, is a form of infestation. In other words, sitting in a draught has produced a slight organic disturbance, which opens the healthy life to invasion by a certain poisonous quality of atomic force, which finds its way from the lower invisible region, where all disease is generated. The fact that it can be cured by external remedies, in no way disproves the fact that the life which comes from above is healthy, while that from below is unhealthy, and that unhealthy life always streams into us when organic conditions admit of its doing so; but that the current of it is checked as soon as the physical balance is restored by remedial agents.

These remedial agents would not be confined to pills and drugs, if the laws which govern the interchange of atomic elements were understood, and, indeed, the efficacy of magnetic and hypnotic treatment in certain cases has long been recognised; but, as I have said elsewhere, it is attended with dangers of another kind, in which evil influences can work more harm than the most conscientious practitioner— as the world is at present constituted—can do good. Divine science, acquired by moral effort, can alone deal satisfactorily with physical disease, and there are men in the profession upon whom this conviction is beginning to force itself with irresistible authority; in illustration of which, I may mention a work by Dr Garth Wilkinson, called 'The Human Body,' in which many of these truths are insisted upon.

At the same time, it should be understood that disease is by no means an unmixed evil; that it is generated by the lower, and not the upper life, is unquestionable: but divine laws perform their functions through the lower as well as through the upper agencies, and the operation of the former is therefore made subservient to beneficent ends. Thus disease, which is, in fact, an effort of nature to throw off poisonous invasive elements, often leaves the organ attacked in a far healthier condition than it was before—in which, possibly, planes existed for moral infestation. A radical change in the organ, produced by disease, often closes the avenue to the invasion. Again, it sometimes happens that when the organism is extremely reduced physically by disease, atomic combinations can be effected in the moral nature, which would be impossible in conditions of robust physical health; and one of the commonest experiences of those who make the violent change in their external mode of thought, aims in life, and daily habits, which is involved in the attempt to rise above the conventional moral standard, and be absolutely and unreservedly self-surrendered to the service of God and the neighbour, is a serious attack of illness, from which they rise with new and higher faculties developed—

the effect of the illness having been to attenuate the gross atomic covering of the finer atomic elements, and so to allow these latter to expand. Sometimes it is the very effort of these to expand which is the cause of the disease. Thus the final effect of disease upon those who are struggling to enter into new and higher conditions is always, in a greater or less degree, to develop the subsurface faculties.

It is for the more gross and infesting class of invisible beings when they are in their earlier stages, that the earth-man can labour, and it is in this phase of their existence that the idea of reincarnation has had its origin; for, as I have already said, the instinct of the depraved, who are recently deceased, is to find for themselves human habitations, and it thus becomes possible, for those on earth who understand these things, to labour for those of their fellows who are thus infested and obsessed. Where their labours are successful, and the man is turned from the error of his ways and reformed, the possessing spirit, who cannot realise in his phantasy that he is not himself the earth-man, becomes captured by the power of the divine energy operating through the human instrument, and is liberated from the thraldom of his vices at the same time as his victim.

Those, on the other hand, who rise, are perpetually increasing in beauty of expression, as their virtues shine from their countenances, and their organisms become refined and purified of all earthly taint by incessant labour for others. These others are not only those whom they left behind on earth, but those in the invisible world who have not yet sunk into irreclaimable depths of vicious self-gratification, and who are painfully and laboriously lifted, by angelic effort, out of regions in which they find alike their misery and their insane delight. There is a point, however, where their insanities become so confirmed, that these efforts are of no avail; where memory fails, and all continuity of individuality is lost. But the divine spark still burns in them—as it does in everything—and their atoms will finally undergo a transformation corresponding to death, by which that spark will be liberated, and the atoms will recombine around it under new and altered conditions. This is the final consummation of that suffering stage of the planet's life through which we are now passing;

the preparation for it formed, as I propose to show later, the one object of Christ's mission to earth, and it will be succeeded by the condition known among theologians as millennial—but the term is misleading, for it has no reference to time, according to our measurement, nor can it be entered upon until that unseen region which forms part of our universe has been purified by the dissolution and reconstruction of the atomic vice-particles, which are the prison-houses at present of the divine elements awaiting their liberation.

At the opposite extreme to the depths of this pit is the ascending scale, which is endless, and where those connected with the earliest stage of our planet, and its subsequent highest religious life, form the connecting links between it and that still higher region which we call heaven.

Midway between the upper and lower regions of our universe is a spiritual tract, which forms a sort of neutral ground, and is more closely attached to our earth than the other two, for it is composed of atomic elements far more nearly allied to our own. It is into this that those who pass from earth immediately enter,—the most highly developed morally, merely to pass through it into the upper region; the most debased to sink with almost equal rapidity into the one below; but the vast majority to linger for a shorter or a longer period, according to their moral conditions, hovering as it were between good and evil, sometimes rising under the attraction of the upper region, and the powerful influences for good which are brought to bear, sometimes sinking under the counter-influence, only to react upwards again. In some instances the organisms of the beings in this region are so coarse, as to be visible to hypersensitive persons on earth, and their occasional appearances have given rise to the belief in ghosts, and the numerous stories of haunted houses and so forth—the atomic influence of earthly localities often possessing such a powerful magnetic attraction, that it is impossible for these unfortunate creatures to liberate themselves from it. It is to this region that the beings from the lower one rise, when, under the operation of angelic love, they are drawn upwards. It is not possible for those who have passed through it into higher conditions to sink back into it again, for the attraction of goodness, in the midst of which they dwell, is too powerful to admit of their doing so; but it is possible for those who have sunk through it downwards to be drawn up to it again, and so finally saved. This is the origin of the doctrine of purgatory.

It is into this region, then, that everybody passes on leaving this world, from still-born children upwards. Infants, on entering it, are tenderly cared for, but not relieved from the responsibility of free-will, when, as they grow up, they become exposed to the attacks of the lower class of influences. They develop there, as they would have done here, the taint of the world into which they were born: their hereditary and inherent tendencies, whether for good or evil, manifest themselves with their earliest consciousness, and they rise or sink in the degree in which they yield themselves to the angelic attraction which draws them upwards, or to the infernal attraction which drags them in the opposite direction. At the same time they are far more favourably situated than they are here, in regard to surroundings; and are so protected, that a child's nature must be very bad indeed to break away from its spirit guardians. We have no reason to regret, therefore, that the proportion of infants born in the slums of great cities, whose only experience of life would be that of squalor and crime, who pass into the other world without knowing anything of this one, should be so much larger than those of the classes more comfortably situated. It is one of the most blessed occupations of good persons who have left this world, to rear and watch over children who come to them from earth. At the same time, those who are atomically connected with them by blood-ties, whether in this world or the other, continue to exercise a most powerful magnetic influence over them, helping them or retarding their progress, according to the quality of their loves and lives.

Parents who have lost children should always remember that the progress of their offspring in the unseen, is much influenced by their own lives here, and that in proportion that they rise here, does the upward attraction increase upon the child there; while many of their own impulses to high and noble action here, may be projected upon them, quite unconsciously to themselves, from children whom they say they have "lost," but with whom they are far more nearly connected than if they had lived—who act as their guardian angels, and to whose ministrations they may possibly owe their salvation.

On the other hand, parents may exercise a most powerful and fatal influence over the future of an infant, by the terrible crimes of infanticide or abortion; for the atomic tie between mother and child is then so very close, that a virulent poison is projected into the infant organism, which infects its psychic atomic structure, and carries its infernal taint with it into the other life—thus, as it were, surrounding it with a barrier to retard its upward progress. This barrier, if the will of the child co-operates with that of its guardians, can be broken down, but it must ever be a great danger and hindrance.

These are very solemn and affecting considerations, and the tie which binds parents to children and infants who have gone before, and the influence they mutually exercise over each other's destiny, should never be forgotten.

From this it will be seen that nothing can be more misleading than the popular conceptions of heaven and hell, which have been constructed out of a grossly superficial and perverted interpretation of Biblical expressions, and made to signify places of reward and punishment, instead of conditions which human beings create for themselves out of their virtues or their vices. Those who do not work out their own happiness by constant endeavour for the happiness of others, but fall under the delusion—which invaded the world in a manner to which I shall refer later—that it could be worked out for its own sake, and at the sacrifice of the happiness of others, continue in this delusion until the vices which it propagates, produce atomic forces which, after causing excruciating suffering, not unmixed with insane delights, finally neutralise each other; but as the divine life-principle in them still exists, it reconstitutes them under entirely new and pure conditions, the only loss being that of conscious continuity of existence on the part of the individual, whose moral, intellectual, and physical nature they composed.

Among the people who can really be said to die, because they finally lose continuity of individual consciousness, are those also who live in the personal desire for immortality, and in the delusion that their own happiness here and hereafter is the one end and aim of existence. But those who are ready and willing to die that they may save others—who have no thought of their own safety or happiness here or hereafter, provided only they can win happiness for their fellows—they are immortal on this earth; and though they may shuffle off what is called their "mortal coil," will never really die, or lose their own individuality, but progress eternally in the joys of service.

This is what Christ meant when He said, "For whosoever will save his life shall lose it: but whosoever will lose his life for my sake, the same shall save it;" and this is the death to which he alluded in the declaration, "Verily I say unto you, If a man keep my saying, he shall never see death;" and again, "There be some standing here which shall not taste of death, till they see the Son of man coming in His kingdom." The Son of man came to them in His kingdom when, after His death, He connected Himself atomically with them, through the pneumatic tie which He had established with them while on earth, and which was magnetically created by the laying on of hands, and transmitted by the disciples in the same manner to those who accepted His teaching. The method, however, soon lost its efficacy through the unfaithfulness of those who practised it, and was superseded by a process more effectual and interior.

It was to this internal contact with Christ that the wonderful success of the early teachers of Christianity was due, and it formed the medium of that manifestation which is described in the second chapter of Acts "as the sound of a rushing mighty wind," and as the appearance of "cloven tongues like as of fire" which "sat upon each of them," the whole occurrence being theologically termed the descent of the "Holy Ghost."

The revolution which was produced by the stupendous moral energy that this psychico-pneumatic force contained, has remained potent in Christendom to the present day. It remains in all the Churches, in spite of the fact that "they draw near unto Christ with their mouth, and honour Him with their lips, while their heart is far from Him," and that "in vain do they worship Him, teaching for doctrines the commandments of men;" for its presence is not banished from the hearts of men because the ecclesiasticisms to which they belong have proved unfaithful; and it remains with those who are outside the Churches, because no human organisation can limit its sphere of operations. It is by virtue of its silent influence, notwithstanding the vices, and the quarrels, and the perversions of Christendom, that a great moral quickening is taking place within it; and it is in consequence of the forces which it has been gathering in the unseen world during nineteen centuries, that a new development of its energy is now impending.

The reason why this could not take place before, is because the atomic chain by which alone it could be conducted from the source of spiritual potency, is only now being completed. It consists of "the spirits of just men made perfect;" and before the great mass of humanity could feel the electric shock which it is destined shortly to impart to the visible universe, the batteries had to be prepared, and the conducting wires led to the hearts of men; and these had respectively to be charged with, and composed of, atoms containing the potential elements of good men who had fought the good fight in their lives here, and had often sunk in the conflict, having apparently accomplished nothing. Such martyrs as Savonarola, Madame Guyon, and, in our own day, General Gordon, supply illustrations; but their names are legion, for the greater part died obscure and unknown, and were accounted nothing in their humble and limited spheres of faithful service. The crown of glory which they have won, is the part they are now playing in the great work of universal redemption, and this great work was begun when He whom Christendom rightly calls its Saviour, brought the restorative vital current into the world, and, by the dissolution of His outward frame, distributed its atoms once for all throughout the decaying structure of the earthly universe, by methods I shall presently describe. Thus the accomplishment of that work, which seemed a failure at the time, is at hand; and thus the bread of His body, which He cast upon the waters, will after many days be found.

Nothing hinders the consummation of His great work more than that misconception of its scope and nature, which forms the basis of the doctrines of the Churches, and which is indeed the "commandments of men." If we would co-operate with Christ, it is not by worshipping the fictitious relics of a cross on which He fulfilled His mission nineteen hundred years ago, or by metaphorically clinging to it now. The solemn words in which He announced His success, though their import was not understood at the time, are pregnant with meaning to us in these days—"It is finished."

Our concern is not what He accomplished then, except as a matter of most sacred history, but what He demands of us now. He did not die to rescue us from the pangs of selfish craven terror, nor to minister to the greed and ambition of egotism. His work was for no one individual, and no one individual has the right to appropriate it to himself, and turn it to his own private and personal advantage. It was for all humanity, and we can only share in it, as we lose ourselves in the great humanitarian need; and the great humanitarian need is not a harp and a crown, but social reconstruction — the extinction of crime, poverty, sorrow, and physical disease, and the substitution for them of sinlessness, health, and happiness.

All such prayers as are daily offered in the Churches, are a direct hindrance to the highest kind of spiritual union with Christ, for they are all tainted by the selfish spirit, and more or less ignore the great co-operative work in which we should be engaged with Him. There is one prayer which Christ adapted in its external sense to the spiritual apprehension of those to whom it was given, which contains a sublime hidden meaning, a garbled version of which is daily degraded by constant and unmeaning reiteration, as if it was a kabbalistic formula, while its sense has been perverted by the Church to suit a still lower class of intelligence than that to which it was originally addressed. There is nothing to justify the translation of ἐπιούσιαν into daily bread. It means, as Canon Carter tells us, "super-substantial," and was so taken by all early Christian mystics. The Roman Church, by substituting "quotidianum" here, (and "carnis" for σώματος in the Creed) brought down the doctrine to the understanding of the vulgar, and lost the inner meaning to a large extent. There are other "orthodox" meanings given to this word—

(1) 'sufficient for sustenance, and necessary to real existence;' and (2) "semper paratus," 'coexistent before all worlds, bestowed in time, but brought into being independently of time and space,' but the Church prefers "daily bread"! It is no wonder that the fearful mockery of beseeching God that His will should be done upon earth as it is done in heaven, half-a-dozen times every Sunday, by ignorant, worldly, and indifferent congregations, who make no effort to do that will, never seems to strike their spiritual pastors and masters. It would be far better never to utter this prayer than thus to insult its author by its "vain repetition." In point of fact and of experience, the man who is atomically united to Christ, and whose sole object in life is to do God's will here as it is done in heaven, does not need formally to pray to Him; for every act is a prayer, and every thought is an aspiration, and every aspiration is an inspiration. His life is hid with Christ in God. All he needs to pray for is, to know from hour to hour what he is to do next, and this—if he is entirely devoid of personal desire and inclination—will always be shown to him.

The service of humanity, which is the only service He demands of us, is instinct in every human breast, and must ever be the source of the highest inspiration; for how sings the poet?—

"Unto each man his handiwork, unto each his crown,
    The just Fate gives;
Whoso takes the world's life on him and his own lays down,
    He, dying so, lives.

Whoso bears the whole heaviness of the wronged world's weight
    And puts it by,
It is well with him suffering, though he face man's fate;
    How should he die?

Seeing death has no part in him any more, no power
    Upon his head;
He has bought his eternity with a little hour,
    And is not dead.

For an hour, if ye look for him, he is no more found
    For one hour's space;
Then ye lift up your eyes to him and behold him crowned,
    A deathless face." [1]

---

[1] Swinburne's Songs before Sunrise.

Let us then rise out of a condition of spiritual mendicity, and the fetich instinct of propitiating a ferocious Deity, into one of divine co-operation—from being beggars for self, into being fellow-labourers with Christ in a great task, where there is no distinction of persons; for the moral atoms of the stupidest and the humblest may be of more value pneumatically than those of the most learned and the most exalted, and may connect him with a far higher group of spiritual beings.

Let no man esteem himself unworthy to be a participator in this divine work: all he needs is an intense longing after God, and a passionate love for his fellow-man. This at once constitutes him a burning-glass, on which must inevitably focalise the ardent rays of the divine affections; for the inspirations of which I have been speaking are not special emanations vouchsafed only to persons peculiarly organised for their reception, but are radiations which fill the spiritual universe; and though they reach human beings through the atomic forces I have described, it needs only the requisite moral attitude to ensure their concentration upon any man who seeks to receive the light and the warmth that they impart; and he will feel their blessed and vivifying influence grow more potent in the degree in which he can shake himself free from the scientific and theological trammels which now impede the development of men's higher faculties, and blind them to the perception of facts, which are only concealed from their finer vision by the prejudices and the superstitions of the learned and the devout.

CHAPTER XI.

THE RELATION OF MAN TOWARDS GOD, CHRIST, AND THE UNSEEN WORLD, HERE SET FORTH, CONFIRMED BY THE INNER SENSE OF THE BIBLE—ALL SACRED BOOKS HAVE THEIR HIDDEN SENSE—TEACHING OF THE KABBALAH AND OF THE FATHERS ON THIS POINT—INNER SENSE OF CHRIST'S TEACHING HAS BEEN LOST, AND THE SYMBOLS AND EXTERNALS ALONE REMAIN; HENCE SUPERSTITION, BIGOTRY, AND HYPOCRISY — FREQUENT ALLUSIONS TO THE "MYSTERY" IN THE NEW TESTAMENT—ST PAUL'S APPREHENSION OF IT—THE MOST ANCIENT RELIGIONS CONTAIN IT IN THEIR UNIVERSAL CONCEPTION OF GOD, AS AN INFINITE PATERNAL AND MATERNAL PRINCIPLE, PERVADING, ANIMATING, AND SUSTAINING ALL THINGS BY THE "WORD"—JUDAISM, WHICH WAS AN IMPROVED RENDERING OF THE EGYPTIAN AND CHALDEAN RELIGIONS, CONTAINED IT CONCEALED IN THE MOSAIC LAW, OF WHICH CHRIST WAS THE FULFILMENT—GENESIS COMPOSED AND COMPILED UNDER A MOST POWERFUL INSPIRATION—MYSTICISM: ITS USES AND ABUSES.

THE view which has been presented of the relation which man generally—but more especially the man who calls himself a Christian—occupies towards God, the unseen world, the founder of his religion, and his fellow-men, while it is essentially unorthodox in so far as the popular theology is concerned, is absolutely in harmony with the spirit of the traditions upon which the greatest religions of the world have been founded, including those of the Bible. For although all these sacred records are full of human imaginings, of contradictory utterances, of unintelligible symbolisms, of mythical legends, and of vague traditions, they all possess to a greater or less degree an inner sense, the meaning of which was generally concealed from the prophets and seers from whom they emanated; and it is the interpretation of this inner sense which has formed the devotional exercise of the mystics from

the earliest times. To this day the Eastern religions retain their associations of "initiated," who are versed in the hidden meaning of their Scriptures. Buddhist and Hindoo, Jew and Moslem, Parsee and Druse—not to mention Ansaryii, Metawalies, Ismailians, and numerous minor sects—all recognise the existence of an esoteric side to their religions; all venerate those who are supposed to be versed in it, and believe that the truths which it contains are of a higher order than those which appear in the external sense of the words. This was also the case with the earlier Christians; and the fact that the Bible possesses this inner meaning is indicated both in the Old and New Testaments. It is recognised in the Talmud, believed in by the Chassidim or orthodox Jews, and strongly insisted upon in the Kabbalah. Thus it is written:
"Woe be to the son of man who says that the Tora (Penta-
' teuch) contains common sayings and ordinary narratives!
' For if this were the case, we might in the present day com-
' pose a code of doctrines which would excite greater respect.
' If the law contains ordinary matter, then there are nobler
' sentiments in profane codes. Let us go and make a selection
' from them, and we shall be able to compile a far superior
' code. But every word of the law has a sublime sense and a
' heavenly mystery. . . . Now the spiritual angels had to put
' on an earthly garment when they descended to this earth;
' and if they had not put on such a garment, they could neither
' have remained nor been understood on earth; and just as it
' was with the angels, so it is with the law. When it descended
' on earth, the law had to put on an earthly garment to be un-
' derstood by us, and the narratives are its garments. There
' are some who think that this garment is the real law, and
' not the spirit with which it is clothed. But these have no
' position in the world to come; and it is for this reason that
' David prayed, 'Open Thou mine eyes, that I may behold
' the wondrous things of Thy law' (Psalm cxix. 18). What
' is the garment under the law? There is a garment which
' every one can see, and there are foolish people who, when
' they see a well-dressed man, think of nothing more worthy
' than this beautiful garment, and take it for the body, while
' the worth of the body itself consists of the soul. The law,
' too, has a body; this is the commandments, which are called

'the body of the law. This body is clothed in garments, which
'are the ordinary narratives. The fools of the world look at
'nothing else but the garment, which consists of the narratives
'of the law; they do not see any more, and do not see what
'is beneath the garment. But those who have more under-
'standing, those do not look at the garment, but at the
'body beneath (*i.e.*, the moral); while the wisest, the servants
'of the heavenly King, those who dwell at Mount Sinai,
'look at nothing else but the soul (*i.e.*, the secret doctrine),
'which is the root of all the real law, and these are destined
'in the world to come to behold the soul of this soul (*i.e.*, the
'Deity) which breathes in the law."[1]

It was in allusion to this hidden meaning that Christ said,
"I come not to destroy the law, but to fulfil it." In what
sense He was the fulfilment of the law I propose to show
later. We learn from the Kabbalah that this knowledge
was made known to the chosen of God after painful initiations.
It was called "the luminous mirror," in contrast with the
non-luminous mirror, the vision of ordinary mortals. It
was called the tree of life, as contrasted with the tree of
knowledge. "Come and see where the soul reaches—that
'place which is called the treasury of life. She enjoys a
'bright and luminous mirror which receives its light from
'the highest heaven. The soul could not bear this light
'but for the luminous mantle it puts on. For, just as the
'soul, when sent to this earth, puts on an earthly garment
'to preserve herself here, so she receives above a shining
'garment in order to be able to look without injury into
'the mirror whose light proceeds from the Lord of light.
'Moses, too, could not approach to look into that higher
'light which he saw without putting on such an ethereal
'garment, as it is written, 'And Moses went into the cloud,'
'which is translated by means of the cloud, wherewith he
'wrapped himself, as if dressed in a garment. At that time
'Moses discarded almost the whole of his earthly nature, as it
'is written that Moses was on the mountain forty days and
'forty nights, and he thus approached that dark cloud whereon
'God is enthroned. In this time the departed spirits of the
'righteous dress themselves in the upper regions in luminous

[1] Sohar, 3. 152 *a*—Dr Ginsburg's translation.

'garments, to be able to endure that light which streams from
'the Lord of light."[1]

Thus it was that Christ retired to a mountain for forty days and forty nights, to receive that law which He gave to His disciples, which, in its outward sense, contains simple ethical precepts which all can understand, though none obey them, while the hidden meaning of it is now waiting to be revealed to those who will internally receive Him. It was to this inner sense that Clement of Alexandria made allusion, when he said that Christ imparted it exclusively to James, Peter, John, and Paul. The inclusion of the last named shows that in the mind of the writer it must have been, in Paul's case, by internal illumination—a statement borne out by Paul himself in his assertion that he was taken up into the third heaven, and heard things which it is not lawful for man to utter. And here I would parenthetically remark, that while a great many of Paul's utterances are, as he says, of himself, and not of the Lord, a great many are pregnant with the deepest internal meaning, and these are for the most part exactly those which have been wrested by the Churches into dogmas dishonouring alike to God, and to Him whom they call their Lord.

Clement says further, in reference to this secret teaching of Christ, "that it was not designed for the multitude, but 'communicated only to those who were capable of receiving 'it orally, not by writing"[2]—allusion to which is made in the Acts, where it is said that after His resurrection, Christ "through the Holy Spirit had given commandments unto the 'apostles whom He had chosen; to whom also He showed 'Himself alive after His passion by many infallible proofs, 'being seen of them forty days, and speaking of the things 'pertaining to God." And Paul describes the difficulty he finds in conveying these higher truths when he writes to the Corinthians: "And I, brethren, could not speak unto you as 'spiritual, but as carnal, even as unto babes in Christ. I 'have fed you with milk and not with meat; for hitherto ye 'were not able to bear it, neither yet now are ye able, for ye 'are yet carnal."

[1] Ginsburg, pp. 37, 38.
[2] See Clement of Alexandria, by Dr Kaye, Bishop of Lincoln, p. 241.

The reason of this spiritual denseness, he proceeds to say, lies in the tendency they had already begun to exhibit, to dogmatise.

The process of unfolding deep spiritual truth to the spiritually evolving man, is beautifully imaged in the Sohar, where the hidden sense is likened to a lovely woman concealed in her palace, who, when her friend and beloved passes by, opens for a moment a secret window, and is seen by him alone, and then withdraws herself for a long time; so the doctrine only shows itself to him who is devoted to her with body and soul, and then only by degrees. First, she beckons the passer-by with her hand; this is the first and most extreme glimpse of truth. Then she approaches closer and whispers, but her face is still covered by a thick veil; this is the second stage of revelation. She then talks to him with a thin veil; this is the third stage. Finally, she shows herself face to face, and intrusts him with the innermost secrets of her heart.[1]

It will thus be seen that, according to the Kabbalah, there are four degrees of the inner sense of the "Word," and to these it furnishes elaborate keys. That the early Christians also recognised an internal interpretation to the sacred record, is indicated by the advocacy of Origen of three senses, which he calls σωματικὸς, ψυχικος, πνευματικος, or earthly, psychic, and pneumatic. "The sentiments of Holy Scripture," he says, "must be imprinted upon each one's soul in a threefold 'manner, that the more simple may be built up by the flesh '(or body) of Scripture, so to speak, by which we mean the 'obvious explanation; that he who has advanced to a higher, 'may be edified by the soul of Scripture, as it were; but he 'that is perfect, and like to the individual spoken of by the 'apostle (1 Cor. xi. 6, 7) must be edified by the spiritual law, 'having a shadow of good things to come."[2]

In the same way, Swedenborg recognises three senses, which he classifies as natural, spiritual, and celestial—of which his books purport to give the spiritual sense, and those of T. L. Harris the celestial; but neither Kabbalists, Gnostics, Swedenborgians, or any other Church or sect have yet turned their knowledge of the hidden treasures, which they admit the Bible contains, to any practical account. And this notwith-

[1] Sohar, 2. 99.   [2] περι αρχων, lib. v. cap. 11.

standing the fact that they have extracted from it moral truths which should revolutionise society, and might help to lay the foundation for that new spiritual departure after which the whole creation is yearning.

As a rule, the very fact that any such inner sense exists, is ignored by the world at large, and in the Churches of Christendom nothing remains of it but the outward symbolisms of the sacraments, the true significance of which has been perverted, until they have dwindled down to mere acts of ceremonial observance, in which a hidden virtue, ensuring everlasting salvation and a present means of grace, are supposed to reside; which, however, produce a scarcely appreciable effect upon the manner of outward living. For, as Paul says, "The kingdom of heaven is not eating and drinking, but righteousness and peace, and joy in the Holy Spirit."[1]

In point of fact, the internal meaning of the Word is neither threefold nor fourfold, but manifold, and to each one who seeks earnestly, will be revealed the internal meaning adapted to his moral and intellectual condition, his past training, and his present capacity for reception.

The reason why those who have sought for light by kabbalistic methods, by the interpretation of symbols, the application of keys, and so forth, have quarrelled among themselves over the meanings of passages, and have failed, with all their occult science, to enlighten the world to its own salvation, has been partly because they have applied their intellect and not their affections to the work, and partly because they were themselves open to the perception of truth in different degrees; and one could see in a passage what was hidden from another, just as an artist, looking at a Raphael, might discover beauties which would be hidden from an ordinary observer, while a peasant might fail to distinguish it from the signboard of an inn. It is the same with spiritual sight; it is as impossible to prove that the internal meaning discovered in a passage of sacred writ is true, to one who can only see its outward meaning, as it would be to try and explain tone and breadth of treatment in a picture to a peasant.

The denseness of spiritual perception of the Jews in regard to sacred mysteries, both in the times of Isaiah and of Christ,

[1] Romans xiv. 17.

is alluded to by the latter in His quotation from the prophet —"By hearing, ye shall hear, and shall not understand; and 'seeing ye shall see, and not perceive: for this people's heart 'is waxed gross, and their ears are dull of hearing, and their 'eyes they have closed; lest at any time they should see with 'their eyes, and hear with their ears, and should understand 'with their heart, and should be converted, and I should heal 'them." These words apply literally to the present day; and "the mysteries of the kingdom of heaven," to which Christ was referring, are as hidden from "the wise and prudent" now as they were then—for they are all summed up in that wondrous Personality, whose nature, achievement, and mission have never been apprehended.

The mysteries which, as Christ said, it was given the apostles to know, are but a fraction of those waiting to be revealed—for they were unprepared for more than a comparatively superficial apprehension of the great work which their Master performed on earth. Therefore He said to them, "There are many things I have to say unto you, but ye cannot bear them now;" and therefore it was, that when He endeavoured to explain to His disciples the greatest mystery of all, which was contained in His death and resurrection, they so little understood it, that Peter "began to rebuke Him, 'saying, Be it far from Thee, Lord: this shall not be unto 'Thee. But He turned, and said unto Peter, Get thee behind 'me, Satan: thou art an offence unto me; for thou savourest 'not the things that be of God, but those that be of men."

The saying of Ezekiel applies with equal force now that it did then, to any man who would try to call Christendom to repentance: "Son of man, thou dwellest in the midst of a 'rebellious house, which have eyes to see, and see not; they 'have ears to hear, and hear not: for they are a rebellious 'house." And the prophets of Christendom are like the false prophets of Israel in those days, "which prophesy concerning Jerusalem, and see peace when there is no peace, saith the Lord God."

The influences which deaden the spiritual perception of a Church and of a people are ceremonial, formalism, priestcraft, dogmatism, and the intolerance which results therefrom. They are accurately described in the first chapter of

Isaiah. "Bring no more vain oblations," says the prophet; "incense is an abomination to me; the new moons and sab- 'baths, the calling of assemblies, I cannot away with; it is 'iniquity, even the solemn meeting. Your new moons and 'your appointed feasts my soul hateth: they are a trouble 'unto me; I am weary to bear them." There is not a Church in Christendom which does not worship God with its lips, while its heart is far from Him; and they all represent, in their several degrees, the various hypocrisies denounced by the prophet. The "oblations," the "feast-days," and the "incense" distinguish one group; the "calling of assemblies" and the "Sabbath" distinguish another, and more especially the Ultra-Evangelicals, Presbyterians, and Dissenters, among whom hypocrisy is more highly developed than among other Christians: this is principally due to the fact that they devote one day in the week more exclusively to the practice of this hypocrisy than other sects, and that day they call "the Lord's." The result is bigotry and self-righteousness, which renders them especially deaf and darkened and foolish spiritually.

All Churches are still blind to the elementary fact that every day is the Lord's, and that it would be better to deny Him any day, than to put Him off with only one. The institution of the Sabbath, or seventh day, which was in existence, as we learn from Accadian records, in the populous city of Eridu, about the time of the creation of the world, according to the Biblical chronology (see Professor Sayce, 'Hibbert Lectures'), had a special internal signification. Not only did it mark seven periods of the world's evolution, but it typifies seven periods of race-history, also seven periods in the history of every human soul. It would occupy too much time to enumerate all the passages in the Bible in which the number seven has an esoteric sense, but there are at least fifty; among the most interesting are those in Revelation, which describe the "Lamb as it had been slain, having seven horns and seven eyes, which are the seven spirits of God," who alone was found worthy to open the book with the seven seals; those referring to the seven angels with the seven trumpets, to the seven thunders, to the beast with the seven heads and the seven crowns, to the seven angels with the seven last plagues, and to the seven vials. When, therefore, the Jews were commanded to keep the seventh day holy, the command was derived from a much older theology, and there was a special mystical reason for it which they did not understand—so, by way of an explanation adapted to their comprehension, they were told that upon that day God got tired with the exertion of making the world, and rested; but the real reason was, that it closed one period of the internal history of the race. This period terminated with the advent of Christ, who practically abolished the Sabbath, when he said, "The Son of man is Lord also of the Sabbath." He did not, however, substitute any other single day for it, but all days; His teaching being that the service of God and the neighbour was a daily duty, and that the "Sabbath was made for man, not man for the Sabbath." The disciples, however, continued to observe the Jewish Sabbath until the destruction of Jerusalem, gradually substituting for it afterwards the first day of the week: since then the whole of Christendom has persistently broken the fourth commandment; while the more unintelligent portion of it, without any Scriptural warrant, applies rules which had reference especially and exclusively to the seventh day of the week, to the first, and even goes so far as to call it the seventh or Sabbath day, instead of by its true Hebrew name.

Christians of all denominations cannot too speedily recognise that their solemn assemblies, as at present conducted—on whatever day they may be held—are an "iniquity." Those who have once experienced the quickening thrill of the divine afflatus, and the actual physical change in external respiration which accompanies it, will bear me out in the assertion, that to enter a Christian Church, unless to carry out some divine mission specially imposed, while what is called "worship" is going on, often produces a sensation of oppression and suffocation which sometimes becomes too painful to endure. I appeal to the testimony of others, because, thank God, the number of those who are physically as well as morally conscious of this increasing respiratory sensitiveness, is daily augmenting.

These things being so, I can scarcely venture to hope that many will realise the truth of the interpretations which I am about to give to passages of Scripture, which their outward sense does not convey. I only refer to the Bible at all, because it is necessary, in writing upon subjects of this nature, to appeal to the authority which the masses still respect, if they do not obey it; and because it is so absolutely confirmatory of views which had forced themselves upon my consciousness, irrespective of the sacred record: but I am always confronted with this difficulty, that the prejudice among men of science, who only judge of sacred books by their external sense, and by their effect upon the lives of so-called believers in them, is so strong, that any appeal to them tends rather to repel than to attract. Nevertheless sacred books, in spite of their imperfections, have had a transcendent value for humanity in the history of the ages, and to ignore them, would be to ignore the most powerful moral engine which has been employed by Providence for the control and restraint of human passions. To treat them with contempt is alike unphilosophical and narrow-minded—the more especially as they contain treasures of knowledge and wisdom for those who know how to dive for them; but in order to do so successfully, they must be taken for what they are really worth—neither elevated into infallible guides on the one hand, nor despised as old wives' fables on the other.

There is an infinite variety in the degree of inspiration in all writings claiming to have a supernatural origin, though the signification of the word "supernatural" depends upon the arbitrary definition we choose to attach to the word "natural." There are parts of the Bible which have been derived from so low a source, that there is very little that is divine in them, and which are calculated to do more harm than good; and there are parts pregnant with the deepest spiritual meaning, and with truths, still unrevealed, of inestimable value. All unfolding of arcana must be purely arbitrary, and can only be judged by the appeal it makes to the respective faculties of the reader; and as these vary infinitely, what is clear to one is obscure to another, and what attracts one, repels the other.

It may safely be affirmed, that the more full a book is of divine truth, the more on its first presentation it will repel the majority. This is as true of a book as of a man, and we know what the result of three years of Christ's teaching was to the Teacher. The best proof, therefore, of its value, will be the violent hostility and antagonism which it will excite. Should what is here written, be received with popular approval, I should require no better evidence of its falsity, and feel that the source from which I had derived my inspiration, was exactly the opposite to that which I believed it to have been.[1]

It may often appear, then, that the meanings which I attach to certain passages in the Bible, may seem strained and fanciful, to those who have regard only to its external sense. If, for instance, I should say that Hagar, Sara's maid, whom Abraham married on her mistress's recommendation, meant really Mount Sinai, and corresponded to Jerusalem, it would seem in the highest degree fantastic, had not St Paul said the same thing. Indeed we find him, in the fourth chapter of Galatians, calling the whole history of Abraham, his wives and children, an "allegory," and he assumes, in the first chapter of Romans, that the most profound mystery, that of the creation itself, may be understood, "For the invisible things of Him (God) are clearly seen, being understood by the things that are made, even His eternal force and Godhead." It seemed

[1] I have been induced to come to this conclusion by some of the criticisms with which 'Masollam' was received, of which I give a few specimens:—

"It is not necessary, or perhaps desirable, to discuss Mr Oliphant's theory; it practically means that men may become on earth what it is taught by theologians the blessed become in heaven. It may be questioned whether such teaching as this can have any healthy effect."

"We have some suspicion of those who profess too all-embracing aims. We think we see the altruistic household in that of Mrs Jellaby."

"On another planet existence so ecstatic might be possible, but on earth it is scarcely even desirable."

"The British Philistine will probably turn away with supreme scorn from a book with which his intellectual development allows but little sympathy."

"The hazy altruism which Mr Oliphant would substitute for the faith once delivered to the saints."

"Mr Oliphant's fad of altruism."

What was the faith once delivered to the saints but altruism? and what was Christ's fad but altruism? Well may Mr W. S. Lilly, in a recent article, talk of the "congenital imbecility of the English mind in respect of eternal and divine things."

relatively simple to Paul, who was probably an Essene, that mysteries which had formed the subject of study from the earliest times, should offer no difficulty to those who now looked into them by the light of that Gospel which Christ had come to teach, and which is described as "the power"— or "force"—" of God unto salvation," endowing man with a wisdom heretofore denied him, "yet not the wisdom of this
'world, nor of the princes (men of science) of this world, that
'come to nought: but we speak the wisdom of God in a
'mystery, even the hidden wisdom, which God ordained be-
'fore the world unto our glory: which none of the princes
'of this world knew: for had they known it, they would not
'have crucified the Lord of glory"[1]—as they do to this day. So then, "he that is spiritual discerneth all things, yet he himself is discerned of no man."

We have a remarkable illustration of the tendency of the early Christian Church to search for the hidden meaning in the Old Testament narrative, in the General Epistle of Barnabas, the 8th chapter and 10th verse, where he says: "Under-
'stand therefore, children, these things more fully, that
'Abraham was the first that brought in circumcision, looking
'forward to the spirit, to Jesus; circumcised, having received
'the mystery of three letters. For the Scripture says that
'Abraham circumcised three hundred and eighteen men of
'his house. But what, therefore, was the mystery that was
'made known unto him? Mark—first the eighteen, and next
'the three hundred. For the numeral letters of ten and eight
'are I.H., and these denote Jesus. And because the cross was
'that to which we were to find grace, therefore he adds, three
'hundred, the note of which is T (the figure of his cross).
'Wherefore by two letters he signified Jesus, and by the third
'His cross. He who has put the engrafted gift of His doctrine
'within us, knows that I never taught to any one a more cer-
'tain truth; but I trust that ye are worthy of it."

It is clear to those who have made a study of the most ancient religions, by the light of their more interior faculties, that they are—not the result of the fetich gropings of primitive man, or were derived from dreams, as Mr Herbert Spencer and other philosophers would have us believe—but

[1] 1 Corinthians ii. 6-8.

the remains of much higher truths that man once possessed, in regard to the nature of God, the creation of the world, the changes it has undergone, the introduction of what we term evil, and the progress of the human soul; and the tradition of this more illumined condition is still preserved in the legend of the "Golden Age."

The religious instinct of man has been devolving, not evolving, though the tide has turned, and the evolutionary period has once more commenced. In all the highest utterances of extinct religions, as well as of those that exist, we find the same leading ideas, all pointing to a common origin, and all presenting the same fundamental principles, though they have been perverted by human imagination into polytheisms and superstitions, and surrounded by myths and legends, which have in some cases almost obscured the primitive worship. It would need a volume devoted to the subject to do justice to it, but modern research is tending strongly in this direction; and provided that those who engage in this study are animated by the right motives, and are thoroughly free from preconceived philosophical or theological prejudices, I have no fear of the assertion I have just ventured to make being confirmed; and I am the more assured of it by the concluding paragraph of Professor Sayce's very remarkable essay on the 'Religion of the Ancient Babylonians.' "This," he says, " is the day of specialists; the increased application
' of the scientific method, and the rapid progress of discovery,
' have made it difficult to do more than note and put together
' the facts that are constantly crowding one upon the other, in
' a special branch of research. The time may come again,
' nay, will come again, when once more the ever-flowing
' stream of discovery will be checked, and famous scholars
' and thinkers will arise to reap the harvest which we have
' sown. Meanwhile I claim only to be one of the humble
' labourers of our own busy age, who have done my best to
' set before you the facts and theories we may glean from the
' broken shreds of Nineveh, so far as they bear upon the reli-
' gion of the ancient Babylonians. It is for others whose
' studies have taken a wider range, to make use of the ma-
' terials I have endeavoured to collect, and to discover in
' them, if they can, guides and beacons towards a purer

'form of faith than that which can be found in the official creeds of our modern world."[1]

When we find a professor of science prepared to look back six thousand years for guides and beacons towards a purer form of faith than can be found in official creeds, and a Canon of the Church prepared to give up the popular view of the atonement and the Trinity, we have evidences of the commencement of an evolutionary epoch tending towards a purer and higher morality, which is infinitely encouraging.

Inquirers in this direction have already discovered that the most ancient conception of the Deity was that of an infinite paternal and infinite maternal principle, united in one, pervading all things, and animating all things, by virtue of an infinite creative and sustaining principle which was called the "Word." As an illustration of the point to which students have already arrived, I annex a table made out by Mr Arthur Lillie,[2] in which, however, he styles the "Word" the solar God-man. Although I do not agree in his classification, the question of nomenclature is purely academic, and does not bear upon the point, which is so highly important, of the prevalence throughout all of the same idea.

	Father.	Mother.	Solar God-Man (or Word).
Rig Veda	Varuna	Aditi	Mitra.
Manu	Brahma	Mâyâ	Brahmâ.
Buddhism	Buddha	Prajna or Dharma	Sangha.
Zoroastrianism	Zervan Akarine	Ardvi Cura	Ahura Mazda or Ormuzd.
Egypt	Amin Ra	Neith	Osiris.
Old Greece	The Serpent	Ceres	Bacchus.
Plato	Father	Mother or Nurse	Logos.
Woden	All Father	Frigga	Woden.
Kabbalah	Ensoph	Sophia	Logos.
Gnostics, perhaps Essenes	Abraxas	Sophia	Gnosis or Christos.
China	Yu	Yang	Taiki.
Babylonia	Bel	Melissa	Tammuz.

[1] Hibbert Lectures.   [2] The Popular Life of Buddha, p. 249.

There is one change, however, I would wish to make, and this is the orthodox Jewish, as well as sometimes the kabbalistic symbol of the Divine Feminine, which is Shechinah, and which, although it signifies tent or covering literally, was used to conceal the ark, in which was contained the mystery of the Divine Feminine. So the Hebrew for "The Word" is Davad, and in the Targum, Memra.

Judaism is nothing more nor less than a Jewish rendering of the ancient Babylonian, Egyptian, Hindoo, and Zoroastrian religions, blended, modified, improved, and inspired to suit the exigencies of the time, and the character of the people for whom it was adapted. Hence we find much of the Levitical law in the Egyptian ritual for the dead, much of the Mosaic cosmogony in the tablets of creation, which have lately been brought to light through the efforts of the late Mr George Smith and Professor Sayce, containing the legends of ancient Accad, and much of the mysticism of the Mazdeans, which more especially pervades the Talmud and the Kabbalah. This in no way affects or reflects upon the value of Biblical cosmogony and theology; it simply proves that God did not leave the world, with its teeming population, and its advanced civilisation, for thousands of years prior to the days of Abraham, without any religion at all, but that such revelations of Him as existed, obscured, perverted, and modified as they were by man's ignorance and inventions, were the remains of a still higher one which had preceded them, and that Judaism was the purest outcome as a reform of those religions, for which society was prepared at the period of its initiation.

From these most ancient sources it is easy now to construct the history of the creation of the world in six days, the story of the fall of man, the account of the deluge, and of the building of the Tower of Babel, which no doubt vary in many particulars, owing to the fact that so far as we know they existed only in oral tradition among the Jews for a long period; the first and second books of the Pentateuch being only committed to writing, according to the conclusions of those who have devoted themselves to research on this subject, about B.C. 800, and some of the others contained in the Old Testament, such, for instance, as the Book of Esther, being disputed as canonical down to the time of Christ.

The books termed Mosaic, though it seems to be generally conceded that they were not written by Moses, are to a great extent practically his, for it was owing to his great learning as a priest of the Temple of the Sun, and as a pupil of Jethro, who was one of the most learned mystics of his time, and as a descendant of Abraham, who was the chief of a society of occultists in Chaldea, that he was enabled, under inspiration, to give his people an account of the creation of the world, and impose upon them a law, both of which have a very profound internal meaning. In fact there are no books in the Old Testament more pregnant with occult divine wisdom than some portions of the Pentateuch, except perhaps the Book of Job; while others, such, for instance, as the books of Chronicles, are entirely devoid of any arcana whatever, and are merely an historical record compiled by Jewish rabbis and scribes, probably not earlier than B.C. 200, and owing to the strong anti-Samaritan bias by which they are disfigured, are historically misleading.

It is evident, however, that the compilers of Genesis, although they incorporated other traditions into those of Moses, were under a most powerful inspiration. The apparent confusion in the record, which has given rise to their division into the Jehovistic and Elohistic accounts, possesses really a deep internal significance. In the Talmud and Kabbalah we have the internal meaning of the Mosaic account of the creation, elaborated in a form of mysticism, which strikes the reader, judging it only by its surface meaning, sometimes as childish, sometimes as fantastic and even revolting, and sometimes as profound. The Talmud especially is full of inspiration from sources in the highest degree misleading; much of it is silly trash, lacking any inner meaning at all, while at other times it contains passages of high significance. The Kabbalah may be said to be the only really valuable *résumé* of ancient mysticism; but while it contains much of the wisdom of the ages, conveyed in a form which is unintelligible except to the initiated, it must always depend largely upon the initiated themselves what hidden meaning they discover in it; and in view of the far more sure and simple method of arriving at divine truth which now exists, its study can scarcely be said to be attended with profit, excepting for reference, and under very special circumstances. Modern criticism has been much exercised as to the date and authorship of the Kabbalah, as if the value of its contents could possibly be affected either by the date at which it was written, or the man who wrote it. Whether Moses de Leon wrote it in the thirteenth century, or Rabbi Simon Ben Jochai in the first, does not in the least affect its intrinsic value; any more than the intrinsic value of the Pentateuch would be affected if it could be conclusively proved that it was written by Ezra, and not by Moses. It would none the less have been founded on tradition which had reached him, and written under inspiration; in the same way some of the apocryphal books of the Old Testament, as for instance the books of Enoch and Esdras, are quite as full of inspiration as any of the minor prophets; but this can only be felt by each, as the divine afflatus which each book contains, may reach the reader according to his moral state. Thus one book will seem inspired to one man, to quite a different degree from that which it may appear to another, and no man can lay down a positive rule, and say this is inspired and this is not. If, in the foregoing remarks, I seem myself to have been doing this with regard to certain books, I do so with the reservation that I distinctly feel them to be so inspired, and am personally conscious of the divine afflatus in some and not in others; but I do not venture to apply my sensations on the matter to others.

It has been necessary to make these remarks, because they suggest large fields of inquiry, that can only be advantageously entered upon by those who have, by long and arduous moral discipline, prepared themselves to seek confirmation of their experiences, and of the conclusions at which they have arrived, by an examination into the sacred writings and mystical records of all religions. They also form an essential introduction to considerations regarding the cosmogony of the world, the early history of man, and his obligations under the new conditions that have now overtaken him, which I am about to present to the reader.

CHAPTER XII.

MASCULINE AND FEMININE ATOMIC ELEMENTS — SENTIENT AND NON-SENTIENT ATOMS — THE DEITY OF THE BIBLE, AS WELL AS OF FORMER SACRED RECORDS, MASCULINE AND FEMININE — EFFECT OF THE DIVINE MATERNITY ON MAN — REVELATION BY THE SPIRIT, WHICH IS FEMININE, A PERSONAL ONE — THIS MYSTERY CONTAINED IN THE HIDDEN SENSE OF BOTH OLD AND NEW TESTAMENTS.

A FUNDAMENTAL difference exists between the atomic elements of the masculine and feminine principles in nature. It is evident that this must be so; because, as a difference exists in the most external male and female forms, the atoms which compose them must be differently combined and arranged.

It is a peculiarity of atoms, well known to chemists, that their properties or behaviour depend upon their arrangement, though their nature is not changed; thus, the difference in constitution between a molecule of ozone, and one of oxygen, is absolutely imperceptible, but they have widely different properties. Why this should be so is a mystery which is perfectly unfathomable to science; and as science generally explains what it cannot understand by a name, it calls this "allotropism." Now the mystery of generation is to be found in the mystery of allotropism.

The nature of the male molecule and of the female molecule is essentially the same, but they possess entirely different properties, and this is due to the arrangement of the atoms of which they are respectively composed. When, in the process of conception, these molecules combine, it depends upon the interlocking of their atomic particles whether the result is a male or a female. It is a mistake to suppose, because science has not been able to discover from any outward manifestation in the embryo, until parturition is far advanced, what the sex is to be, that this has not been determined from the beginning. The influence which controls this result is the great dual influence which pervades all nature, and which imparts to every object in it, even to those which we call inanimate, its twofold sex-life.

It was by the operation of this twofold principle that external nature, as we see it, was called into existence; and it is by its constant operation that it is sustained. Its origin and source we call God.

This sex-principle pervades the dynaspheric force atoms, which may be divided into two categories—those which are sentient, and those which are not sentient. Non-sentient atoms are those which compose what we term inorganic matter, and pervade the material forces of which we are cognisant—such as electricity, material magnetism as distinguished from animal magnetism, light, heat, and so forth. Sentient atoms are those which operate in animal magnetism, in the will, intellect, and emotions; but they are graduated downwards in infinite variety to the non-sentient atoms, as animal life is linked by zoophytes to vegetable life. The lowest form of atoms which animate the human race, are in the shape of infusoria or predatory animalculæ, corresponding in appearance to its worst vices and passions, for every thought and emotion is represented structurally in invisible substance; the highest and purest emotions and intellectual aspirations consist atomically of bisexual human beings, patterned after the shape of primal man. These, however, can only display their force in, and operate through, mortals here, who are struggling to regain the lost bisexual condition in a manner presently to be described. This is the new force of which it is the purport of this book to treat. It has only commenced to operate in the world within the last few years, excepting in very rare instances, but it was fully manifested in the person of Christ. What is called by theologians His second advent, consists in His personal operation through this bisexual force, in the organisms of those who, after long preparation, have received it, and invoke His presence by virtue thereof. Hitherto the purest force known consisted of unisexual homuncules, and this force it is which operates generally in the organisms of all good and unselfish individuals. These atomic male and female divided entities are susceptible of transmutation into bisexual human atoms; but they can be only thus transmuted by severe moral discipline and suffering on the part of those individuals who, having given themselves to the service of humanity, struggle to effect this organic change in the forces of which their own emotions, passions, and volitions consist.

The person in whom this change has been accomplished, is conscious of it through the new sensations which begin to vibrate in his nervous centres—affecting more especially the solar plexus—by the inspirations by which they are accompanied, and by which he can be guided in his everyday life; as well as by the new potency with which he finds himself endowed for the performance of his various duties, and the imparting of moral and physical vitality into the organisms of those who seek to approach these new conditions, and whose progress he is thus enabled to assist. He is also able in certain cases to heal disease, as I have myself experienced; but this only under a very powerful internal guidance, and in very special circumstances, as no man is a judge when, by an act of his own will, disease should be checked. Physical malady often produces atomic structural changes of the highest moral value, and should be allowed to run its course for that purpose. It also produces death at a critical period of the soul's history, when to prolong natural life would be to affect most injuriously the immortal body; but this is no reason why remedies, in which the forces consist of non-sentient atoms, should not always be employed, because they act irrespective of human volition, and are controlled by the unseen agencies which operate through them, independently of the selfish ambitions, interests, or affections of human beings. The only magnetism which it is safe for one person to impart to another, is that in which the atomic forms are bisexual, because they contain the Christ element, and because they refuse to be imparted, except where the volition is under divine control—in other words, the operator feels his will resolutely set against imparting it, except when he is internally ordered to do so. The quality of a healing magnetism which is imparted for purposes of pecuniary gain, is generally morally debased, sometimes containing atomic creatures of a ferocious and sanguinary moral type, which, although wonderful physical cures may be accomplished through their agency, continue to affect the soul long after it has left the body which had thus been temporarily healed.

It is evident that these considerations must have an important bearing on the origin and conditions of physical life.

The hypothesis that because, where 36 atoms of carbon, 26 of hydrogen, 4 of nitrogen, and 10 of oxygen, are found in combination, you get a substance exhibiting visible life, and call it protoplasm—which I believe is now being split up, and explained by the word "plastogen"—therefore protoplasm or plastogen is the source of this great twofold sustaining and animating principle in nature, is the most stupendous fallacy which it has entered into the mind of man to conceive, though some have indulged it to the extent of expecting the day to come, when they will be able to make living protoplasm.

Such a notion would not have been possible, had not the rational atomic structure of the persons holding this view been altogether disintegrated by overstrain, and by the entire repudiation of the controlling function which the atoms of the moral structure exercise, by divine prerogative, over those of the reason. There can be no better illustration of the fantasies of which the human mind is capable, when left to itself, than the theory that protoplasm is the origin of life; and yet it is one which finds wide response among what are called "the intelligent classes," and who call those who can see a little further into the nature of matter than they can with their microscopes, Visionaries! Let them accept rather the teaching of the Psalmist than of these philosophers, when he says,—" I am fearfully and wonderfully made: mar-
' vellous are Thy works; and that my soul knoweth right
' well. My substance was not hid from Thee, when I was
' made in secret, and curiously wrought in the lowest parts
' of the earth. Thine eyes did see my substance, yet being
' unperfect; and in Thy book all my members were written,
' which in continuance were fashioned, when as yet there was
' none of them."

The principle of bisexuality is even in the amœba, and it is by virtue of it that it is enabled to multiply itself by fission.

There is no more potent argument in favour of design in the order of the universe, than is supplied to us by the existence throughout it of the sex-principle; and the fundamental truth that it emanated from a bisexual source, the Father and Mother of all Life, Two-in-One, finds expression, sometimes mystically, sometimes in distinct language, in the most ancient of religions. I will confine myself to a very few illustrations in support of this assertion; but those who consider these religions of value as a confirmation of its truth, will find it in them all, in one form or other.

Thus in Buddhism there are two Pâramitas, Upâya and Prajnâ, which represent the Fatherly and Motherly principles. " From the union of Upâya and Prajnâ," says an old Buddhist book, cited by Mr Hodgson, "proceeded the world."[1] Prajnâ is the exact equivalent of the Hebrew Chokmah and the Alexandrine word Sophia — Wisdom imaged as a woman. Upâya is variously translated; its literal meaning is "approach."[2] Upâya Prajnâ with the Buddhists is similar to the Ardha Nâri (literally half-woman) of the Brahmans— the Cosmos imaged as a bisexual God.[3] While in that most ancient religion of Accad which Professor Sayce has been revealing to us, he tells us that "it was believed that 'Ana Sar was the male principle which, by uniting with 'the female principle (ana) ki-sar," (the goddess of) the earth (and) the hosts of heaven, "produced the present 'world. It was to this old elemental Deity that the great 'Temple of Esarra was dedicated, whose son was said to be 'the God Ninip or Adar"[4] (the Word).

A recognition of this truth is to be found in the Talmud, while the Kabbalah discourses on the subject very elaborately. Thus in the Sohar we find that from the boundless En Soph emanated the Sephiroth, consisting of masculine and feminine principles, of which the first were Wisdom, represented by the divine name Jah (masculine), and Intelligence, Jehovah (feminine), and it is from a union of these, which are also called Father and Mother, that the remainder proceeded, or, accord-

---

[1] Hodgson's Essays, p. 88.   [2] Buddhism in Christianity, p. 91.
[3] Hodgson's Essays, p. 78.   [4] Hibbert Lectures, 1887, p. 125.

ing to the same authority, "When the Holy Aged, the concealed of all concealed, assumed a form, he produced every- thing in the form of male and female, as things could not continue in any other form. Hence Wisdom, which is the beginning of development, when it proceeded from the Holy Aged, emanated in male and female, for Wisdom expanded, and Intelligence proceeded from it: and thus obtained male and female—viz., Wisdom the Father and Intelligence the Mother—from whose union the other pairs of Sephiroth successively emanated."[1]

These are either masculine, feminine, or two-in-one. Thus "love" is masculine, "justice" feminine, and they are united in "beauty," the whole composing a figure somewhat after the Grand Man of Swedenborg, and each triad of Sephiroths giving birth respectively to the intellectual, moral, and material worlds. There is, moreover, a trinity of triads, and, above all, a supreme trinity of crown, king, and queen.

I mention this, not relying upon it in any way as an authority, but merely as illustrating what a prominent position the divine feminine held in the most ancient conception of the Deity—for whatever may be the date of the Kabbalah in its present form, there can be no doubt of the antiquity of the traditions which it contains.

The Kabbalists to this day pray for "the reunion of the Holy One, blessed be His name, and His Shechinah : I do this in love and fear, in fear and love, for the union of the name [masculine] הו with הי [feminine] into a perfect harmony;" for they imagine in their conceit that the afflictions of the race proceed, not from the fact that they have lost their biune God, but that He has lost His Shechinah, or feminine principle.

"For some reason best known to themselves," says Mr Macgregor Mathers, in his introduction to his very interesting work, 'The Kabbalah Unveiled,' "the translators of the Bible have carefully crowded out of existence and smothered up every reference to the fact that the Deity is both masculine and feminine. They have translated a *feminine plural* by a *masculine singular* in the case of the word Elohim. They have, however, left an inadvertent admission of their

[1] Sohar, iii. 290a.

'knowledge that it was plural, in Genesis i. 26, 'And Elohim
'said, Let us make man.' And again (verse 27), how could
'Adam be made in the image of Elohim, male and female,
'unless the Elohim were male and female also? The word
'Elohim is a plural formed from the feminine singular ALH—
'*Eloh*—by adding IM to the word. But inasmuch as IM is
'usually the termination of the masculine plural, and is here
'added to a feminine noun, it gives to the word Elohim the
'sense of a female potency united to a masculine idea, and
'thereby capable of producing an offspring. Now we hear
'much of the Father and the Son, but we never hear anything
'of the Mother in the ordinary religions of the day. But in
'the Kabbalah we find that the Ancient of Days conforms
'himself simultaneously into the Father and Mother, and thus
'begets the Son. Now this Mother is Elohim. Again, we are
'usually told that the Holy Spirit is masculine. But the
'word RVCH — Ruach—is feminine, as appears from the
'following passage of the Sepher Yetzirah, ʻACHTH RVCH
'ALHIM CHIIM — A Chath (feminine, not masculine)
'Ruach Elohim Chiim—One is *she*, the Spirit of the Elohim
'of Life.'"[1]

And again (page 25): "This Sephira completes and makes
'evident the supernal Trinity. It is also called Ama,
'Mother, and Aima, the great productive Mother, who is
'eternally conjoined with Ab, the Father, for the mainten-
'ance of the universe in order. Therefore is She the most
'evident form in whom we can know the Father, and therefore
'is She worthy of all honour. She is the supernal Mother,
'coequal with Chokmah, and the great feminine form of God,
'the Elohim, in whose image man and woman are created,
'according to the teaching of the Kabbalah, *equal before God*.
'*Woman is equal with man, and certainly not inferior to him*,
'as it has been the persistent endeavour of so-called Chris-
'tians to make her. Aima is the woman described in the
'Apocalypse (ch. xii.) . . . She is the supernal Mother, as
'distinguished from Malkuth, the inferior Mother, Bride,
'Queen." This inferior Mother, Bride, or Queen is, as will
presently appear, the feminine principle of the Son, or the
Word made flesh. I have thought it worth while to quote

[1] The Kabbalah Unveiled, p. 22.

in full some passages from 'The Kabbalah Unveiled' concerning the androgynous character of the Son, which will be found at the end of the Appendix.

This truth was contained in the hidden meaning of the law which Moses gave his people, and in the arcana of numberless passages of the Old and New Testaments, especially in the Book of Job and the Revelation. It was held by the mystical sect of the Nazarites, for it formed part of the lore which they had received from the mystics of Egypt, Chaldea, and Persia; it was well known to the Essenes, who succeeded them, and to the Pythagoreans; while in the Orphic poems, Zeus, who is "one force, one spiritual being, great rector of all things," is described as being at once a male and an immortal nymph. And again he calls Jupiter the divine husband and wife—$Z\epsilon\hat{v}_S$ ἄφοην γενετο, $Z\epsilon v_S$ αμβρωτος επλητο νυμφη, The Osiris-Isis of ancient Egypt, and the Iswara Prakriti of ancient India, represent the same truth.

The twofold character of God was held by the Therapeuts and Gnostic sects, and it was not until the suppression of the latter that Christendom may be said to have lost its God, and adopted the God of the Jewish Pharisees and Sadducees; the cruel, implacable, vindictive, unjust male monster, which exoteric Judaism created after its own image, and which was the hideous legacy they left to the civilised world on their own extinction as a nation. If the ignorance, bigotry, and cruelty of Christendom, have made the Jew a martyr for well-nigh two thousand years, amply has he revenged himself upon it by presenting it with his God, as material out of which to invent a Trinity.

Both Jews and Gentiles have yet to find the Infinite Father and Mother whom they have lost. Among a sect of the former, it is true, He exists theoretically in His twofold essence; but Christians have only a faint emblem of it in the person of the Virgin Mary, who, as the mother of Christ, occupies the same relative position to a minute fraction of Christendom—which still finds a profound mystical meaning in some of the dogmas of the Church—that Maya does, as the mother of Gautama, to Buddhists; but to Christendom at large, this is not comprehended even as a symbol.

In proportion as a Church loses the infinitely tender element of the divine maternity, and substitutes for it the character of an unjust judge, does it become harsh, self-righteous, and arrogant. We see evidence of this in what are called the evangelical sects of the West, whose hatred of Popery has led them to repudiate the feminine element in it.

If we accept the idea of a Deity at all, as a great First Cause, or creative principle, it is surely rather a self-evident proposition than a mystery, that the twofold principle of life must emanate from Him, and that if He is our infinite Father He must also be our infinite Mother, though the idea is so foreign to us, that we have no pronoun in our language to attach to a bisexual being.

To him who seeks his God by the light of this truth, will its substantial verity be revealed in ways of which he can little dream; for it is evident that a conception of the Deity, even if it be vague, which contains a vital truth, furnishes a foundation-stone for a living faith; and two incomprehensibles which form one, by virtue of a combination of two principles which we all understand, form a basis more solid to build upon, than three incomprehensibles which form one, by virtue of three principles which none of us understand. Beyond this no human mind, as at present constituted, can furnish to another any adequate conception of the great First Cause; though Churches have endeavoured to define Him, and have dared to stigmatise what they call pantheism, or the belief that His essence must be present everywhere, and that nothing can be where He is not, as error. That a dual principle should be all-pervading, and yet constitute a personality, is only incomprehensible to us, because we cannot emancipate ourselves from the false perceptions which attach to our limitations in time and space. And as, while these perceptions are relative to our senses, it is impossible that this should be otherwise, the revelation of His nature by God to man must always be a personal one, conveyed to his affections through the subsurface faculties which those affections can alone develop.

Those to whom God has revealed Himself in His divine womanhood, become conscious of a new tenderness stealing over them, which embraces the whole visible world. The beauties of nature now become invested with an indescribable attraction. The swelling hillsides, the craggy rocks, the undulating ocean, the rustling foliage, are all palpitating with God in a way they never did before; and the life which is in them seems to blend mysteriously with the affections. They do not need to be told that nature has a soul, for they feel themselves to be united in most loving sympathy with it.

If this is the case with what is called "inanimate creation," how much more strongly is it the case with all living things! and how intense becomes the compassion and the yearning over the fellow-man, irrespective alike of colour, race, or condition in life! It was this Divine Feminine which spoke through Jesus, when He called the little children toward Him; when He refused to condemn the fallen woman; when He brooded as a mother over Jerusalem, and drew the beloved disciple to His bosom. It was this tenderness which evoked a response from the hearts of women, such as no prophet or teacher had ever evoked before, and prompted Him, in the moment of His supreme agony, to utter the sublime ejaculation, "Father, forgive them; for they know not what they do."

It is this revelation of the divine maternity to the soul of man that brings with it a new sense of spiritual potency, and that enables those who have received it to exercise an indefinable influence over those who are being prepared for its reception: it is the infusing of a new warmth into nature, the dawning of a new brightness upon the soul's horizon, the palpitating of a new joy throughout all the being. To those who have rejected the theological Christ, and misunderstood His work, and His true relation to God and man, it is an inspiration which sweeps away old prejudices, and lifts the veil that has hidden the animating principle of His personality from our gaze. We see Him now, no longer through a glass darkly, but face to face, and we feel the infinitely sweet touch of a nature, in which the Divine Feminine has been developed, and which can reach us through atomic sympathy by the appointed channels, because He was Himself once tempted in all points like as we are.

It is by the light of this revelation that we can judge of the work of the great religious reformers and teachers of the world; and while to some of them we accord a majesty of inspiration and a dignity of effort which claim our highest respect and veneration, we are enabled to perceive that though they in some instances recognised the existence of this principle, and taught it as a mystery, to none was given the highest illumination that it imparts.

This internal illumination can only be attained by an occult union with the bisexual Deity, for which the world was not yet prepared, and for which the elements did not exist in nature. Therefore it was that the efforts of the mystics in this direction proved of comparatively little advantage to the world at large; and that the attempts of those who now seek by the methods which they employed, of asceticism, dirt, self-concentration, and so forth, to attain the same end, will be of no avail, unless they recognise the supreme function of Christ, as the divinely appointed channel by which this union can alone be won by the elements which he imparted. Nevertheless He can visit those who have not so recognised Him, and the visitation will, sooner or later, convey the revelation.

If the intelligent classes in Christendom understood that there was an esoteric sense in the letter of the Bible, and if this fact had been recognised as essential to its true comprehension by the Church, materialism and scepticism would not have assumed the proportions they have attained during this century; and instead of searching for arguments to prove the scientific absurdity of Biblical statements, men would have devoted themselves rather to the task of discovering what that inner meaning was.

If the Churches had not lost the inspiration of the Holy Spirit, that can only operate in man through the Divine Feminine, which Christ was the first to embody on earth, they would have been able to oppose a barrier to the flood of infidelity which now threatens the submergence of all religion; and it is with the object of urging all those who are animated by a sincere love for their fellows, to search for this hidden wisdom, not in the Bible alone, but in their own hearts, that this book is written.

So long as those who regard the Bible as an authority, attempt to meet the conclusions of science by clinging to the literal interpretation of records, adapted in their outward form to the ignorant, credulous, and superstitious conditions which existed among the common people three thousand years ago, so long will they get worsted in their endeavours, and build up scaffoldings of fallacies for their opponents to pull down.

When, on the other hand, there are to be found in those records concealed verities, which are only true to those to whom they have been revealed, and which therefore make no appeal to the unenlightened reason of those who seek to dictate to the world, from the lofty summits of their darkened intelligence, these latter are deprived of all the weapons of argument or demonstration, and are perforce driven to silence, or to the more congenial armoury of gibes and sneers.

I have more than once remarked that the religion of the future will be founded on personal revelation and personal experience. It will not be a subject which can be discussed in the schools, nor ventilated in the public press, nor defined by Convocation in catechisms. The only catechism which the religious man, animated by the quickening life that is now descending, needs, his own conscience will formulate; the only doctrines are those which will be shown him by the effort of doing the will of his Father; the only demonstrations upon which he will rely to convince the unbelieving, will be "the demonstrations of the Spirit with power"; and the force of his arguments will lie in the force of his sympathies.

He will draw men to him, not by "the enticing words of wisdom which man speaketh," but by the magnetic attraction of his atomic elements, which are the same in their nature as those which enable men and women to attract each other, or, in other words, to fall in love; but are altogether different in their properties and behaviour, as those who are searching into the mysteries of allotropism will understand to be possible.

Read only by the light of the external meaning of the word, the first few chapters of Genesis are not only opposed to all the conclusions of science, but to common-sense: or, as Origen says, "What person in his senses will imagine that 'the first, second, and third day, in connection with which

'morning and evening were mentioned, were without sun,
'moon, and stars?—nay, that there was no sky on the first
'day? Who is there so foolish and without common-sense
'as to believe that God planted trees in the garden of Eden
'eastward, like a husbandman; and planted therein the tree
'of life, perceptible to the eyes and to the senses, which gave
'life to the eater thereof; and another tree which gave to the
'eater thereof a knowledge of good and evil? I believe that
'everybody must regard these as figures, under which a recon-
'dite sense is concealed."

I will therefore give such of the inner sense of these chapters as has been shown me, premising that though it is in some extent supported by the Kabbalah, it is in no way drawn from it, though its confirmation is not without its value. Nor would I enter upon a subject so recondite, were it not necessary to do so, for the purpose of explaining the origin of the moral malady from which the world is suffering, in order to elucidate the nature of the remedy to be applied, for it is impossible to cure a disease, unless it be in the first instance diagnosed, and this diagnosis involves a glance at the early history of the planet, the story of its creation, and of the evils which befell it.

At the same time, I make no claim upon the credulity of my readers, nor expect those to believe me who hear no whisper within them, urging them to make the experiments here suggested for verification; but some there may be, so internally prepared already, that they will desire to respond at once to the call to consecrate themselves to the life which is here proposed. And to those it will be shown how they may extricate themselves from the worldly complications which may seem to bar the way to the absolute self-surrendry which it demands; or how, at all events, to manage their lives in the midst of their surroundings, as God may direct, with the view to their ultimate emancipation. For, however vaguely hitherto they may have been conscious of the influence in their affairs of an overruling Providence, however insufficiently they may have found guidance and direction when sought for in difficulty, when once they have decided to allow nothing to interfere with an immediate response to the voice within them, all doubt and uncertainty on this head will cease. God will prove to them that He exists by unmistakable evidence, that He hears, that He answers, that He directs, that He consoles, that He sympathises. But to obtain this consciousness, the dearest earthly affections must be sacrificed, the most trying ordeals must be endured, the most intense faith must be exercised, the most unflinching courage displayed, and a fortitude à toute épreuve must be exhibited.

The words of Christ, which have never been acted upon yet, must be put in force now: "For if any man come to me 'and hate not his father, and mother, and wife, and children, 'and brethren, and sisters, yea, and his own life also, he cannot 'be my disciple."

Even now "the abomination of desolation spoken of by Daniel the prophet," is "standing where it ought not," as it was prophesied by Christ that it would, and many are coming in His name, saying, "Lo, here is Christ, or lo, He is there." It is time, therefore, for those who are in the Judæa of the theologies of Christendom, to flee to the mountains of spiritual truth, and this they can do by discovering each for himself where the true Christ is; but to those alone will He reveal Himself, who literally follow His precepts—which are now ignored—and who are prepared to sacrifice everything they hold dear, to find Him.

As spiritual impressions and mediumistic communications increase, will the difficulty become greater, for the evil ones take advantage of the ignorance and credulity of those they can influence directly, to speak in the name of Christ, and to "show signs and wonders, and to seduce, if it were possible, even the elect." There is no way of escaping from deception, except by efforts of verification, which will involve tremendous personal sacrifice. Should those who have made such efforts find, as the result of them, that what is here written contains error, I should be the first to co-operate with them in the attempt to correct it; for I make no claim for it, except that it is the highest truth that I have been able to reach. I am well aware that it is rudimentary. It is not until such an effort has been made, that any one is in a position to search for the hidden wisdom contained in those sacred records, which one class of minds regards now with a blind unbelief, and another with an equally blind credulity; and to estimate at their true value such interpretations as may be submitted to them.

Any criticisms, therefore, which may be offered upon the interpretations of sacred records I am now about to offer, by persons who have not fulfilled those conditions, are absolutely worthless.

PART II.

CHAPTER XIII.

THE GENERATION OF UNIVERSES—FIRST CHAPTER OF GENESIS DESCRIBES THE CREATION BY EMANATION OF A PREVIOUS UNIVERSE—ANALYSIS OF ITS HIDDEN MEANING—THE REBELLION OF LUCIFER—ARCHANGELS OR SERAPHIM, AND ARCH-DEMONS OR SIDDIM—THE FIRST ADAM, OR ADAM CADMON.

UNIVERSES come into being under the fixed, orderly, and predetermined operation of law. They are not the result of arbitrary acts, or catastrophic interventions of Providence, but of a process of combined emanation and creation, or fashioning, which is in eternal and infinite progression, through the agency of other universes and their inhabitants. For as life is eternal, and matter is indestructible, and as life is twofold, and therefore generative, procreation is incessant, and its manifestation is by emanation.

The faculties and potencies of the loftiest orders of beings on the highest universes are inconceivable by man, as is the material of which those universes are composed, which would not be cognisable to his present senses. None of the heavenly bodies, therefore, that we see are in this category; but they are, like our own earth, emanations from these unseen universes. The scientific theory of the nebular hypothesis, and of the gaseous incandescence which was the primal substance out of which they took form, is, so far as our senses are concerned, in the main correct; but even in that condition they were only the outward manifestation of an unseen archetype. The connection between these two conditions of the same universe is inseparable; their interaction is incessant, and their dependence upon each other absolute. But it varies in degree, so that in some instances the difference between the outer manifestation and its archetype is apparently very great, and in others scarcely perceptible.

These conditions depend on those of the universes from which they emanated, and on the intelligences which controlled their development and evolution. These intelligences, who are the agents of the divine will and operation, are in atomic affinity with the universe which is called into existence, through their fertilisation of the atomic particles composing the substances of those materials, which first take the form to human consciousness of incandescent gases.

This cosmic ether, or biod, or biogen, or protyle, or by whatever name it may be called, is, in fact, world-seed;[1] each atomic germ-cell containing in its essence a twofold masculine and feminine principle. These evolve, according to the conditions which presided over their generation, and these again differ infinitely in their variety. Hence there are no two worlds alike.

This is the "fiery cloud" of Professor Tyndall, and when he says that "human mind itself, emotion, intellect, will, and all their phenomena," were once latent in it, he catches a glimpse of a great truth.

The processes of generative emanation, as well as of subsequent evolution, are protracted over a period of almost unimaginable duration.

The foundation of a universe under these conditions is recorded in the first verse of the first chapter of Genesis. It was an emanation from the infinite Elohim, or Two-in-One, through the agency of the Elohim, a race of beings of an inconceivably high type, inhabiting a universe beyond our ken, but whose life and potency are visible to us in the sun of our own system. They are one of the angelic hosts, of whom ten, according to the Kabbalah, compose the "world of formation." The angelic hosts—like all beings in their essence—are bisexual.

The world which was called into existence through their operation was prior to our earth. It was formed of substance beyond the range of our cognisance, and took countless ages to evolve before it was ready to receive the race which was prepared for it, called Adam in the Bible—and "Adam Cad-

[1] The world-seed is the Golden Germ of the Rig Veda.

mon" in the Kabbalah, to distinguish it from the subsequent race of the same name—which is, in fact, only the Hebrew word for red earth, and who were patterned bisexually after the Elohim.

It is not possible with our limited faculties to form any mental image of the nature by which this race was surrounded, because every object in it, animate or inanimate, was, so to speak, an *eidolon*—that is to say, the representation of an idea.

The classification of these is indicated in the distinction drawn between those brought forth by the waters and those brought forth by the earth, also between those that had "souls" and those of which this is not said. Thus we are told that God said, "Let the earth bring forth grass, the 'herb yielding seed, and the fruit-tree yielding fruit after his 'kind, whose seed is in itself, upon the earth." This represented one class of moral and intellectual conceptions, and physical faculties and energies; and again, "Let the waters bring forth abundantly the moving thing that hath soul," represents another class; and "let the fowl fly above the earth in the open firmament of heaven," has reference to those forces which are connected with the operation of the will-principle, represented by the word firmament; but it is impossible for us, with our finite perceptions, to form any notion of the character of the potencies, faculties, conceptions, and ideas here indicated. Thus the expression rendered by our translators "great whales" represents another class; and the things brought forth by the earth, "the living creature after his kind, and cattle after their kind, and everything that creepeth on the earth after his kind," another class.

The repetition that everything was after its respective kind, is an accentuation of the distinctions of the different principles contained in these ideas. Lastly came man, representing the divine idea, and controlling the forces, moral and intellectual, which pervaded the nature over which he was given dominion; and to whom was given, together with the superior animal forms representing the highest conceptions, the principles symbolised by the herbs, the trees, and their fruits, as moral sustenance. The whole of nature being, as it were, a book, representing the sublimest truths in a pictorial form, of the divine life and love principles, living, moving, and having their being in the bosom of the infinite Father and Mother of all, and being, in fact, an embodiment of the creative fiat or word,[1] and of the Divine Masculine and Feminine principles.

That the emanation occurred through the operation of these principles in the Elohim, through whom it took form, is indicated in the first verse, "By wisdom God created the heavens and the earth."[2] The word "heavens" here signifies force, and "earth," substance. It is a fact well known to those conversant with the ancient religions, and with mystical interpretation generally, that force is deemed to be masculine, and substance feminine, whether it be solid or liquid. Hence we have the earth called Prakriti, or the Mother, in the Vedas; and water is almost always symbolised by a goddess in the old mythologies, as in Zoroastrianism by Anahita, and in the Kabbalah by Aima, "the great sea."

The Divine Feminine principle represented by "substance" is love. The Divine Masculine principle represented by "force" is operation. In other words, the divine wisdom, love, and operation, which are ever present in the infinite Elohim, acting upon and through the representative Elohim, called into existence a universe, by forming a conjunction of atoms appropriate to its new conditions, and which emanated from them.

The statement that "the earth was without form, and void; and that darkness was upon the face of the waters," signifies that the bisexual principle was not yet in operation. "The Spirit"—or Ruach—"of God moving upon the face of the waters," signifies the quickening by the divine potency of the

---

[1] According to the Hindoo cosmogony, Prajapati, getting tired of his solitude, "emits," that is to say, draws forth from himself, everything that exists, or who begets it, after having divided himself into two, the one half male, the other half female.—Barth's Religions of India, p. 69.

Irenæus, speaking of our own universe, says, "God made the world by means of the Word and Wisdom" (Hær., 4. 28).

[2] The word Berashith, which Onkelos, Le Septagius, and others, including our own translators, render "in the beginning," is translated in four different ways by Grotius, Tertullian, Rabbi Bochai, and Simeon respectively; but the Jerusalem Targum, which may be esteemed the highest authority, renders it "by wisdom."

feminine principle in the universe. "And God said, Let there be light: and there was light," signifies that the divine life now animated the universe. Hence John says, "And the life was the light of men." The division of the light from the darkness signifies the division between the bisexual principle operant in God, and the bisexual principle which was to be operant in the universe, under the conditions of free-will. The "firmament," by means of which this division was brought about, signifies the principle of free-will. The collection of the waters into one place, and the appearance of dry land, signifies the conditions under which the bisexual principle was to operate in nature. The passage from the 15th to the 19th verses contain arcana in regard to the processes of love, wisdom, and operation, represented by the "greater" and the "lesser" light, and the stars in the firmament, or free-will, by means of which three great principles, operating in freedom, the universe was to be governed.

This is the universe which has given rise to the tradition of the fallen orb, to which allusion is made by the prophet Isaiah in the 14th chapter, where he says, "How art thou "fallen from heaven, O Lucifer"—or Day-star—"son of the 'morning! how art thou cut down to the ground, which didst 'weaken the nations! For thou hast said in thine heart, I 'will ascend into heaven, I will exalt my throne above the 'stars of God: I will sit also upon the mount of the congre-'gation, in the sides of the north: I will ascend above the 'heights of the clouds; I will be like the Most High. Yet 'thou shalt be brought down to hell, to the sides of the pit. 'They that see thee shall narrowly look upon thee, and con-'sider thee, saying, Is this the man that made the earth to 'tremble, that did shake kingdoms; that made the world as a 'wilderness, and destroyed the cities thereof; that opened 'not the house of his prisoners?" The special interest of this passage consists in the fact that it is a prediction of the judgment which is to overtake the powers of darkness on the occasion of the Messianic advent, as distinctly foreshadowed in the Revelation, which will clearly appear when we come to consider the 20th chapter of that book.

The story of the rebellion of Lucifer and his host, of their habitation in a lower world, of their invasion into this one, of the archangels who remained loyal, and were saved, together with that part of the inhabitants of the orb who did not take part in the rebellion, with many legends of great interest, are to be found in the sacred literature of the Hebrews, and especially in the Book of Enoch, while the Bible contains many allusions to it. Thus the Psalmist says, "I said, Ye are 'gods; and all of you the children of the Most High: yet ye 'shall die like men, and fall like one of the princes." And Jude, quoting from the Book of Enoch, thus alludes to this event: "And the angels which kept not their first estate, but 'left their own habitation, He hath reserved in everlasting 'chains, under darkness, unto the judgment of the great day;" and again,—"Yet Michael the archangel, when contending with 'the devil, he disputed about the body of Moses, durst not 'bring against him a railing accusation, but said, The Lord 'rebuke thee." The greater part of the Revelation contains in its hidden meaning the narrative of events which have transpired, and will yet transpire, in the world of which the first chapter of Genesis records the creation, sometimes under a very thin veil; as, for instance, where it is said, "And there 'was war in heaven: Michael and his angels fought against 'the dragon; and the dragon fought and his angels, and pre-'vailed not; neither was their place found any more in 'heaven. And the great dragon was cast out, that old serpent, 'called the Devil, and Satan, which deceiveth the whole 'world: he was cast out into the earth, and his angels were 'cast out with him." And says Peter, "If God spared not 'the angels that sinned, but cast them down to hell, and de-'livered them into chains of darkness, to be reserved unto 'judgment." And Job, comparing the people of this world with those of its predecessor, says, "Shall a man be more 'pure than his Maker? Behold, He put no trust in His 'servants; and His angels He charged with folly: how 'much less in them that dwell in houses of clay, whose foun-'dation is in the dust, which are crushed before the moth?"[1] The enormous structural difference between existing man, whose bodily tenement is of clay, and the nature of the fallen angels is here alluded to. They were, in fact, patterned closely after the divine image, with an absolute freedom of will, and

[1] Job, iv. 17-19.

powers of a stupendous character. In accordance with the divine method of rule, there was one among them in whom supreme authority was vested. His faculties transcended anything of which we have any idea, and in him originated the idea that his will, which was free, was his own, and not God's freedom acting in him. The consequences which resulted to humanity from this false conception we shall see later. It produced a conflict in the "Day-star," to use Isaiah's nomenclature, and there was " war in heaven," Michael and those who clung to the true conception of free-will, rebelling against the authority of the Prince of Darkness, who is since known as Satan. It was the supreme position with which the latter was endowed, which gave rise to the tradition, recorded in Jude, that Michael, disputing with Satan "about the body of Moses, durst not bring against him a railing accusation," but could only say, "The Lord rebuke thee."

This passage is deeply interesting, as throwing light upon the relations which subsist between the fallen and the unfallen parts of the preceding, or Elohistic, universe. Though divided into two hostile camps, and though it underwent a violent atomic dislocation on the occasion of the conflict which took place between the opposing will-principles, it still forms but one universe, and the collision continues between the antagonistic forces; nor can the magnetic contact by which they are united be severed. This contact is both direct and indirect. Direct as between the two hostile portions in the region they occupy, and indirect through both the visible and invisible portions of our universe.

And here I feel compelled to make a statement which it has been necessary thus to lead up to, but which does, in fact, furnish us with a key to the mystery of our complex earthly existence.

Races are generated through a primal pair. The primal pair, in the case of the world preceding our own, were called Adam, or Adam Cadmon. And it was the perversion of the will-principle by this Adam Cadmon, who was supreme in his universe, which produced the catastrophe. In other words, the first Adam mentioned in the Bible, has become the Devil or Satan, who wages perpetual war against his Maker, and

P

whose rebellion was succeeded by an atomic dislocation in his outer organism, which involved a divorce from his own feminine complement; and by a conflict between the male and female principles in that region of the fallen universe in which he still exercises rule. Nevertheless in its deep interior the bisexual principle remains intact.

It is important that this should be understood, because there has been in the minds of intelligent people, a very natural reaction against a narrative which, taken in its literal sense, seems so fantastic, that with the rejection of the talking serpent, has followed that of a personal devil, largely, because he is invested in the popular imagination with horns, hoofs, and a tail; but the whole Bible teems with references to this personality, and it stands to reason that, to use Paul's expression, if "the rulers of the darkness of this world" exist at all, there must be among them some who are more powerful and intelligent than others. In the Talmud and Kabbalah these have names, just as among the Seraphim or unfallen angels we have the archangels Michael, Gabriel, and others. So there are arch-demons, and, besides Satan, we read in the New Testament of Beelzebub and Apollyon, and in the Talmud of Ashmedai, Samael, and others. Ashmedai is the Asmodeus of Tobit, iii. 8, vi. 14, &c. The Kabbalah gives us a list of ten archangels and ten orders of angels, and of ten arch-demons and ten orders of demons.

But the ruler of all is generally known as Satan, and his power may be inferred from the verse, "And God said, Let us 'make man in our image, after our likeness; and let them have 'dominion over the fish of the sea, and over the fowl of the 'air, and over the cattle, and over all the earth, and over every 'creeping thing that creepeth upon the earth." This signifies that the first Adam, or Adam Cadmon, was invested with powers almost equal to the Deity—that he could control all the principles represented in the nature by which he was surrounded, and that he possessed the divine attributes to such a high degree, that when his will became perverted, he imagined himself to be equal, if not superior, to God.

On this insane delusion taking possession of his mind, and the Divine Feminine principle within him having become perverted, he represented instead the infernal feminine or lust principle, as his name Satan implies. This will appear later, when we come to consider the threefold nature of the Deity.

Henceforth the object of the infernals was to close the creation which was about to come into existence—and which is our world—to the operation of the Divine Feminine, and to substitute for it the infernal feminine; and the struggle between the Seraphim and the Siddim,[1] or the unfallen and the fallen angels, has been carried on in man over this principle ever since. For the Seraphim never lost their divine bisexual nature in their outer organisms, and are the guardian angels of our planet. Satan, on the other hand, controls that section of the world which fell with him, and is regarded by the Siddim as the Deity—a delusion in which he is himself fixed. Hence all the abominations perpetrated through their agency are justified on the highest moral grounds; and the effect of their inspiration in the religions of the world is to be seen in the atrocities which have been committed in the name of religion, as, for instance, those under the Inquisition. All crime becomes lawful as the means to the end, which appears to their perverted imaginations to be divine. Their strongholds upon our earth are the religions which flourish largely under their ægis, and, as we shall see later, especially the Churches of Christendom.

It has been necessary to dwell upon the nature of the catastrophe which overtook the Elohistic universe, because our own fortunes are inextricably bound up with it; and a knowledge of its history and present condition, forms an indispensable preliminary to an apprehension of the nature of the destiny reserved for our own world, and of the struggles and duties which await us. It has also been necessary, because it is to be hoped that the attempt to reconcile a chronicle of cosmogony which has no reference to our own world—except indirectly—with the conclusions of modern science, will be abandoned, as one of the most fatal blows which can be struck at those parts of the Bible which contain divine truth in their hidden meaning. It gives scoffers most unnecessary occasion for satire, so thin, that it would lose all its point if the subject satirised was not considered sacred; and it brings the intelli-

[1] Note for the origin of the words Satan and Siddim. See Appendix.

gence of those who cling to the external sense of the record, from habit, prejudice, or panic, as the case may be, into a contempt which even they might be spared.

The effect of the violent shock which this former universe sustained, as the result of the conflict between the Seraphim and the Siddim, was to shatter it, in so far as the original arrangement and combinations of its atomic structure was concerned, and it passed through a stage corresponding to what we call death, shedding off its grosser atomic particles, while those which were finer, rearranged themselves according to their moral attraction, and ultimately formed themselves into two widely opposite systems, of extreme good and extreme bad, with an intermediate region of a mixed character.

These three regions are connected atomically with three corresponding regions in our own invisible universe; and although we on earth are practically cut off from direct contact with the inhabitants of the previous world, there have been in former periods exceptional instances of visitations by them. Thus we have records of Satan appearing to Job and to Christ; and of messages borne to it by Gabriel to Zacharias and to the Virgin Mary; and upon two occasions to Daniel, in order to explain visions to him; while Michael is mentioned as "the great prince that standeth up for the people," with especial reference to a period of moral and physical revolution which was in store for our own universe.

CHAPTER XIV.

SECOND CHAPTER OF GENESIS DESCRIBES CREATION BY EMANATION OF OUR WORLD—ANALYSIS OF ITS HIDDEN MEANING—THE CREATION OF BISEXUAL MAN—ANCIENT BELIEFS IN HIS ANDROGYNOUS NATURE—STORY OF HIS FALL—AND SEPARATION INTO TWO DISTINCT SEXES—STRUCTURAL CHANGES CONSEQUENT THEREON.

The narrative of the creation of the world which succeeded that which underwent atomic dislocation, under the circumstances above described, commences at the fourth verse of the second chapter of Genesis. It contains in its internal meaning a description of the process by which the new generative emanation took place, which forms the basis of existing matter.

On the dislocation of the previous world, its physical *débris*, consisting of those grosser particles which it had shed off at the time of its dissolution, now solidified into cosmic ether, or a "fiery cloud" of unparalleled density, and formed world-seed of a debased and corrupted quality, composing a matrix, out of which should condense a nature of a type corresponding to the unhappy mixed conditions to which it owed its origin.

It will be observed that the narratives of the two creations bear no similarity to each other. There is no mention in the second of the number of days in which the world was made, nor of the order of creation; and especially is the distinction marked in all that concerns the creation of man. We are not told that he was made in God's own image, nor that he was given dominion over the nature by which he was surrounded, as was the case with the preceding Adam. The narrative commences abruptly—

"These are the generations of the heavens and of the earth, *in the day* that Jehovah Elohim made the earth and the heavens." "These are the generations of the heavens and the earth," signifies the nature of the generative process by means of which force and substance—in other words, "matter in motion"—underwent violent transformation in the case of the world, whose creation is now being described; in contradistinction to the process of gentle emanation from the Elohim, by means of which the preceding world had been called into existence.

"In the day that Jehovah Elohim made the earth and the heavens." The transposition of substance and force indicates the nature of the new atomic combination, which was effected "under the immutable operation of divine law, by the combined, but, at the same time, antagonistic, agency of the angels, fallen and unfallen, of the former universe."

"And every plant of the field before it was in the earth, and every herb of the field before it grew," signifies the prior existence in another form of substance, of the nature which was now being created, and indicates the slow and gradual character of the process.

"For Jehovah Elohim had not caused it to rain upon the 'earth, and there was not a man to till the ground. But there 'went up a mist from the earth, and watered the whole face 'of the ground," signifies that the only feminine principle which vivified nature, was that which ascended to it through the substance of the previous world—man not having yet been formed—and the new feminine principle which was to descend through him not having yet done so.

"And Jehovah formed man out of the dust of the ground"—in other words, fashioned Adam out of Adamah—signifies that the substance of which he was made, was far more gross and material than that out of which the previous Adam had been formed, and closely allied in its atomic structure to the nature by which he was surrounded. It is worthy of note that in the first instance the Hebrew word meaning "created" is used, and in this case another word, which can best be translated by "fashioned," is employed, indicating a different process of formation.

"And breathed into his nostrils the breath of life," signifies that this process of fashioning was by exhalation—that is, that the divine afflatus or pneuma, passing through the Elohim into the Seraphim, contained within it the vital principle by which the new man was to be animated. It also indicates that these principles differed in quality from those of which the former race had been composed.

"And man became a living soul," signifies that now, instead of partaking of the nature of the Elohim, as in the first instance, he partook of the nature with which the creeping things of the water and of the earth, who were called "living souls," had been endowed in the former creation; for atomic affinity existed between him and the beings of the fallen world, as well as between him and the Seraphim.

"And Jehovah planted a garden eastward in Eden, and there he put the man whom he had formed," signifies a specially protected region set apart for man, and indicates the relation which it bore to the rest of the universe.

"And out of the ground made Jehovah Elohim to grow every tree that is pleasant to the sight, and good for food," signifies that in this region was provided all the moral sustenance necessary for man, to enable him to accomplish the high purpose for which he had been placed in it.

"The tree of life also in the midst of the garden," signifies the mystery in which lies hidden the secret of the creative potency, and the conservation of energy by atomic combination, which renders impossible the destruction of the human personality. In other words it typified the bisexual body.[1]

"The tree of knowledge of good and evil," signifies the knowledge of the fact that the newly created world was already in atomic contact with both regions of the previous world, and in danger from the one that had fallen. It typified, therefore, the separated body.

"The river that went out of Eden to water the garden," and "was parted into four heads," signifies the divine life-current, which, flowing from the specially protected centre of the universe, divided into four vitalising streams; one flowing

---

[1] In the Kabbalah it is said, "But whensoever the colours are mingled together then is He called Tiphereth, and the whole body is formed into a tree (the Autz Ha-Chaiim or tree of life), great and strong, fair and beautiful." Dan. iv. 11; p. 336, Mather's Kabbalah.

into the surface of so-called inorganic nature, one into the vegetable creation, one into the inferior animal creation, and one into man.

"And Jehovah Elohim took Adam, and put him in the garden of Eden to dress it," signifies the duties and functions which now devolved upon man in the nature by which he was surrounded, with a view to its ultimate restoration to perfect conditions.

"And Jehovah Elohim commanded the man, saying, Of 'every tree of the garden thou mayest freely eat: but of the 'tree of the knowledge of good and evil, thou shalt not eat of 'it: for in the day that thou eatest thereof thou shalt surely 'die," signifies that if man wilfully opened himself to direct atomic contact with the beings of the lower world, he would imbibe a virus, which would prove destructive to his natural life, and result in the sexual separation of his body.

"And Jehovah Elohim said, It is not good that man should be alone; I will make an help meet for him," signifies that up to this time man had been unconscious of the feminine principle that had been enfolded within him, and that God was about to impart to him a consciousness of it, as without it it would not be possible for him to fulfil the great function that devolved upon him.

"And out of the ground Jehovah Elohim formed every beast of the field, and every fowl of the air," signifies that this creation differed from the one that preceded it by the composition of its atoms, which were nevertheless a reconstitution of those which had previously existed; but the process of this reconstitution had been slow and gradual, having been evolutionary in its character, and having been developed from the principles of the ideas which had been contained in the representations of them in the previous world. They were, nevertheless, still the symbols of those ideas.

"And brought them unto Adam to see what he would call them: and whatsoever Adam called every creature, that was the name thereof," signifies the apprehension by man of the symbolical meaning of the creation.

"And Adam gave names to all cattle, and to the fowl of the air, and to every beast of the field: but for Adam there was not found an help meet for him," signifies that the feminine principle appropriate to man was not to be found in the lower animal creation—the feminine principle of which was contained within itself. It also indicates the great difference which existed between man and the animal creation, the latter having evolved from pre-existing types, through the agency of the life-current flowing through the Elohim, and thence through the combined operation of the Seraphim and the Siddim, while the latter had been generated subsequently by an altogether different process. For not only was the feminine principle inferior in the animals, but it had become polluted; the new creation having from its outset suffered from the influence of the poison of the infernal feminine which pervaded its atoms, by reason of their affinity with the atoms of the fallen region of the previous world. Hence carnivorous and other disorderly species had evolved.

It was the function of man by his efforts to regain the ground that had been lost, and this could only be achieved through the orderly operation of the combined masculine and feminine principles within him, and by abstention from the tree of knowledge of good and evil, which contained within it the infernal principle that had become interwoven in the universe, by reason of the complex conditions under which it came into existence. In other words, it behoved him to avoid all contact with the Siddim. For as he himself had been generated through the ultimate operation of the preceding human type, he was in atomic affinity with the lower intelligences; from invasion by whom he could only be saved by implicit obedience, and the preservation of the purity—with which he had been endowed—of the Divine Feminine principle. A specially protected region was therefore set apart for his habitation, called "the garden of Eden."

"And Jehovah Elohim caused a deep sleep to fall upon
'Adam, and he slept: and He took one of his ribs, and closed
'up the flesh instead thereof; and the rib, which Jehovah Elo-
'him had taken from man, made he a woman, and brought
'her unto him."

This signifies the process by which the atomic elements constituting the feminine principle, which had been combined with those forming the masculine principle—thus rendering man bisexual—were so altered in their combinations, that without being internally disassociated, they could be externally separated. The nature of their new association being such that they could interweave themselves, or separate themselves at pleasure. Thus presenting the appearance either of a man and a woman apart; or of a man infused, as it were, by a woman—the two forming one. This permeation of atoms by one another, being possible in the case of beings whose atomic structure differs essentially from ours as theirs did, or, in other words, were four dimensional.

"And Adam said, This is now bone of my bone, and flesh of my flesh: she shall be called Isha, because she was taken out of Ish," signifies the comprehension by man of the nature of the bisexual principle with which he was endowed, and which, although externally he might appear as two persons, rendered him substantially one; and the names which he gives these principles, signifies his perception of the fact that the feminine principle is contained within the masculine.

"Therefore shall a man leave his father and his mother, and shall cleave unto his wife," signifies that these principles are absolutely inseverable, and are inherent in every man and every woman long before the moment of birth. Though neither may know in mortal life who the complementary being is, each person is born with an atomic structure, the particles of which are interlocked with those of the complementary being, and must be so to all time; for there is no such thing, either in this world, or those that are invisible—fallen or unfallen—as a being who is unisexual in essence, though all sense of bisexuality has long been completely lost, and almost the only external trace of it that remains is the male rudimentary breast. Nevertheless it is in this deeply seated principle that all our affections, emotions, and passions originate; and sooner or later the complementary being is found, with whom we are each internally, and as yet unconsciously, atomically interlocked, proving, if the scene of meeting be the upper world, a source of infinite joy; if the lower, a cause of intense misery. Hence the whole struggle of the Siddim is against bisexuality.

It is not possible, however, for two beings who are thus interlocked, to pass into two opposite regions; for inasmuch as an internal attraction is constantly drawing their souls together, though their bodies may be far apart, and inasmuch as the atomic quality of their affections or passions is essentially one, they always develop in the same direction. The upward or the downward tendency is common to both, because they are essentially not two but one. Christ quoted the words here put by the inspired writer into Adam's mouth, to the Pharisees, for He understood the profound truth which they contained, when He said: "Have ye not read, that He 'which made them at the beginning made them male and 'female, and said, For this cause shall a man leave father and 'mother, and shall cleave to his wife: and they twain shall 'be one flesh? Wherefore they are no more twain, but one 'flesh. What therefore God hath joined together, let not man 'put asunder." He does not say what the Church has joined together, or the priest hath joined together, but what God hath joined together; and the presumption of Churches and priests, that God joins the male and female principles together through their agency, betrays an ignorance equal to its arrogance.

If Christ denounced an attempt to put them asunder—which is an impossibility—it was only because it was necessary, in the cause of morality, to meet this question on the low plane of His interrogators, and allow the allusion to have reference to external wives; but even here some of the Churches called by His name repudiate His teaching, and deliberately sanction adultery, by marrying those who are divorced, in express defiance of His command to the contrary—and these they say solemnly, in a temple dedicated to Him, God has joined together.

In point of fact, though it was not understood by the Pharisees, the bisexuality of man was held among the initiated, both by the Nazarites and afterwards by the Essenes, and is to be found alluded to in the apocryphal writings of the early Christian Church. Thus Cyril of Jerusalem calls "the Anointed" male and female; and in the second Epistle of Clement of Rome we find, "The Lord Himself was asked by 'some one when His kingdom should come; and He said, "When the two shall be one, and the external as the internal, 'and the male with the female, neither male nor female.'" Clement of Alexandria repeats the saying—"When Salvine 'asked, when these things of which she was asking should

'be known, the Lord said, Whensoever ye shall have trampled
'down the garment of shame; and whensoever the two have
'become one, and the male with the female, neither male nor
'female."[1]

The explanation of Christ's saying that in heaven there will be neither marrying nor giving in marriage, is evidently in allusion to the fact, that it would no longer be in the power of men to unite in a disorderly way, those who had been eternally divided by God. The popular idea that angels are sexless, can only be held by those who are entirely closed as to their subsurface, or supersensuous, vision; but so many are open now sufficiently as to their subsurface faculties to be convinced by their own experience and observation that this is a delusion, that it is scarcely necessary to insist upon a point which it is impossible to prove to those who cannot see behind the veil.

Those, however, who care to look into the testimony of ancient writers, will find much curious lore upon the subject. Thus the Naassene is represented as a believer in man becoming androgynous when he is "passed over 'from the earthy range of the nether world to the eternal 'substance above, where there is neither male nor female, 'but a new creature, which is androgynous."[2] Simon Magus, in the 'Great Announcement,' says, concerning a class of spiritual beings, that "they possess a bisexual power and 'intelligence, whence they form a mutual apposition . . . 'being one . . . so it is, therefore, that likewise their 'manifestation, while actually one, is found to be two; a bi- 'sexual being, holding the feminine within itself."

This doctrine is to be found among the Pythagoreans, while Plato devotes many pages of his 'Symposium' to its elucidation. "In the first place," he says, "the sexes were originally 'three in number, not two, as they are now. There was man, 'woman, and the union of the two, having a name correspond- 'ing to this double nature."

In the Egyptian ritual of the dead, perhaps the earliest known tradition on the subject, we find—"I, Ra, appeared be- 'fore the sun, when the circumference of darkness was opened; 'I was as one among you (the gods). I know how the woman

[1] Strom., iii. 13. [2] Hippolytus, Ref. Hær., 5.

'was made from the man." It was taught by Zoroaster in the
'Arda Viraf' (iv.), in a mystic way; but it is strongly insisted upon in the Kabbalah. Thus the Sohar tells us, " Each
' soul and spirit, prior to its entering into this world, consists
' of a male and female united into one being. When it de-
' scends on this earth, the two parts separate, and animate two
' different bodies. At the time of marriage the Holy One—
' blessed be He who knows all souls and spirits—unites them
' again as they were before. And they again constitute one
' body and one soul, forming, as it were, the right and left of
' one individual. Therefore there is nothing new under the
' sun. . . . This union, however, is influenced by the deeds
' of the man, and by the ways in which he walks. If the
' man is pure, and his conduct is pleasing in the sight of God,
' he is united with that female part of his soul which was his
' component part prior to his birth."[1] The marriage here
alluded to is that which takes place after death. So Rabbi
ben Jochai talks of his death as entering into his nuptials
(see Appendix).

This view is maintained by many Jewish rabbis of the
present day, outside of those who are learned in the Kabbalah,
and finds expression in the Talmud, as, for instance, where
the Rabbi Samlai says, "Man is impossible without woman,
woman without man, and both without the Shechinah."

"And they were both naked, the man and his wife, and
were not ashamed," signifies the absolute and essential purity
of the divine bisexual life-principle.

"Now the serpent was more subtil than any beast of the
field which Jehovah Elohim had made," signifies that the invasion of the lower animal creation by the Siddim, enabled
them to use it as a channel by which to approach man; for
before man had appeared upon the world, it was already
poisoned with ferocity and lust, with the exception of that
region which had been specially set apart as the centre, from
which the deliverance was to be achieved by man.

"And he said unto the woman, Yea, hath God said, Ye
shall not eat of every tree of the garden?" signifies the method
of approach by which the Siddim sought to invade the
feminine principle in man, and to introduce into his organism

[1] Sohar, i. 91b.

the impure forces which had been developed in the fallen world, where the bisexual principle had become debased, and, by the disorderly practices of the infernal feminine, had generated the fatal passion of lust.

It was by means of the introduction of this inverted sex-principle into the newly created universe that the Siddim sought to achieve its conquest, and thus extend the sphere of their own influence and domination. The story of what is known as "the Fall" records in allegorical language the success of this attempt. It is not necessary to describe, by giving at length the internal signification of each verse, the method by which this was done. Enough has been written by way of interpretation, to indicate the nature of the veil by which the external sense shrouds the inner meaning, and to dispose for ever of the doubts and difficulties which arise in some minds, because they are unable to reconcile this mask of words, with either reason or common-sense. Suffice it to say, that the Siddim clothed themselves with atomic particles drawn from the organisms of the lower animal creation of earth, and were thus able to make an intrusion into that part of the universe which, up to that time, had been the habitation of the infancy of the Adamic race, whose intercourse had been confined to the Seraphim, from whom they had emanated.

This resulted in an unholy union between the celestial feminine, represented by Isha, and the infernal masculine, represented by the serpent.

The effect of the impregnation of the pure feminine principle, by the virus thus injected into humanity through the lower animal creation, was to infect the divine bisexual life-current at the fountain-head in our world; and the four rivers of the garden of Eden became polluted with a poison, pregnant with increased disaster to the universe through which they flowed.

The rush of this tainted torrent into nature, when once the sluice-gates were opened by sex-intercourse by the human race — represented by Adam and Eve — with the Siddim, was almost more than the delicate atomic structure of man could bear. He now perceived the consequences of his act, and he sought to protect himself from the destruction which seemed about to overwhelm him, by increasing in some way his organic power of resistance to infernal invasion.

This is indicated in the words, "And the eyes of them both were opened, and they knew that they were naked; and they sewed fig-leaves together, and made themselves aprons." Nevertheless the effect of the introduction of an opposing current into the organism, threatened an absolute atomic wreckage. Man found himself between the opposite poles of an electric battery, and his extinction under existing circumstances seemed imminent; for it was only by an atomic dislocation of the earthly human structure, tantamount to the physical death of man, that he could be assimilated to the organisms of the Siddim, and so become completely enslaved by them, unless he could protect himself from this fate, by acquiring the hidden knowledge concealed in the mystery of the tree of life. He would thus have gained not merely power to protect his life, but have augmented his faculties so enormously by infernalising the quality of the pure bisexual principle which it contained, that he would have become even more highly diabolised as the Siddim, and more potent for evil. Not only would this world have been lost, but the means provided in it for the salvation of the former one, would become instead the means of sinking it still lower.

This danger is indicated in the verse, "And Jehovah 'Elohim said, Behold, the man is become as one of us, to know 'good and evil: and now, lest he put forth his hand, and take 'also of the tree of life, and eat, and live for ever: therefore 'Jehovah Elohim drove him forth out of the garden of Eden, 'to till the ground from whence he was taken." It also signifies that the celestial or seraphistic conditions, by which man had been surrounded for his protection, had become intolerable to him, and that he would now find himself condemned to a perpetual struggle with the evils in his own organism, or to "till the ground from whence he was taken."

The diminution in his faculties for controlling not only his own nature, but the nature by which he was surrounded, is indicated in the words, "Cursed be the ground for thy sake; in sorrow shalt thou eat of it all the days of thy life," and the two following verses.

The organic change which the human race underwent is

indicated in the words, "Unto Adam also and to his wife did Jehovah Elohim make coats of skins, and clothed them." This signifies that every atom of the human structure, was now enclosed in another atom composed of elements drawn from the atoms of the lower animal creation, and that thus was formed a more solid material frame, still, however, far more highly attenuated than the fleshly covering which we now wear. The enclosed atoms which remained intact, correspond more nearly to the material composing our psychic bodies or souls, or, in other words, the frames we carry with us when we undergo the process of change called death, and pass into the invisible part of our universe.

The relatively dense bodies of the Adamic race, are the coats of skins above mentioned, and the fact is alluded to more than once in the Kabbalah, as it was known to the ancient mystics, of whose knowledge this obscure record is largely a repertory. So we read in the Sohar—" When Adam dwelled
' in the garden of Eden, he was dressed in a celestial gar-
' ment, which is a garment of heavenly light; but when he was
' expelled from Eden, and became subject to the wants of this
' world, what is written? Jehovah Elohim made coats of
' skins unto Adam and to his wife, and clothed them, for
' prior to this they had garments of light—light of that light
' which was used in the garden of Eden."[1]

This transformation did not merely affect the whole nature of man, and prove the indirect cause of certain modifications in the earth's crust, but it also had a most direct effect upon the fallen world. This is indicated in the words, "And Je-
' hovah Elohim said unto the serpent, Because thou hast done
' this, thou art cursed above all cattle, and above every beast
' of the field; upon thy belly shalt thou go, and dust shalt
' thou eat all the days of thy life: and I will put enmity be-
' tween thee and the woman, and between thy seed and her
' seed; it shall bruise thy head, and thou shalt bruise his
' heel."

The atomic connection which had been established between our universe and the fallen world by sex-intercourse, rendered this inevitable: no such change, as that involved by the solidification of the human organism, could take place

[1] Sohar, ii. 219*b*.

without having a direct influence upon these nether regions which had now become inextricably interlocked with our own. The result has been incessant warfare. Warfare there, and warfare of another kind here. The warfare here is of another kind, because it is the effect of a conflict between divine and infernal atomic forces—in other words, between good and evil; while there it is the clash of angry passions, developed by the principle of lust,—the insane struggle with each other, of lunatics.

The time is approaching when on our globe the conflict will enter upon a new phase, for the atomic conditions are undergoing change, the effect of which will be to increase our sensitiveness to influences from both worlds, and therefore to intensify, as it approaches its climax, the stupendous struggle of which our universe has been the theatre. The progress, and some of the results of that great struggle, are detailed at length in the inner meaning of the book of Revelation, as well as in some of the prophetic writings of the Old Testament.

The cherubim with the "flaming sword which turned every way, to keep the tree of life," signify the divine dual principle through which alone man can win his way to immortal life; and the flaming sword signifies the penetrating quality and heat of the force contained in this twofold principle, which has barred the way to man to a knowledge which should enable him to take in the immortal life-principle, which lies concealed behind it. But, as we learn elsewhere in Scripture, this flaming sword is not to bar the way for ever, for it will be grasped by the hand of the Messiah, and prove the sword of victory.

Thus did man lose his original likeness to God. From this time, owing to the separation of the sexes into two solid halves, neither knowing which belonged to the other, man's life on earth has been one of sorrow, disease, and sin, for each half is now the receptacle of an impure sex-force, instead of a pure one. So man procreates impure and diseased offspring; he violates the laws of nature, and gives vent to the passions of rapine and violence which infernal lust has generated in his organism.

It is only by man's own effort that he can win deliverance from this condition of things; and he will be supplied with the forces requisite for the combat, which will precede the victory. It is because the days are at hand, when those who desire to be fighting on the right side will need all the spiritual weapons that can be forged in the white heat of the divine affections, and all the potency for action which those affections can impart, that I have felt myself impelled, by no force of natural inclination, to attempt to explain the origin and nature of the warfare upon which we are entering, and to reveal, so far as is permitted, the secret of the world's malady.

CHAPTER XV.

THE ORIGIN OF EVIL—MIXED CONDITIONS IN THE GENESIS OF EARTH—EVOLUTION OF THE FIRST FORMS OF LIFE, UNDER THE OPPOSING INFLUENCES OF SERAPHIM AND SIDDIM—THE GARDEN OF EDEN—MAN'S MISSION—METHOD OF ITS ACCOMPLISHMENT—THE EARTH-MALADY CAUSED BY THE POLLUTION OF ITS SEX-LIFE—ITS PURIFICATION POSSIBLE—NATURE OF THE STRUGGLE FOR PURITY THUS INVOLVED.

HAVING in the previous chapter attempted to give, in as condensed a form as possible, the account of the cosmogony of the world, contained in the first three chapters of Genesis, as read by the light of the inner meaning of the terms employed, it may be well to recapitulate it as shortly as possible, in a form more adapted to the mind of the present day, and reconcile with it, so far as may be, the discoveries of modern science, without adopting necessarily the conclusions which have been arrived at as a consequence of those discoveries, and which are generally hypothetical; though it will be necessary, in continuing to follow the history of the human family, constantly to refer to the inner meaning of the Biblical narrative.

In making this attempt I shall invoke not merely the sacred record on the one hand, nor scientific discovery on the other, but such aid as may be vouchsafed for the purpose.

The method of operation of the divine love, wisdom, and proceeding, is hidden from the angels who inhabit the invisible region of our world; but it is known to them that a universe was called into existence by the creative fiat, prior to our own; that, owing to the extraordinary faculties with which the beings who peopled it were endowed, and the entire freedom of will which—as it is an essentially divine attribute — is inherent in every created being, certain of the beings who inhabited this prior world, appropriated these faculties to themselves, not recognising the fact that while they felt themselves free, they did not belong to themselves, but to the Great Cause of their existence, whose freedom was in them, and therefore not their own, excepting as they remained in Him. Hence arose a divergency in the will-principle, which induced a conflict within itself. And this engendered a sense of independence, which in its turn generated separation, isolation, pride, love of dominion, and introduced a disorder, which finally ended in a disruption between the antagonistic will-principles, and which penetrated to the very foundations of the universal structure, culminating at last in two regions of the same world, dominated by opposing principles,—the ruling sentiment in the one being love of God and the neighbour, and in the other, love of self to the exclusion of the neighbour; these two remaining nevertheless in atomic affinity, and being united by an intermediate region.

As the reproducion of life in new forms is a universal law of nature, there evolved from the wreckage which resulted from the catastrophe above alluded to, a new substance or world-seed, the atomic elements of which contained principles inherent in the material of the opposing sections of the universe which had given it birth.

The fertilisation of the world-seed of our universe, under the rival operation of the Seraphim and Siddim, took place, therefore, under conditions in the highest degree disorderly and antagonistic. And as the Siddim could act more powerfully upon the lower forms of nature, for reasons which will presently be explained, than their unfallen opponents, there resulted a chaotic and relatively disorderly evolutionary process, which, although it took place under the laws which controlled it, exhibited—in the features of disturbance which characterise the solidification of the earth's crust, in its primitive atmospheric conditions, and in the debased forms of early animal life, which alone could exist in them until they underwent modification—all the evidences of an almost overpowering infusion of that corrupt atomic force which we call evil.

The result was the generation of many forms of vegetable and animal life which are now extinct, and which were more in affinity with the lower than the upper world. As these evolved, the infernal force increased its hold on nature, because the action of the Seraphim is from above through the highest form of living being, which is man, who had not yet come into existence; while that of the Siddim is from below, through the lowest forms of nature. The tendency of the Siddistic force is to disintegrate; that of the Seraphistic is to unite. The former endeavoured, therefore, to introduce into nature the principle of unisexuality, they having lost all consciousness of their own bisexuality; while the Seraphim opposed their effort with the force of bisexuality, which, being derived from the source of all nature, was impregnable to their attacks in its centre, though open to them on its circumference.

Species developed under these complex and disorderly conditions; hence we find in vegetable nature so many plants bisexual, side by side with others which are male and female, while in many of the lower forms of animal life, beginning with the amœba itself, from which we are supposed by evolutionists to have sprung, the bisexual principle is retained, though concealed from the scientific eye, and each specimen is furnished with the reproductive powers necessary for its own propagation by fission. As larger forms evolved, the division of the sexes became manifest, and the action of the Siddim became more apparent in the hideousness of the monsters, of which we find the remains so far back as the palæozoic period. Nor is it unlikely, although we have no direct evidence of it, that at that period transmutation of species may have taken place.[1] The aspect of nature prior to the

[1] A tradition of the confusion which now reigned is evidently contained in the cosmogony of Eridu, professed to have been inscribed by the god of Eridu himself, and which was long anterior to the Mosaic cosmogony: "There was a 'time in which there existed nothing but darkness and an abyss of waters, 'wherein resided the most hideous things, which were produced by a twofold 'principle. There appeared men, some of whom were furnished with two 'wings, others with four, and with two faces. They had one body, but two 'heads—the one that of a man, the other that of a woman. They were like-'wise, in their several organs, both male and female." Here is a distorted allusion to the biune composition of the first human pairs as they originally

appearance of man in it has been graphically portrayed for us by science, and there is no reason to think that the picture is in any important respect inaccurate; but it is impossible to conceive of anything more weird, desolate, and forbidding than this world was under the influences which were now controlling its evolution. It was when it had reached its extreme stage of disorderly development, that man appeared upon the scene, in a region more highly favoured than any which has been pictured by the pen of science. It was one upon which the Seraphim had concentrated the divine energies for this purpose, and was upon a continent which has since been submerged. Here both fauna and flora were of a fairer type than in other parts of the world, the seasons less inclement, and the conditions of existence in every way more favourable.

The great contrast which existed between the primitive condition of man, and that of the nature by which he was surrounded, arose from this fact, that the formative or evolutionary action of the Siddim was diffused, that of the Seraphim was concentric. The one set of influences acted on the circumference, their life-emanations germinating in the very lowest forms of nature, and on its most external expanses,—the other set, focussing as through a burning-glass the rays of the divine vitality on the *anima mundi*, or world-soul, and thus developing life from the centre outward, from whence it radiated to all parts of those outer expanses in which the Siddim were so busily employed, infusing a divine element into their field of labour, and preparing it for the special vitalising force which man was destined to bring

emanated from the Seraphim, mixed up with that Siddistic invasion to which we owe the monsters of the period prior to the appearance of man upon earth, and which are thus described: "Other human figures were to be seen 'with the legs and horns of a goat; some had horses' feet, while others united 'the hindquarters of a horse with the body of a man, resembling in shape the 'hippocentaurs. Bulls likewise were bred with the heads of men, and dogs 'with fourfold bodies terminated in their extremities with the tails of fishes. 'In short, there were creatures in which were combined the limbs of every 'species of animal. In addition to these there were fishes, reptiles, serpents, 'with other monstrous animals, which assumed each other's shape and coun- 'tenance—of all which were preserved delineations in the Temple of Belos in 'Babylon."—Hibbert Lectures, 1887, p. 369.

to bear upon it through the principle of bisexuality. For this purpose a concentration of divine force was directed upon that locality on the earth's surface symbolised by the garden of Eden, which was in fact the point of external magnetic contact with the upper world, and hence the myth which has located it in the vicinity of the Pamir plateau, in the Hindoo Koosh, which is sometimes called "the roof of the world," and sometimes its navel; for it may be said that the umbilical cord which connected this world with the one which was unfallen, was attached by the atomic chain of the Seraphim, who, in spite of the more finely attenuated substance of which they were composed, were able to visit it, and to a certain extent make it their abode. They were, in fact, the progenitors of the human race; giving birth to our first parents, not by any process of propagation known to men in these days, but by what I have already called generative exhalation.

The near relations which the Siddim bore to primitive man is indicated in the sixth chapter of Genesis, where it is said that "the sons of God saw the daughters of men that they were fair; and they took them wives of all that they chose." This, however, was after man had succumbed as to his feminine principle, to infernal invasion. The consequences of this sex-contact on the part of the Siddim I shall allude to presently. They were called sons of God, although Siddim, because originally made in His likeness. Although, as I have explained, the generation of man took place through the Seraphim, in a region specially prepared for him, and he was surrounded by a nature in strong contrast to the rest of the world, the greater part of which was so miasmatic and pervaded by infernal poisons, that it would have been uninhabitable by him, his position was in the highest degree critical. Even though he had been preserved free from taint, the exquisite nature by which he was environed was not; for even though surrounded by sea, the continent figured under the name of the garden of Eden, had its roots in the poisoned earth-crust, and its atomic particles were pervaded by the virus, though to a far less extent than elsewhere, which infected the whole creation.

The persistent attacks which the Siddim brought to bear

upon this portion of the earth's surface ultimately caused its submersion. Still man was provided with protection from the dangers arising from this source, which are symbolised in the tree of the knowledge of good and evil. In other words, he was intuitively conscious of the laws which ensured his safety, and of the consequences of disobedience. Moreover, he was in constant relations with the angelic visitors to whom he owed his origin, and of whose frequent visitations he was externally cognisant. This is indicated by the internal meaning of the words, "And they heard the voice of Jehovah Elohim walking in the garden in the cool of the day," and in the narrative of the conversation which followed, which they recognised as a divine inspiration through the Seraphim.

The substance of the Adamic man, although grosser than that of his angelic progenitors, was far more attenuated than that of the nature by which he was surrounded, which was permeable to it; he was, in fact, more nearly allied to that of a being who has passed away from this world, than to one now on it, or, to use a term now in common use, he was fourth dimensional. His partial supremacy over nature was due to this fact; and it was by virtue of the potency with which he was thus endowed, that he was intrusted with the lofty mission of purifying the earth, or rather of preserving his own bisexual purity, in order that through it the ardours of the divine energy might descend, and thus restore this universe to the primal condition of our parent world, and so reconquer and redeem the region of it that had fallen.

In a word, the whole story resolves itself into this:—

Worlds generate worlds. In our case the world that brought us forth involved itself in a catastrophe, consequent upon the violation of a law controlling the operation of the will, by which its freedom is lost so soon as it ceases to be a divine freedom, and becomes a personally appropriated freedom. It was not possible for God to endow man with His own will, which is free, and at the same time so to limit it that its recipient should be deprived of the sense of individual freedom, which would naturally take the form of personal independence, were it not held in check by the constant recollection of its origin. The indulgence of this sentiment of independence is the first step to a separation from God, which, in the case of such stupendously endowed beings as those who inhabited the world prior to our own, would at first unconsciously develop into pride, and so gradually into a more or less conscious antagonism. This is the origin, so far as our universe is concerned, of what is called "evil." As the offspring of that world we inherit its taint, and, indeed, are impregnated with it to such an extent that few among us have yet learnt that we have no freedom of will of our own, apart from the divine will which should be freely operating through us.

It is by the recovery by man of God's freedom of will, that he can recover his own; and this can only be done by regaining the condition he has lost, with all the potencies inherent to it. He then becomes the instrument, not merely of the redemption of his own world, but of the one that gave it birth. To these contending streams of energy,—one from below, tainted with the poison of evil; one from above, containing within it concealed potencies of unknown capacity for good,—is due the complex character of the universe in which we dwell; with its death-dealing and health-giving properties of plants and minerals; its noxious and revolting insects, and those that charm the eye with their beauty of form and colour; its animals that war upon man, and those that serve him; and lastly, man himself, aspiring or debased, gentle or ferocious, as the case may be.

This nature it is now man's function and mission to purify and redeem; and to this end he must understand, first, the secret of its malady, secondly, the causes that produced it, and lastly, the remedy which it is in his power to apply. He must no longer allow his prejudices, derived from the very finite and imperfect observation of his senses, to close his eyes to the fact that we are in direct *rapport* with two opposite classes of invisible beings, and that upon the relation which we occupy towards them everything depends. This is a truth that Christians ought to have no difficulty in accepting, for it is taught in almost every page in the Bible. He must also realise that these two classes consist, on the one hand, of those who have lived upon this earth, and who have, by the exercise of will in the right direction, placed themselves in close atomic union with the inhabitants of that superior region which preserved its first estate, and who are in relation with the Elohim, and so with the infinite Jehovah Elohim; and on the other hand, of those who have, by the exercise of the will in the wrong direction, placed themselves in atomic union with the inhabitants of that lower region which lost its first estate, and who use every effort to oppose the vital life-current that descends through the first-mentioned class of beings, by a counter-current, which, meeting in man, produces the incessant conflict of which he is the victim, and which is known as the struggle between good and evil. This assertion is not one which is susceptible of mathematical proof, but it is one which it is open to every man to verify by his own personal experience by a moral process, the nature of which will always be made clear to every man who honestly sets to work to discover it.

In the course of his effort to verify the existence of these rival influences, which will bring him into violent and painful internal conflict, he will become conscious of the truth of the next statement, which is, that the root of the moral disease in himself, and which is also the seat of the malady in nature, is the poison which has polluted the vital or generative principle in his organism. The most powerful current in nature is the life-current—that which propagates and sustains; for it is by the force inherent in it that worlds generate worlds. If this is impure, vitality is poisoned at its fountain-head; but inasmuch as this force, like every other force, is atomic, and depends for its impurity upon its present atomic combinations, it is evident that the introduction of new force of the same essential quality, but with different properties, would involve chemical changes and a recombination of elements, by means of which those which are now impure might be relieved of their taint, and the character of the whole vitalising current altered. The man engaged in the moral experiment of discovering in his own person what this force is, and how it may be applied for the "restitution of all things," without taking thought for himself in the matter, will soon discover that while it is of sex-quality, it is of a different sex-quality from any of which he has hitherto had any knowledge; and he will find himself entering upon a region of investigation from which he would gladly turn aside, for it will expose him to attack, misconstruction, and persecution from many quarters. It is also one in which snares, pitfalls, and dangers of every description abound; and it would be better far never to enter upon it, than to do so unimpressed with the fearful responsibilities it involves, with the solemn issues which are at stake, and with the utter unworthiness of any human creature to tread upon such holy ground, until he has prepared himself, by long and arduous combats for purity, and has placed himself in such relations with his protecting and assisting angels, as will assure him against overwhelming attacks by the infernals.

Having thus fortified himself both from within and from without, and having steeled himself against charges of impurity on the part of those he is giving his life to purify, he may venture, tentatively and cautiously, upon this dangerous ground; but he will immediately become aware that it is not safe to do so alone, and that he must be upheld, guided, and assisted by those who have trodden it before him, and who have learnt to discriminate between the divine bisexual force, and the unisexual simulation of it projected from the lower world.

Those who, from fear of a public opinion impregnated with impurity, shrink from grappling with the disease inherent in the generative and reproductive principle of the universe, after they have become convinced that the only hope of the world's redemption lies in its purification, will reap the reward of their timidity when they pass into another life, and find the problem of their own purification presented to them under conditions much more trying than those which surround it here. But those who are willing, inspired by love for humanity, to place themselves in God's hands as ready sacrifices for the advancement of this great work, will find a consolation in the supreme peace and joy which will flood them, that will more than compensate for the rage that will be concentrated upon them by the infernals, and which will find expression through their agents in this world, generally among those most noted for what is called their "piety" and "good works."

As in the days of Christ, so it will be again; the most bitter enemies of him who tries to bring new life and love into the world from the source of life and love, will be the Churches, and the Pharisees by whom they are haunted.

The problem of the origin of evil has long been the one which has vexed the soul of humanity: we now see that evil may be extirpated from its origin, which is no lower than the fallen part of a universe which has assisted in the development and evolution of our own, in which will, asserting that it possessed a personal freedom inherent in itself, independently of the divine freedom, separated itself from God, and thus from the quality of love which is in God. For in the degree in which man feels that his will is God's will operating in him, does he feel that his love is God's love operating in him, and the nature of that love is all-embracing, and its quality is out-giving. But the man who feels that his will is his own, feels also that his love is his own, and the nature of that love is exacting, and its quality in-taking. Therefore it is evident that in the degree in which man feels that he has no other will but God's, does the potency of that will increase; and in the degree that the divine love flows into him by the channel of that will, does it flow out of him upon the nature and the humanity which is so dear to God; and he will recognise in its ardours an uncontrollable desire to serve his fellows, and can discriminate it thereby from that false love, which, having its root in the principle of personal human will, is essentially parasitical, and sustains itself by the life which it drains from others, thus perverting the principle of divine love, and transforming it into infernal lust.

The evolutionary period is now commencing when, if we look in vain for help from theology, we may at least hope for sympathy from science; for even it will admit that if electric and other forces contain, as has been suggested by science itself, "files of particles," the most powerful force in nature, which is the sex-force, must also be atomic. And indeed, considering its natural results in the shape of offspring, this is an almost self-evident proposition; for it cannot be doubted that the character of the offspring is determined by the quality of the masculine and feminine atoms which combine to form it, and it is the knowledge of this fact which governs the breeding of stock, accounts for the phenomena of heredity, and explains the varieties of species, both in vegetable and animal nature. If, then, a new atomic force can be introduced into man's organism, of a higher and purer quality than any of which we have any cognisance, it is evident that a new door of evolution is open to him. He will survive, not because he is able to destroy more of his fellow-creatures in a given time by means of a curiously invented gun than other men; not because he is the pioneer of a civilisation so deadly in its character, that the Red Indian or Australian perishes before it as before a pestilence; not because he has greater facilities than his fellows for starving others that he may enrich himself; not for these, and many other kindred reasons, will he survive; but because he will find himself endowed with the vigours derived from a new and pure sex-potency, which will enable him ultimately to produce offspring of a loftier physical and moral type, possessing those finer faculties of a supersensuous kind, which were lost when the Adamic race closed all the subsurface region of its consciousness, and stupefied alike its moral instinct and its rational intelligence, by absorbing a current of lust from the lower animal creation.

To those who have had the patience to follow me thus far, the question will now naturally suggest itself, By what process can the pure bisexual force be introduced into the organism? and what channel of descent has been provided for it? Before reaching this point it will be necessary briefly to revert to the history of the race from the period of the commencement of the new conditions under which it was destined to exist. The internal meaning of the Book of Genesis records the story with much elaborateness of detail, as handed down by tradition on which was grafted the inspiration of the writer; but it is foreign to the purpose of this book to do more than notice the points which have a practical bearing upon the special subject we are discussing.

It has been said that the process of atomic accretion, which resulted in the materialisation of the particles in their present form, was a slow and gradual one, and during its progress the struggle between the Siddim and the Seraphim over the sex-principle in man—the one still further to debase it, the other to preserve it—was fierce and incessant. It resulted in the division of the Adamic race into two opposing forces, represented by Cain and Abel, the one dominated by the Siddim, the other under the influence of the Seraphim. Up to this time physiological birth was unknown, the human race being, by means of the respiratory organs, propagated in pairs, the male with the female, who formed the complete being, though it was divided materially as to the surface substance.

The tradition of this exists in the Talmud, where it is said that both Cain and Abel were born with twin sisters;[1] and it has been handed down to us from the most ancient times as one of the signs of the zodiac, though mystics apply it also to the progress of the soul.

The individuals of the Adamic race were also, owing to their atomic composition, endowed with vitality which protracted existence over long periods of duration; the tradition of this accounts for the longevity ascribed to the patriarchs. The idea of procreation by respiration will of course seem fantastic to the natural mind, until it reflects upon the fact that we actually do procreate by respiration every day of our lives. This is only brought forcibly to our notice in cases of infectious maladies, for nothing is more certain than that the exhalations of diseased persons are charged with microbes or bacilli, or minute living organisms which carry with them the germs of death, which are, so to speak, hatched in our bodies, and which we breathe out into nature, thus becoming their human parents. There would therefore be nothing strange in the phenomenon of similarly generated organisms being life-giving, instead of death-dealing: such do in fact exist in the sentient atoms of healing magnetism, the quality of which largely depends on the respiratory processes of the operator. In proportion as the breath is long and deep, is the magnetic current powerful and effective. I am able to state this from personal experience. As the inhalation of infinitesimal living organisms, which generate in the lungs, produce consumption, and as the exhalation of them propels their life into other human organisms, so the human soul-germs were propelled from the creative source into the respiratory organs of those beings of a former world, where

[1] Sanhedrim, fol. 38, col. 2.

they generated, and from which they issued in a bisexual aromal form, filled with the breath of life, and acquired, by atomic condensation and combination, the structural conditions necessary to their growth and development. It was thus man was first generated through the Seraphim; it was thus, though under somewhat different conditions, that he was procreated throughout the early stage of his existence on earth—and this is the mystery of the origin of man.

CHAPTER XVI.

THE FIRST PERIOD OF THE RACE—ESOTERIC SENSE OF THE CONFLICT BETWEEN CAIN AND ABEL—THE MARK OF CAIN—THE INTRODUCTION OF PHYSIOLOGICAL BIRTH—OF POLYGAMY—THE FATE OF THE LAMECH RACES—INVASION OF THE PLANET BY THE SIDDIM—THEIR MIXED PROGENY—THE BOOK OF ENOCH—THE DELUGE—EARLIEST COSMOGONIC TRADITIONS—THE GOLDEN AGE.

In order to trace the early history of man to historic times, it is necessary that I should enter upon a somewhat detailed examination of the esoteric sense, contained in the Biblical narrative up to the period immediately succeeding the deluge.

Geologists admit the existence of a miocene continent which has been submerged, and which has received the name of Atlantis. From the evidences which have been obtained as to the conditions of nature upon it, there is nothing impossible in supposing it to have been the scene of the catastrophe called the Fall, and of the subsequent experiences of the Adamic race.

Eastern occultists of the modern school throw back the first appearance of man upon earth to a period far anterior to this: though they insist strongly on his androgynous composition, they hold that the separation of the sexes took place with the third root-race—the Lemurians of the secondary geological epoch. Physiological birth was, according to them, unknown to the second race, who were androgynous, and will close before the sixth race.

Without entering upon this theory, it is interesting, as pointing to a common origin in tradition, and a certain similarity in detail; for the change in the method of reproduction is symbolised in the story of Cain and Abel.

As the processes of nature are gradual, the events which preceded this episode—namely, the expulsion from the garden of Eden, which consisted in a modification of the earth's crust; and the clothing with skins, which consisted in a slow atomic change in the organism of man—was extended over a protracted period, as measured by our standard; during which time a constant separation was being effected between the masculine and feminine principles, until it reached the point signified in the fourth chapter of Genesis, by the birth of Cain and Abel. Cain, as his Hebrew name implies, signifying the male principle—therefore when Cain was born, Eve said, I have gotten a man of the Lord; and Abel, as his name implies, signifying the breath (pneuma) or female principle.[1] "And Abel was a keeper of sheep, but Cain was a tiller of the ground," signifies the difference between the interior functions of the feminine principle and the exterior functions of the masculine. "And Cain brought of the fruit of the ground an offering unto the Lord," signifies the desire of the masculine to approach God directly, and not through the feminine, which is the divine order, and thus to dominate the feminine. Abel's sacrifice signifies adoration by the human feminine. "And God had respect unto Abel and his offering," signifies the union of the divine masculine with the human feminine; "but unto Cain and to his offering he had not respect," signifies the divine repudiation of the disorderly attempt of the human masculine to unite itself with God, otherwise than through the feminine. "And Cain was very wroth, and his countenance fell," signifies the revolt of the male principle. "And the Lord said unto 'Cain, Why art thou wroth? and why is thy countenance 'fallen? If thou doest well, shalt thou not have the excel-'lency? and if thou doest not well, sin lieth at the door, and 'he shall be subject unto thee, and thou shalt rule over him," signifies that God does not interfere with the freedom of man's will, but allows him to take the consequences of his own acts. Therefore in this case the human masculine principle violated the divine order, and asserted its supremacy over the feminine, thus pointing to the fulfilment of the

---

[1] *The marginal translations* of both names are not quite correctly given in the Bible.

condemnation of Eve, to whom it was said in the sixteenth verse of the previous chapter, "and thou shalt be subject to thy husband, and he shall rule over thee." In other words, the feminine principle had, by this act of fatal disobedience, incurred subjection to the masculine.

The conflict between Cain and Abel signifies the struggle between the two principles, and the murder of Abel or the "breath," signifies the conquest of the female by the male principle, and the extinction of the respiratory generative process which had hitherto prevailed. Cain's exclamation in answer to the demand of God after the feminine, "Am I my brother's keeper?" signifies his repudiation of the relation of guardianship, which, in the divine order, the masculine principle bore to the feminine. "The voice of thy brother's blood crieth unto me from the ground," signifies the complaint of the feminine upon being thus animalised by the masculine.

"Now thou art cursed from the earth, which hath opened her mouth to receive thy brother's blood from thy hand," signifies the degradation which would ensue to man through an atomic change of particles of a still grosser material character, by which his organism and its functions would become nearly allied to those of the lower animal creation. "When thou tillest the ground, it shall not yield thee her strength," signifies that it would be impossible for man to draw from the principle which he had thus debased the divine nourishment, as he had hitherto done. "A fugitive and a vagabond shalt thou be in the earth," signifies that by this act man had separated himself from internal union with God. Cain's exclamation, "Behold, Thou hast driven me out this day from the face of the earth; and from Thy face shall I be hid; and I shall be a fugitive and a vagabond upon the earth," signifies the despair of the race at finding the change which had supervened in consequence of the extinction of the external manifestation of the Divine Feminine principle, and of the method of procreation thereby previously existing; thus involving man in a period of spiritual desolation, and of rapid decay as to his natural life, and, as he supposed, of cessation from race reproduction. "And the Lord said, Therefore whosoever slayeth Cain, vengeance shall be taken on him sevenfold," signifies that the sex-principle would be preserved notwithstanding that it had been thus debased, and could only be further prostituted on the penalty of a still heavier punishment than that which had befallen the race already.

"And the Lord set a mark upon Cain, lest any finding him should kill him," signifies that a method of procreation had been provided, suitable to the new organic conditions which had now been introduced, allied to the lower animal creation; and that the physical organism of man underwent the change as to the formation of his body, which thus constituted the outward mark of his animal degradation.

This change could only be effected under the conditions which the introduction of the Siddistic virus into the human system imposed. It was a slow and gradual process of devolution from the more plastic or fluid man, downward to the gross and solid brute creation, and involved a structural change in his organism almost as complete as if he had evolved upwards from the amœba. It involved a corresponding mental and moral degradation, and extended over an immense period of time, during which the forces of the Siddim were incessantly active, until, at last, man was almost reduced to the condition of a monkey. Being, however, originally atomically constituted as to his moral and reasoning faculties on a fundamentally different basis, it was not possible for the moral and intellectual chasm which separates him from the brute creation to be bridged over. During all this time the process of procreation underwent a gradual change, developing new conditions which entirely altered its character, until it became enshrouded in the secrecy and the shame which the mark of Cain bears with it to this day.[1]

The physiological change culminated at the race of Seth,

---

[1] " St Augustine makes Abel the type of the new regenerate man ; Cain that of the natural man."—(De Civ. Dei, xv. 1.)

' The oriental Gnosticism of the Sabæans made Abel an incarnate æon, and
' the Gnostic or Manichæan sect of the Abelitæ in North Africa, at the time of
' Augustine (De Hær., 86, 87), so called themselves from a tradition that Abel,
' though married, lived in continence. In order to avoid perpetuating original
' sin, they followed his example ; but in order to keep up their sect, each mar-
' ried pair adopted a male and female child, who in their turn vowed to marry
' under the same conditions." See Smith's Dictionary of the Bible. The above tradition evidently had relation to the change in the sex-relation concealed in the allegory of Cain and Abel.

as we read in the 25th verse of the same chapter, "And 'Adam knew his wife again; and she bare a son, and she 'called his name Seth: For God, she said, has appointed me 'seed otherwise,[1] instead of Abel, whom Cain slew." These words signify the completion of the change, and the name Seth implies the nature of the change, which may easily be deduced from the Hebrew.

The birth of Seth marks a new departure for the race, which is indicated in the first verses of the next chapter, in which we are told that Adam " begat a son in his own likeness," in contradistinction to the immediately preceding verse where it is said, " In the day that God created.man, in the likeness of God made He him; male and female created He them; and blessed them, and called their name Adam." It is scarcely possible to have a statement emphasising and recapitulating more strongly the bisexual nature of the first created man than this. For, though it refers to the first Adam, or Adam Cadmon, it is expressly repeated to give point to the great change which had taken place in humanitary conditions, and which resulted in a man being no longer born in the divine likeness as two-in-one, but in that of his father alone. Hence the son of Seth was called " Enos," a word signifying " a man of sorrow."

" Then men began to call upon the name of the Lord," signifies the effort man made to unite himself with God in his new condition.

We are given the pedigree of Lamech, the seventh from Adam, up to Cain, and also of another race Lamech, the ninth from Adam, up to Seth, in order to mark the two opposing moral currents, which had resulted from the new organic conditions that now controlled the human race.

It should always be borne in mind that these names in their deepest signification indicate principles, and in their more external sense mean races. In the descendants of Cain we trace the lower or material development of man, in that of Seth the higher or spiritual one. Thus, in one case, we have Enoch, the father of Irad, and the third from Adam, establishing the selfish lust-principle as a vital energy in the organism; which is represented by Cain, or the masculine

---

[1] The Biblical translation is incorrect.

principle, founding a city in his name; and in the other we have Enoch, the son of Jared, and the seventh from Adam, representing the absolutely pure divine love-principle; for we are told that he "walked with God: and he was not; for God took him," which signifies that at this period of the race, a certain specific manifestation of the pure love-principle which had lasted up to this time became temporarily extinguished; but only temporarily, for this principle is one of the two witnesses mentioned in the eleventh chapter of the Revelation, in which, "after three days and a half the Spirit of life from God shall enter," and these three days and a half are even now terminating. The second witness is Elijah, who represents another principle; as it is written, "Behold, I will send 'you Elijah the prophet before the coming of the great and 'dreadful day of the Lord: and he shall turn the heart of the 'fathers to the children, and the heart of the children to their 'fathers, lest I come and smite the earth with a curse." The precise signification of the two witnesses will be explained later.

We have further, in the descendants of Cain, the vices indicated which characterised the material progress of the race, and in their most external sense that progress itself. Thus the names of the three women mentioned mean respectively, "adornment," "music," and "beauty"; while the occupations which are given of the three sons of two of them, indicate the state of civilisation at which the world had arrived. All these names have, however, other inner meanings.

The names of the descendants of Seth indicate the moral condition of the race, and such virtues as it still retained.

Up to this time, although the process of procreation, which characterises the lower animal creation, had been introduced by the catastrophe represented in the legend of Cain and Abel, the external marriage-tie which had resulted therefrom had been strictly monogamic, and an essential principle of the Divine Feminine had thus been retained.

It was reserved for the race, signified under the name Lamech, seventh from Adam, to destroy this last vestige of purity by the introduction of polygamy. "And Lamech said unto his wives, Ada and Zillah, hear my voice; ye wives of Lamech, hearken unto my speech: for I have slain a man to my wounding, and a young man to my hurt." The presence of the two wives, and the fact that the speech is addressed specially to them, imparts a peculiar significance to the confession of Lamech. The man slain to his wounding, and the young man to his hurt, signifies the monogamic principle, as represented by Cain, who was thus in his turn slain.[1] "Therefore," he continued, "if Cain shall be avenged sevenfold, truly Lamech seventy and sevenfold." In other words, so little of the divine purity was now left, that if the destruction of what Cain preserved deserved a sevenfold vengeance, the extinction of the slight semblance of it still retained by Lamech, deserved one much heavier.

The reason why the crime of Lamech exceeded, if possible, that of Cain, was because, so long as the monogamic principle lasted, it represented, however feebly, the original dual constitution of man, a principle embodied in the "Word" or the creative "Two-in-One," proceeding from the infinite Father and Mother, incarnated at last on earth as Christ. This is remarkably illustrated by the records which have reached us of the most ancient Accadian religion of Eridu, as elucidated by Professor Sayce, from which the allegories contained in the Pentateuch are derived. Tammuz, as we know, was the sun-god, or "Word," proceeding from the two-in-one, Ea and Dav-kina, the sources of life, and represented in Genesis, according to Professor Sayce, "by the two varying forms of Methuselah and Methusael," which in Assyrian should be Mutu-sa-ilati, "the husband of the goddess"—*i.e.*, Tammuz, the husband of Istar, who was his feminine complement. We learn from the same authority that Lamech would be the Semitic equivalent of Lamga, a name of the moon-god; that "Adah and Zillah, his wives, would correspond" with Edu and Isillu, "darkness" and "shade"; that "Jabal and Jubal 'are merely variant forms of the same word, which is evi-'dently the Assyrian Ablu, 'son,' from Abalu, to 'bring down,' 'hence Abel. Ablu refers us to the only son Tammuz, who 'was a shepherd like Jabal and Abel, whose untimely death 'was commemorated by the musical instruments of Jubal," and that "there are some who would aver that the Tubal-'cain of Genesis is but the double of Cain, and that it was

[1] According to the Talmud Cain was slain by Lamech.

'he, and not his father Lamech, who had slain the young 'man" (Yeled, Assyrian, ilattu, a title of Tammuz). The patriarchs of the Pentateuch thus became deities in the more ancient religion, but there runs through all its mythology the thread of the same idea, that a great sacrilege had been committed in regard to the sex-principle, which was typified by Tammuz and Istar, by Venus and Adonis, Isis and Osiris, Baal and Beltis, and elsewhere; but the Accadian mythology is especially interesting, because the Abel slain by Cain, and the young man slain by Lamga, the moon-god, are in both instances Tammuz, the sun-god, or Word. With regard to Enoch, Professor Sayce says: "If I am right in identifying 'Unuk with the Enoch of Genesis, the city built by Kain in 'commemoration of his first-born son, Unuk must be regarded 'as having received its earliest culture from Eridu, since 'Enoch was the son of Jared, according to Genesis v. 18, and 'Jared or Irad (Genesis iv. 18), is the same word as Eridu."[1]

It was part of the great mission of Christ, by His life and death, in preparation for a much greater event which was to follow, to restore the monogamic principle; and it was reserved for Mohammed and Joseph Smith to receive inspirations from the lower regions of our universe, which proclaimed as a divine revelation, the essentially infernal principle of polygamy.

Christ's reply to the Pharisees, that in heaven there was neither marrying nor giving in marriage, had reference to the condition of the race before the introduction of marriage, that followed on the procreative method resulting from the suppression of generative exhalation, and which implied that bisexual union, where male and female principles form one indissoluble being.

We hear nothing more of the polygamous races, whose lapse is thus recorded; nor of their extinction as separate nationalities, which is figured under the death of each patriarch, because they spread over the face of the habitable globe, and became literally fugitives and wanderers, soon losing the last traces of any civilisation they may have possessed, and sinking to the lowest depths which it is possible for humanity to attain. We have traces of them to

[1] Hibbert Lectures, 1887, pp. 185, 186.

this day in the remains of palæolithic man—in the rude implements and debased physical conditions which characterise the earliest specimens that have been found of the human race.

It was otherwise with the race Lamech, the ninth from Adam. Their organic conditions still admitted of a close external contact being maintained between the beings in the fallen and unfallen regions of the world which had preceded. Hence we read in the Biblical narrative "that the sons of God saw the daughters of men that they were fair." The sons of God here mentioned were the Siddim or fallen angels of the previous world, the term "sons of God" merely signifying their divine origin, although now debased and corrupted. The Book of Enoch, referred to by Jude, contains many chapters describing this event in detail. I will quote part of one of them, from which their general tenor may be gathered.

"It happened after the sons of men had multiplied in those
' days, that daughters were born to them elegant and beautiful.
' And when the angels, the sons of heaven, beheld them, they
' became enamoured of them, saying to each other: Come, let
' us select for ourselves wives from the progeny of men, and
' let us beget children. Then their leader Samyaza said to
' them, I fear that you may be perhaps indisposed to the per-
' formance of this enterprise, and that I alone shall suffer for
' so grievous a crime. But they answered him and said, We all
' swear and bind ourselves by mutual execrations, that we will
' not change our intention, but execute our projected under-
' taking. Then they all swore together, and all bound them-
' selves by mutual execrations. Their whole number was two
' hundred, who descended upon Ardis, which is the top of
' Mount Armon. That mountain therefore they called Armon,
' because they had sworn upon it and bound themselves by
' mutual execrations. These are the names of their chiefs—
' Samyaza,[1] who was their leader, Urakabarameel, Akibeel,
' Tamiel, Ramuel, Danel, Azkeel, Sarakuyel, Asael, Armers,
' Batraal, Anane, Zavabe, Samsaveel, Ertael, Turel, Yomyael,
' Arazyal. These were the prefects of the two hundred angels,
' and the remainder were all with them. Then they took
' wives, each choosing for himself, whom they began to

[1] Samyaza may possibly be the Samas of the Accadians.

'approach, and with whom they cohabited, teaching them
'sorcery, incantations, and the dividing of roots and trees; and
'the women conceiving, brought forth giants." These are the
Nephilim or giants alluded to in the fourth verse of the sixth
chapter of Genesis.

The efforts of Michael, Gabriel, Raphael, Suryal, and Uriel,
and the unfallen angels to intercede for those who had committed this wrong, and to preserve the earth from the fatal
consequences of the act which involved the race in destruction, are fully recounted in this rejected book, which, however,
was undoubtedly anterior to Christianity, was accepted as inspired by Jude, Tertullian, Irenæus, Clement of Alexandria,
and other early Christians, and what is more important,
alluded to in the Sohar of the Kabbalah, "The Holy and
'Blessed One," it is said, "raised him, Enoch, from the world
'to serve Him, as it is written, for God took him. From that
'time a book was delivered down, which was called the Book
'of Enoch. In the hour that God took him, He showed him
'all the repositories above. He showed him the tree of life
'in the midst of the garden, its leaves and its branches: we
'see all in this book." The Book of Enoch loses none of its
interest from the fact that it cannot possibly have been
written by Enoch, but by some Jew, probably about two
centuries B.C., who fancied himself inspired by Enoch, and
whose inspirations, from whatever source, certainly possess a
high interest and value, as having both an internal sense of
their own, and throwing light upon the internal sense of
those included in the canon of Scripture. According to the
Accadian cosmogony, the Siddim or fallen angels are represented by the Anunagi, the Seraphim by the Igigi, the
deluge was caused by Mul-lil, who was the devil, and whose
wife, Nin-lil, is the Lilith of the Hebrew tradition, the first
wife of Adam of the Talmud, and the "bright monster,"
mentioned by Isaiah, ch. xxxiv., v. 14.

The result of this contact between the Siddim and the
human race tended rapidly to infernalise the latter. Hence
we are told that "every imagination of the thoughts of his
'heart was only evil continually. And it repented the Lord
'that He had made man on the earth, and it grieved Him to
'His heart."

Making allowance for the anthropomorphic conception of the Deity which pervades this passage, we gather from it plainly, that it was thus that the great change which was impending, was afterwards accounted for; as the idea of the inevitable operation of law was foreign to the mind of the writer. What really happened was this; the conflict of currents, which had been for cycles in antagonism in the organism of man and of nature, now again culminated, and a new chemical change was operated throughout the universe, by which it was once more convulsed; of this convulsion the records are to be found in the glacial epoch, in the submergence of some of the earth's surface, and in many other evidences of disturbance and modification, both of a physical and climatic nature. Under this influence the especial region that may be said to have been the seat of the disease—for it was the point of contact between the opposite poles of the battery—disappeared beneath the ocean. Hence come the traditions of the flood, which are to be found in some form or other in all the most ancient religions, which had derived them, as well as the knowledge of the high truths which had been imparted by the Seraphim to the submerged races, and of which the remains have been handed down to us in the religions of the East, from a fragment of the race which survived the catastrophe, known under the name of Noah.

"And the Lord said, I will destroy man whom I have 'created, from the face of the earth; both man, and beast, and 'the creeping thing, and the fowls of the air; for it repenteth 'me that I have made them," signifies the confusion which had been created upon the Edenic continent by the commerce of the Lamech race with visitants from the previous world, whereby physical and animal nature was becoming tainted, and the action of the Siddim which had been centred upon it, with a view to its destruction, finally culminated in catastrophic changes upon the earth's surface, above described, resulting in the more or less gradual submergence and upheaval of certain portions of it, and in the extinction of the races which had become entirely dominated by them.

The protection afforded to the race of Noah, who alone retained a knowledge of divine primitive truth, is figured by the ark, into which the animals entered by pairs, thus symbolising the principle of pure bisexual love, which the Noachic race still preserved as a religious belief, and which therefore constituted their salvation, and that of the region in which they found a refuge. It was this ark which was destined to preserve for humanity all its most profound religious ideas; for all the leading religions of the world owe their parentage to the knowledge of divine truth which this race transmitted from the most ancient times, and in which they had been instructed by the Seraphim.[1] From this time forth these angel visitations were destined to be comparatively rare, though the legends of mythology are based upon them, and we have no fewer than a hundred and sixteen allusions to angels in the Bible, either as recording instances of their appearances to man, or as referring to their functions in his behalf.

Meantime those portions of the earth's surface which were unaffected by the catastrophe known as the flood, were inhabited by the descendants of the polygamist Lamech race, who, having lost every vestige of divine truth, had long before sunk to the promiscuous condition of almost brute beasts, with their cannibalism, their fetich-worship, and other unholy rites. It is from the crude perverted instincts of these races that Mr Herbert Spencer and other philosophers have built up an evolutionary theory of the religious sentiment in man, deriving it, if we trace the theory to its origin, from the moral instinct of the amœba. Professor Max Müller, in his 'Chips from a German Workshop,' discussing the ancient religions of the East, on the same lines, ascribes to the earliest Vedas an antiquity of only about B.C. 1500, and in his 'Science of Religion,' he tells us that the polytheism and mythology that they contain are the childish prattle of religion. "The world had its childhood, and when it was a child it 'spoke as a child, it understood as a child, it thought as a 'child"; but differing totally from Mr Herbert Spencer, he continues, "and I say again in that it spoke as a child, its 'language was true, in that it believed as a child, its religion 'was true. The fault rests with us if we insist on taking the 'language of infants for the language of men. . . . The 'language of antiquity is the language of infancy. . . .

---

[1] Hence we find the ark preserved in the Egyptian and Babylonian religions, as a sacred symbol, long before the time of Moses.

'The childish prattle of religion is not extinct, witness the religion of India."[1] Geological science here, at all events, comes to our rescue, and proves to us that the human race was hoary-headed, having been many hundreds of thousands of years upon the earth in the year B.C. 1500, when the Professor calls it in its infancy. In the last three thousand years, after a childhood of unexampled length, the race has suddenly shot up into a man, and these learned professors are the result. So blind is science, when it leaves facts and begins to formulate theories, to the logical absurdities into which it is driven by its own discoveries. It is, however, some satisfaction to obtain from science the admission that the religion of the world's infancy was true.

We are now able to trace profane history with tolerable distinctness to the year 1500 before the flood, as given in the Biblical chronology, which places the birth of Enos at a period as nearly as possible contemporary with that which Professor Sayce assigns to the Hymns of the Sun-God of Sippara at the court of Sargon of Accad, which, he considers, marks the period of the commencement of Semitic literature.

The Biblical chronology, therefore, with many of its time-honoured illusions, must be abandoned as being several hundred thousand years out of date, if we are to take the geological evidence furnished by the miocene flints found at Thenay, and which were undoubtedly shapen by human hands, possibly of the race of Lamech; while the fact that Eridu, now twenty-five miles inland, was, at the date assigned to the creation of the world, the seaport of the Euphrates, and the seat of Babylonian commerce with Arabia and India, is now pretty well established.

Professor Sayce, however, seriously interferes with Professor Max Müller's ethnological theories, when he describes our ancestors as a "fair-haired, blue-eyed, light-complexioned, dolichocephalic race, which is still found in its greatest purity in Scandinavia."

Referring to this and other utterances of the Hibbert lecturer, the 'Times' says: "These are some of the instances 'which show how science advances and changes. What was

[1] The Science of Religion, p. 278.

'thought to be demonstrated in 1861, is now known to have
'been little more than brilliant guesswork. Facts accumulate,
'and old theories are proved by them to be untenable.
'Meantime the world takes us to new positions; but it is
'just as well that it should admit that they, too, are only
'provisionally occupied." But this is exactly what the world
does not do. It is as difficult for a philosopher to learn humility in this respect, as a bishop.

The formulating of theories is especially dangerous where they refer to the religious instinct of man, and are based upon the evidences of that instinct which he may have left, either in the shape of carved monuments and hieroglyphs, as in Egypt, or engraved tablets, as in Babylonia and Assyria. Because the earliest record from the modern point of view superstitious belief in evil spirits, and forms of exorcism and magic, and the great Deity is veiled under symbols which have an inner meaning, which is quite beyond the reach of "professors," it by no means follows that their conclusions as to the religious ideas of the initiated classes in those early days is sound. Indeed the very fact that the ancients believed in possession by evil spirits, and used methods of exorcism, shows a far more accurate knowledge of the mysteries of nature than is possessed in these days.

The faculties do not exist in the learned men of our time for tracing the history of religious thought. To do so involves a moral training which is incompatible with the requirements of modern civilisation, and with a residence in the vortex of its superstitions, its infidelity, and its corruption. This applies no less to the theologians than to the men of science; and to understand the profound conceptions which underlie the symbols and carvings, the prayers and the legends, of the religions of Egypt and Babylon, requires not only the diligence, intelligence, and skill which have enabled those who have devoted themselves to the study, to decipher the external meaning; but that divine intuition by which alone light can be obtained that shall enable them to apprehend their esoteric sense.

In point of fact, the religions and superstitions of the world spring from two sources. No philosophic analyses of them, or deductions in regard to them, drawn from analogy, possess any value, which do not recognise their twofold origin, and the nature and operation of the influences from the invisible world to which they have been subjected.

The great majority of the races we call savage—that is, of those which compose the lowest human type, and whose superstitions are the most debased, revolting, and inhuman—are descendants of the antediluvian races, who, as I before explained, fell under the curse attaching to the polygamous crime of Lamech, and who, being specially open to Siddistic invasion, have introduced the insanities, cruelties, and lusts of the fallen region into this world, and thus minister to an ignorant, degraded, and absolutely perverted religious instinct. They continue to derive their inspiration from the lower invisible region of our universe, where the same practices prevail.

The other class of religions, which may be traced back through Egypt, Babylonia, and India, although in the most degraded expression of them which has reached us, they may offer some analogy to the debased superstitions of which we have been speaking, owe this degradation also to Siddistic invasion, which, however, was never able absolutely to obscure the remains of the religion of the Noachic race, which was a far purer, loftier, and more sublime spiritual conception than any of which we have any idea; and the period immediately following the deluge is that which has been handed down to us by tradition, as the period of the "golden age"—a period indicated in Scripture by the words, "And the whole earth was of one language and of one speech."

Once more humanity made a new departure—from a lower level, it is true, than that which had characterised the earlier stages of its existence, but still on a far higher level than that to which it afterwards sank; and it is to this subsequent history that we must now turn our attention.

CHAPTER XVII.

THE NOACHIC RACE—THE GUARDIANS OF THE MYSTERY—TRANSMITTED TO THE ABRAMIC—MAGNETIC CONDITIONS OF THE HOLY LAND—THE DIVINE TRINITY OF THE EARLY RELIGIONS—ANALOGY OF THE RELIGION OF ACCAD WITH THAT OF THE JEWS—THE SECRET CONTAINED IN THE LAW OF MOSES—THE FULFILMENT OF THE LAW—EFFECT OF MODERN CRITICISM ON JUDAISM.

WE are now approaching the historic period, though the date of the catastrophe alluded to in the last chapter, and the golden age which succeeded it, was a great many thousands of years prior to that assigned to it in the Biblical chronology. The region occupied by the Noachic race and its subdivisions was all that part of Central Asia, extending from Persia to China, including Thibet, Turcomania, and Northern India. The legend of the Tower of Babel, which subsequently found a literal expression in Chaldea, symbolises the pride and arrogance by which this race began to be puffed up, in consequence of the high pitch of moral, intellectual, and material development to which they had attained; and the "confusion of tongues" signifies the quarrels which ensued, and the religious schisms resulting therefrom, which finally culminated in widespread migrations even as far as Scandinavia—giving rise to those divisions in the human family which are known somewhat incorrectly among us as Aryan, Semitic, Turanian, Dravidian, and so forth; and to sundry religions, in all of which were to be discovered the fundamental ideas upon which the Noachic religion was founded, but which by degrees became so distorted and debased, in order to meet the popular comprehension, to subserve local conditions, and to pander to priestly ambition, that they ended by presenting widely different superficial conceptions, and became degraded into polytheisms, idolatries, and superstitions, of various types and character.

The most remarkable feature, however, of these early religions was the prominent position assigned to the vital principle. Emblems of reproduction were almost invariably objects of religious worship. Mysteries were celebrated in their honour, and much of the most profound occult lore was devoted to the conservation of secrets which had been derived from the Noachic race on this subject. Any one who will take the trouble to study the early religions, especially if they are at all initiated into their internal or mystical sense, will find that this is so, and I need not dwell upon it more particularly now; my object being to show that a special method had been provided for the preservation of the most profound mystery of all, from the knowledge of the vulgar, until the time had arrived when it might be revealed; and the transcendent value of the Bible, over other sacred books, consists in this, that it is the only one of them which contains in its inner sense, the history of the conservation of the secret, as well as the secret itself, which has defied the penetration of the ages, and which had to be preserved in a form that could afterwards be unfolded. It concealed the kernel, of which the literal meaning was the husk; and mankind has behaved in regard to it very much as a savage might, who was intrusted with a bottle containing spirits of wine as a remedy for his ailment, but which was corked in such a manner, lest the spirit should escape before he was intelligent enough to know how to apply it, that he ended by thinking that the virtue lay in the bottle, and that by keeping tight hold of that, he could be cured.

But not only was it necessary to embody it in a written record, but to find a custodian for it, and for that purpose a special race was chosen to whom it should be confided, and the history of that race, which was contained in that record, was to symbolise the history of human development in regard to the mystery they guarded; and a man of that race was to appear at a precise period of that history, who should embody in his life and death the occult fulfilment of it, and prepare mankind for its full revelation in his own person; and inasmuch as the special race failed to recognise the fulfilment of their law—which more especially contained the mystery—in the person of Him whom they crucified, those who are called by His name now also guard the sacred book, become doubly sacred, since it contains the record, however imperfect, of the life and death of Him whose life was destined to be the light of men, and whose death their redemption.

On the dispersion of the Noachic race, those who retained the fullest measure of the divine truth were those who remained behind, and who transmitted it to their descendants, among the earliest of whom were Rama and Chrishna, who were turned into mythological personages, but through whom came the traditions which afterwards found expression in the Vedas. By this time, however, they had become corrupted, and overlaid with myth, by human transmission and reproduction, and were only preserved in a comparatively untainted form, by a small group of persons who were the descendants of those who had filled exalted priestly functions during the golden age, and who had migrated to Palestine and established themselves at Jerusalem, where they retained a knowledge of the secrets which had been transmitted to them in their purity. This sect is internally signified in the Bible by the name Shem.

Meantime we find relics of them in Chaldea, and subsequently in Persia, where a highly inspired teacher and sage appeared in the person of Zoroaster, who reformed to some extent the Vedantic religion, and reproduced some of the old truths in the Zend-Avesta and other Mazdean writings, thus founding a new school of mysticism, the influence of which was speedily felt in Assyria and the neighbouring countries.[1]

At this time there lived in Chaldea a sect who had also preserved many of these truths, and who warmly identified themselves with the attempt of Zoroaster to revive them; but the Chaldeans resented any interference with the abuses they had introduced, and with the superstitions of a debased type to which they clung, and hence arose a strife, to which the Talmud contains many allusions; for the leader of these re-

---

[1] A much later date is usually assigned to Zoroaster than the period above indicated, which is rather in accordance with Parsee tradition than learned conjecture.

formers is known to us in the Bible as Abram, who found himself compelled, with his followers, to quit the country of his birth and seek a refuge in Egypt. The whole of the history of Abram, Sarai, and their posterity, contains, as Paul tells us, an interior or allegorical meaning, bearing upon the nature of the great trust which was to be confided to him and to his descendants, and which was to prove a blessing to all humanity. Therefore God is reported to have said to him, "In thee shall all the families of the earth be blessed."

The affinity which still exists between the Parsee and Jewish religious ideas may be traced to this early connection between Abram and Zoroaster, and the parallelism which has attended the fortunes of the two peoples. The exclusiveness and fidelity with which they have both clung to their ancient traditions, is not without its significance. As, at this period, the priests of Egypt were deeply learned in the occult lore of Chaldea, Persia, India, and Thibet, the expelled sect was led thither by Abram, but were received coldly. The internal signification of this journey is the rejection of the principle of the pure Divine Feminine, represented in the person of Sarai, by the Egyptians.

Returning to Canaan, Abram was received at Jerusalem by the last representative of that group of holy men to whom had been intrusted the divine mysteries, to whom I have already referred as having migrated thither long previously, and who throughout the period following the confusion of tongues, had preserved the truth intact. Their mission, represented by the person of Melchizedek, had now come to an end, while that of the Jews, represented in the person of Abraham, their father, was to begin.[1] Abram, therefore, rendered the most

[1] The Talmud has a tradition somewhat confirmatory of this. Rabbi Yochanan ben Nuri says: "The Holy One, blessed be He, took Shem and 'separated him to be a priest to Himself that he might serve before Him; He 'also caused his Shechinah to rest with him, and called his name Melchizedek, 'Priest of the Most High and King of Salem. His brother Japhet even 'studied the law in his school until Abraham came and also learned the law in 'the school of Shem, where God Himself instructed Abraham, so that all else 'he had learned from the lips of man was forgotten. Then came Abraham and 'prayed to God that the Shechinah (Divine Feminine) might ever rest in the 'house of Shem, which was also promised to him, as it said, Thou art a priest 'for ever after the order of Melchizedek."—Avodash Hakkodesh, Part III., chap. 20.

divinely gifted man then alive the homage which was his due, and paid him tithes, and was instructed by him in the knowledge which he had been brought to this sacred spot to acquire; for Jerusalem had even then been chosen as a local focus of inspiration, and prepared, by the residence on it of those devout men who had been the depositaries of divine truth, to be the territorial centre of the race that had been selected to succeed them as its custodians. It is for this reason that the rare allusions to Melchizedek which the Bible contains are pregnant with the deepest meaning, and that Christ is called "a priest for ever after the order of Melchizedek." That the true significance of his character was known to the Jews, is evident from the reference made to him by the writer of the Epistle to the Hebrews: "To whom also Abraham 'gave a tenth part of all; first being by interpretation King 'of righteousness, and after that also King of Salem, which is, 'King of peace; without father, without mother, without 'descent, having neither beginning of days, nor end of life; but 'made like unto the Son of God, abideth a priest continually."

In order to apprehend the full significance of this passage, we must refer to the origin of the word Melchizedek, as understood by the light of its inner meaning. We find in the 9th chapter of 'The Lesser Holy Assembly,' concerning the Son and His Bride, who are concealed in the last two letters of the Tetragrammaton IHVH (Jehovah), an explanation of the 14th verse of the 89th Psalm, *Tzedeq Va-Meshephat*, "Justice and judgment are the abode of Thy throne;" *Chesed Va-Emeth*, "mercy and truth shall go before Thy countenance;" from which we gather that from the Father of all light there proceedeth light, for which "two light-bearers are found, which 'are the conformation of the throne of the King, and they are 'called Tzedek, justice, and Meshephat, judgment. And they 'are the beginning and the consummation. And through 'them are all the judgments crowned, as well superior as 'inferior. And they are all concealed in Meshephat. And 'from that Meshephat is Tzedek nourished.

'And sometimes they call the same Meleki Tzedek, Melek 'Shalem, Melchizedek, King of Salem." Thus Christ was the Light of the world, emanating from the Father of lights, to whom the light-bearers were justice and judgment, and thus was He a priest for ever after the order of Melchizedek; but, as we shall see from what follows, because the female principle had not been conjoined to the male, disorder ensued.

"When the judgments are crowned by Meshephat, all 'things are mercy; and all things are in perfect peace, 'because the one tempereth the other.

'Tzedek and the Rigours are reduced into order, and all 'these descend into the world in peace and mercy. And 'then is the hour sanctified, so that the male and the female 'are united, and the worlds, all and several, exist in love and 'in joy.

'But whensoever sins are multiplied in the world, and 'the sanctuary is polluted, and the male and the female are 'separated;

'And when that strong serpent beginneth to arise, Woe 'unto thee, O World! who in that time art nourished by this 'Tzedek. For then arise many slayers of men and execu'tioners (of judgments) in thee, O World! Many just men 'are withdrawn from thee.

'But wherefore is it thus? because the male is separated 'from the female; and judgment, Meshephat, is not united 'unto justice, Tzedek."[1]

It was to restore this balance between justice and judgment that Christ came into the world, and to lay the foundation of that union between the male and female principles which should enable Him to return as Melchizedek, King of peace, so that, in the words of the Psalmist, mercy and truth should go before His face, and "that great serpent" be overthrown. The whole of this will be more fully made manifest when we come to consider the nature of Him who is called the Son of God.

I may here remark parenthetically, that the three books of the New Testament which were written under the most powerful inspirational descent, and which are therefore most pregnant with hidden truth, are those, the authorship of which is most shrouded in mystery—namely, the Gospel of St John, the Epistle to the Hebrews, and the book of the Revelation.

Jerusalem had now become, and has ever since remained, in spite of the vicissitudes through which it has passed, the

[1] Mather's Kabbalah, p. 293.

most sacred spot on the earth's surface, for here the sublime tragedy was afterwards enacted which was the occult fulfilment of the law that contained the mystery; and this Holy City is destined yet to play a part in its final revelation. It is thus that surface nature is enlisted in the service of divine design, and that the highest forms of inspiration can only descend, when the magnetic conditions of soil and climate are favourable to certain combinations of the atomic elements of the moral, psychical, and physical organisms of those who seek it. Medical science recognises this fact in a degree, when it recommends change of air and scene as being good for the health and spirits; and few persons are so dense organically, as not to be conscious that a heavy damp air and a light dry one affect them differently—while, if their attention was sufficiently turned to it, they would also perceive that the influence of a heavy clay soil was different from that of a light sandy one.

If this relation between soil and climate and health and spirits, is sufficiently palpable for persons who are perfectly closed as to their interior faculties to appreciate, it will easily be understood that when once these are opened, the organic sensitiveness increases to such a degree, that quite a different set of sensations may be perceived in one country, from those which are felt in another. This is, no doubt, largely due to the magnetism radiating from the inhabitants, according to their quality. When these are in strong contrast, they become appreciable even to dense persons; thus there is a sensible difference of sensation between walking in the streets of London and those of Canton. People have just as much right to deny that this is so, as to deny the existence of an odour because they cannot smell it, though others can.

The magnetic conditions which conduce to inspirational receptivity, are warmth, light, clearness, and a certain amount of rarefaction of atmosphere, and therefore of elevation, with a light soil and a nature sparsely inhabited, or, in other words, as free as possible from human taint. But there are other essential conditions of a more internal kind, which are connected with the history of the locality, as affected by the character of the influences which have at different times centred upon it. Thus, wherever an opening has been made by a stream of inspiration upon it more or less constant, there nature is peculiarly bounteous in her response to the man who is struggling to offer himself to the highest sources of light; for her atoms always retain the original impregnation of the divine life, which descended through them to the hearts and brains of men, who received their inspiration in her solitudes. For although, as I have said, preparation for the highest inspiration must be acquired in the busy hum of men, and in active service for them, as well as in occasional retirement, the descent itself can only take place in comparative solitude, in conditions of environment peculiarly adapted to it, and in the especial locality indicated: therefore Moses ascended Mount Sinai, and remained there for forty days and nights; and Christ withdrew for the same period to a solitary mountain before He began His ministry; and Buddha retired for forty-seven days into the wilderness of Uravila to be tempted of the devil.

I have been led into this digression, because it has been necessary to account for the flood of inspiration which descended upon the Jewish prophets during the residence of the race in what is called the Holy Land, and also to explain why, when that race had proved itself unworthy of the high mission which had been confided to it, it was necessary to banish it from the land, in order that the elements which existed there suitable for inspirational descents, should be purified and restored, for they had already suffered corruption. Therefore it was that the land was condemned to a period of desolation—for nature, like man, requires to be devastated in order to be purified: and this land, once so densely populated, has had to lie fallow for fifteen hundred years; its flourishing cities heaps of ruins, and its population dwindling down to a mere fraction of that with which it formerly teemed. But this period of desolation has drawn almost to its close, and new conditions have been induced, which will fit it once more for its high destiny.

The future of the race to whom it once belonged must depend upon themselves. In order to show why this is so, we must recur to their history from the time when the land was given to Abram and his seed for an heritage. With Abram himself a solemn covenant was made, the terms of which are contained in the first fourteen verses of the seventeenth chapter of Genesis, and the confirmation of which was the change which took place in the names both of himself and of Sarai—in the case of Abram, by introducing the feminine letter "he," and in that of Sarai by cutting off the masculine letter "jod," and adding "he," thus signifying that to them and to their seed, was intrusted the guardianship of the mystery of the Divine Feminine being concealed within the Divine Masculine.

It is worthy of note that on the occasion of this covenant we, for the first time, find the word "Shaddai" used as a name for the Almighty,—a word of the deepest and holiest import, for in its internal meaning it signifies the Divine Feminine. We now know God in one aspect of His Trinity; as Elohim, when He created the first world; as Jehovah, when out of its wreck He reconstructed, and then destroyed, a great portion of the world which succeeded it, and again when He destroyed Sodom and Gomorrah; and now we hear of Him as Shaddai, in connection with the peopling of the world, because not only in His promises to Abram, but in other places where this name is mentioned it is generally in a similar connection; thus He says to Jacob in the thirty-fifth chapter of Genesis: "I am Shaddai; be fruitful and multiply." In the Hindoo religion we find the same Triad, represented by Brahmâ, Siva, Vishnu—the Creator, the Destroyer, the Preserver; in the case of the latter he is often represented in Hindoo temples as having many breasts,—an idea which was signified by the word "Shad," meaning in Hebrew a breast. Each member of the Hindoo Triad is androgynous,—Brahmâ, with His complement, Sarasvati, and here we have them represented almost identically in the words Abraham and Sarah, as the earthly prototype; Siva, with his complement, Devi; and Vishnu with Lakshmi. The Sakti or feminine complement of the Deity with whom she forms one, "has its roots," Mr Barth tells us, "far away in those ideas, as old as India it-
'self, of a sexual dualism placed at the beginning of things
'(in a Brahmâna of the Yajur-Veda, for instance, Prajapati
'is androgynous), or a common womb in which beings are
'formed, which also is their common tomb."[1]

The parallel between the two religions, as showing how

---

[1] The Religions of India, p. 200.

much of the Jewish nomenclature is derived from one still older, and containing the same idea, may still further be illustrated by the name given to Jacob when he struggled with the "man,"—who was in fact one of the Seraphim,—and who changed his name from Jacob to Israel: the masculine principle is called in the Vedas, Iswara, which is allied with or encloses the feminine Prakriti, hence we get Iswara-El or Israel. Therefore Jacob raised an altar which contained the whole mystery in its name, and called it El-Elohe-Israel.

But the time was at hand when this mystery was going to be embodied more permanently and elaborately than by an altar, and for this purpose a man was specially prepared, of remarkable character and attainments, who was destined to become celebrated as the great lawgiver of Israel, and the reputed author of the Pentateuch, and who is always called in Scripture the "man of the Elohim," which, as before remarked, is a feminine plural. The training of Moses as a priest of the Temple of the Sun in Egypt, the high protection he enjoyed as the adopted son of Pharaoh's daughter, and his own force of character and abilities, singularly qualified him for his lofty mission. For this he was still further prepared by his long residence with his father-in-law, Jethro, the priest of Midian, who was more deeply initiated than any man at that time in the most hidden knowledge which he imparted to Moses. This is indicated by the deference which the latter paid to his advice, and the authority with which he tendered it, as when he says: "Hearken now 'unto my voice, I will give thee counsel, and God shall be 'with thee: Be thou for thy people God-ward, that thou 'mayest bring the causes to God."[1]

The mysteries which Moses had received from the traditions handed down from Abraham and his sons, together with the stores of occult knowledge he had acquired from Jethro, and from his training in the mystical lore of Egyptian worship, especially qualified him for the task of perpetuating

---

[1] There is a curious kabbalistic legend as to the connection which subsisted between Moses and Jethro, according to which, Cain had robbed the twin sister of Abel, and therefore his soul passed into Jethro. Moses was possessed by the soul of Abel, and therefore Jethro gave his daughter to Moses.—Yalkut Chadash, fol. 127, col. 3.

them, for preservation by his people, in a form by which they should be concealed in the letter of the law, and the ceremonial observances which symbolised its deeper meaning; and this had become the more necessary, as the Jews had fallen into the habits of worship of the common people among the Egyptians, and were losing their sense of the majesty of God, in their veneration for His attributes under the forms of animals.

It is desirable here to notice the many similarities which exist between the Mosaic theology and that of Accad, from which, as well as from the funereal ritual of Egypt, it was in great part derived—more for the sake of directing attention to them, than with any view of following them into detail, which would occupy too much space. The most ancient religious observance of which we have any record is that of the Sabbath. It was strictly enforced upon the people of Eridu more than a thousand years before it was enjoined as a commandment upon Moses. So we have records at the same period of vicarious sacrifices, of distinctions made between clean and unclean animals, and of the rite of circumcision; while here, as in Egypt, we have the Ark and the Temple, with its Holy of Holies, with its veil which concealed the mysteries. "Within," says Professor Sayce, "the Temple 'bore a striking likeness to that of Solomon. At the ex-'treme end was the Paraku, or Holy of Holies, concealed by a 'curtain or veil from the eyes of the profane. . . . There 'seems to be evidence that the institution of the shew-bread 'was known in Babylonia—'On the high altar mayest thou 'found a place of feeding'—*i.e.*, a table of shew-bread. . . . 'The coffer of the little temple of Imgur-Bel, or Balawat, 'resembled in form the arks or ships, as they were termed, in 'which the gods were carried in religious processions. It 'thus gives us a fair idea of what the Israelitish Ark of the 'Covenant must have been like." [1]

So we have the Kerubu or Cherubim, whose function it was to guard the mysteries of the Temple, while the duties and ranks of the hierarchy bear a striking resemblance to that of the Jews. In fact it is clear that, whether they understood it or not, the Egyptians, the Babylonians, and the Hindoos

[1] Hibbert Lectures, pp. 64, 65, 66.

were all ancient custodians of the mystery which was now to be confided to Moses, under an outward symbolism and ordinance analogous in externals to that under which it had always been concealed.

The time has now arrived to explain the secret which the law that Moses gave to his people contains. It is described in a few words by Paul in the third chapter of his first Epistle to Timothy, though the translators of the New Testament have apparently for ecclesiastical purposes cut off the first line of the sixteenth verse to which it belongs, and added it on to the end of the fifteenth, thus making the last lines of the latter read—" Which is the Church of the living God, the pillar and ground of the truth;" whereas the pillar and ground of the truth is not applied to the Church at all, but to the mystery of godliness, and the sixteenth verse should read—" The pillar and ground of the truth—and undoubtedly great—is the mystery of godliness."[1] The apostle then goes on to tell us what this mystery, which is the pillar and ground of the truth, is—" He who was manifested in the flesh, justified in the spirit, seen of angels, preached unto Gentiles, believed on in the world, received up into glory." This mystery was revealed to Paul, but only in so far as the world to whom he preached could apprehend it—though we have indications that he himself perceived more of its real significance than externally appeared in his writings—as, for instance, where he says: " If ye have heard of the dispensation of the grace of God ' which is given me to you-ward: how that by revelation He ' made known unto me the mystery; (as I wrote afore in few ' words, whereby, when ye read, ye may understand my know- ' ledge in the mystery of Christ;) which in other ages was not ' made known unto the sons of men, as it is now revealed ' unto His holy apostles and prophets by the Spirit."[2] And Paul describes the revelation made to him when he was caught up into the third heaven, and heard " unspeakable

---

[1] This tendency of the translators, possibly unconscious to themselves, to give inaccurate renderings of the original, so as to support ecclesiastical dogmas, of which many instances occur both in the Old and New Testaments, even in the revised version, is very unfortunate and misleading.

[2] Ephesians iii. 2-5.

words" which it was not lawful for him then to utter; so again he alludes to the mystery "which had been hid from 'ages and from generations, but now is made manifest in the 'saints, and to the revelation of the mystery which was kept 'secret since the world began."

This mystery is dwelt upon with great power and detail in the Book of Enoch. Considering that this book was undoubtedly written before the advent of Christ upon earth, the numerous references which it contains to the Messianic function and secret are in the highest degree interesting. I will content myself, however, with one quotation: "In that 'day shall all the kings, the princes, the exalted, and those 'who possess the earth stand up, behold, and perceive, that He 'is sitting on the throne of His glory; that before Him the 'saints shall be judged in righteousness; and that nothing 'which shall be spoken before Him shall be spoken in vain. '. . . One portion of them shall look upon another. They 'shall be astonished and humble their countenance, and 'trouble shall seize them when they shall behold this Son of 'woman sitting upon the throne of His glory. Then shall the 'kings, the princes, and all who possess the earth, glorify Him 'who has dominion over all things, who was concealed; for, 'from the beginning, the Son of man existed in secret, whom 'the Most High preserved in the presence of His power, and 'revealed to the elect. He shall sow the congregation of the 'saints, and of the elect, and all the elect shall stand before 'Him in that day. All the kings, the princes, the exalted, 'and those who rule over the earth, shall fall down on their 'faces before Him, and shall worship Him. They shall fix 'their hopes on this Son of man, shall pray to Him, and peti-'tion him for mercy."[1]

The Messiah of Enoch is the Messiah in which the orthodox Jews still believe. As Professor Marks tells us: "The more 'troublous the time, the more hostile fanaticism waxed, the 'closer the Jew clung to the hope that persecution would 'gradually abate, although its spirit might flicker at intervals; 'and that the crowning scene of the Messianic drama would 'realise the Psalmist's anticipation of mercy and truth meeting 'together, and righteousness and peace being locked in fond

[1] Book of Enoch, chap. 61.'

'embrace. This idea finds its most intense expression in the 'apocalyptic books of Daniel and Enoch, Sirach, and the 'Sibylline Leaves, all of which date downwards from about 'the year 170 before the Christian era."[1]

The Kabbalah, in the Sohar, alludes to the Book of Enoch as having been "carefully preserved from generation to generation."

The fact that the Messiah is called the Son of woman and the Son of man in almost the same passage, and the assertion that notwithstanding He was the Son of woman and of man, He had existed in secret from the beginning as such, indicates on the part of the author of this book a very deep intromission into the sacred mysteries.

This mystery, which has generally been assumed by theologians to be the scheme of the atonement, contains, in fact, another and altogether different signification; though, in its primitive sense, the word atonement, or at-one-ment, is exactly applicable to it. That different sense is to be found in the inner meaning of the law of Moses, which while it contains arcana too profound for us yet to penetrate, still supplies us with all that is needful for our present requirements, for it shows us how Christ was its fulfilment, as He said, "I came not to destroy the law, but to fulfil it." It shows us how "the law having a shadow of good 'things to come, and not the very image of the things, can 'never with those sacrifices which they offered year by 'year make us perfect;" it shows us how "Christ is the end of the law unto righteousness, unto every one that believeth." It shows us how, what "the law could not do, in 'that it was weak through the flesh, God, sending His own 'Son in the likeness of sinful flesh, and for sin, condemned 'sin in the flesh: that the ordinance of the law might be 'fulfilled in us, who walk not after the flesh, but after the 'Spirit;" and Christ Himself said, after He was risen, to His disciples, "These are the words which I spake unto you, while 'I was yet with you, that all things must be fulfilled which 'was written in the law of Moses, and in the prophets, and 'in the Psalms, concerning me." But although we are told

---

[1] Professor Marks on the Jews in modern times—'Jewish Chronicle,' 17th February 1885.

that He opened their understanding that they might understand the Scriptures, the time had not come for them to penetrate its meaning. He had to adapt the fulfilment of the law to their gross conceptions, as Moses had been obliged to adapt the law itself to the moral and intellectual condition of the people to whom he gave it. The apostles' minds were still too much impregnated with the Jewish conception of the Deity, as a god in the likeness of a man, with all the passions of anger, jealousy, and vindictiveness, delighting in the blood of bulls and of goats, and of propitiatory sacrifices, to conceive of any other fulfilment of the law but that of a stupendous sacrifice which should take the place of all these, and therefore they imagined that this fearful Deity could derive satisfaction from the sacrifice of His own Son, as a propitiatory offering for the sins of the race He had Himself created. This darkened their understanding; and hence their conception of "repentance and remission of sins," which "should be preached in His name among all nations, beginning at Jerusalem," resolved itself into an elaboration of this propitiatory scheme, which has ever since been received among Christian Churches as the fulfilment of the law, accomplished in the person of Christ, and has thrown a veil over their moral vision, which has prevented men from recognising what the real internal meaning of the law was, in what the fulfilment consisted, and what was the true nature of that mystery which has "been kept secret since the world began," which could only be revealed by the apostles through the imperfect medium that their own crude moral condition provided, and which, had their perceptions been more deeply internal, would have been premature, and unfitted them to appeal to the moral and intellectual capacity of the congregations they addressed.

Nevertheless, much of the spirit of their teaching has been overlooked, and the literal meaning of their words strained in a wrong sense, into the construction of dogmas foreign to the whole tendency of their thought. Many passages have seemed obscure, which, read by the light which a knowledge of the mysteries throws upon them, become not only comprehensible, but indicate that the apostles themselves knew a great deal more than they could give to the people; and this is confirmed by the fact, which a study of the early history of the Church will reveal pretty plainly, that there was among themselves a class of initiated, who met for secret rites and worship—a fact which is not denied by Tertullian, as we read of "mysteries which were to be kept secret and 'concealed from all except the faithful, inasmuch as to others 'the very manner and method of their actions were unknown, 'which was observed by the pagans, who objected to the 'Christians and the secrecy of their mysteries, which charge 'Tertullian does not deny, but, confessing it, answers that it 'was the very nature of mysteries to be concealed, as Ceres 'were in Samothracia."[1] But these Christian initiates were in advance of the age, and were crushed by the early Church as soon as it had firmly established itself at Rome. Paul, indeed, alludes to the incapacity of the converts generally to receive truth in its more essential degree, when he told them that he could only feed them with milk, not with meat, for they were not able to bear it—"Nay, not even now are ye able to bear it, for ye are yet carnal." It has taken nearly two thousand years for the meat which was withheld by the apostles, and which is therefore not contained exoterically in their teaching, to be food adapted for the mind of the educated classes; but a new dispensation is dawning upon the world, and therefore it is that the mystery may be revealed; for the religious instinct craves earnestly for new food, and that food is contained in the internal meaning of the law of Moses, and of the Psalms, and of the Book of Job, and in the prophets, and in the New Testament.

It is not necessary for those who seek this new food to cast away the book they have so long cherished in the letter, but rather for some who receive their spiritual enlightenment in that way to study it; while to others it can be imparted otherwise, more secretly and more effectively, and to them the book will ever be a blessed confirmation of their own discoveries and experiences, but it will not be necessary for them, any more than a stick which has been a support to

---

[1] An Inquiry into the Constitution, Discipline, Unity, and Worship of the Primitive Church within the first Three Hundred Years after Christ. Published 1692.

an invalid is needful when he has acquired strength enough to walk alone.

It is, however, of inestimable value to those who are attempting to lead others by the light of the arcana which it contains, and to trace in it the history of the mystery which it has preserved, and which, so far as the race to whom it was confided is concerned, culminates in its first important stage with the two covenants which God made with them, and the terms of which are recorded in the 29th and 30th chapters of Deuteronomy. The curse attached to the first covenant contained in the 29th chapter was fulfilled after the crucifixion of Christ, when the second temple was destroyed and the dispersion of the race among all the nations of the earth was accomplished. For they did not recognise in the Jewish carpenter the fulfilment of the law. Therefore, when the tragedy was consummated, the law practically disappeared from outward observance. They had allowed the spirit to evaporate from the flask of which they were the guardians, and the flask was taken from them, to be restored to them, according to their belief, when they are themselves restored to their own land; but this restoration can only take place upon condition that they fulfil the second covenant, which is contained in the 30th chapter. It is too late now to give them back the letter of their old law: in these enlightened days they would not know what to do with it if they had it. It is impossible to conceive the civilised Jew of the present day returning to Levitical observances, sacrificing lambs as trespass-offerings, and having some of the blood put upon the tip of his right ear, and some upon the thumb of his right hand, and some upon the great toe of his right foot, and so forth. Either they must be content to remain exiles, and practically abandon the law—which is, in fact, the one thing that makes them Jews—or they must recognise the fact that the law was a mere outward ceremonial, which only involved obligations so long as it contained a mystery, but that with the revelation of the mystery, the law and the obligations attached to it ceased to have any *raison d'être*. But more than that: if the law and the obligations go, then so far as the Jews are concerned, the book must follow; and if the book goes, there will be nothing left of the Jew. Unless an inner meaning can be found for the book, and it is rescued from the attacks made on its literal and historical value, it must certainly perish as divine authority, from Christians no less than from Jews.

Symptoms of uneasiness are already beginning to manifest themselves among the more intelligent Jews in this direction, as is evidenced by a recent article, which I regret is too long to quote at length, but from which the following extract is well worthy of reproduction. After discussing the effect of modern criticism upon the Biblical record, the writer, Mr Alfred Henriques, says: "As to the effect of this new 'learning upon Judaism, a few remarks will now be offered. 'It is proper to observe that the patriarchs are rejected as 'entirely unhistoric characters, and are relegated to the region 'of myths and legends. If this destructive criticism can be 'maintained, the miraculous call of Abraham and the promises 'made to him must be abandoned. Doubtless these conclu- 'sions will greatly surprise pious Hebrews. The unhistoric 'character of the Biblical account of the exodus, and of the 'tremendous events said to have taken place at Sinai, is, 'however, fatal to the claims of dogmatic Judaism. It has 'long been believed that the authorship of the Ten Command- 'ments has to be sought in Egypt, where the Book of the Dead 'gives some remarkable parallelisms. These are the great 'questions on which Jewish thought has to be concentrated. 'In the present condition of Biblical criticism, it would be 'most unwise to form inflexible opinions or to assume un- 'changeable positions either favourable or antagonistic to the 'new learning. The object of the writer will be fully attained 'if he succeed in directing a very much larger share of public 'attention to questions which are vital to Jewish belief, and 'which in the near future will imperatively press for solution. 'They are questions which cannot profitably be set aside or 'ignored. The Hebrews are the people of the Book. By the 'Book dogmatic Judaism must stand or fall. It is needless 'to point to the immense antiquity of Judaism and to the 'severe trials it has gone through. Antiquity in many aspects 'is an element of weakness, not of strength. No danger that 'Judaism has ever escaped is as formidable as the present 'one. Judaism has in the past entered into contest with 'rival creeds, has overcome them all in solid argument; but the approaching combat will be of a totally different kind. None of the old weapons will avail, none of the old arguments will succeed, against an array of learning which the world has never before equalled. The field of the combat has also changed. It will not be a challenge of a doctrine or of a text, or of the interpretation of a prophecy—it will be a challenge as to the value of the records upon which *all* is founded. If the Book be unhistoric and incapable of sustaining the pretensions of dogmatic Judaism, pious Hebrews need not be disheartened. The fundamental beliefs need no historic records to validate them. A new foundation must be sought for the ancient faith, and it will no doubt be no less potent to concentrate religious fervour, than that which may be lost. For indeed, on the failure of dogmatic Judaism to fulfil the intellectual needs and aspirations of the coming generation, a new and more solid and also a more rational basis may be found for the grand and simple faith, which, rejuvenated by the infusion of modern knowledge, may still continue to give comfort and solace to those of the ancient race who cannot conscientiously sacrifice their reason or their standard of historic truth in favour of records, however ancient their origin or however beautiful their contents."[1]

The foundation for the ancient faith which Mr Henriques seeks is not a new one, for it is to be found in the principle which sustains the universe, and in the revelation of the mystery contained in the law which Moses, who was without doubt an historical personage, gave to his people. It is none the worse for being in some measure derived from the Egyptian funereal ritual, for that also contained the mystery; but its presentation will discover features calculated to touch the race, to whom the lofty mission is offered of laying this foundation for all humanity, in its most sensitive point, and to offend prejudices so deeply rooted that the operation of the Divine Spirit can alone remove them.

It is in the earnest hope that I may be guided by that same Spirit, that I now venture to approach this most profound and vital subject.

[1] The Jewish Chronicle, July 22, 1887, "Modern Biblical Criticism." Alfred Henriques.

CHAPTER XVIII.

THE MISSION OF THE JEWS—THE MYSTERY OF THE DIVINE FEMININE CONFIDED TO THEM—THE VISION OF ISAIAH—THE DIVINE FEMININE ENFOLDED IN CHRIST—THE METHOD OF HIS BIRTH—JEWISH BELIEF IN THE MESSIAH—THE VIRGIN MARY—NATURE OF THE DESCENT OF THE FEMININE PRINCIPLE—COVENANTS WITH THE JEWS—REASONS WHY THEY SHOULD RECOGNISE IN THIS PRINCIPLE THEIR MESSIAH.

THE life of a nation differs from the life of an individual in this, that the individual frequently escapes the results of his own misconduct in this world by passing away from it before the consequences, which must always, sooner or later, follow the infraction of divine laws, can overtake him; but these consequences pursue him into the next phase of his existence, and he undergoes there the penalties they involve, from which he can only escape by his own efforts, and by going through that severe disciplinary process to which he refused to submit in mortal life. The nation, on the other hand, perishes in this world, by reason of its collective violation of those same laws. History testifies to the decay and final disappearance of one form of civilisation after another, and of the nations which represented them, by reason of the vices inherent in them, and the corruption which, in some instances slowly, and in others with greater rapidity, putrefied the whole social and political system.

A special destiny was reserved, however, for the race which was intrusted with the guardianship of the Sacred Mystery; for the external form in which it was veiled, and which was called the law, was so framed as to ensure the tribal distinctiveness of its custodians, and thus endowed them with an element of cohesion which is lacking in other nations and the religions they profess. This developed a tenacity of race that has resisted the fiercest persecution—which, indeed, only had the effect of cementing it more strongly—and has tided it through epochs which witnessed the rise and fall of mighty empires.

The history of all nations is a history of moral discipline, if they would but see it. Their wars and revolutions, their pestilences and famines, are all so many moral lessons to warn them against prominent national vices, and so to give them an opportunity of averting the judgment which the indulgence of those vices must inevitably entail. But the Jews alone were carefully instructed in this fact, and were privileged in possessing a class of men who preached, and warned, and denounced incessantly,—a class of men of whom history contains no similar record, who were perpetually reminding their nation of its lofty mission, and prophesying the calamities it would bring upon itself if it proved unfaithful to it. The Jews alone recognised as a nation their sacred character, and gloried in it; calling themselves a people chosen by God, and pointing with pride to the covenants which they believed He had specially made with them, and to the infraction of which such fearful penalties were attached.

But whilst conscious that this was so, they persisted with a singular infatuation in violating even the letter of their law; in allying themselves with the natives of the land which they had received as an inheritance, contrary to the divine command; in adopting the worship of their gods, and in manifesting their contumacy in many ways.

Notwithstanding the severe affliction they underwent in their banishment to Babylon, and in the numerous hostile invasions to which their land was subjected, they remained stiff-necked to the last; their worship sank to a mere formalism, their conscience became deadened, and their spiritual perceptions so utterly blunted, that, with the exception of a very small group of persons connected with a mystical sect who devoted themselves to the study of the internal meaning of the law, there were none among them who were sufficiently illuminated to perceive that the period of the fulfilment of the first covenant was at hand, and that the time had arrived when, if they did not apprehend its inner sense, they were to be " rooted out of the land " and " cast into another land," as it is this day. Yet, notwithstanding this, they were promised that the revelation of the mystery contained in the law should still remain their inheritance, for it is written in the following verse: " The secret things belong unto the Lord our God: but those things which are revealed belong unto us and to our children for ever, that we may do all the words of this law." [1]

The reason that the history of the Jews contains a record of exceptional infidelity and backsliding, is because upon them was concentrated a terrific and sustained infernal attack. The powers of darkness well understood the loftiness of their mission if they themselves did not; the former knew the mystery contained in the law of which the latter were the guardians, and how it was to be fulfilled, and all their ingenuity was expended in blinding the eyes of the Jews to its fulfilment, and in perverting their moral sense by tempting them to repeated infractions of the outward law, with the view of destroying them utterly as a nation before it was fulfilled. In this they succeeded with nearly all the tribes; while the minority, who remained faithful to it, have never to this day recognised its fulfilment.

Not only did God treat them with infinite tenderness and long-suffering, out of compassion to the exceptionally difficult position in which they had been placed, but He made another covenant with them containing a blessing, even as the former covenant contained a curse, compliance with which would ensure their return to their own land. " If any of thy out-
' casts be in the utmost parts of heaven, from thence will the
' Lord thy God gather thee, and from thence will He fetch
' thee: and the Lord thy God will bring thee unto the land
' which thy fathers possessed, and thou shalt possess it; and
' He will do thee good, and multiply thee above thy fathers." [2]

But this blessing is made conditional on the recognition of the "Word"; and the Word, they are told, is to be found in the heart of him who opens himself to its influence. " It is not
' hidden from thee, neither is it far off: it is not in heaven, that
' thou shouldest say, Who shall go up for us to heaven, and bring
' it unto us, that we may hear it, and do it? Neither is it beyond
' the sea, that thou shouldest say, Who shall go over the sea for

[1] Deuteronomy xxix. 29. [2] Deuteronomy xxx. 4, 5.

THE FULFILMENT OF THE LAW.

' us, and bring it unto us, that we may hear it, and do it? But
' the word is very nigh unto thee, in thy mouth, and in thy
' heart, that thou mayest do it." What this Word was, was
at once recognised by some of those among the Essenes who
had studied the mysteries, and were familiar with the divine
Triad of Wisdom, Love, and Operation, and who could recognise the Word in that "Operation"; whether it took form
in a law, or in a man, or in a mystery contained both in the
law and in the man. Therefore, says Paul, who never saw
Christ, but who perceived a part, but only a part, of the sense
which is now fully to be revealed, in which Christ was the
fulfilment of the law, " For Christ is the end of the law for
' righteousness to every one that believeth. For Moses de-
' scribeth the righteousness which is of the law, That the man
' which doeth those things shall live by them. But the right-
' eousness which is of faith speaketh on this wise, Say not
' in thine heart, Who shall ascend into heaven? (that is, to
' bring Christ down from above;) or, Who shall descend into
' the deep? (that is, to bring up Christ again from the dead.)
' But what saith it? The word is nigh unto thee, even in
' thy mouth, and in thy heart: that, is, the word of faith,
' which we preach."[1]

Now the mystery which the law contained was, I have already said, the Divine Feminine principle, and the mystery in
Christ was concealed in His androgynous nature. He was the
second Adam in this, that He contained within Himself the
Divine Feminine principle enfolded within His external masculine. Moses, however, could not have given the law, had he
not contained the principle organically within his own atomic
frame. This principle has never been absolutely and entirely
withdrawn from earth, and a latent atomic connection has always been maintained with human organisms, but only in very
special cases has it been manifested. Of these the most remarkable Biblical instances were Melchizedek, Moses, Elijah,
and John the Baptist. I do not include here the founders or
sages of other religions, in whom it was more or less developed,
or Christ, who possessed another principle in addition to it.
But the case most undoubtedly interesting to the Jews is that
of Moses, of whom we are told that God " buried him, and no

[1] Romans x. 4-8.

man knows his sepulchre to this day." This signifies that the altogether exceptional development of the principle in him, and which culminated in him during his retirement on Mount Sinai, was withdrawn from earth; as it was also in the case of Elijah, on the occasion of his withdrawal. The account, to which I have already alluded, of the dispute which took place over the body of Moses between Michael and Satan, was for the possession of these Divine Feminine organic elements.

The fact that we never read of the death of those thus exceptionally favoured, implies a peculiar transference of atomic elements, under conditions which should protect them from infernal appropriation, for they contain potencies of which the Siddim were deprived by their rebellion, and which they have always desired to regain, in order that they might pervert them. Could they succeed in this, their victory over man would be assured. Hence it is that the potencies of the Divine Feminine have been so carefully guarded, and that Moses was not allowed to enter into Palestine, charged as he was with so large a measure of them, as they would have superinduced magnetic conditions in the country, too powerful for the people to bear. As it was, we owe the prophets, with their remarkable utterances, to this influence. There is a curious passage in the Talmud bearing upon this subject: "Six months did the Shechinah (or Divine Feminine) hesitate 'to depart from the midst of Israel in the wilderness, in hopes 'that they would repent. At last, when they persisted in 'impenitence, the Shechinah said, May their bones be blown; as 'it is written, Job xi. 20, 'The eyes of the wicked shall fail, 'they shall not escape, and their hope shall be as a puff of 'breath.'"[1] The puff of breath is the false or infernal pneumatic afflatus, as contradistinguished from the true and divine pneuma or breath.

It was thus that the Divine Feminine was only allowed to enter the promised land in the person of Joshua and some of the priests, in whom it was tempered and suppressed, and only made itself manifest in certain persons,—as, for instance, in Samuel, whose birth was attended by circumstances somewhat similar to those of John the Baptist, and whose mother bore

[1] Rosh Hashanah, fol. xxxi., col. 1.

a child in her old age, because, we are told, "the Lord remembered her"; and in the case of Isaiah, who received an inspiration on the subject for a special purpose, which bears so directly on the present position of the Jews in regard to this important matter, that it is necessary to examine the inner meaning of the sixth chapter, which contains it.

The prophet narrates a vision in which he saw the "Lord sitting upon a throne, high and lifted up, and His train [or the skirts thereof] filled the temple." The train or the skirts thereof signify the Shechinah. "Above it stood the seraphim: each one had six wings; with twain he covered his face, with twain he covered his feet, with twain he did fly." The first pair of wings signify "adoration," the second pair "abasement," and the third pair "obedience." "And one cried unto another and said, Holy, holy, holy, is the Lord of hosts: the whole earth is full of His glory." The three holies apply to His threefold nature—to Jehovah, masculine and feminine combined, to El, masculine, and to Shaddai, feminine. The "glory" is the glory of the Shechinah.

"And the posts of the door moved at the voice of him that cried, and the house was filled with smoke," signifies the physical and psychical effects of the Divine Feminine upon nature.

"Then said I, Woe is me! for I am undone; because I am
' a man of unclean lips, and I dwell in the midst of a people of
' unclean lips: for mine eyes have seen the King, the Lord of
' hosts." This signifies the seer's consciousness of his impurity, in the absence of the Divine Feminine principle in his organism.

The "Lord of hosts," signifies the divine male generative principle. (See chapter quoted from the Kabbalah in the Appendix.)

"Then flew one of the seraphim unto me, having a live
' coal in his hand, which he had taken with the tongs from
' off the altar; and he laid it upon my mouth, and said, Lo,
' this hath touched thy lips; and thine iniquity is taken
' away, and thy sin purged," signifies the atomic contact of the Divine Feminine with the organism of the seer.

"Also I heard the voice of the Lord, saying, Whom shall I
' send, and who will go for us? Then said I, Here am I;
' send me. And He said, Go, and tell this people, Hear ye

'indeed, but understand not ; and see ye indeed, but perceive
' not. Make the heart of this people fat, and make their ears
' heavy, and shut their eyes; lest they see with their eyes,
' and hear with their ears, and understand with their heart,
' and convert, and be healed." This signifies the impossibility
of conveying to the Jewish race at that time any conception
of the Divine Feminine.

"Then said I, Lord, how long ? And He answered, Until
' the cities be wasted without inhabitant, and the houses
' without man, and the land be utterly desolate, and the
' Lord have removed men far away, and there be a great for-
' saking in the midst of the land," signifies the desolation
which was to overtake Palestine, and the dispersion of its
race, before the knowledge of the Divine Feminine should be
conveyed to them.

"And yet in it shall be a tenth, and it shall return, and
' shall be eaten : as a teil-tree, and as an oak, whose substance
' is in them, when they cast their leaves: so the holy seed
' shall be the substance thereof," signifies that the principle
shall be preserved in Palestine, and shall form the sustenance
of those who accept Him who sowed its sacred seed in that
holy land by His death, and of those also, who, if they are
unable to accept Christ in His first advent, will open themselves to the reception of the Divine Feminine.

I may here note incidentally, in illustration of the degree
of sanity which characterises the religious instinct of the
present day, that if any man now was to say that he had
seen such a vision as the one above narrated, or indeed such
as any of those recorded by the prophets, he would instantly
be put into a lunatic asylum. The lapse of a certain number
of years makes divine revelation at one time what would be
madness at another. What is divine revelation, and what
insanity, is left to be determined by the clerical and medical
professions, who have in this nineteenth century compounded
between them the strangest jumble of childish superstition
and ignorant scepticism which the world has ever seen. It is
to their guardianship, assisted by courts of so-called justice,
that the consciences and the liberties of unfortunate human
beings are confided.

The fulfilment of the law, then, consisted in the advent to

earth of a Being atomically bisexually constructed, whose nativity took place under circumstances which ensured His complete union, through the operation of the Divine Feminine, with His own feminine complement.

Christ thus approached, as nearly as external conditions admitted, the primitive man, and in this sense was a second Adam. This completion of His twofold nature, however, did not take place until He ascended out of the water, after being baptised by John the Baptist, when we have it recorded that the spirit, or pneuma, descended upon Him in the form of a dove. This was the outward symbol of His own feminine complement, and in recognition thereof there was heard a voice from heaven saying, "This is my beloved Son, in whom I am well pleased."

It will be explained later how John was specially prepared atomically by the circumstances of his birth, for the important function he was called upon to perform, which was to impart a special pneumatic element contained in his organism, to that of Christ—the outward and visible sign of the interior contact thus established, being figured by the rite of baptism. This was, in fact, a baptism of the Holy Spirit and of fire.

The real signification of baptism consists in its typification of the descent of the Divine Feminine; for water was an emblem of that principle. Thus *Aima*, the Supernal Mother, who is eternally conjoined with *Ab*, the Great Father, is sometimes called "The Great Sea," and to her are attributed the divine names, Elohim and Jehovah Elohim.[1] This rite had been understood and practised by the Jewish sect of Essenes, to which John the Baptist belonged, and by other sects which had preceded it, from ancient times; but its signification was soon lost in the early Christian Church, though certain of the apostles, who had been instructed in the hidden mystery by Christ, understood, when they were commanded to baptise in the name of the holy pneuma or *Ruach*, that this spirit was the feminine principle of God, as the feminine Hebrew word *Ruach* implies. In this sense, baptism typified the regenerating influence of the Divine Feminine principle in man, though the Church soon con-

[1] Mather's Kabbalah, p. 25.

verted it into a mere formal ceremony, by means of which man was to be saved from eternal torment in hell-fire.

It is not to be wondered at that the Jews failed to recognise their Messiah in Christ, for it involved the belief in a double Messianic advent, which is nowhere clearly prophesied in the Old Testament, excepting to those who could interpret the hidden meaning of the visions and predictions of its seers. The necessity for the first Messiah was to sow the seed of the Divine Feminine, the harvest of which the second Messiah, whose approach is now at hand, was to reap. But as real belief cannot be acquired by an intellectual effort, but descends by inspiration to the affections, a belief in the first Messiah is not necessary to those who desire to form the first-fruits of that harvest. When once such persons, of whatever race or religion, have prepared themselves by the necessary discipline, to receive the Divine Feminine into their organisms, their subsurface faculties will be opened to the apprehension of all mysteries appertaining to the proper exercise of the new forces which will descend upon them, for the more perfect service of God, their race, and of humanity at large. The Jews will not be judged because they failed altogether to apprehend the nature and mission of the first Messiah; but let them beware how they turn their backs upon the second, who now invites them to receive Him atomically in the inmost recesses of the organism, in His twofold nature—as Bride and Bridegroom, as King and Queen.

Here I must refer to the belief of certain initiates among the kabbalistic Jews in regard to the Messiah. As a rule, the sentiment of the nation at large upon this point is very vague, and based upon divers renderings of Talmudic traditions, while some among the more advanced of Western Jews, who, however, are still called by that name, go so far as to repudiate any anticipation of a Messiah at all. But the mystical, oriental, ultra-orthodox Jew, who is profoundly versed in the Kabbalah, entertains secret views in regard to its meaning of which his co-religionists know nothing; and he, although disbelieving most profoundly in the Messianic character of Christ, whom he holds in horror, does nevertheless believe that the tetragrammation contains the

Messianic mystery. Now, the tetragrammaton consists of the four letters which compose the name of Jehovah, IHVH— or Yod (masculine), He (feminine), Vau (masculine), He (feminine). These possess a great variety of significations, according to the order in which they are placed, while the word itself is too holy to be pronounced; nor is it supposed that any, except a few initiated, know the sacred pronunciation. Read in their proper order, they signify kabbalistically, *Yod*, the Father; *He*, the mother; *Vau*, the Son; and *He*, the Bride— that is, the Bride of the Son, with whom *He* is eternally and androgynously united (see Appendix). Therefore the Kabbalists to this day accept the belief of the ancient rabbis, that the Messianic advent will be the descent of the Divine Feminine, as it is written in the Book of the Greater Holy Assembly: "And in the days of King Messiah there shall be no need 'that one should teach another; for that one Spirit, who in 'Herself includeth all spirits, knoweth all wisdom and under- 'standing, counsel and might, and is the spirit of science and 'of the fear of the Lord, because She is the Spirit compre- 'hending all spirits."[1] And again, in the 'Book of Concealed Mystery,' where the "horn" mentioned in the Old Testament is interpreted as meaning "influx from the Mother," as in the 132d Psalm, 17th verse: "'There shall the horn of David flourish'—that is, the Queen (the Bride of the Son) shall receive influx from the Mother;" and again, in paragraphs 41, 42: "For it is written, Josh. vi. 5, 'And it shall be when the 'horn of jubilee is sounded.' This is the splendour of the 'jubilee, and the truth (path) is crowned by the Mother '(that is), the horn which receiveth the horn and the spirit, 'that it may restore the spirit of *Yod He* unto *Yod He* (that 'is, when the spirit is to be given to the Son, His Mother 'contributed as much—which is the horn, the brilliancy—as 'the increase which He receiveth from the Father). And 'this is the horn of jubilee, . . . and *He* (fem.) is the spirit 'rushing forth over all (because the Mother is the world to 'come, when in the resurrection all things will receive the 'spirit), and all things shall return into their place (like as in 'the jubilee, so in the world to come)."[2]

The jubilee here alluded to corresponds to the millennium

[1] Mather's Kabbalah, p. 133.   [2] Ibid., p. 107.

of the Christians. The whole of these obscure and mystical writings, which are replete with the most profound inspiration, though they are altogether repudiated by Western Jews as possessing any authority, are full of arcana containing the mystery of both the first and second advents of the Son and the Bride, contained in the last two letters of the tetragrammation, which are concealed from the most learned Kabbalists in the absence of the key furnished by the first advent. The fact, however, that they understand what the nature of the approaching Messianic advent is to be, places them in a far more favourable position for the reception of the Bride and Bridegroom, than their advanced and civilised co-religionists of Western countries, who ignore it.

Nevertheless, though the Jews of every shade of opinion may refuse to accept our explanation, we must, for the sake of Christians, return to the details of Christ's appearance upon earth, in order to show how the Messianic advent, which so many of them are looking for, has become possible.

Upon the completion of His bisexual nature, through atomic contact with John the Baptist, Christ retired for forty days into the wilderness to be tempted of the devil. In the internal meaning contained in the record that has been given us of His temptations,—which was, in fact, His own description of them to His disciples,—we have conveyed to us a summary of the nature of the trials, temptations, and ordeals through which every man and woman will have to pass, who receives the bisexual life which is now descending upon the world, whereby we are entering the path which is leading us back to an approximate image of our Maker.

It was a dim perception of the Godlike nature that Christ had thus acquired, which caused His deification by His apostles, and in the religion which they founded; but though His actual nature differed from ours in this respect, and also in respect of His origin, it did not make Him God, except in the sense that any man who can embody this Divine Feminine principle can become absorbed in God.

The profound significance of Christ's mission on earth, consists in the fact that it is through Him that the channel for it is provided. In order to explain this, I must again revert to the atomic structure of the universe, and of all that it contains.

I should be considered a lunatic if I ventured to assert the possibility of a man coming into the world otherwise than by the ordinary process of procreation, or of his passing away from it otherwise than by the ordinary process of corruption, were it not fortunately the case that this is admitted, or professed to be admitted, by all who call themselves Christians. What they would deny is that this should be possible without violating any law of nature. Now, not only is this perfectly possible under natural law, but the day is not so very far distant, when the organic changes, which are now in their incipient stage, will have reached such a point that this possibility will be made manifest. I have already described how the human organism became as it were locked up by a winter frost, which set in to arrest its control in its fluid condition, by the lower region of the previous orb. Since that time it has strained against its icy fetters, unable to free itself from the bondage of incrustation of gross atomic substance, and enthralled by the limitations of surface sensuous perceptions. This is what Paul means when he says, " For ' we know that the whole creation groaneth and travaileth in ' pain until now. And not only they, but ourselves also, which ' have the first-fruits of the Spirit [or the Divine Feminine], ' even we ourselves groan within ourselves, waiting for the ' adoption, to wit, the redemption of the body,"—which can only be achieved by its operation.

But the thaw is setting in, the atomic incrustation is becoming attenuated, witness the phenomena of hypnotism, telepathy, spiritualism, and those attendant upon various phases of what are called "nervous" maladies. The effect of this is to bring about great variations in the conditions under which atomic force manifests itself in the human organism. I have already described the three methods of contact between the visible and invisible worlds, and will presently enter with more detail into the process by means of which this force acts, through pneumatic-atomic interlocking, and thus imparts a new vitality to our frames, and a new potency to our faculties. It is to this change that Paul alludes when he says, " for the earnest expectation of the creature waiteth for the manifestation of the sons of God." This manifestation of the sons of God will enable them once more to unite themselves with the daughters of men, as they did in old time, and once more visitants from the nether sphere will appear on earth, and it will become the arena of the conflict at which I hinted in the introductory chapter, and those who will engage in it are thus described in the Revelation: " For they ' are the spirits of devils, working miracles, which go forth ' unto the kings of the earth and of the whole world, to ' gather them to the battle of that great day of God Almighty. ' Behold, I come as a thief. Blessed is he that watcheth, and ' keepeth his garments, lest he walk naked, and they see his ' shame. And he gathered them together into a place called ' in the Hebrew tongue Armageddon."

Now it is quite within the bounds of possibility that this atomic change for which the world is being gradually prepared, may have taken place under very exceptional circumstances, and in a single instance, nearly nineteen hundred years ago; for there is scarcely a law in nature that is not subject to irregularity and variation, and this is especially true of the laws which govern the will and the emotions in their relation to the reproduction of life.

In order to apprehend this, it is necessary to understand that the propagation of every human soul into the visible part of our universe, is preceded by its generation into that which is invisible. As by death we are born again from this world into the other, so by birth here we die out of the other, after having been generated into it from the Infinite Source of all, by the interaction of successive male and female atomic elements, through a long series of beings, as a vital spark or soul-germ, which is finally let down into human organisms, there to receive from the earthly parents an atomic overlay, derived more or less from their physical and moral natures, but still retaining its own essential characteristics as to atomic sensibility and capacity for recombination. The moral and intellectual condition of a being born into this world depends not so much on its human parents, from whom it has derived its fleshly covering and many of its hereditary characteristics and resemblances, as upon its more immediate invisible progenitors, who are usually in blood affinity with its parents, and who by similarity of moral constitution and temperament are atomically allied with them. It is for this reason we often find that after three or four generations even physical resemblances will be reproduced. It is perfectly possible, therefore, for a child to be born here, whose immediate invisible progenitors were exceptionally gifted with the faculty of endowing a soul-germ with a peculiar receptivity to atomic combinations, which should render it sensitive to direct special operation upon its organism, and this receptivity might be still further developed by growth and cultivation.

It is thus that mediums appear every now and then capable of achieving the most phenomenal results—by no effort of their own, but simply because their atomic elements are so constituted that they can be invaded by those of invisible beings, who, in cases of materialisation, literally clothe themselves externally with those elements. The bodies thus formed are composed of materials drawn from the grosser atoms of physical nature; but in such cases the contact is made by surface adhesion, not by internal combinations.

Where, however, a soul-germ is projected into the world by progenitors who have attained lofty spiritual conditions, through natural parents who have also been especially prepared by moral training and previous insemination of vital currents from a pure source, that soul-germ would, upon being let down into them, in its turn develop into a mortal exceptionally endowed with atomic sensitiveness and receptivity to vital forces directed from the beings to whom it owed its origin in the invisible world, and with whom an interior atomic combination would be effected.

This was the case with the Virgin Mary, and thus it was that a soul-germ was projected into her organism by invisible agency, and clothed upon with fleshly particles without the aid of human instrumentality. Buddhists in the same way maintain that Gautama was born of a virgin.

It follows as a matter of course that the atomic structure of a child born under these conditions differs from that of ordinary men. It was open to the in-flowing of energies from the invisible world, and possessed a capacity for their distribution and radiation which resulted in those phenomena called "miraculous," by the aid of which the sick were healed, the elements dominated, material substance indefinitely increased, natural life restored, and invisible transference effected from one locality to another; and it further follows that the process of translation from this world was also attended with different atomic conditions, from whence resulted the phenomena which succeeded the crucifixion of Christ, and the death of His natural body, but not its corruption in the usual course of nature.

The fact that it was only through the descent of the Divine Feminine principle into the organism of the Virgin, that it could become enfolded into that of her babe, invests her with a character of peculiar sanctity, and with spiritual functions, having reference to this world, of a very high order. It is due to a sort of dumb consciousness of this fact, that she occupies such a prominent position in the worship of the Greek and Roman Churches, and which, in the latter, has found expression in the dogma of the Immaculate Conception. She is the atomic link between the invisible progenitor and the "Son of man"—so called because the source of His being had been Himself a man. She now presides with Him over that divine descent into the world which first touched her organism; and is worthy of all the worship and adoration which she receives at the hands of those who have exalted her into her rightful position of an intermediary, but who wrongly style her the Mother of God. The peculiar relation which she bears to Christ, is a mystery which can only be apprehended by those who have received into their organisms that most sacred principle which she represents, and against which the prejudices of what is called Protestant Christendom, have erected a serious barrier. Nevertheless, those who honour the Virgin Mary, and invoke the potencies of that life which she imparted to her Son, will progress far more rapidly in bisexual life than those who do not.

This explanation of the functions of the Virgin, and the birth of Christ, is not derived from any preconceived idea, based on the Biblical statement that He had no natural father; for until I began to write this account of His birth, I did not believe that statement, it never having been shown to me before that it was a true one. I feel therefore impelled to make it against my preconceptions in the matter; but as I do so, the certainty arises in my mind that Christ was thus exceptionally born into the world, in order that a contact of a new kind might be established between Him and the inhabitants of those regions, who form an atomic chain which finally attaches itself to the Almighty. He thus, in conjunction with the Virgin, becomes the essential connecting-link between all human beings, and the universal Father and Mother; and there is no phrase which more accurately expresses His intermediate position than that which is used when prayers are offered "through Jesus Christ our Lord." Thus He is the mediator or intermediary between God and man; and thus so many of those texts with which the New Testament teems, and from which the false doctrine has been coined that He was a blood-offering and a sacrifice for guilty man to appease an angry God, receive their literal and exact application. In one sense He was a blood-offering and a sacrifice, but not in the sense usually received, but in one quite different. It was necessary that He should shed His blood, not to appease an angry God, but in order to distribute into nature the atomic elements of the Divine Feminine with which He was charged. Therefore He said, " Verily, verily, I say unto you, Except a corn of wheat fall into the ground and die, it abideth alone: but if it die, it bringeth forth much fruit."

The atoms of that blood, and of that fleshly covering, which passed into nature, were like a drop of some potent medicine infused into the decaying structure of the world's vitality. Ever since it has been silently imparting its health-giving vigours. It is true there has been a long period of apparent religious stagnation since that sublime event, but it has only been apparent. The seed seemed dead, but it was all the time germinating; and the energies had been slowly storing themselves in preparation for a great crisis foretold by Him in the words: "Now is the 'judgment of this world: now shall the prince of this world 'be cast out. And I, if I be lifted up from the earth, will 'draw all men unto me." For this purpose He needed to be born into the earth through a natural woman, and to die, and be lifted up from it, because He could only thus acquire an atomic construction which would enable Him to come into close affinity with man, and so draw all men unto Him. There is no other being in that world, constituted as to His organic elements with reference to ours as He is; and hence

He is our Saviour, to whom alone we must cling, and through whom alone we can draw the vital currents which will impart the potency necessary for the salvation of the race.

But while this applies to Christians, who are thus exceptionally favoured in that they can invoke Christ, with a full understanding of their reason for doing so, it does not exclude those who have no intellectual appreciation of, or belief in, it. A method has been provided, in the infinite love of God, by which the Divine Feminine principle can descend, through Christ, to all who love the neighbour better than themselves, and are ready to give themselves for humanity—whether they be Materialists, Agnostics, Jews, Moslems, Buddhists, or of any other religion, or form of philosophy or superstition.

There were two reasons why what seems to us so long an interval should elapse between Christ's sacrifice of Himself, and His return in the plenitude of His might, to accomplish, through the organisms of those who yield themselves to Him, the work which He had begun. One was, that it has taken all these years for the seed which He sowed in the world, through His body and blood, to germinate. The other is, that it has taken all these years before a sufficiently powerful pneumatic battery could be charged, and an atomic chain could be prepared out of the organisms of those who have passed into the invisible world in the faith and love of Christ, to transmit the forces which are necessary for the world's redemption. This vital energy had to be stored both here and there. It is through the chain thus formed that we reach Christ, and that He reaches us; and it is through atomic sympathy, by means of the energies stored here, that those who feel the truth of what is here written, will be attracted to each other. As soon as the earthly battery is powerful enough to draw down the life which is waiting to be poured out upon us, those which have been hidden from us by death hitherto will be made manifest. This is "the manifestation of the sons of God," and when the atomic combinations are complete between ourselves and those which have gone before, "then 'we which are alive and remain shall be caught up together 'with them in the clouds, to meet the Lord in the air: and so 'shall we ever be with the Lord." This does not, of course, mean a literal ascension in our present bodies, but an atomic modification of them, which will altogether alter our relations to matter in its existing form, and enable us to exercise the same powers, which are not unknown to fakirs in the East and mediums in the West, though it will be under conditions altogether different from those which operate in their case, and enable us to unite ourselves with those who are in approximately like condition with ourselves.

Then we shall be able to bear, what it is not possible for us to bear now, a more direct contact with Him who will return in glory to lead this great redemptive movement, and be our leader in the great battle which is impending. This is what is called by theologians "the second coming of Christ," and it is in anticipation of this event, now not far distant, that we are called upon to engage without delay in the work of preparation. For even now He begins, by a process presently to be explained, to steal into the hearts of each one of us; silently, but surely, to those who open themselves to Him. Therefore He says,—"Behold, I come as a thief; blessed is he that watcheth."

The reason that this warning, while it applies with the utmost force to all of us, should be especially heeded by Jews, is because they, as the custodians of the mysteries contained in Christ and in their law, are called upon to lead into the world the full revelation of them; and because failure to do so will bring upon them the judgment pronounced in the second covenant. For what is the doom attached to the non-fulfilment of their part of this covenant? "But if thine 'heart turn away, so that thou wilt not hear, but shalt be 'drawn away, and worship other gods, and serve them; I 'denounce unto you this day, that ye shall surely perish, and 'that ye shall not prolong your days upon the land whither 'thou passest over Jordan to possess it." The gods here spoken of are not the gods of other religions, which have long since lost all attractions for the Jews; but the great god Mammon, whom they have worshipped more devoutly and more successfully than the people of any other race do; to such an extent, that the wealthy, civilised, and intellectually cultured Jew has not only lost all patriotic sentiment in regard to the land of his forefathers, but shrinks with dismay from the prospect of the coming of that Messiah whom he expects, and from the sacrifices and obligations which the advent of the Prince of Peace would involve. Such are they who desire only to be left to wallow amid the flesh-pots of Egypt; and any Moses who should arise and bid them to follow him to the desert of personal suffering, discipline, and self-sacrifice, as a needful preparation for entering the promised land and welcoming their King, would be rejected as a fanatic, and denounced as a traitor to that golden calf which they have set up as their god, and which they so diligently worship.

It is most likely, if this appeal finds a response in any Jewish heart, it will be rather amongst those who pray for the reunion of the Jehovah with the Shechinah, than among those who have lost all interest in the inner meaning contained in the law, who are rapidly abandoning even its letter, and who can regard with composure the disappearance of the Book itself, and the prospect of "a new and more solid and more rational basis" than the Book affords, "for the grand and simple faith" of their forefathers.

But the Book itself, when rightly understood, affords this new and solid and rational basis. Unfortunately it is a basis which can only be built upon by those who are not utterly blinded by prejudice. For, in the words of one of your own prophets, "the Lord hath poured out upon you the spirit of 'deep sleep, and hath closed your eyes: the prophets and 'your rulers, the seers hath he covered. And the vision of all 'is become unto you as a book that is sealed, which men 'deliver to one that is learned, saying, Read this, I pray thee: 'and he saith, I cannot; for it is sealed."[1] And yet, if the eyes of your inner understanding could be opened, and you could as a race adopt the view of the descent of the Divine Feminine here set forth, you would be the direct means in God's hands of overturning every Church in Christendom; for that view is as much opposed to their theology and to their prejudices as it is to yours, and the first achievement of those of your people who can see in Christ the channel for it, will be the destruction of that so-called Christian creed which has for so many centuries persecuted you in His name.

[1] Isaiah xxix. 10.

For the benefit of those oriental Jews who still accept the Kabbalah as authoritative, I will here insert a fragment of its teaching on the subject of the nature and operation of the Divine Feminine :—

"Come and behold! When the Most Holy Ancient One, 'the Concealed of all Concealments, desired to be formed 'forth, He conformed all things under the form of Male and 'Female; and in such place wherein Male and Female are 'comprehended.

'For they could not permanently exist save in another 'aspect of Male and Female (their countenances being joined 'together).

'And this wisdom, embracing all things when it goeth 'forth and shineth forth from the Most Holy Ancient One, 'shineth not save under the form of Male and Female.

'Therefore is this wisdom extended, and it is found that 'it equally becometh Male and Female. Chokmah Ab Binah 'Am. Chokmah is the Father, and Binah is the Mother; 'and therein are Chokmah, wisdom, and Binah, understand-'ing, counterbalanced in perfect equality of Male and Female. 'And therefore are all things established in the equality of 'Male and Female; for were it not so, how could they sub-'sist?'[1] This beginning is the Father of all things—the 'Father of all fathers; and both are mutually bound together, 'and the one path shineth unto the other—Chokmah, wisdom, 'as the Father; Binah, understanding, as the Mother.

'It is written, Prov. ii. 3, 'If thou callest Binah, the 'Mother.'

'When they associated together they generate, and are 'expanded into truth.

'In the teaching of the school of Rav Yeyeva, the Elder, it 'is thus taught: 'What is Binah, the Mother of understand-'ing?' Truly when they are associated together.

'Assuredly Yod, I, impregnateth the letter He, H, and 'produceth a Son, and She Herself bringeth Him forth.

'But they both are found to be the perfection of all things 'when they are associated together, and when the soul is in 'them, the Syntagma of all things findeth place.

[1] Here is authority derived from the most ancient tradition for "woman's rights."

'For in their conformations are they found to be the 'perfections of all things—Father and Mother, Son and 'Daughter.

'These things have not been revealed save unto the Holy 'Superiors, who have entered therein and departed there-'from, and have known the paths of the Most Holy God '(may He be blessed), so that they have not erred in them, 'either on the right hand or on the left."[1]

There are two reasons why this lofty mission has been in the first instance offered to the Jews. The first is, because Christ was a Jew, and He is thus enabled to occupy an exceptional relation to His own race by reason of atomic affinity, even though they may not consciously accept Him. This exists to a greater or less degree among all nations and races, but among none to the same extent that it does among the Jews. Therefore it is, that it has been imposed upon them to keep themselves exclusively apart, so that their blood might not be tainted with intermarriage, and that this internal structural condition might be maintained, by which they could be interiorly and atomically united with the channel for the Messianic descent of the Divine Feminine, and could therefore be acted upon by Christ with a more direct potency and energy than those who are not of His own blood. And the second reason is, because the law not only contains the mystery of His bisexual nature, by means of which this potency can be brought to bear, but it also contains the whole method of the construction of Messianic society upon a theocratic basis, differing from anything that the world has ever seen, and which will contain within itself the solution of all those social and political problems which have distracted the civilisation of the nineteenth century, and which threaten now to overturn it.

Therefore it was prophesied that the day should come when ten men should "take hold out of all languages of the nations, 'even shall take hold of the skirt of him that is a Jew, saying, 'We will go with you; for we have heard that Elohim is 'with you.'"[2]

---

[1] Mather's Kabbalah, chap. viii. of the 'Book of the Lesser Holy Assembly,' p. 281—" Concerning the Father and Mother in special."
[2] Zechariah viii. 23.

The task of the reconstruction of this new society will be committed to the Jews, to be built up by them in conformity with the instructions concealed in the hidden meaning of their law, for it is thus, and thus only, that the temple can ever be rebuilt in Zion, and thus, and thus only, that the words of the prophet Isaiah can be fulfilled, "that the 'mountain of Jehovah's house shall be established in the 'top of the mountains, and shall be exalted above the hills; 'and all nations shall flow unto it. And many people shall 'go and say, Come ye, and let us go up to the mountain of 'Jehovah, to the house of Elohim of Jacob; and He will 'teach us of His ways, and we will walk in His paths: for 'out of Zion shall go forth the law, and the word of Jeho- 'vah from Jerusalem."[1]

The Book of Ezekiel is full of prophecy regarding Israel's restoration, and the visions, from the fortieth chapter to the end especially, contain arcana, concealing under the figure of the rebuilding of the temple, instructions for the rearing of a social structure upon a divine model, which shall be theocratic in its form, hierarchic in its constitution, and co-operative in its organisation.

The modern Jew can expect no literal fulfilment of this mystical symbolism. He must either accept some such interpretation as is here offered, or discover another, and this I am not aware of his having yet attempted to do. It will not do for him to sit down apathetically and wait for some unknown fulfilment, for in that case he will never recognise it when it comes. It is only by ardent and disinterested service of God and the neighbour, that his eyes can be opened, and his ears quickened, and his heart softened.

Excepting among the more "advanced" section of Western Jews, the advent of the Messiah is still universally believed in by the nation; and although I have explained in this chapter, that those who apprehend what I believe to have been the true nature of the work of Christ on earth, will see in it the preparation for His second coming, I repeat that it is not necessary that Jews who desire to receive an inflow of Messianic or Divine Feminine life now, should begin by doing violence to their prejudices, and accept the view of Christ's

[1] Isaiah ii. 2, 3.

work which has here been set forth. What is above all things necessary is, that they should recognise the feminine element in the Messiah whom they expect; that they should divert their gaze from the angry vindictive Father, upon whom it has been so long riveted, to the tender loving Mother, the mystery of whose nature was concealed in the Shechinah, and of whose secret presence among men, they have been the ancient and unconscious guardians. It is in Her outstretched arms that they will find their Messiah; and if, when the revelation is made of His twofold presence among them, they are unable to recognise in it the human form whom we call Christ, He will still remain Christ to us, while to them He will appear as the long-looked-for conqueror, and their deliverer from the social and spiritual bondage from which they have so long suffered.

Although these prophecies seem sure, they cannot override the free-will of those concerning whom they are made; for there are others equally explicit, foreshadowing the judgment which will follow non-compliance with the covenant, which only made these blessings conditional on its fulfilment. It is expressly stated, in the event of unfaithfulness to this trust, "I denounce to you this day, that ye shall surely perish." And this consummation must inevitably follow upon the abandonment of the Book, and the adoption instead of that "new and more solid and more rational basis" for the "grand old simple faith," when it is "rejuvenated by the infusion of moral knowledge," as proposed by the writer of the article already quoted. I have shown what the value of modern learning in matters of religion amounts to, and it would be difficult to imagine a greater act of sacrilege than that of supplanting the Book by the 'Origin of Species' or the 'Descent of Man.' This is being drawn away and worshipping other gods, and serving them with a vengeance. As surely as this is done, must the race perish, for there will be nothing left to hold it together. The law will vanish with the Book, and the children of Abraham will take unto themselves wives from the women of the lands in which they dwell, and be lost for ever in the society which they have helped to corrupt.

If the Book be abandoned, the law spurned, and its fulfilment denied, there is no way by which this fate can be averted. Nor can the Book be retained, the law preserved, and its fulfilment accomplished, excepting as here set forth. "I call 'heaven and earth to record this day against you, that I have 'set before you life and death, blessing and cursing: therefore 'choose life, that both thou and thy seed may live."

CHAPTER XIX.

THE TRUE POSITION OF WOMAN—THE FALSE POSITION ASSIGNED HER BY CIVILISATION—HER NEW FUNCTIONS IN LIFE—THE DESCENT OF THE DIVINE FEMININE THROUGH HER—THE CO-OPERATIVE STRUGGLE OF THE SEXES FOR PURITY—WOMAN'S RIGHTS—THE TRUE HIGHER EDUCATION OF WOMAN.

ALTHOUGH the Jews may thus be intimately associated with the great scheme of the elevation of humanity to new and higher conditions, it need scarcely be said that it in no way depends upon them, and that it is they, and not the world, that will suffer by their not co-operating in it.

The earth received an electric shock when contact was established with the battery of the Divine Femininity, by the death of Christ upon it; and it is in no human power to impede the storage of that transcendent energy which has ever since been transmitted, or to hinder its ultimate manifestation.

It is to this manifestation that Christ alluded so frequently to His disciples, though they did not perceive the interior meaning; as, for instance, when He explained to them the parable of the tares and wheat. And this is "the good seed," of which He spoke, when He said, "He that soweth the good seed is the Son of man;" and this is the "kingdom of heaven" which He likened to "treasure hid in a field, the which when a man hath found he hideth, and for joy thereof goeth and selleth all that he hath and buyeth that field;" and to "a pearl of great price;" and to "a net that was cast into the sea;" and to "a grain of mustard-seed, which, when it is ' sown, it groweth up, and becometh greater than all herbs, ' and shooteth out great branches; so that the fowls of the air 'may lodge under the branches of it;" and to "leaven which 'a woman took and hid in three measures of meal, until the 'whole was leavened."

It is to this indestructible and all-pervading principle that man will owe his salvation, and it is to its method of operation that we must now turn our attention.

It has already been shown how the poisonous element which we call evil, and which is the cause of all the crime, disease, poverty, and suffering in the world, entered into it through the organism of woman, and tainted the springs of human life. The immediate effect of the woman's fall was to abase her before the man, who visited upon her the affliction she had brought upon him, and the internal separation from himself which was the consequence of it, by reducing her to a position of inferiority.

Hence it is that, as far as we can trace back in history, woman has in all countries been regarded as man's inferior, and this tradition exists most strongly in the East, and in the vicinity of those regions which were the cradle of the Noachic race. In some of the sects in these countries woman is not even supposed to have a soul; she is not instructed in matters of religion, or allowed to take part in worship; and in all of them she is treated as a slave, and ground down under the iron heel of a social, if not always a domestic tyranny. In the most civilised countries of the West, the state of the law as regards woman and her relations to man, especially her husband, is a disgrace to our age. Her most sacred instincts are violated, her inmost shrine of purity is legally outraged, and she is dragged through the mire of law courts, a spectacle for gods and men. There is no fouler stain upon that dishclout covered with spangles, which we call our civilisation, than the position which it still assigns to woman; nothing more anti-Christian—for it prostitutes the principle embodied in Christ, and which He sanctified upon earth by the sacrifice of His body and blood. But now its pent-up energies are finding irregular and disorderly vent in woman herself. Already she is beginning to make efforts, more or less frantic and misdirected, to assert her rights; but in default of any interior perception of what these rights are, she will only succeed in creating confusion and producing discord. The hope for woman lies in the recognition by man of the Divine Feminine principle in God. When once he clearly perceives that God is a dual Being, containing within Himself woman as well as man, as the word "Jehovah" signifies, he will see that —as it is impossible for one part of God's being to be inferior to another part—woman must be essentially man's equal.

The mistake that woman now makes is to suppose that, feeling herself to be man's equal, she is therefore qualified to exercise the same functions as man, to engage in the same pursuits, and to compete with him in the same avocations. Her province is to inspire man, not to rival him, to strengthen him by her love, not to drain him of the elements which he needs for his work in life, by struggling to surpass him in it. Woman represents the affectional side of humanity, whilst man represents its intellectual faculty and executive capacity. Woman, therefore, as the Divine Feminine descends, will be exonerated from the hardening cares of material productiveness, and will now stand, God willing, in growing grace as those lilies of the field, while man remains their outer providence. They will train themselves to watch for the tracings of God's workmanship in man, and to offer to that their reverence and the sustaining power of their affections; they will not regard themselves as the immediate instruments for the divine application of power to the world's needs. They will feel no responsibility in devising the ways and means of external existence, nor suggesting the plans and movements for it. They will not venture to formulate opinions as to how men should act in great things or in small; they will feel that they stand as media for the transmission of a moral force which makes true action in the men a possibility; and when, in loyalty to their own internal insight and to their outgoing love, they give to men prepared to receive them, some fresh perceptions of greater or lesser truth, it will be by appreciation of some force or growth or desire in man's nature, which he failed to recognise, which her love discerns, but which he alone knows how to apply in life's activity. She can reveal him to himself as she learns meekly to look in him for signs of how God works through him; but the true woman owns not the harsher intellectual faculty required for making active impress on the external world. The machinery of her nature is not constructed for direct contact with the resistances excited in external life by human activities, and she does herself deep injury if she exposes herself needlessly to such contact. But in direct ratio with her conception of the vastness of man's work in all the universe, which she feeds with elements that she alone can draw from the divine immensity, will be the delicacy of her succouring service. She will train herself to take up the minute tenderness of the divine currents, and apply them to those intricate necessities of men, for which they are destined. With the expanding of her bosom-love will come the multiplication of her sensitive atomic fibres, and their vibratory capacity. She will thus grow, educating herself by the whisper of God's love that she will hear every hour, more watchful, more gentle, more tender, more reverential, as she becomes more potent to all men, and as she seeks to know all the fulness and all the littleness of the divine service. In the degree in which she does this, will the man, who is opening himself to the same influence, recognise in her the divinely appointed channel for the transmission of that force by which his intelligence can be inspired, and his creative faculties operate; and he will reverence her not only as his equal, but as his presiding genius, drawing from God those rich stores of life with which he is supplied through her. He will feel her to be his indispensable copartner in the great evolutionary task to which he has set his hand, while he becomes in turn the medium through which her love flows out upon humanity; inspiring him the while with an exquisite sense of unison with her, and revealing to him unsuspected depths of capacity for enjoyment, in the absolute unselfishness of a love that demands nothing, but that floods him with its life by the very act of pouring through him. Such a love the world at present knows nothing of; but Christ knew of it, when he said, "Behold, a new commandment I give unto you, that ye love one another; as I have loved you, that ye also love one another." Had it not been that the love was new—for His love contained in it the Divine Feminine—there would have been nothing new in the commandment; for people had always been in the habit of loving each other, after their own selfish fashion. The newness of the commandment consisted in the newness of the love, which was to be fashioned after His bisexual love; which should banish, by the quality inherent in it, all those exacting passions of envy, jealousy, craving, and suspicion, which characterise what still goes by the name of love, and which, by reason of its perverted nature, carries desolation into homes that might otherwise be happy, poisons the very springs of pure affection, and prompts to murder, suicide, and all manner of crime.

It is evident that, as through woman disease entered into the world, it is through woman that the remedy must be provided, and that it is by uniting herself with the Divine Woman, that the force will descend which will expel the impurities which now taint her organism. The link which has been furnished to form this union is to be found in the person of Christ; therefore He repeatedly calls Himself the Bridegroom, and illustrates His relation to the race by the parable of the wise and foolish virgins. It is through this interior union with Christ, that the Church, of which woman is the feminine principle, becomes the Bride, the Lamb's wife. To those who can see with their eyes, and hear with their ears, and understand with their hearts, the book of Revelation is full of this mystery; therefore, "Let us be glad and rejoice, and give 'honour to Him: for the marriage of the Lamb is come, and 'His wife hath made herself ready. And to her was granted 'that she should be arrayed in fine linen, clean and white: 'for the fine linen is the righteousness of saints."[1] The "fine linen, which is the righteousness of saints," signifies the atomic overlay with which she becomes clothed by the operation of those who have passed into the other world, and by whom alone she can be prepared for her union with Christ; it is they who furnish her with the wedding garment; and herein lies a great mystery, for, as I have said before, it is impossible for any man or woman in their present condition to come into direct relations with Christ. The rays of His glory are too intense for any human being to support, without the modifying influence of a transmitting medium. This transmitting medium is composed of the spirits of just men made perfect, and their relation to us is fully described in the Epistle to the Hebrews. They are those who have "all died

[1] Revelation xix. 7, 8.

'in faith, not having received the promises, but having seen
'them afar off, and were persuaded of them, and embraced
'them, and confessed that they were strangers and pilgrims
'on the earth;" and again, "these all, having obtained a
'good report through faith, received not the promise; God
'having provided some better thing for us, that they without
'us should not be made perfect."[1]

The reason that the saints who died in faith received not the promise, but only saw it afar off, is that the visible and invisible parts of our world do in fact only form one universe, so intimately interlocked atomically, that it is not possible for one part of it to be redeemed without the other. Therefore, although this "great cloud of witnesses" by whom we are encompassed have "received the promise" of the Divine Feminine which they saw afar off, and are persuaded of it and have embraced it, so that they have become the media of transmission for its descent, they cannot enter into its fulness, unless we who are on earth enter into it also. Therefore it is said that "God has provided a better thing for us, that they without us should not be made perfect." This "better thing" is the ultimate victory to be accomplished through us, and they "cannot be made perfect without us," because our organisms contain certain elements essential to the perfection of theirs, of which they were deprived by the process of natural death. In a word, they are still suffering from the infernal virus which has poisoned the whole universe, both visible and invisible, and which can only be expelled by the combined operation of those in the flesh, with those who have parted from it.

There has been so much delusion concerning all these things, that although they seem very clear to the babes to whom they have been revealed, it is difficult to make them so to the wise and prudent from whom they are hidden; chiefly because it is characteristic of those who are wise and prudent to feel a very profound contempt for babes, and an equally profound respect for their own superior wisdom and prudence. The propositions, therefore, that an invisible region exists, that it is only invisible to the multitude because they are short-sighted, and that it is not a different world from the one

[1] Hebrews xi. 13, 39, 40.

visible even to the short-sighted, but is an integral part of it, are not likely to be accepted, excepting by those who *feel* that this must be so by a higher faculty than their reason supplies; but to them it will not seem strange that the conditions there are not very widely different from those which exist here; that the struggle between good and evil goes on there as it does here; that Christian Churches continue to fight, heathen to rage, and the people to imagine a vain thing; while occultists mystify, Buddhists contemplate and beg, and learned professors and metaphysicians investigate and discuss. Only the conditions differ, the attraction of affinity is stronger, and the forces are ranged against each other more systematically, especially in the higher and lower regions, where the union of the good, and the consolidation of the bad, are each more powerful respectively.

Numerically the population of the seen part of the universe is, of course, but a fraction of that which inhabits the unseen; and the forces in operation there are therefore infinitely more powerful than they are here. Nevertheless, its progress and fortunes are absolutely dependent upon those of the earth we inhabit, and the regeneration of the universe can only take place through the instrumentality of man upon our own orb. The reason that this is so is, that upon it the disease entered; and it is through the influence of woman upon man, that the leaven is to be introduced which will leaven the whole lump, as it was through the influence of woman upon man that the virus entered by which the whole was infected. It is in order to endow the woman with a new force which will enable her thus to act upon man, that the chain of saints has been established, by means of which the Divine Feminine elements may be transmitted to her directly from Christ.

As once she listened to the voice of the tempting serpent, so now she must tune her ear to the whisper of the tender angel. As once she felt the shock of an infernal vibration, convulsing and debasing her organism, so now she must invite the thrill of a divine impulse to purify and uplift it. As once she gave to the man the fruit of the tree of knowledge of good and evil, so now she must give to him the fruit of the tree of life, which is freely offered to her.

And as once she deceived him with lying speech, so now

she must inspire him with the true Word itself. As to her was due his expulsion from the garden of Eden, so to her must be due his restoration to it. She is the priestess of the shrine at which man is henceforth to worship, and represents there the High Priest, her Bridegroom. These are woman's rights, and this is woman's mission.

"Having therefore, brethren, boldness to enter into the ' holiest by the blood of Jesus, by a new and living way"— *i.e.*, the atomic distribution of the elements of the Divine Feminine into nature—"which He hath consecrated for us ' through the veil, that is to say, His flesh"—or His human organism —"and having an High Priest over the house of ' God; let us draw near with a true heart, in full assurance ' of faith, having our hearts sprinkled from an evil con- ' science, and our bodies washed with pure water"—*i.e.*, divine purity—"let us hold fast the profession of our faith ' without wavering; for He is faithful that promised."

The atomic overlay, to which allusion has been made as the bridal investiture of woman, consists of elements introduced into the present gross animal atomic covering of feminine passion, whereby a chemical change takes place in them of a sublimating and purifying character. This is a slow and gradual process, and the preparation required for it is one of severe self-discipline of the affections. All natural affections must be subordinated to those which are divine. Those instincts which have hitherto been considered the highest and purest in human nature, must give way to others, higher and purer still; thus the love of children for their parents, of a wife for her husband, of a mother for her children, must be relegated into the second rank. This is what Christ meant when He said, "Every one that hath forsaken ' houses, or brethren, or sisters, or father, or mother, or wife, ' or children, or lands, for my name's sake, shall receive an ' hundredfold, and shall inherit everlasting life."

The tie at present existing in these cases is magnetic, and the *rapport* which constitutes it is direct. This direct *rapport* must be broken, which is a most painful process, as it involves a certain amount of atomic dislocation. Between husbands and wives, where this is sometimes of a very intimate kind, the suffering caused seems almost unbearable;

but I can assure those who have the courage to make the attempt, from personal experience, that a satisfaction will come later, that will more than compensate for any suffering that may be thus incurred. The woman who would convey the right kind of love to those she loves must make it pass through Christ. She must detach her affections from the beloved object, and attach them to Him. She is aided in doing this by the chain of saints who connect her with Him. Her love, thus purified, passes back again to earth through the same channel to the loved one here, who begins to feel conscious of a totally different quality in it, and whose impulse it is to return it by the same channel; for if it is a man, he also can come into relations with Christ by a similar chain, and be acted upon as to his affections by the same process; but this he must do under female guidance.

When once the new magnetic tie is established between earthly man and woman, they are in a position to co-operate together in their struggle after purity; for, in both cases, this conjoint male and female co-operation is an essential preliminary to receiving the complete angelic atomic overlay. It may last a lifetime, or it may be accomplished in a comparatively brief period. This depends upon the condition of the atomic particles, which vary in every one, according to temperament, the modifications they may have undergone by the habits of a lifetime, their inherited character, and many other causes, which operate in life to create organic changes. But in every case, so far as my present experience testifies, a long period is necessary of entire suppression of all passional instincts, and of abstinence from indulgence in them. There are plenty of persons in the world to carry out its peopling, without those who have decided to enter upon this struggle after renovated life-currents, contributing to the population with their old ones. A pause is absolutely necessary before a new departure, and it is not for us to judge how long that pause may be. One thing, however, is quite certain, it must last until the overlay is completed, and that cannot commence until much preparatory work has been gone through, not only in the purification of the sex-magnetisms, but in all those which have been superinduced by social contact, general environment, and the pursuits and habits of a lifetime. In many cases the work of preparation has been progressing, unconsciously to the person in whom it is taking place, during a long course of years, and will account for much suffering which seemed cruel and superfluous at the time. Indeed it may be remarked, parenthetically, that all losses, sorrows, illnesses, or suffering, moral or physical, are designed to convey lessons, and can be turned to most valuable account by those who regard them in that light.

There are many women who, on reading these lines, will feel that they appeal to an inner sense, which will at once make response, but who are so hedged in by the circumstances of their surroundings, so entangled by family and other complications, that it seems absolutely impossible for them to give effect to their aspirations, or to enter upon the mission which they instinctively feel is their true one, and to which they would gladly at all costs dedicate their lives and energies. Let such take comfort; if their present duties and position render the abandonment of home-ties impossible in a world as yet unable to appreciate their sense of what their highest aspirations demand, it is because they themselves are not ready, and because further preparatory work has yet to be accomplished. This internal preparation any earnest woman can continue for herself, no matter what the complications which fetter her freedom of action may be. Trials will be sent her, duties imposed upon her, and sorrows encompass her about, in which she will find her discipline, if she only looks for it. She must kiss the rod, remembering that it is not sent to chastise her in the way of punishment, but to purify her affections and to fortify her will. She has got to learn the important lesson of self-reliance, and to accustom herself to the thought that in this great new moral departure upon which the world is entering, it is she, and not the man, who must lead the way; it is she who must be his strength, and not he hers, as he has hitherto been. She must give up leaning upon him, and learn to support him; it is she who must supply him with courage, endurance, and aspiration. Even his intelligence he must derive from her, though she knows it not; for he draws from her unconsciously the elements necessary to complete his own, as well as the energies which shall enable him to give practical effect to the ideas thus derived. And yet she must not consider herself upon this account in any way superior to man, but simply the complementary half of his being—she having inherently in herself none of the faculties which would enable her to grapple successfully with the problems of life, or to organise the reconstruction of society upon that new basis, which alone can be accomplished by her supplying man with the materials for the purpose.

At present women are reversing this process, and, by reason of their absorptive capacities, are unconsciously draining man of the elements of his moral and executive faculties. By this inverted method of procedure, they are enabled to compete with more or less success in the intellectual and executive paths of life; but in the degree in which they succeed in this, do they stunt and destroy their own higher faculties, and interpose a barrier which will close the avenues to the descent of the Divine Feminine. This practice is much to be deprecated; and those colleges for the higher education of women, which attract a certain class of the sex, are nurseries of hybrids, which turn out an inferior species of man-woman. They promote evolution utterly in the wrong direction. Woman must evolve in the realm of her affections, which is especially her kingdom, and develop those faculties, which are essentially hers, for the aid of man; and man must evolve in his own empire of thought, and develop those which are essentially his, for the aid of humanity at large. In no case should either sex invade each other's territory in a struggle for any personal advantage, or in a spirit of rivalry; but the two should always be found fighting side by side for the universal good, in a spirit of mutual love and co-operation.

It has been said that the circumstances of each case are different. No rule, therefore, can be laid down for the guidance of those who are desirous of opening themselves to the Divine Feminine, beyond the general principle of individual training and discipline above stated. But it may be remarked that though this discipline is always attended with more or less suffering, this varies much in degree; and there are those who have become conscious of the divine descent, whose atomic condition was such, that the change in the elements could be effected without any of that acute pain which attends the process in other instances.

In order, however, to understand how this consciousness manifests itself, it will be necessary to enter upon a consideration of the next stage of feminine evolution, as bearing not only upon her own development, but also upon the new and higher conditions which await the advancing man.

CHAPTER XX.

METHOD OF THE DESCENT OF THE DIVINE FEMININE—AND OF ITS RECEPTION BY WOMAN—THE SYMPNEUMA—INTRODUCTION OF THE DIVINE FEMININE INTO THE WORLD, THROUGH THE BIRTH, LIFE, DEATH, RESURRECTION, AND ASCENSION OF CHRIST—THE OUTPOURING ON THE DISCIPLES ON THE DAY OF PENTECOST—THE SYMPNEUMATIC CONSCIOUSNESS.

THE two dogmas of the Churches of Christendom that operate most powerfully against the descent of the Divine Feminine, which now seeks to impart its purifying and regenerating influence to the "Bride, the Lamb's wife," are the atonement as popularly understood, and the Trinity; for it is mainly to these dogmas that the present debased and degraded condition of the religious instinct is due. I have already shown the fatal effect which such a thoroughly false conception of the Deity as that which the doctrine of a propitiatory sacrifice of the just for the unjust presents, must exercise upon His worshippers.

The dogma of the Trinity, according to the theology of Christendom, operates no less injuriously, though in a different way. Its tendency is to confuse the faculty of spiritual perception to such an extent, that it is extremely difficult for those who have incorporated it into their religious belief, to apprehend the true nature of God.

It was, in fact, a dogma projected, from a lower source than that which inspired Arius, into the mind of Athanasius, and the majority of the Council which supported him, in the earlier part of the fourth century after Christ; but it is not to be found even in the external sense of the New Testament, though insidious attempts have been made to introduce it;

as, for instance, in the seventh verse of the fifth chapter of the First Epistle of St John, which was such an evident interpolation that it has been altogether omitted in the Revised Version; and in the manufacture of that strange expression, "the Holy Ghost," which to the popular mind conveys a somewhat different idea from the Spirit of God, partly owing to the unwarrantable use of capitals where none are used in the original, and partly to special occasions being selected for its application.

There is no possible excuse for the word πνεῦμα being sometimes translated "spirit" and sometimes "ghost," nor is there the slightest reason for supposing that when Christ commanded His disciples to baptise in the name of "the Father, the Son, and the Holy Spirit," He was then, for the first time, imposing upon them a triune God, in the sense which has since been invented. The expression signified God; Humanity, as typified by Himself; and the Spirit or pneuma by which alone they could be united through Him.

The pneuma is, in fact, the spirit which conveys to man the consciousness of the Divine Feminine, by a process presently to be described, as it did to Christ when it descended upon Him in the form of a dove; and it is by its operation in the organism of man, that the new revelation descends to him, and conveys to him the fundamental truth that he is a biune being in the service of a biune God, and that, until he regains the lost image of his Maker, he can never be reunited to Him.

In the first instance, the Divine Feminine descends to woman, and the method of its descent is through Christ, masculine and feminine Himself, the biune Word. From Him it descends through angelic pairs in the upper region of the invisible world to pairs beneath them, becoming tempered as it passes earthwards, till it reaches that pair which has been divinely commissioned for its final transmission to the woman on earth, in whom they have been labouring during her preparatory and disciplinary stages, and with whom they are in special structural atomic affinity.

When a sufficient change has been effected in the gross passional particles of her nature, for physical sensation to be conveyed, she becomes conscious, for the first time, of a peculiar vibratory motion in her nervous centres, affecting the whole organism with thrills of exquisite delight, the absolutely pure and divine character of which are quite unmistakable, if the work of preparation has not been unduly hurried; but inasmuch as it is in the power of human beings who have not the necessary experience, or whose zeal outruns their discretion, to precipitate results, too much care cannot be taken in these early stages not to anticipate, by hypnotic suggestion or otherwise, the divine process. Any human interference with these is in the highest degree dangerous, as advantage can be taken of it by the evil ones, who are on the alert, and whose whole effort is to simulate these sensations by others which are nearly allied to them, but which are antagonistic in their operation, and which, if encouraged, would end in terrible disaster.[1] If, however, the perils by the way are to daunt those who are prepared to sacrifice themselves in the effort to purify and renew the human life-currents, it would be better that they never entered upon the struggle; for, after reaching a certain stage, they will only encounter greater dangers by turning back, than by pressing forward. They need have no fear if the motive be kept absolutely pure: it is better, by excess of daring, to risk encountering a pitfall, than by excess of timidity to step backwards into one. The outstretched hand is never shortened that it cannot save; and however dexterously the snares are concealed, they are always visible to the eyes illumined by the light of love and faith.

Progress in this difficult path is zigzag. We advance by the very force of our blunders, for they mean experience. We first try in one direction, and finding that we are getting off the track, we try another, till we are checked again by some mistake, and so on; but on looking back, we find we have made progress: it is like tacking in the teeth of a gale of wind, and it sometimes seems slow work, for often we may lose a little way, but this is our own fault. We have failed to keep up the incessant strain which the effort requires, have

---

[1] The chronicles of the Roman Catholic Church contain numerous instances of obsession, by Incubi and Succubi, of the nature here indicated, among its devotees.

thought we would run into some little harbour to take breath and find shelter, only to discover that it was a pirate's cove, and that our only safety was once more to face the storm; but when we feel quite exhausted, and a further combat with the elements seems impossible, then, in the most unexpected way, at the very crisis of our despair, land appears, and we are gently wafted into the harbour of refuge which has been prepared for us, there to taste delights which compensate for all our perils and fatigues—delights which are indescribable, because they are the revelations of the divine mysteries, which can only be understood by those who have, by long and arduous effort, won their way to initiation into them. But of this whosoever has tasted them feels sure, that they are divine, in that they excite an all-absorbing desire of service, with an all-embracing love of humanity; and in that they convey an ineffable sense of personal union with Christ, and a peace that literally passes all understanding.

These are results that the evil ones cannot simulate — though it is not impossible that the pioneers into this new and unexplored land of the purest and loftiest affections, may have tumbled into one of their traps. If so, they have gained an experience which, however agonising it may have been at the time, will be of great value when they have effected their escape; and, indeed, when they have reached a certain point, they find that they have passed a whole class of dangers, and can breathe again, and, like Christian in 'The Pilgrim's Progress,' can go on their way rejoicing.

The woman, then, pursuing this upward path, encased in the panoply of the purity she has so long struggled for, and vigilant at all points, boldly presses onwards, inspired by a heroism which increases with every effort that she makes, and radiant with the ardours of new affections, which she feels glowing within her.

With this fire of the new life burning in her, will dawn upon her awakened consciousness the absolute conviction of the duality of her nature. She will know—not because it is to be found in the Bible—not because her reason suggests its truth—but because her physical organism forces the fact upon her, that she is the feminine half of a twofold being, and that her completion consists in union with her masculine complement; and as she progresses, that union will take form in a manner which she cannot mistake, though it will remain veiled from her who he is, whether he is in this visible world or has passed away from it. This is kept a secret for her own protection, for woman must be far advanced before she can resist the tendency to imagine that he who is to be hers for all eternity, and who was part of her from the first conception in the creative womb of the biune soul-germ, is not the man she most loves or has loved on earth. This may or may not be the case; but she is not allowed to know it while he is on this earth, although in rare cases, and for very special purposes, it may be made known to others. When, however, she has reached a certain stage of progress it may be revealed to her, if he has passed away from it. In that case he will himself reveal it to her, when her natural affections have been so uplifted out of all personal desire that it is no longer dangerous to her.

It is through the operation of the biune principle of the divine affections, transmitted in the manner described to her physical, moral, and psychical nature, that this consciousness of the complementary being, whom we call the "Sympneuma," is attained; and thus it is that the revelation of this sympneuma is effected through the operation of the "pneuma" or "spirit" of God, with which it is so absolutely identified, that the union with the sympneuma seems identical with a union with Christ; and therefore it was that Saint Theresa, Madame Guyon, and other devout persons, whose exceptional temperament and organisation permitted of such revelations, felt themselves to be brides of Christ. Such instances in time past were very rare; but, owing to the organic changes which are taking place in the world, they are every day becoming more common.

It is to the divine pneumatic operation, which can only be effected by the channel provided by His organism, that Christ alluded when He said, "But the helper, which is spirit, which is holy, whom the Father will send in my name, it shall teach you all things;" and therefore it is said of Christ Himself, that He was conceived of a holy spirit, because it was by this "operation" that He was brought into being in the womb of the Virgin. And so again He said, "But when the helper is 'come, whom I will send unto you from the Father, even the 'spirit of truth, which proceedeth from the Father, it shall 'testify of me."

The evidence that this divine biune descent is the spirit of truth of whom He here speaks, is that it does most emphatically testify of Him in the organism of every one whom it visits; but the world could not receive it in His day, for He tells His disciples, when they dreaded losing Him, that He " will pray the Father, and He shall give you another helper, ' that it may abide with you for ever, even the spirit of truth; ' whom the world cannot receive, because it seeth it not, ' neither knoweth it; but ye know it, for it is abiding by ' your side, and shall be in you." And He explains that this promise cannot be accomplished, unless He dies as to His outer frame here, and passes into the invisible world: "Never- ' theless I tell you the truth; it is expedient for you that I go ' away: for if I go not away, the helper will not come unto ' you; but if I depart, I will send it unto you. And when it ' is come, it will convict the world of sin, and of righteous- ' ness, and of judgment."

We read of the partial fulfilment of this promise in the account of the descent of the cloven tongues of fire in the book of the Acts. It was necessary that Christ should die first, because only by the dissolution of His outer frame could the particles containing the Divine Feminine principle be distributed, and atomic affinity established between them and His disciples. "But ye know it," He says, "for it is abiding by your side, and shall be in you." That is to say, whilst Christ was still on earth, abiding by the side of His disciples, the pneuma, being in Him, was thus abiding by them; after His departure, the pneuma, emanating from Him, should enter into and be in them. The atomic *rapport* was theirs whilst He spoke; but the combination consequent on that *rapport* could not be effected, until the particles of His own frame had been liberated, and those who were most conscious of this *rapport* were the women who clung to Him to the last, and especially that one woman who early felt the pure attraction of the peculiar magnetism with which He was endowed, and whom, when she anointed His feet, with a divinely inspired prescience of the change peculiar to it which

His body was to undergo during interment, He commended to all who should believe in Him, saying, "Wheresoever this 'Gospel shall be preached throughout the world, there shall 'also this, that this woman hath done, be told for a memorial 'of her." It was no wonder, then, that she was not only the first to see Him, but also to speak to Him in His subsurface body, when she was attracted in the early morning to His sepulchre, and when He said, "Touch me not, for I am not yet ascended to my Father;" for her organism could not have borne the contact, while His needed translation into the higher sphere, before He could allow the elements it contained to stream forth upon man.

The significance of the descent of the cloven tongues has never been recognised by the Churches, owing to their darkened condition as to the nature and functions of the Holy Spirit; and even the disciples themselves did not fully apprehend it. Peter saw in it the fulfilment of the prophecy of Joel, which had reference not to that manifestation, but to the evolutionary epoch upon which we are now entering. It is evident, from the epistles in the New Testament and the writings of the period which have been handed down to us, that the general impression among the disciples at this time was, that the final catastrophe was at hand; and that the second coming of Christ was to occur within the lifetime of some of them. This appears very strongly in the 3d chapter of the Second Epistle of Peter, and in some of the writings of Paul. It was based upon the statement that Christ made to some of those to whom He was speaking, that they should not taste of death until they should see the Son of man coming in His kingdom; and again, upon His promise, just before His crucifixion, that "in a little while" they would see Him again.

The apparently miraculous powers that accompanied the manifestation of the cloven tongues confirmed this impression; though these were the results, under natural law, which must of necessity have attended the introduction of this new vital energy into the organisms of such of the disciples as had been prepared, by daily magnetic contact with Christ, to receive it; and we are told that when the disciples asked Christ, "Wilt Thou at this time restore the kingdom to Israel?" He said,

"It is not for you to know times or seasons, which the Father hath settled on His own authority."

In point of fact, the promises of Christ in regard to the advent of the "helper," as preceding His own coming, had reference to two separate events. The one was the initiation of His great work; the other, its accomplishment. This great work was not, as has been before remarked, His death upon the cross as a "propitiation" for our sins, but His death, burial, resurrection, ascension, and descent upon His disciples in fiery potency. It was in the sequence of these events that the distribution of the atomic particles of His biune nature could be accomplished, and the elements of the Divine Feminine could be incorporated into the organism of man.

Each of these events contained a mystery, too profound to be entered upon at length here. By His death—and each account of it contains an interior signification, which I may perhaps be permitted to write about at some future time—He distributed the atomic elements of the Divine Feminine into nature. By His burial, He was enabled to descend into the lower unseen region of our universe, and distribute them there; for its redemption would be impossible, unless atomic affinity had been established between the particles of visible and those of invisible nature. By His resurrection He came into physical relations with His disciples, and thus was enabled magnetically and inseverably to attach His sub-surface body to their grosser organisms. Without this the descent of the pneuma would have been impossible. By His ascension, He inaugurated a new method of translation from the visible to the invisible world, and became the first-fruits of them that slept. And by His descent on the day of Pentecost, He completed His first mission to earth.

The internal meaning of the manifestation which took place when the disciples were gathered together, fully explains its nature. The "sound from heaven as of a rushing mighty wind" signifies the new spiritual birth of those who came under its influence; the necessity and character of this spiritual birth was explained by Christ when He said, "Mar‘vel not that I said unto thee, Ye must be born again. The ‘wind bloweth where it listeth, and thou hearest the sound

'thereof, but canst not tell whence it cometh, nor whither it
'goeth: so is every one that is born of the Spirit."

The "cloven tongues, like as of fire," were cloven to symbolise the two-in-one nature of the principle they represented; they were of fire, because that principle was the ardour of bisexual potency; and they were in the form of tongues, because the "Word" itself was thus manifested. This was the fulfilment of Christ's promise, that His disciples should see Him again, although it was stated so enigmatically that they were mystified. "And they said therefore, What is this that He saith, A little while? We cannot tell what He saith." And it was plain that He perceived that they misunderstood his explanation, for He said, at the end of it, "These things have I spoken to you in proverbs: but the time cometh, when I shall no more speak unto you in proverbs, but I shall show you plainly of the Father." That time came to them when they passed away from the earth; it is coming to us now.

Had the apostles and these disciples understood that the cloven tongues contained a far deeper meaning than the faculty they acquired of speaking in foreign languages, healing the sick, prophesying, and so forth, and had they perceived, in the new forces they thus acquired, the principle of the Divine Feminine operating through them, as it had through Christ, they would not so soon have lost their powers, which scarcely lasted their lives and those of their immediate followers.

But though the outward manifestation of its potency disappeared, the great work of Christ—the planting of the divine spark of that fire of love for the race, with which He burned, in the human organism—had been accomplished; and it is because it has been kindling and burning ever since, that men are now beginning to feel its heat, and to know what that heat means.

So it is that much that must have been obscure to the disciples, is, by the light of this revelation, made plain to us. As, for instance, when he says, "I have yet many things to 'say unto you, but ye cannot bear them now. Howbeit 'when the Spirit of truth is come, it will guide you into all 'truth: for it shall not speak of itself; but whatsoever it shall 'hear, that shall it speak: and it will show you things to come.

'It shall glorify me; for it shall receive of mine, and shall 'show it unto you." This passage refers to the method of inspiration which reaches man through the "operation" of the spirit of truth, which reveals the existence of the Sympneuma, and by virtue of that revelation opens to him an avenue of inspiration which he never before possessed; therefore Christ says of the spirit, "It shall not speak of itself; but whatsoever it shall hear, that shall it speak"—that is, inspiration will be adapted to the recipient through the appointed channel. "For it shall receive of mine, and shall show it unto you," signified that this biune principle, operating between the pair in the invisible world, and the person acted upon by them on earth, reveals to that person the Sympneuma. So Christ is glorified in the spirit of truth or the "helper." And so of all His other promises and prophecies, of which His disciples expected to see the fulfilment; we see them in the descent of the Divine Feminine by the operation of the "helper," and they come as an individual revelation to the heart of every one that is open to it. The sign of the times in which we live, and of the end of this dispensation of darkness, which is popularly called "the end of the world," is to be found in the fact that this is the commencement of the great era of personal revelation.

Therefore when Christ "was demanded of the Pharisees, 'when the kingdom of God should come, He answered 'them and said, The kingdom of God cometh not with obser-'vation: neither shall they say, Lo here! or, lo there! for, 'behold, the kingdom of God is within you."

When, by the operation of the Pneuma, the Sympneuma is revealed to woman by atomic contact with the pair in the invisible world divinely commissioned for the purpose, she becomes conscious of an immense increase of faculty, and this lies chiefly in the direction of correcting the faults of her nature which she was unable to grapple with before. Heretofore the experience of the most earnest and excellent people has been that in spite of the energetic endeavours of a lifetime, they have been unable to eradicate from their natures their besetting sins. They accounted for this by the fact of all sin being "original," and in this they were right, for it was an inherited taint of virus from the fallen world, projected through the animal creation into this one; and they comforted themselves by the reflection that it was washed out in the blood of the Lamb, and in this, again, they were right, for it is by the distribution of the atomic elements of the Divine Feminine contained in His blood, that the redemption of both the visible and invisible worlds has become possible.

The great work of Christ was to bring the Divine Feminine within reach of every human being here, and this the woman is the first to find out when the Sympneuma is revealed to her, because that revelation brings to her consciousness the biune principle through which she derived her life, even when she was unconscious of it; but it is not until she becomes conscious of it that she is taught how to employ its vigours for the expulsion of her own evils—indeed those evils cannot be fully revealed to her until then.

I am alluding exclusively to woman, because I shall treat of man separately in his new relation to her. It was to her that the revelation contained in this book was first made, and it is upon her that the responsibility is laid of first evolving in accordance with the principles which she derives from it. Not only does she acquire new powers of introspection, new weapons for combat, and new dexterity in using them, but she acquires also increased capacity of subsurface vision, increased intelligence for understanding what she sees, increased potency of sympathy, and increased ingenuity in discovering methods by which that sympathy can be imparted to encourage, to support, and to uplift.

I will here quote some words which my wife dictated to me on this subject before leaving this world:—

"Woman will soon be called to deep and solemn duties, 'in which nothing can take the place of her own effort, for 'she must, all alone, in her appointed time and place, bear 'the consciousness of the growing Word of God within the 'inner frame, that forms as Sympneumata unite. She must, 'for this end, stand in isolation from all the currents of the 'outer world; she will soon stand in sweetest contact with 'the currents of the heavens.

"The woman who is becoming sensitive to sympneumatic 'life, need change in nothing of her ministrations of hand

'and head, so far as she gives out life, thought, pity; but let
'her not dare to *take in* aught from friend or world—only
'and alone from the life of the higher beings whom God brings
'now to those who seek to rise. Every thought of the natural
'man or woman, not yet instructed in the heavenly education,
'is poison to her mind; every highest feeling in them, is now
'insufficient as food for her aspirations. She must case herself
'with steel against the whole mental, moral, and physical
'movement of life around her, for it is positive and literal
'death to her, and to the growing formation within her frame,
'which is the tender sweet growth of the Beloved One, from
'whose presence opens all the being to the influences of the
'great Two-in-One.

"Great pity should be felt towards those called to minister
'to others in their incipient stages of growth, and who have
'learnt to stand in the region of the forming beings, as to
'deeper consciousness; but who suffer into 'outmosts' from
'every variation in the states of those they are called upon
'to uplift and to encircle, and with whom the rejection of
'the growth into highest life would now be almost death;
'because their love seeks to flow out towards their charge,
'and any unwillingness to open the whole organism to
'that love, whether conscious or unconscious, tortures and
'crucifies.

"Of inner laws which women must know for themselves,
'there are these: however deep within the nature that point
'may be at which occurs an interchange of love—that is, life
'—between the closest bound of souls, fraternally, conjugally,
'or otherwise, in the case of the woman there remains beyond,
'a depth into which man can never penetrate;—in that
''within' she is eternally alone with God.

"What she knows within that depth is for ever to man a
'mystery, save for what God, for ends of service, instructs
'her to set forth; but it can never be known to man except
'through woman. In the deep and inward man-woman
'union of pure essences, she touches God herself: through
'whatever atomic chain of beings this union is effected, man
'touches God through her.

"Hence arises a most solemn science, in which she must

'be educated now by the wisdom of the angelic womanhood,
'—for without her understanding it, men cannot be saved.
'The inner life-currents of God, which are the interior spirit
'and power of all others, pass out through the woman's form
'radiating from her centre, to which no other life-currents
'can have access but the divine one. She is properly and
'only a radiative orb, and her life is passed immediately into
'the enveloping outer form of herself,—her Sympneuma; and
'then mediately, by countless methods of distribution, into
'the universe at large.

"Let woman, with spirit consecrated to the Holy One who
'first designs to love and visit her, seek for her world-service
'that it may no longer be hourly violated, as it is now, by
'every method and custom of the man-womanhood of the
'race."

Much more could be written on this subject, but this is not the place to say it; nor would it be appropriate, except to those who have given proofs of their devotion and sincerity by passing successfully through those earlier trials which no human will can impose upon them, but which, in the course of the divine training, they may be called upon to encounter.

Enough has been said to appeal to the nobler instincts of every pure woman; for those instincts must be revolted by the relations which she bears to man under existing conditions. It needed not this book to tell her that they must be the result of a foul inversion; that, though the source from which the generative principle of life emanated, is infinitely pure, its current has been perverted. The maiden shrinking which many an innocent girl feels at the prospect of marriage, is a testimony to the fact that the animalism which has degraded the union which her purer nature craves, to one she dreads, is not what was originally intended, but that it has become corrupted through an infernal and poisonous element which has been introduced into it, and which it is her function now to expel. If the picture which I have attempted to draw of woman's present position, and of her relation to man, may seem harsh in some respects, it is not to discourage her, but to stimulate her to redeem that position, and to reform those relations; and my experience of the patience, the courage, the fortitude, and the heroism of woman, convinces me that this appeal will not only find a responsive echo in her breast, but will rouse her to exertions which will finally culminate in triumph. It can only be by her efforts that man can be lifted from the slough of ignorance and sensuality into which she first dragged him, and where he now tramples upon her.

CHAPTER XXI.

THE SYMPNEUMATIC DESCENT—ITS INFERNAL SIMULATION—THE FUNCTION OF BISEXUAL ATOMS—CONTACT WITH PNEUMATIC CENTRES—SOCIAL CONVENTIONALITIES IMPEDE MALE AND FEMALE CO-OPERATION — INSANE DELUSIONS — THE RELATION OF CHRIST TO MAN THROUGH WOMAN ILLUSTRATED BY ST PAUL—KABBALISTIC INTERPRETATIONS.

IT is about fourteen years ago since the consciousness of the sympneumatic presence was first awakened—in the organism of a devout pure-minded woman of about sixty-five years of age, who has now passed away—in its present fulness, and as the inauguration of a new revelation on the subject; for, although history from a very remote period records visitations somewhat similar in character, which degenerated into the most filthy and obscene mysteries, and though they have been known in later times, as in the cases I have already cited, as well as in infernal obsessions, the time had not arrived for such manifestations to be understood, and they were too full of danger to be permitted, except under very special conditions. Now, however, they have become absolutely necessary to counteract the invasive sex-current, which has already begun to work much mischief among persons of sensitive temperament, especially in spiritualistic circles; many of whom are under the impression that their experiences are from celestial sources, and who will only find out the grievousness of their mistake when it is too late.

Theology and science alike are powerless to grapple with this danger; the former denounces it as of the devil,—which is true, but which carries no conviction to the mind of the subject, who probably does not believe in a devil, or who may easily mistake him for an angel of light, and who feels that his clerical adviser is merely using a Church formulary, and is probably utterly ignorant of the whole matter so far as his personal investigation is concerned.

Indeed, the class of persons among whom these experiences occur, as a rule keep them profoundly secret: they are constantly increasing, however, both in England and America, especially in the latter country, and statistics on the subject, could they be obtained, would astonish the sceptical, and afford an extensive field of operations for the Psychical Research Society, who, nevertheless, would escape from the dilemma in which they would be placed, by the easy expedient of calling them subjective; a term which explains nothing.

Science is, of course, powerless to meet the evil: for, in the first place, it denies that it exists; and, in the second, if it was forced upon its notice, it would be explained by some long word, of which neither those who invented it, nor anybody else, would understand the meaning. It will not be possible, however, much longer to maintain the reticence which has hitherto been observed on the subject, as the effect upon the human organism is sooner or later certain to produce physical or mental disturbance. This has already been the case in numerous instances; and if medical men do not talk of them, it is either because the cause has been concealed by the patient, or because it is regarded as merely the *result* of a cerebral disturbance instead of its *origin*.

But neither priests nor doctors will be able to stem the tide as it grows in volume: it is a bane which can only be met by its antidote; and as it is the result of the direct operation of invisible beings from the nether region of our own world, it must be met by the direct operation of invisible beings from the upper one. Persons must therefore be found who will brave the dangers, suspicions, ridicule, or obloquy with which they will be assailed in their attempt to acquire the powers that will not only enable them to beat back this invading influence, but to draw down into the world such currents of divine purity as shall cleanse the foul magnetisms which taint all social and domestic relations, and to which all the miseries and woes of humanity are primarily due.

Almost immediately on the sympneumatic descent, above

alluded to, taking place, many persons—myself and wife among the number—became conscious of it. During the fourteen years which have elapsed since then, new developments have occurred; but the time had not come until now to give to the world the manner in which these have taken form in my mind, under the influences which have directed this statement, although, three years ago, some conclusions and explanations arrived at then were given, as far as possible, in the book called 'Sympneumata,' the method of production of which I have described in the fourth chapter of this book. It deals exclusively with the practical bearing of this new advent upon the fortunes of the race, and I would earnestly recommend it to the perusal of such of my readers as may have had their interest sufficiently aroused by the subject treated of, to follow me thus far.[1]

A few words, however, are necessary to explain, so far as language enables me to do so, the difference between pneumatic-atomic interlocking and pneumatic-atomic combination; the former being the special characteristic of sympneumatic contact, as contradistinguished from the only contact which has been heretofore possible between man and the beings in the unseen.

I have already alluded to the difference which exists between sentient and non-sentient or moral atoms; if I have shrunk from entering more fully into the subject, it is not because I feared the mockery and ridicule which this book is certain to evoke, but because I did fear that if I made too great a demand upon the credulity of my readers, many, who might be disposed to accept some of the truths which I feel it contains, would reject them if they were called upon to believe too much. As I cannot offer them any proof for what I am about to state, I do not ask them to believe it, but merely to assume it as a possible hypothesis, just as they have assumed Darwin's hypothesis as to the origin of man.

The fact, then, which has been so clearly shown to me in regard to these moral atoms that I cannot doubt it myself, is, as I have already said, that they are all sentient beings, and that they correspond in appearance to the moral qualities

---

[1] Sympneumata; or, Evolutionary Forces now Active in Man. William Blackwood & Sons.

which they represent. Thus, all those representing virtues are exquisitely beautiful, whilst those which correspond to vices are monstrously hideous. We have a faint analogy to this in terrestrial insect life. A great variety, again, are of a mixed character: the elements of which they are composed form combinations according to structural affinity, and the result upon man is an infinite variety of complex emotions, violent passions, lofty aspirations, and, in fact, all that goes to make up what we call character and temperament.

Those corresponding to the purest and most celestial attributes are in pairs, representing man's original dual nature; but these exquisitely formed bisexual beings were unable to make their abode in man until he himself had become open to the divine bisexual life, or, in other words, until he became prepared by Christ's work on earth, for sympneumatic consciousness. They were expelled from man when he was expelled from Eden, and enfolded in the all-sheltering embrace of the Divine Feminine, where they remained protected until the time arrived when they were once again to be let down into a human organism. They made their advent into the world through the womb of the Virgin, in the person of Christ, and after His death were distributed into nature, on the occasion of the descent of the cloven tongues. Since then they have been incessantly labouring in the human organism, endeavouring to arrange themselves, like particles in an iron bar, under the influence of Christ the Divine Magnet. This process, however, had first to be accomplished through a long series of beings in the invisible world; and these bisexual atoms form, in fact, the medium of transmission of the divine sympneumatic potency to earth. It is only, however, since that potency has been active in man, that it has been possible for him to transmit them to other organisms. These infinitesimal biune innocencies are in human form, and the fact of their existence was one of the secrets known to the ancients, and was handed down by tradition by them. They only form a transmitting chain for the divine vigours when they are in conjugal union, and hence they differ from the chain formed by atomic combination, where the union is not bisexual, but according to affinity. This statement may perhaps not seem so fantastic to scientific men as to the world at large, for they are familiar with the idea of the generation of human life by means of infinitesimal living entities in the vital fluid, and of disease by microbes, which propagate in the human organism, and with the fact that certain diseases thus produced affect the moral character and temperament, rendering persons violent, irritable, melancholy, nervous, and so forth. Thus vices may, in the first instance, be sometimes traced to the action of animalculæ, of which there are in fact three classes—those which are atomically connected with the structure of the outer organism, those which are atomically in affinity with the psychic organism, and those which actually form the atoms of the pneumatic organism.[1]

I must here insert an explanation which would have appeared more appropriately on page 162, with regard to the method of the approach of the highest form of inspiration into the pneumatic centre of the human organism, as con-

[1] With regard to the transmission of thought, which is one of the results of this atomic combination, I am confirmed in my contention that the transmitting force has its origin in the invisible world by the following passage from a remarkable pamphlet published since this book was written, by a French writer, entitled, 'Esquisse d'une Démonstration Scientifique de l'Existence de la Vie Future. Suivie d'une courte appréciation des conséquences qu'aurait sur la Littérature et les Arts une démonstration complète (Geologie, Magnetisme, Hypnotisme, Génération, &c.): par P. C. Revel.' Taking as his basis the axiom that effects which are similar to each other are due to causes which are similar to each other, he remarks that if we apply this law to thought-transmission, we arrive at this remarkable result:—

"The visible brain is the instrument of an invisible body, in which reside 'memory, intelligence, will, or, in other words, the faculties termed intellectual. 'In fact, physiology teaches us that intelligent phenomena have the brain as 'their point of departure. Now, in experiments of thought-transmission, the 'intelligent phenomena which the magnetised person exhibits, have for their 'cause, as experience unquestionably demonstrates, *the influence* of the magnetiser.

"Therefore the brain of the person magnetised is *the instrument* of the magnetiser. But we have said effects which are similar to each other are due to 'causes which are similar to each other, from which we conclude that the 'brain in its ordinary condition is *the instrument of a particular body* belonging 'to the invisible world, which body acts upon the brain, in the same manner 'that the magnetiser himself acts in his experiment upon the brain of the 'magnetised person."

Monsieur Revel then points out that the difference between the action of the brain of the magnetiser and magnetised person is more apparent than real, and arrives at the conclusion that this forms a complete refutation of the theory which establishes the visible human brain as the sole direct cause of the effects produced.

trasted with the disorderly inspirational approach towards that centre from the circumference. In the latter case all the defences of the human pneuma are broken through by the current which invades the organism from an invisible source, resulting in those psychic phenomena with which we have lately been familiar, and which are attracting increasing attention. In the other case, the human will, which is the central and most potent principle of the human pneuma, attracts by the force of its aspiration, when it is fixed in the service of God and humanity, the divine potency with which it is in affinity. It is owing to this attraction that persons who rise in prayer to the highest states of devotion, receive what they feel to be answers to their supplications, and are inspired thereby to great acts of religious fervour and heroism; but these do not break down any of the barriers which guard the inmost shrine, but reach it subtly and silently, by reason of its elevation, by long psychic and corporal discipline; fortifying rather than otherwise those defences through which they have so mysteriously penetrated. This faculty of permeation is due to the composition and nature of the sentient atoms of which the purest and loftiest inspirations are composed. Once lodged in the inmost centre of the human structure, they press outwards towards the circumferences of it, transmuting the atomic particles, first of the pneumatic dialectric, then of the psyche, then of the psychic dialectric, then of the natural body, and finally of the sphere which surrounds the natural body, thus repelling disorderly invasion, and slowly but surely, if the human will is vigorously co-operating, making all things new.

There is no greater mistake than to suppose that human organisms which are called "sensitive"—or which, in other words, are mediumistic—are in more favourable conditions of receptivity to the divine touch, than those which are organically dense, and closed to psychic influences. On the contrary, the latter expand from the centre more perfectly, and develop into more powerful pneumatic batteries than those where the external breaches have first to be repaired. On the other hand, this latter class of organism has its advantages when those breaches have once been repaired, and can be used for purposes for which the previous class is not adapted. All have their special functions, and all can co-operate in the great service which should be dear to them. But it is most important that those who desire to be engaged in this service, should not imagine that they are qualifying themselves for it by what is usually termed "developing their sensitiveness." They should seek rather to close it to all external psychic influence. Hence, I repeat, and I cannot insist upon this too strongly, that all dabbling in spiritualism, hypnotism, and what is called magic, or experiments in occultism, is attended with serious danger to the progress of the soul, which can only safely develop under the direct operation of the spirit of God acting upon its will-centre, through the channels provided for it, and more especially through that new and powerful sympneumatic descent which, in these latter days, has been vouchsafed to the world, to reinforce the will, purify the affections, and arm for the fray those who have decided to invoke its energies, that they may become instruments in the divine hand for the restitution of all things.

I have alluded to the pneumatic organism; by it I mean the spirit which abides in the soul of man. Pneumatic atoms form the battery which acts upon psychic atoms. It is not possible for sympneumatic force to act upon man upwards from the lower invisible world, because there is no bisexual transmitting chain; but it is possible for earth contact to exist with that world by pneumatic-atomic combination, and promiscuous unions are used for that purpose. The communications which have reached the world in the form of revelations have depended for their value and character, not only upon the pureness and elevation of the earthly recipient, but also of the atomic beings, because they represent the nature of the invisibles from which they emanated.

When, however, two human beings occupy sympneumatic relations to each other on this earth, without being conscious of it, there is always the danger of their both falling under delusions—even after they have been opened sympneumatically to the divine descent—and being deceived by infernal simulations. The result in this case is very disastrous, for they still remain magnets, and for some time they can be used as such by the infernal agencies. Not for long, however, for the effect of the disorderly contact into which they are now brought, must surely demagnetise them, and, although they may still remain powerful media for infernal spiritual influx, the special quality which carries conviction to the hearts of men will be wanting, and sooner or later they will become powerless. During the period of their obsession they remain more or less insane, but as their mediumistic faculty dies out, their moral balance gradually reasserts itself, and they may be restored to the sympneumatic consciousness they lost, if not in this life, in the next.

The main obstacle to the rapid evolution of sympneumatic life in the world is to be found in its existing social conditions, and the conventionalities which have sprung from them. These are naturally based upon the perfectly correct hypothesis, that man is such an essentially impure creature that it is dangerous to leave two persons of opposite sexes alone together in a room; while if they should happen to travel for a couple of days upon the most sacred mission, the vilest suspicions are aroused. This surrounds the co-operation of any man or woman, unless they happen to be married, with the gravest difficulty. It was right and proper that this should be so, for these conventionalities are the result of the experience which gave rise to them, and which furnishes all the evidence required to prove that a society in which they are needed, is quite incapable of criticising the motives and actions of those who have sought and achieved a purity of which it knows nothing, after long and arduous struggles of a kind to which it is a stranger, and which have lasted over a long period of years.

I say advisedly that the world is ignorant of the nature of this purity, because I have never heard of, nor read of, nor met with, organic conditions such as may be induced by the special training by which alone it can be acquired. Yet, to attain to it has been a motive by which the highest and purest men and women that the world has known, have been inspired; but they sought it in seclusion and abstinence, and the coldness and deadness which they attained, they called purity. Whereas the highest purity means heat and life. It is not the extinction of the generative principle within us, but its restoration to divine conditions. Men and women can never find purity by keeping apart from one another; they must train for it together. And this training is of such a nature as to cause a suffering far more acute than all the self-imposed rigours and penances of monks and nuns. It may consist of a variety of disciplines—as, for instance, when two young people, who are both in quest of this pearl of great price, and who are passionately attached to each other, feel that they must marry if they would win it, and yet never know in this life what the marriage relation, as commonly understood, is. Or it may consist in intimacies which, though pure and innocent, are calculated to arouse jealousy in quarters where it would be legitimate under ordinary circumstances, and excite suspicions which nothing but supreme faith can banish; to say nothing of other ordeals to be undergone, which differ in each case, but are always of a character to try most severely the peculiar quality of the temperament to which they are applied. For the position of man in relation to woman, in this particular struggle, is reversed. It is she who, when she has herself attained to the consciousness of sympneumatic life, must lead him to it. From first to last he must be a passive instrument in her hands; under her guidance he must crush out of his nature every instinct of animal passion, and become dead to all the old sensations, before he can become alive to the new.

The man who has undergone this training finally becomes absolutely impervious to, and case-hardened against, the subtle magnetisms which radiate from ordinary women. He forgets at last what the emotion of being what is popularly called "in love," was like; no charms can captivate his outer senses, no feminine sympathy, based on a mere personal sentiment, can penetrate into that inmost shrine, which he has dedicated to the worship of the Divine Feminine. His reverence for woman has never stood so high as when woman has become nothing to him personally, but everything to humanity at large. His attachment to woman depends solely upon her attachment to Christ as the universal Bridegroom, and upon his deep internal tie with her as an indispensable colleague and copartner in the stupendous mission which has been imposed upon her.

Men and women who have arrived at these new relations

towards each other, enjoy a happiness in them which compensates for all the suffering they have undergone to reach it —a happiness which would be shattered at a blow, if they could be guilty of any such act of physical gratification as the closeness of their external relations would justify the world in attributing to them. And yet the progress of the work in which they are engaged, involves an intimacy as close as that between sister and sister, or mother and daughter, and as pure; for the needful interchanges of magnetism can only be effected by constant and close proximity, by which new electro-magnetic forces can be generated, sufficiently powerful to resist the invasion of the infernal lust-currents which are now struggling to make an entry into the world, through the organisms of "sensitives," who are ignorant of the nature of the forces which are accomplishing their subjection. To rescue such, when their eyes have been opened; to close up the rupture in their odylic sphere which has given entrance to the invading tainted magnetic current, and to restore them to physical health and moral sanity, is one of the most blessed duties which devolves upon those who are labouring in this new sphere of action; for it is one which medical science, with its present limitations of ignorance and prejudice in such matters, is quite unable to undertake.

But the co-operation of persons of opposite sexes, who have attained to sympneumatic conditions, extends far beyond this: they have undertaken no less a task than the reconstruction of society from its foundations, upon the cornerstones of purity and co-operation, which must begin by the grouping of individuals socially who are prepared to enter upon it, under the conditions of self-sacrifice already described, and who will have the courage to face the unholy conjectures, the bitter sneers, the unjust criticism, and the violent opposition, not only of the world at large, but of their own friends and families. Once again, the man or the woman who has determined to abandon the profession of being a Christian for the reality, must be prepared to share the real Christian's fate; for the time has come, which was predicted by Christ when His disciples asked, "What shall be the sign when all these things shall be fulfilled?" and Jesus, answering them, began to say, "Take heed lest any one deceive you; for many shall come in my name, saying, I am Christ, and shall deceive many." Those who have come in the name of Christ, and have deceived many, are all the existing Churches and sects in Christendom without exception; until the conscience of the whole civilised world has been drugged by their dogmas and their formularies. The result of that conscience being quickened, must inevitably lead to the overthrow of the ecclesiasticisms which have held it so long in bondage, and to the discovery that the Christ whom they proclaimed was a false one.

But inasmuch as the infernals are intrenched more strongly in the Church than anywhere else, and can fight against the true Church more effectively under the banner of the false one than under any other, the hostility of the priesthood and ministry in all countries will be more bitter against those who are struggling for purity, than that of any other class. It will not be in music-halls or on race-courses that this effort will be denounced, but in cathedrals and conventicles; and the true Christ again will find His home, not among the Scribes and Pharisees, but among the publicans and sinners.

What is stranger still is, that, while materialists are treated with comparative tolerance by these Christians and dignitaries of the Church, who lavish the highest ecclesiastical honours they can bestow upon the burial, and read funeral eulogies over the grave, of the prophet of a No-God like Mr Darwin, they will furiously resent the teaching of those who believe that the mission of Christ was to introduce into the world the purity of the Divine Feminine; and they will traduce all who should offer themselves, under a guidance which they believe to be divine, to be the instruments for its introduction to fallen man; because it is not possible to do so without violating the conventional relations of the sexes which impurity has established, and denouncing Churches which cement adulterous marriages. But those who have received the Sympneuma by the channel of Christ and the Holy Pneuma need not fear, for He says: "When they shall 'lead you, and deliver you up, take no thought beforehand 'what ye shall speak, neither do ye premeditate; for what-

'soever shall be given you in that hour, that speak ye: for
'it is not ye that speak, but the Holy Pneuma. Now the
'brother shall betray the brother to death, and the father
'the son; and children shall rise up against their parents,
'and shall cause them to be put to death. And ye shall
'be hated of all men for my name's sake: but he that shall
'endure to the end, the same shall be saved."

That these prophecies did not refer alone to the persecutions which the disciples were afterwards called upon to suffer, is evident from the context.

The reason why the true Christ has been lost is, because the Churches have never understood the full significance of the fact that He alone, of all the world's great teachers and regenerators, of all the founders of religion, was never married, and preserved Himself wholly untainted as to the flesh.

This was because the true order of the relation which should subsist between the sexes had been reversed by their separation; and as He contained enfolded within Himself His own feminine complement, or Sympneuma, all other women were to Him, like all other men, objects of his disinterested love and compassion. The restoration of the sympneumatic union involves, sooner or later, the restoration of the divine conditions of procreation; but herein lies a great mystery, the revelation of which is reserved for One who has retained the Christ-like condition, concerning which it is not expedient to write further at present than to say, that the period when this revelation will be made does not seem very remote. But before it can be made, it will be necessary for the two or three who have passed away from this earth in full sympneumatic consciousness, to be reinforced by the addition of others now alive who have attained the same state.

As it was impossible for Christ to send the "Helper" until He died, and ascended into the invisible region of our universe, there to form a new atomic combination and generate a new force, which took form in the descent of the fiery cloven tongues, so now we, who are called upon to prepare the way for a second and more triumphant descent of the Word-made-flesh, as Conqueror and as Bridegroom, must expect soon to be summoned to strengthen the battery of sympneumatic life beyond the tomb. We are like mariners swimming from a wreck to the shore with life-ropes; and it is not until sympneumatic groups, more numerous than yet exist, are formed both in the seen and the unseen, that the next revelation can be made.

There is no more profound delusion than that which prevails in certain quarters, that a crisis is at hand which will sweep all humanity from the face of the earth, except a chosen few, who will be preserved immortal amid the general crash. A crisis is undoubtedly at hand, but it will not be catastrophic or outside of natural law. It will consist simply in the further development and collision of those forces which are already exhibiting themselves in unknown and startling phenomena; and the day will no doubt come when the conditions of death will undergo the change predicted in the Bible, and when it will be swallowed up in victory.

But this cannot be until the victory has been won; and the victory cannot be won until the forces on the other side of the grave have established sympneumatic connection with those on this side; until both have learned thoroughly how to co-operate with each other, and have acquired the necessary combined potency. For any man who has attained sympneumatic conditions, or who thinks he has attained them, to desire immortality, or to suppose that he has already achieved it, is to nurse himself in a delusion as ignorant as it is selfish. It is one which has been projected into the minds of those who are in close psychic *rapport* with the lower region of our universe, and is suggested by the certainty they have acquired of an approaching collision between the forces, hitherto latent, which are now developing with such remarkable energy.

To this collision I referred in the introductory chapter to this book; and in a subsequent chapter I quoted the testimony of medical science in France, to the effect that these forces had already developed to such an extent, that it had become possible by hypnotic suggestion for an operator to arrest the vital functions of a patient, and to put an end to natural life. Similarly there also resides in those forces latent potencies for prolonging it. It is to obtain the control of these potencies that the struggle will take place. The effort of the infernals is to acquire it by pneumatic propulsion and psychic impact of atoms, and by the subsequent absorption of the principle of human vitality into themselves, from those over whom they have thus acquired control, whereby they would reinforce the electro-magnetic force of their own organisms, and then, by a simulation of the sympneumatic descent, connect themselves so indissolubly with their victims on earth, that these latter would become instruments in their hands for shortening or prolonging human life, to suit their own purposes. There are those now on earth who are rapidly approaching this condition, and who have arrived at the conviction—no doubt sincere—that they are not only immortal themselves, but that they can control the vitality of others. Of this—which must seem in the highest degree fantastic to the general public—I have had personal experience, and have got written evidence of it in my possession. The fact that the world may call them lunatics, does not invalidate the danger of the delusion, nor of the insanities to which it may give rise, since, as I have shown, men of science have experimentally tested the nature of the forces upon which it is based, and have proved that by their operation they can either arrest life, or prolong it as they are every day doing in several French hospitals, by using them for the cure of disease.

It is to meet this danger that the sympneumatic descent has become necessary; but the man who is vitalised by it seeks no immortality for himself, nor does he desire to be the means of controlling the vitality of others. He knows he has become impervious to anti-sympneumatic attack, or to hypnotic suggestion from any quarter, whether seen or unseen, which can limit the divine freedom within him. He would not consciously shorten the life of an agent in this world of the powers of darkness, even if he were able to do so, nor attempt to prolong his own, by the avoidance of any risk he should incur in the service of his Master.

It is in this that those who have received the true sympneumatic consciousness, can be distinguished from those who have only received the infernal simulation of it, or who have had it and lost it—that the former have no desire for length of days on earth; but, asking only to be God's instruments, place themselves unreservedly in His hands, and are equally ready to go or stay. All that they seek is to be shown His will, from hour to hour, and to do it effectually.

It is by this earnest effort alone that they can keep their lamps trimmed and burning, and clothe themselves in the wedding garment; and this wedding garment is the sympneumatic overlay with which their particles can be clothed as effectively in another life as in this; for all, whether they be on this earth or not, are invited to the feast of the Bridegroom and the Bride. "And he saith unto me, Write, 'Blessed are they which are called unto the marriage supper 'of the Lamb. And he saith unto me, These are the true 'sayings of God."

In the internal meaning of the book of Revelation, the views which have been set forth in the preceding pages may be clearly found; though, as much which that book contains refers to the future, and some of it conceals mysteries which are still veiled, its study can only be pursued under conditions which require long preparation. Nor is it even expedient that all the results which may have been arrived at should be made public, for much that is hidden is too sacred; while any attempt to unravel the future by intellectual interpretations of its symbols, springs from a morbid curiosity, which will certainly not be gratified by revelations that can be relied upon.

This has been abundantly illustrated by the utter failure which has hitherto attended the numerous endeavours that have been made to fix dates, and predict political events by human interpretation of prophecy, whether in the Old or New Testament.

In attempting, therefore, to unfold the inner meaning of such passages as have been shown to me as being appropriate to these pages, I shall confine myself to those to which I feel most strongly impelled to call the attention of my readers; and as it would occupy too much space to quote the entire text, I must leave them to do that for themselves. At the same time, I would remind them that a mere intellectual apprehension is of very little avail; and that, in such matters as those dealt with in this book, it is better to reject the inspiration it contains, than to think it true as a matter of theory, without at once acting upon it. Nor can any one judge of its value, one way or another, except those who have already subjected themselves to a severe course of moral discipline, or have inwardly decided to sacrifice all that they may find truth.

Before, however, entering upon this task, I must once more refer for confirmation of what has been stated in the foregoing pages, to the writings of St Paul as well as to the Kabbalah.

The sympneumatic nature of man, and his relation to Christ in the twofold quality of his love, is very clearly indicated in the 11th chapter of First Corinthians, where the apostle says, " Nevertheless neither is the man without the woman, neither the woman without the man, in the Lord." In other words, as the Lord contains within Himself the bisexual nature, it is not possible for those to be absolutely and completely united to Him, who are not themselves similarly united as to their masculine and feminine principles. It is not possible for the man alone to be *in* the Lord, nor for the woman alone to be *in* the Lord. They may separately and individually be attached to Him by a certain external atomic adhesion, as all good people who love Him are; but they can never know the bliss of the deep interior atomic interlocking, which seems to melt them into His ineffable Personality, unless they come to Him as two-in-one; for the masculine cannot unite itself to the masculine principle in Him, excepting through its own feminine complementary half; and the feminine cannot unite itself to the masculine principle in Him, excepting through its own masculine complementary half. This is what is meant by the expression "neither is the man without the woman, neither is the woman without the man, in the Lord." And he goes on to say, " For as the woman is of the man, even so also is the man by the woman; but all things of God." The two being inextricably interwoven by God, from the day that they were created two-in-one by Him.

The chapter in which these verses occur furnishes a very remarkable illustration of the mixed inspirational influx, to which I have already alluded as characterising all the earliest Christian writings which are assumed to be infallible. The apostle is discussing a subject which would seem unaccountably trivial, were it not that a spiritual significance attached to it, the nature of which he did not himself fully comprehend. The position of woman having become changed by the work which Christ had already done on earth, the apostles felt themselves spiritually impressed to change the Jewish custom by which the men while they worshipped remained covered, while the women were compelled at all times to shave their heads—a custom which prevails in orthodox Jewish communities to this day. The new order now introduced was that the men should worship uncovered, and the women allow their hair to grow.

This was evidently a shock to the Jewish mind, and Paul attempts to give an explanation of the reasons which involved it, in his Epistle to the Church at Corinth, which doubtless contained Jews. His mind, however, was still too deeply imbued with the social prejudice which prevailed throughout the whole East, and was by no means confined to the Jews, of the inferiority of woman, to understand the full significance of the change. He considered that the woman being taken out of the man stamped her with inferiority, not realising that the most interior principle must be in some senses the superior, and that her apparent inferiority was in fact the result of a previous catastrophe which involved the appearance of man upon our earth under conditions different from those which had characterised his previous creation, but which in no way affected the broad fact that the Divine Feminine must always be equal to the Divine Masculine in God, and therefore in all His created beings. A dim consciousness of this forces itself upon him, however, when he says, "But all things of God"; and again, "For this cause ought the woman to have power on her head because of the angels." This verse has been so utterly enigmatical to the translators, and so apparently contradictory to what has preceded it, that they have ventured on an explanation in the margin. "That is," they say, "a covering, in sign that she is under the power of her husband." Now the meaning of ἐξουσία, rendered "power" in the authorised version, is really "authority." By no possible licence or contortion of terms can it be made to mean "covering." Still less is there anything to justify an explanation which is in palpable opposition to the words of the text. There can be no better illustration of the pride and ignorance with which man, even to our own day, insists upon woman's subjection to him, than that he should presume to put in a marginal note, which in the minds of the ignorant has almost the authority of the text itself, in explanation of the words, "For this cause ought woman to have authority on her head because of the angels," this means, "A covering, in sign that she is under the power of her husband." Had women been the translators, the explanation would have been different. The true internal significance is, that woman is the connecting-link between man and the angels, and that it is through her affectional atomic union with them that a channel is formed by which alone the Divine Feminine can descend to man; and the reason why the apostles were divinely impressed to forbid the women to shave their heads was, in the inverse sense, analogous to that which caused Delilah to shave the head of Samson when she wished to deprive him of his strength. There is a certain quality which pertains to the electricity that resides in hair, as to its essential atoms, of which, if I spoke further, I should only excite, still more than I have already done, the ridicule and scepticism of men of science, for it is far beyond their ken, which renders it an important factor in the transmission of force derived from those whom Paul calls "the angels," and to tamper with this transmitting medium of electric magnetic force is to limit woman's power, and therefore her authority in her own special sphere of operations, over man.

But there is another far more internal meaning connected with the word "hair" as applied to woman, which will appear when we come to consider a passage in the chapter I am about to quote from the Kabbalah, "Concerning the Bride of the Son, or 'Lesser Countenance,'" which also throws remarkable light upon the inner meaning of the Apocalypse. From this it will be seen in what manner the hair of the woman signifies the male Sympneumata, and why the expression of St Paul in a previous verse, that "the head of the woman is the man," does not imply his lordship over the woman, but signifies the nature of his organic relationship to her, which is that of the intellect; while of him it might in like manner be said, "the heart of the man is the woman," in allusion to the affectional character of her functions towards him. It is probable, however, that Paul himself was too much impregnated with the prejudices of his race on the subject fully to apprehend the true significance of his own words.

I have already said that, according to kabbalistic interpretation, the four letters of the Tetragrammaton, IHVH, which compose the word Jehovah, indicate the Father, the Mother, the Son, and the Bride or Son's Wife—the two latter, VH, being emanations of the former. And here I would remark that Christ, in whom the Bride was enfolded, was an emanation from and manifestation of VH in the sense—modified by the peculiar circumstances attending His birth—in which we can all become manifestations of VH when once we have acquired the twofold nature with which our Lord came to endow humanity; and to that degree, and only to that degree was He divine. The ineffable divinity of IHVH, in His fourfold comprehensiveness, it is beyond the grasp of the human mind to fathom.

This being so, I will quote the dark sayings of the Book of the Lesser Assembly on the subject:—

"Unto His (the Son's) back adhereth closely a ray of 'vehement splendour, and it flameth forth, and formeth a 'skull concealed on every side.

"And thus descendeth the light of the two brains, and is 'figured forth therein.

"And She (the Bride) adhereth to the side of the Male; 'wherefore also she is called my dove, my perfect one '(Cant. v. 2). Read not 'Thamathi,' my perfect one, but "'Theomathi,' my twin-sister, more applicably." Therefore after the baptism of Christ by John, the Divine Feminine was seen descending in the form of a dove.

"The hairs of the Woman contain colours upon colours, as 'it is written (Cant. vii. 5). 'The hair of thy head like 'purple.' But herewith is Geburah, severity, connected in 'the five severities (*i.e., which are symbolised in the numerical 'value*, 5, of the letter H, final of IHVH, which is the Bride), 'and the Woman is extended on Her side, and is applied to 'the side of the Male."

This passage—and indeed the same may be said of the whole Kabbalah,—contains arcana referring to Christ in His conjoined Masculine and Feminine nature, which has been concealed from the most learned students of that Book of

Mystery, owing to the veil which hid from their view the true nature of that wonderful Personality. The symbolism contained in the words "the hairs of the Woman which contain colours upon colours," will be understood when we refer to what is said of the hair of her Spouse in the chapter "concerning the hair of the Son or Lesser Countenance," p. 307.

"From the skull of the head (of the Divine Son, the Spouse) 'depend all those chiefs and leaders (otherwise all those 'thousands and tens of thousands), and also from the locks of 'the hair, which are black, and mutually bound together, and 'which mutually cohere.

"But they adhere unto the Supernal Light from the Father 'AB, which surroundeth His Head (*i.e.*, is the Son's), and unto 'the Brain, which is illuminated from the Father.

"Thencefrom, even from the Light which surroundeth His 'Head (*i.e.*, the Son's), from the Mother AIMA, proceed long 'locks upon locks of hair.

"And all adhere unto and are bound together with those 'locks which have their connection with the Father."

The chiefs and leaders spoken of above, as being thousands and tens of thousands, symbolised by the locks of hair which are black, are the male sympneumatic complements of earthly women, as the hairs of the Bride, containing colours upon colours, are the female sympneumatic complements of earthly men here, which all depend originally from the Great Father and Mother, Two-in-One—AB and AIMA; "the colours" are the germinating essences, and the five severities are the evils which afflicted the world, because the balance has been lost in it owing to the absence of the Divine Feminine principle, the separation of the sexes, and the inferiority in which woman has been placed, and which is symbolised by the words, "and the Woman is extended on Her side, and is extended by the side of the Male," and these severities will continue until, in the words of the next sentence, "She is separated from His side, and cometh unto Him, so that She may be conjoined with Him face to face." It was to prepare the way for this union that Christ appeared on earth. Therefore continues the Kabbalah, "And when they are conjoined together, they appear to be only one body.

"Hence we learn that the Masculine, taken alone, appeareth

‘ to be only half the body; so that all the mercies are half;
‘ and thus also is it with the Feminine. But when they are
‘ joined together the (two together) appear to form only one
‘ body. And it is so.

"So also here. When the Male is joined with the Female,
‘ they both constitute one complete body, and all the universe
‘ is in a state of happiness, because all things receive blessing
‘ from their perfect body. And this is an arcanum."

The arcanum is simply the sympneumatic descent, and herein is its secret revealed—for it will result in the union on earth of the halves hitherto divided, whereby man will regain his lost condition. Nevertheless, this arcanum has never before been revealed to Jewish students of the Kabbalah. Now will commence the Sabbatic year spoken of therein as follows:—

"And therefore it is said 'Tetragrammaton (IHVH, or
‘ Jehovah) blessed the seventh day, and hallowed it.' For
‘ then all things are found (*to exist*) in the perfect body; for
‘ Matronitha (*i.e., the Inferior Mother, the Bride*) is joined unto
‘ the King, and is found to form one body with Him. And
‘ therefore are there found to be blessings on this day. And
‘ hence that which is not both male and female together, is
‘ called half a body. Now no blessing can rest upon a muti-
‘ lated and defective being, but only upon a perfect place and
‘ upon a perfect being, and not at all in an incomplete being.

"And a semi-complete being cannot live for ever, neither
‘ can it receive blessing for ever. The beauty of the Female
‘ is completed by the beauty of the Male. And now have
‘ we established these facts (concerning the perfect equality
‘ of Male and Female), and they are made known unto the
‘ companions.

"With this Woman (the Bride) are connected all those things
‘ which are below: from Her do they receive their nourish-
‘ ment, and from Her do they receive blessing; and She is
‘ called the Mother of them all.

" Like as a mother containeth the body (of her child before
‘ birth), and that whole body deriveth its nourishment from
‘ her (otherwise containeth a garden, and the whole garden
‘ is from her), thus is She unto all the other inferiors.

" It is written (Prov. vii. 4), 'Say unto Chokmah (wisdom),

' Thou art my sister.' For there is given one Chokmah (male), ' and there is also another Chokmah (female)."

" And this Woman is called the Lesser Chokmah, in respect ' of the other.

" And therefore it is written (Cant. viii. 8), ' We have a little ' sister, and she hath no breasts.'

" For in this exile (*i.e.*, separated from the King) she appear- ' eth unto us to be our little sister. At first, indeed, she is ' small; but she becometh greater and greater, until she be- ' cometh the spouse whom the King taketh unto Himself."

Then is she the Bride, the Lamb's Wife—the city of the New Jerusalem arrayed as a Bride to meet her Husband, for this is the restitution of all things.

We will now turn to the book of Revelation, in which the ultimate triumph of this Divine Feminine principle on earth is described.

CHAPTER XXII.

THE TWELFTH AND THIRTEENTH CHAPTERS OF THE BOOK OF REVELATION INTERPRETED—THE EFFECT OF CHRIST'S MISSION TO EARTH UPON THE UPPER INVISIBLE REGION OF OUR WORLD—CONCEALMENT OF THE DIVINE FEMININE—THE TWO WITNESSES—THE FUNCTIONS OF JOHN THE BAPTIST—HIS RELATION TO CHRIST—TEMPORARY TRIUMPH OF THE INFERNAL FEMININE—THE BEAST, ANTI-CHRISTENDOM, OR THE GENTILE CHURCH—THE MARK OF THE BEAST, THE FALSE CROSS—MAN'S PRESENT RELATION TO CHRIST.

THAT portion of the book of Revelation, of which the inner meaning bears more particularly upon the subject of the present volume, commences with the 12th chapter.

"The mother, the woman clothed with the sun," who was "with child and pained to be delivered," is the Divine Feminine.

The dragon, waiting "to devour her child as soon as it was born," is the Prince of the fallen region of the previous world, and of the Siddim.

The child which was "brought forth," and "caught up unto God and His throne," was Christ.

The "wilderness" into which the woman fled, and "was sustained for 1260 days, in a place prepared for her," is the hearts of the saints, in which she has found refuge and sustenance since her descent, through Christ, into the human organism.

The "war in heaven" between "Michael and his angels" and "the dragon and his angels," was the struggle between the Seraphim and the Siddim over the Divine Feminine, in the invisible part of our universe, to preserve its atomic elements in the organisms of those who, having received it here, had passed away from earth.

"And the great dragon was cast out, that old serpent, called the Devil, and Satan, which deceiveth the world; he was cast out into the earth, and his angels were cast out with him," signifies the victory of the Seraphim, and the final expulsion of the Siddim from the upper invisible region of our universe, and the transference of the struggle to earth.[1]

This was what Christ meant when He said, "I saw Satan, like lightning, fall from heaven."

"And I heard a loud voice saying, Now is come the salva-'tion, and the force, and the kingdom of our God, and the 'authority of His Christ: for the accuser of our brethren is 'cast down, which accused them before our God day and 'night," is the song of triumph of the Seraphim at the salvation, which had been accomplished through the mission of Christ to earth, of the upper region of the invisible world in which the supremacy of Christ, as ruler, is henceforth established.

"And they overcame him by the blood of the Lamb, and by the word of their testimony; and they loved not their lives unto the death," describes the process by which the early Christian martyrs, who had received into their organisms the atomic elements of the Divine Feminine, which had been distributed throughout humanity by the actual blood of Christ, redistributed them by their own death as martyrs. This has given rise to the saying that "the blood of the martyrs is the seed of the Church."

"Therefore rejoice, ye heavens, and ye that dwell in them," signifies the completion of Christ's work so far as regards our own invisible upper world.

"Woe to the inhabitants of the earth and of the sea! for the devil is come down unto you, having great wrath, because he knoweth that he hath but a short time," indicates the violence of the struggle which was now to take place over the Divine Feminine on earth.

---

[1] The whole of this combat is described in the Babylonian mythology in the legend narrating the conflict between Bel or Merodach and Tiamat the Dragon of Darkness (Sayce, Hibbert Lectures, p. 102); and indeed many most interesting analogies can be traced between the myths of Accad and Babylonia, the Dhammapada of the Buddhists in which a city resembling the New Jerusalem is described—and the Revelation.

"And when the dragon saw that he was cast unto the earth, he persecuted the woman which had brought forth the man-child," signifies the infernal attack made to prevent the introduction on earth of the Divine Feminine.

"And to the woman were given two wings of a great eagle, ' that she might fly into the wilderness, into her place, where ' she is nourished for a time, and times, and half a time, from ' the face of the serpent," signifies the means which were adopted to conceal the Divine Feminine from the infernals; and indicates the nature and period of duration of the struggle.

The next two verses contain arcana, as to the method of the infernal attack and the means employed to meet it.

"And the dragon was wroth with the woman, and went to make war with the remnant of her seed, which keep the commandments of God, and have the testimony of Jesus Christ," indicates that the infernal attack was especially concentrated upon those few who had "the testimony of Jesus Christ"—in other words, had received the atomic elements of the Divine Feminine distributed by Christ into their organisms.

This vision terminates here. It must be remembered that the order in which the different visions occur in the book, have no reference to any relation which they bear to each other in order of time.

The next vision is that of the Beast, who rose from the sea, "having seven heads and ten horns, and upon his heads the names of blasphemy."

This beast symbolises the infernal lust-principle introduced by the Siddim into humanity, with the six other deadly sins, at the period known as "the Fall." The source from which this beast derived his origin is signified in the words, "And the dragon give him his power, and his seat, and great authority."

"And I saw one of his heads wounded as it were to death; and his deadly wound was healed: and all the world wondered after the beast," signifies the wound which this lust-principle received by the advent of Christ into the world, and the subsequent healing of the wound by the suppression of the Divine Feminine. The worship of the dragon by the world, the power he exercised, and the evil that he wrought, are described in the following verses. The duration of his reign is given as three years and a half, which is half of the mystical number seven, that signifies perfection, and which corresponds to the three days and a half during which the dead bodies of the two witnesses were to "lie in the street of the great city, which spiritually is called Sodom and Egypt, where also our Lord was crucified" (chapter xi. 8).

Here I feel compelled to make a digression concerning these two witnesses, and the relation they bear to the work of Christ.

The two witnesses represented typically by Enoch and Elijah are the Sympneuma, or complementary being which completes man's bisexuality, and the Holy Spirit, the Pneuma or Divine Feminine, through the operation of which the Sympneuma—so called because it is the companion of the Pneuma—is united to man. Of Enoch we read that "he walked with God, and he was not, for God took him." This signifies that traces of sympneumatic life lingered in the world, notwithstanding the fatal wounds it had received, first, by the disobedience of woman, and secondly, by the slaughter of a vital principle in it, typified by Abel, until the race called "Enoch," when it was finally withdrawn from the human organism. The races in the invisible world, prior to this date, who passed away from this earth in sympneumatic conditions, however imperfect, are differently constituted atomically from all those who passed into it subsequently, and remained therefore as a witness of that sympneumatic life which again descended to earth in the person of Christ.

The whole history of Elijah, which, if the events recorded ever really happened, would be one of the grossest cruelty and vengeance, is in reality pregnant in its inner sense with the most profound spiritual significance; for the operation of the Divine Feminine is concealed in the legendary history of the prophets, but more especially in that of Elijah, who was charged with a fuller measure of it than any man had been, from the days of Moses to those of John the Baptist. The pneuma, of which Elisha is said to have received a double portion, differed in quality from that which Elijah carried with him on his departure from earth, which was of the fiery potency which characterises the ardours of a high degree of the Divine Feminine, and which, reinforced by elements received from earth, returned to the invisible world, thence to be once again projected into this one through the organism of the Baptist. Hence we find all the most striking episodes of Elijah's career accompanied by a fiery manifestation.

It is fire from heaven which consumes the sacrifice on Carmel; it is fire from heaven which consumes successively two captains of fifty with their men; it was after a great strong wind, and an earthquake and fire, that he heard the still small voice; and it was in a chariot of fire that he disappeared from the gaze of Elisha. Therefore he typifies the fiery pneuma of God, whose purifying flame is about once more to touch the hearts of men, either to kindle in them divine ardours, or to devastate them and lay them waste.

We read that the dead bodies of the two witnesses, the Sympneuma and the Pneuma, were to lie for three days and a half "in the street of the great city, which spiritually is called Sodom and Egypt, where also our Lord was crucified." The Sympneuma was trampled upon by the sin of Sodom;[1] the Pneuma was crushed out of man's consciousness in the early Church by the dogma of the Trinity, which owes its origin to Egypt.[2] But in its larger sense the "great city" signifies the gigantic imposture called "Christendom," where our Lord is being daily crucified, and in whose streets the dead bodies of the two witnesses are still lying.

The representative of Elijah was John the Baptist, and it is very important that his relationship to Christ should be understood.

The Gospel of St John introduces him as a "man from God," or, as the Greek preposition $\pi a \rho a$ with the genitive implies, "from alongside of" God.

The angel Gabriel, in announcing his birth to his earthly father, Zacharias, says: "Thou shalt call his name John, and 'there shall be joy and gladness to thee; and many shall 'rejoice at his descent [that is, the source from whence he shall 'come]. For he shall be great in the presence of Jehovah, 'and he shall by no means drink wine or intoxicating liquor; 'and he shall be filled with a holy pneuma, even from his 'mother's womb. And he shall turn many of the sons of

---

[1] See Appendix. [2] See Appendix.

'Israel to Jehovah their God. And he shall proceed in His
'presence, in Elijah's presence and force, to turn the hearts
'of parents to their children, and unbelievers by means of the
'intelligence of just ones, to make for Jehovah a people fur-
'nished" (or constructed as a dwelling-place), Luke i. 13-17.
These words are almost textually those of the prophet Malachi
predicting the same event.

"John" signifies the "gift of God." "Many shall rejoice
at his descent," signifies that the progenitor of John in the
invisible world being Elijah, the potency of the pneuma in
him would cause many to rejoice who came under the influence of the Baptist.

Although true and complete sympneumatic union does not
fully exist in the invisible part of our world, among the descendants of races which have passed into it since its final extinction on earth in the Enoch race, yet there is a degree in
which it exists, which is awaiting completion, through the co-
operation of earthly mortals, who contain elements necessary
thereto, "for they without us could not be made perfect."
The fact that some have passed recently into the invisible
world, who had attained to sympneumatic consciousness here,
has already operated powerfully on sympneumatic conditions
there; but John, although of such high descent, came into
the world through human parentage, and his progenitor—
though filled with so large a measure of the Divine Feminine
—had not attained to full sympneumatic consciousness. Nevertheless, John proceeded in Jehovah's presence, and in Elijah's
pneuma and force; the pneuma being the feminine, and the
force the masculine element, by means of which he was generated through Elijah. Hence, too, from his mother's womb,
he was to be filled with the Divine Feminine, and to be called
the "gift of God." The important significance of this appellation was attested by the dumbness of Zacharias, and which
was removed as soon as he wrote, "His name is John."

"To turn the hearts of the parents to their children," signifies the yearning of the saints who form the pneumatic chain,
over their children whom they are labouring for here; "and
unbelievers by means of the intelligence of the just ones,"
signifies the effect of inspirational impression by the saints
on the hearts and minds of unbelievers.

"To make ready a people furnished," signifies that the effect of John's advent would be to prepare men to receive the sympneumatic life, which would be distributed by Christ; and indicates also the power of the Divine Feminine, when operating in the hearts of men, to make them wise unto salvation.

Therefore it was, when the disciples who were present at the transfiguration asked Christ, saying, "Why say the scribes that Elias must first come?" He answered and said unto them, "Elias truly shall first come, and shall restore all things. 'But I say unto you, that Elias has come already, and they 'knew him not, but have done unto him whatsoever they listed. 'Likewise shall the Son of man suffer also of them. Then 'His disciples understood that He spake unto them of John 'the Baptist."

These disciples were at the time under the influence of a very powerful descent of the Divine Feminine, which had overshadowed them on the occasion of Moses and Elias appearing with Christ on the Mount of Transfiguration. The effect of this remarkable event was not only to charge them with the Divine Feminine, but to reinforce the elements which Christ contained in His own body, prior to their distribution into nature; therefore Moses and Elias, who appeared "in glory," or in an outward manifestation of the Divine Feminine, "spake of His decease which He should accomplish at Jerusalem;" and this influence was so powerful that "Peter said 'unto Jesus, Master, it is good for us to be here; and let us 'make three tabernacles, one for Thee, and one for Moses, and 'one for Elias, not knowing what he said." The tabernacle was, as we know, the abode of the Shechinah—one of the Hebrew terms for the Divine Feminine—and this utterance was forced from his unconscious lips by its presence at the moment within him. The visible evidence of which was "that while he thus spake, there came a cloud and overshadowed them, and they feared as they entered into the cloud;" and from the cloud was made the same announcement which accompanied the descent of the dove on the occasion of Christ's baptism, "This is my beloved Son; hear Him."

It was this perceptible influence which radiated from the principle with which Elijah and John the Baptist had been filled, that invested the personality of Christ with so much mystery among the Jews, so that when He asked His disciples, " Saying, Whom say the people that I am ? They ' answering said, John the Baptist; but some say Elias, and ' others say that one of the old prophets is risen again. He said ' unto them, But whom say ye that I am ? Peter answering, ' said, The Christ [or anointed] of God." He then goes on to describe the nature of the sufferings He will be called upon to endure in order to fulfil His lofty mission, and strictly charges them to keep the revelations He makes to them on this mysterious subject a secret.

The parentage of Christ in the invisible world is hidden from us. All that is shown to us is that He was generated directly by the Seraphim, in complete sympneumatic biunity. This is indicated by the terms of the angelic announcement to Mary, who was told that a "holy pneuma" should come upon her, and that "force of the Highest" should overshadow her; the pneuma and force being the Divine Feminine and Masculine principles respectively. It was by means of this powerful bisexual concentration upon a prepared virginal organism that, as I have already described, Christ's descent into the world without a human father was effected.

Nevertheless, before His sympneumatic complement could internally manifest herself to Him, it was necessary for certain atomic combinations to be made by elements derived from a human organism, specially filled with divine pneumatic life for the purpose. These elements were contained in the organism of John. It was the pneuma residing in John's yet unborn personality which recognised the superior sympneumatic personality of Christ Himself, at the time undergoing conception in the womb of the Virgin Mary, which caused the babe to leap in Elisabeth's womb, and called forth the exclamation, " Blessed art thou among women, and blessed ' is the fruit of thy womb. And whence is this to me, that the ' mother of my Lord should come to me ? For, lo, as soon as ' the voice of thy salutation sounded in my ears, the babe ' leaped in my womb for joy."

It was to effect this atomic combination, that it was necessary for Christ to be baptised of John, and when the latter remonstrated, saying, "I have need to be baptised of thee, comest thou to me?" "Jesus answering said, Suffer it to be so now: for thus it becometh us to fulfil all righteousness." Christ needed baptism by the Pneuma to develop the full consciousness of the Sympneuma in Him, which descended in the form of a dove. When this had taken place, John recognised the sympneumatic nature of Christ at once; for when the Jews came to him, pointing to Christ as a rival who was also baptising—though there were good internal reasons why He should not baptise, but only His disciples—"John 'answered and said, A man can take unto himself nothing, 'except it be given him from heaven. Ye yourselves bear me 'witness, that I said, I am not the Christ, but that I am sent 'before Him. He that hath the bride is the bridegroom: 'but the friend of the bridegroom, which standeth and heareth 'him, rejoices greatly because of the bridegroom's voice. This 'my joy therefore is fulfilled." It is impossible to have a clearer testimony to the sympneumatic nature of Christ, and the completion of His bisexuality, than is afforded by this allusion to His bride by the only man then alive capable of apprehending this profound mystery.

Christ himself recognises His twofold character when He says to His disciples, "Can the children of the bride-chamber 'mourn, as long as the bridegroom is with them? but the 'days will come, when the bridegroom shall be taken from 'them, then shall they fast." In this saying He foresees that the children of the bride-chamber, whom He called by that name because He was preparing them to receive sympneumatic life, would soon lose the slight consciousness of it they possessed, when His presence was removed from them, and mourn and fast for lack of the vivifying principle which that life imparted; and this in fact they did, only sustaining themselves by the delusive hope of His reappearance among them during their lifetime.

We are now in a position to understand the meaning of Christ's statement, "Verily I say unto you, Among men that 'are born of women there has not risen a greater than John 'the Baptist; yet he that is least in the kingdom of heaven 'is greater than he." John the Baptist entered this world endowed with a loftier invisible parentage than any human being who had preceded him; but inasmuch as he lacked the Sympneuma, he failed on earth in his biune perfection, and the least of all the sympneumatic subjects of the kingdom of heaven must be greater than the greatest of those who have not yet entered into sympneumatic conditions. That John recognised this most fully, is evident not only from the words I have already quoted, but from his saying, " I indeed baptise ' you with water unto repentance; but he that cometh after ' me is mightier than I, whose shoes I am not worthy to bear. ' He shall baptise you with the Holy Pneuma and with fire." It is this baptism with fire that every one of us, who are struggling to enter into that condition which John had not attained, must be baptised with; and it is that Holy Pneuma, through whose operation alone we can regain the lost image of our Maker, that we must invoke.

It was the Divine Feminine, which so powerfully impregnated the nature of John, that aroused against him the fury of the infernal feminine principle which infested Herodias and her daughter Salome, and caused them to contrive the beheadal of the Baptist, in order to secure the withdrawal from the earth of the Divine Feminine potency which resided in him.

This tragedy was followed shortly afterwards by the crucifixion of Christ, and the two witnesses lay dead in the streets of the great city. But the time is accomplished, and the hour of the second woe is come, when we are told that "the Spirit of life from God entered into them, and they stood upon their feet; and great fear fell upon them which saw them."

The final catastrophe is described in a few words, when the seventh angel sounded, and there were "great voices in ' heaven, saying, The kingdoms of this world are become the ' kingdoms of our Lord, and of His Christ; and He shall reign ' for ever and ever."

But a great deal is to happen between the resuscitation of the two witnesses and this glorious climax, and in order to apprehend it, we must return to the chapter in the Revelation, from which we have digressed.

While the witnesses are lying in the streets, the dragon is reigning, and the fourth and three following verses describe the triumph of the lust-principle on earth, and the worship of it by all those "whose names are not written in the book of life of the Lamb slain from the foundation of the world." This indicates that from the time when our universe emanated from the previous one, it was foreseen that its redemption could only be accomplished through the means that were then provided in the person of Christ.

"He that leadeth into captivity shall go into captivity: he that killeth with the sword must be killed with the sword. Here is the patience and the faith of the saints," signifies that it will also be their final triumph.

"And I beheld another beast coming out of the earth; and he had two horns like a lamb, and he spake as a dragon." This second beast signifies the Antichrist, which Christendom has represented to this day. This beast is a false Christ; therefore it is said to be like a lamb. His two horns signify lust and pride; but his voice is the voice of Satan.

"And he exerciseth all the power of the first beast before him, and causeth the earth and them which dwell therein to worship the first beast, whose deadly wound was healed," signifies that the world was apparently as much under infernal influence, after Christ's advent, as before, and as much a slave to the lust-principle; for it was the unfaithfulness of the early Christian Church which healed the deadly wound of the beast.[1]

The remaining six verses of this chapter contain arcana, which I would gladly have been spared interpreting; but the pressure upon me has been so strong not to shrink from what has been presented to me, however unpalatable it may be to some, that I have no alternative but to obey it.

"And he doeth great wonders, so that he maketh fire come
'down from heaven on the earth in the sight of men, and
'deceiveth them that dwell on the earth by means of those
'miracles which he had power to do in the sight of the beast;
'saying to them that dwell on the earth, that they should
'make an image, which had a wound by the sword, and did
'live,"—signifies that the Christian ecclesiastical organisations which sprang up on the ruins of Christ's teaching, by the suppression of all its inner meaning, and the perversion of its outer sense for sacerdotal purposes, speedily began to prosti-

[1] See Appendix.

tute their holy office by imposing upon the popular imagination by so-called miracles, and such superstitious practices as may be witnessed in the Greek and Roman Churches to this day—using the sacred authority to cover or enforce the vilest crimes of cruelty, ambition, lust, and avarice, and setting up the emblem of Christ's death as an object of worship. Banners bearing the cross of Christ were flaunted over armies engaged in bloody wars waged in His name—as, for instance, at the time of the Crusades; false relics of the cross were scattered broadcast over Christendom as objects of worship, and the ignorant masses prostrated themselves before them in adoration; processions of priests bearing crucifixes led hundreds of victims to be burnt at the stake in the name of Christ. Whenever a crime was to be perpetrated by the Church, whether Eastern or Western, the cross was exalted, as furnishing the warrant for it; and the body and blood of Christ were thus, so to speak, trampled in the mire in effigy by the very persons who believed that, every time the sacrament was administered, that body and that blood underwent a miraculous change, which enabled them to eat the one and drink the other.

"And He had power to give life unto the image of the beast, ' that the image of the beast should both speak, and cause that ' as many as would not worship the image of the beast should ' be killed."

The power to speak, with which the image of the beast was thus endowed, signifies the abominations which have been perpetrated in the shape of dogmas under the claim of infallibility, the tyranny which has been exercised by Papal bulls, and the profanity which has suggested that the cross gave any man authority to assume the title of Christ's vicegerent on earth. The image of the beast, then, signifies the false Churches of the false Christ throughout so-called Christendom.

"And he causeth all, both small and great, rich and poor, ' to receive a mark into their right hands or on their fore- ' heads; and that no man might buy or sell, save he that had ' the name of the beast or the number of the name."

The mark of the beast on the forehead signifies the false cross made at baptism, and the mark of the beast into the right hand signifies the sign of the false cross. This spurious cross has for eighteen centuries been the trade-mark of anti-Christendom. No salvation was worth anything unless it had received its brand. Its devotees are taught that out of the Church there is no salvation; that "two sacraments are necessary thereto—Baptism and the Supper of the Lord;" and that "they that have done evil, shall go into everlasting fire. 'This is the Catholic faith; which except a man believe faith-'fully, he cannot be saved. Glory be to the Father, and to 'the Son, and to the Holy Ghost."[1]

But the Calvinists vie with the Romanists in the cruelty and bigotry of their creed, as will appear from the following quotations from the 'Presbyterian Confession of Faith':—

"Although the light of Nature, and the works of creation 'and Providence, do so far manifest the goodness, wisdom, and 'power of God as to leave man inexcusable, yet they are not 'sufficient to give that knowledge of God and of His will 'which is necessary to salvation. . . .

"By the decree of God, for the manifestation of His glory, 'some men and angels are predestined unto everlasting life, 'and others foreordained to everlasting death. These angels 'and men, thus predestined and foreordained, are particu-'larly and unchangeably designed, and their number is so 'certain and definite that it cannot be either increased or 'diminished. . . .

"Men not professing the Christian religion cannot be saved 'in any other way whatsoever, be they never so diligent to 'conform their lives according to the light of Nature. We 'cannot by our best works merit pardon of sin. There is no 'sin so small but that it deserves damnation. Works done 'by unregenerate men, although, for the matter of that, they 'may be things which God commands, and of good use both 'to themselves and others, are sinful and cannot please God, 'or make a man meet to receive Christ or God. . . .

"The souls of the wicked are cast into hell, where they 'remain in torment and utter darkness, reserved to the judg-'ment of the great day. At the last day the righteous shall 'come into everlasting life, but the wicked shall be cast into 'eternal torment and punished with everlasting destruction, 'The wicked shall be cast into hell, to be punished with un-

[1] Athanasian Creed.

'speakable torment, both of body and soul, with the devil
'and his angels, for ever. . . .

"At the day of judgment you, being caught up to Christ
'in the clouds, shall be seated at His right hand and there
'openly acknowledged and acquitted, and you shall join with
'Him in the damnation of your son."

No man is to be allowed to buy salvation except stamped thus, and no Church to sell it. Until quite recently, any man in Christendom who had not been baptised, or who denied that he was a Christian according to this faith, was an outcast; and a few hundred years ago would not have been allowed to exist. Jewish persecutions up to the present day testify to the cruelty of "the beast."

Dr Edward Irving, one of the noblest men and greatest spiritual geniuses which this century has produced, was penetrated with the conviction that Christendom was the beast, and gave vent to that conviction in the following words: "The present visible church of the Gentiles, which hath been
'the depository of the oracles and the sacraments and the
'ordinances since the Jewish state was dissolved—I mean
'the mixed multitude which are baptised in the name of the
'Father, and the Son, and the Holy Ghost under that seal,
'including Protestants, Roman Catholics, Greek Church,
'Arminians, and all the sects of each, as Scottish, English,
'Irish, Lutheran, and Calvinistic Churches, with the dis-
'senters and seceders from each. This body of baptised men,
'which I call the Gentile Church, who should every one of
'them have been a saint, being by baptism ingrafted into
'Jesus Christ, to be made partakers of His justice, whereby
'our sins are covered and remitted, standeth threatened in
'the Holy Scriptures because of its hypocrisies, idolatries,
'superstitions, infidelity, and enormous wickedness, because
'it hath transgressed the laws, changed the ordinance, and
'broken the everlasting covenant (Isa. xxiv.), with such a
'terrible judgment, as hath not been, nor ever shall again be
'seen upon the earth; in the which deluge of wrath she shall
'be clean dissolved, as the synagogue was heretofore in the
'destruction of Jerusalem, when she in like manner had
'filled up the measure of her iniquity; which fearful con-
'summation I judge to be close at hand, both by the signs of

'the times, and from the prophetic numbers expressly given
'to guide us in the anticipation of these great Gentile judg-
'ments which are mentioned in Scripture wherever and
'whenever the coming of the Lord is mentioned."

Those who dare to denounce the perverted theology and false dogmas which have led to such results, must be prepared to meet the storm which will be roused against them by what the same writer calls "the British Inquisition, 'whose ignorance of truth I know to be equalled only by 'their malice against everything which touched the infalli-'bility of their idol PUBLIC OPINION. I mean," he continues, "by the British Inquisition, that court whose ministers and 'agents carry on their operations in secret; who drag every 'man's most private affairs before the sight of thousands, and 'seek to mangle and destroy his life as an instructor, trying 'him without a witness, condemning him without a hearing, 'nor suffering him to speak for himself; intermeddling in 'things of which they have no knowledge, and cannot on any 'principle have a jurisdiction; and defacing and deforming 'the finest beauty and the profoundest wisdom by the rancour 'of their malice. I mean those who set principle, who set 'truth, who set justice, who set everything sacred up to sale: 'I mean the ignorant, unprincipled, unhallowed spirit of 'criticism, which in this Protestant country is producing as 'foul effects against truth, and by as dishonest means, as ever 'did the Inquisition of Rome."[1]

"Here is wisdom. Let him that hath understanding count the number of the beast: for it is the number of a man; and his number is six hundred and sixty-six."

If we take the numerical value of the Hebrew letters, according to the usual methods of kabbalistic or mystical interpretation, we find this name to signify the offspring of the polluted Pneuma and the inverted Shaddai.

It must be remembered that the denunciations, in the subsequent chapter of Revelation, of those who worship the image of the beast, and have received his mark, do not apply to the ignorant and superstitious masses, but to those who are responsible for the gross perversions and flagrant iniqui-

[1] Preliminary Discourse to Ben Ezra's work on the Second Advent, by the Rev. Edward Irving, pp. 5 and 22.

ties which have characterised the religion, almost ever since it has been called by the name of Christ.

The history of the Roman and Greek Churches is a hideous record of blasphemy and crime, of the most wanton desecration of the name and teaching of Christ, of the foulest hypocrisy, of unbridled lust, and of relentless cruelty. It is only held in check now by the requirements of modern civilisation; but the old spirit is still latent, and in the eastern parts of Europe and west of Asia, Christendom is inferior to most Eastern religions, and in fact scarcely removed from the paganism of the savage. At the same time, among its devotees, as among the devotees of all religions, whether lay or clerical, are to be found the "salt of the earth," whose intuitive instinct it is to discover what is good in their religion, by whatever name it is called, and to practise it. Anti-Christendom abounds in true Christians. Many of these will feel a pang at the idea of giving up the beloved symbol, which has proved so often a solace to them in suffering, and an encouragement to them in effort; but one of the most powerful hindrances to the approach of Christ the Bridegroom, is this constant clinging to the cross of Christ the victim.

It is a hindrance for two reasons. One is that the majority of people cling to the contemplation of the sacrifice of Christ, because they believe that by doing so they will escape eternal damnation. In the first place, there is no such thing as eternal damnation; and in the second, if there were, they could not fit themselves for it more aptly than by making use of a perfectly innocent victim, for purely selfish purposes, in order to appease the wrath of an angry God. The stagnant and utterly feeble condition of Christ's Church on earth is well expressed by the line of the popular hymn—

"Simply to Thy cross I cling."

To hang on to it like a drowning wretch is considered the highest evidence of piety, and the noblest effort man can make for his afflicted fellow-men. Though it has not been without its value as a moral agent and an emblem of self-sacrifice, it has now become a mere drag to hold man back from the side of his Master, who is thus placed like a magnet in the remote past to attract Christians backward, or root them to the ground, and the lofty inspirations and high endeavours for humanity of those who love Him thus become paralysed.

But the standard of Christ is floating before us, and not behind us; and on its folds is emblazoned the Dove, the emblem of His Bride, the Sympneumatic Church—and not the Cross.

The second reason why the cross of the victim operates as a hindrance to the approach of the Bridegroom is, that it falsifies our entire conception of Christ as He is now, and His present work, and of our duties in regard to it. He is a conquering warrior, summoning us to the battle which is to precede His nuptials. We get near Him just in the degree in which we realise that this is the case, and, "forgetting 'those things that are behind, and reaching forth to those 'things that are before, press towards the mark for the prize 'of the high calling of God in Christ Jesus."

It is not on the wound that our General received on the first day of His first battle, that we are to fix our minds if we would co-operate with Him, but on the orders which we receive in the struggle in which we are now engaged under His leadership, and in a determination to do or to die, as He did; and by our deaths, if necessary, to help to win salvation for the race.

The last chapters of the Revelation, to which we must now return, describe the overthrow of His enemies, and the descent of His Bride.

CHAPTER XXIII.

THE FOURTEENTH AND FOLLOWING CHAPTERS OF REVELATION INTERPRETED—COLLISION ON EARTH BETWEEN THE SYMPNEUMATIC AND ANTI-SYMPNEUMATIC FORCES — CATASTROPHIC CHANGES IN CONSEQUENCE—THE FATE OF THE SIDDIM—THE TRIUMPH OF THE SAINTS—THE SECOND ADVENT, AND THE DESCENT OF THE BRIDE—RECAPITULATION.

THE first five verses of the fourteenth chapter have reference entirely to the joys of the saints in the invisible part of our universe, who "were redeemed from among men, being the first-fruits unto God and the Lamb." "The angel that flew 'in the midst of heaven, having the everlasting gospel to 'preach unto them that dwell on the earth, and to every 'nation, and kindred, and tongue, and people, saying with a 'loud voice, Fear God, and give glory to Him; for the hour 'of His judgment is come," signifies the proclamation of the Sympneuma to man, and the advent thereof.

The angel that follows, saying, "Babylon is fallen, is fallen, that great city, because she made all nations drink of the wine of the wrath of her fornication," signifies the proclamation of the overthrow of anti-Christendom, with its existing ecclesiastical organisations. The expression "wine of the wrath of her fornication" seems to have no sense, on account of its incorrect rendering. It is literally the "wine of the essence of her fornication," and has reference especially to the desecration of the sympneumatic elements contained in the blood of Christ, by the ecclesiastical dogma, which transmutes ordinary wine into His actual blood.

"The same shall drink of the wine of the wrath of God" should in the same way mean "of the essence of God";

"which is poured out without mixture into the cup of his indignation" is also a misleading translation, "indignation" meaning more properly "temperament," and referring not to God, but to the temperament of the man who drinks of the essence of God. In other words, these verses signify a collision between the divine pneumatic force and the infernal ecclesiastical one; and the "torment with fire and brimstone" signifies the acute suffering caused by this collision; "torment" meaning literally "testing by suffering," which will overtake every one "who worships the beast or 'his image, or receives his mark on his forehead or into his 'hand," and who refuses the gift of sympneumatic life now offered to him.

"Here is the patience of the saints: here are they that keep the commandments of God, and the faith of Jesus," signifies the trials which those who have accepted this gift will be called upon to endure.

"And I heard a voice from heaven saying unto me, Write, 'Blessed are the dead which die in the Lord henceforth, saith 'the Spirit, for they rest from their labours; and their works 'do follow them," signifies that those who have received this gift enter the invisible world under different conditions atomically from those who predeceased them, in ignorance of sympneumatic contact. "And their works do follow them," signifies that their efforts here receive their full fruition by a perfect sympneumatic union hereafter.

The remainder of the chapter contains an account of judgments to come; but it must be remembered that none of these judgments are in the sense of punishment or vengeance, but are the inevitable results of the infractions of law. The Greek word $\kappa\rho\iota\sigma\iota\varsigma$, which is usually translated judgment, would be more correctly rendered by a word which did not carry with it the idea of condemnation.

The following chapter refers entirely to the upper region of the invisible portion of our universe. It must be borne in mind that the words "heaven" and "hell" in the Bible always include the upper and lower portions of our world, and sometimes refer to them exclusively.

The seven plagues of the sixth verse are various methods of operation of divine pneumatic force, which, antagonising the corresponding methods of infernal pneumatic force, bring man to a crisis for violating law.

The sixteenth chapter contains an account of the crises which have overtaken man, both in the visible and invisible portions of our universe, and of the violent disturbances thus produced; also of those which are yet to follow.

The first, second, and third vials have reference to events which have already occurred, in consequence of this collision, on earth.

The fourth vial refers to crises which have overtaken the race in the lower invisible region of our universe.

The fifth vial refers to crises which are about to overtake anti-Christendom.

The sixth vial refers to crises which are about to overtake Islam and the Eastern religions; the three "unclean spirits," which are "the spirits of devils working miracles," are the polluted pneumatic forces working in man by three different modes of operation, and which are being projected by the Siddim, through the lower invisible region of our universe, into this world; "which go forth to the kings of the earth, and of the whole world, to gather them to the battle of that great day of God Almighty (Shaddai)," signifies that these forces are about to precipitate the crisis, to meet which the pure sympneumatic forces are now being developed in man.

"Behold, I come as a thief," signifies the secrecy with which these forces steal into the organism. "Blessed is he that watcheth, and keepeth his garments, lest he walk naked, and they see his shame," signifies the necessity of protecting the sympneumatic force by vigilance, purity, and discretion.

"And he gathered them together into a place called in the Hebrew tongue Armageddon," signifies that the battle-field will be, as the name implies, masculine strength and feminine fruitfulness.

"And the seventh angel poured out his vial into the air; and there came a great voice out of the temple of heaven, from the throne, saying, It is done." This signifies the second coming of Christ into the world, and the final accomplishment of His work in man.

The next three verses describe the troubles which will ensue to humanity, not in anti-Christendom alone, from the terrific projection of pneumatic force consequent on Christ's descent; these are likened to voices, thunderings, lightnings, and a great earthquake.

"And there fell upon men a great hail out of heaven, every
' stone about the weight of a talent: and men blasphemed God
' because of the weight of the hail; for the plague thereof was
' exceeding great," signifies the descent, from the upper invisible portion of our universe, of a great company of saints, in sympneumatic relations with those here, and the impotence of men animated by the infernal pneumatic forces to resist them.

The seventeenth and eighteenth chapters describe the final extinction and destruction of the Gentile Church, which exists now, and is called by the name of Christ, with all its dogmatic ramifications, ecclesiastical organisations, and sects, tawdry ceremonials, and empty formulas. This inversion is figured as a "woman, sitting upon a scarlet-coloured beast, full
' of names of blasphemy, having seven heads and ten horns,
' arrayed in scarlet and fine linen, decked with gold, and pre-
' cious stones, and pearls, having a golden cup in her hand
' full of abominations and filthiness of her fornication." By a certain section of Christians this is applied to the Church of Rome; but it applies to themselves as well, for the whole spirit of existing Christianity is one of rank blasphemy, inasmuch as it is based on the anti-Christian principle of enlightened selfishness. The social and political systems, involving bloody wars and hideous immoralities, constructed upon this basis, they call by the most holy name of Christ; thus crucifying Him afresh, and putting Him to an open shame.

There is no language which can fitly describe this gross profanation; but the seer has designated it by the name written upon the forehead of the woman, which is—

"MYSTERY, BABYLON THE GREAT, THE MOTHER OF HARLOTS AND ABOMINATIONS OF THE EARTH."

"Mystery" here signifies darkness. I have in a previous chapter described the aspect of Christendom, as seen from the invisible portion of our universe, under its black pall of atomic infusoria. "Babylon the great" signifies that the inversions are as pagan in their essence as those which characterised the inversions of the Babylonian religion, after it lost its primitive purity; and it is called "the great," because it includes all Christendom, and not any one section of it. "The mother of harlots and abominations of the earth," signifies that from its womb have sprung impurities and crimes of the blackest description.

The rest of the chapter contains arcana with reference to these, which it is not necessary here to specify; nor is it necessary to enter upon the details of the nature of the crises by which anti-Christendom or the Gentile Church will be overtaken, contained in the eighteenth chapter.

It is a relief to turn from so painful a subject to the description given in the nineteenth chapter of the final preparations for the marriage supper of the Lamb, which signifies the union of Christ with His sympneumatic Church, and the conquest of the Siddistic infestation of humanity.

The twentieth chapter foretells a period of repose into which the world will enter owing to this victory, and the reign of Christ and the sympneumatic Church upon the earth for a long period, which is popularly known as the Millennium. During this time the earth will be open to the upper invisible region of our universe, to whom, as to their atomic structure, the inhabitants of the earth will be likened. This is signified in the words, "Blessed is he that hath part in the first resur-
' rection: on such the second death hath no power, but they
' shall be priests of God and of Christ, and shall reign with
' Him a thousand years."

The earth during this time will not only be impervious to Siddistic attack, but to invasion from the inhabitants of the lower invisible region of our universe. This is signified in the words, "But the rest of the dead lived not again till the thousand years were finished." At the expiration of the period here mystically indicated, the earth will be exposed to a new Siddistic attack, which is signified in the words, "And when the thousand years have expired, Satan shall be loosed out of prison."

The result of the struggle which will then ensue will be a victory over the Siddim, which will be accomplished by the descent of the Seraphim—a word meaning "fiery creatures"—

to earth. This is signified in the words, "And fire came down from God and out of heaven and devoured them."

Their subsequent fate is signified in the words, "And the 'devil, that deceived them, was cast into the lake of fire and 'brimstone, where the beast and the false prophet are, and 'shall be tested day and night for ages of ages." The words, "tormented for ever and ever," contained in the English version of the Bible, are a strained translation of the original, to accord with the idea of eternal punishment, which is a radically false one. The literal translation is the one given above, and signifies the long period of probationary discipline through which the Siddim must pass before they can be finally redeemed. This is the necessary consequence of the lengthened duration of their wilful inversion of truth, and violation of law; but the final and ultimate extinction of the world they inhabit, and the liberation of their wills from the prison-house of self in which they have been so long confined, and their reabsorption into the will of the infinite All-Father and All-Mother, however long delayed, is certain. The extinction of the invisible portion of our universe will also take place simultaneously with the conquest over the Siddim; some of those, who were too fixed in their vices to be restored, having their future lot cast with the latter in the region of testing or purification, signified in the words, "lake of fire"; and others being restored to our own world, as is signified in the words, "And the dead were judged out of those things which were written in the books, according to their works."

The change which will thereby be effected is signified in the words, "And death and hell were cast into the lake of fire."

The final union of Christ with His Church is described in the next chapter. By this time the animal, vegetable, and mineral worlds will have undergone atomic transformations of so vast a kind that they are indicated by the seer in the words, "And I saw a new heaven and a new earth: for the first heaven and the first earth were passed away; and there was no more sea." This last sentence signifies that the ocean which now separates the visible from the invisible will no longer exist. The universe will again form one, visible to all its inhabitants, for the atomic accretion will have been removed, faculties which are now subsurface or supersensuous, will be developed, the conditions of life and of translation to the new heaven, which is the unfallen region of the former world, will be altogether changed. And this change will no less affect the animal creation, which will also develop new faculties and instincts, losing all those which are predatory or carnivorous, and fulfilling the prophet's words that "the lion shall lie down with the lamb."

Therefore, "He that sat upon the throne said, Behold, I make all things new"; and there was a "great voice which cried out of heaven, saying, The tabernacle of God is with men."

These are the most pregnant words in the whole book; for they signify the presence of the Divine Feminine, because the tabernacle was the abode of the Shechinah. The elaborate instructions given to Moses during his retirement of forty days and nights on the top of Mount Sinai, in regard to the construction of the tabernacle, contained the mystery which the cloud concealed, out of which God called to Moses,[1] when "the sight of the glory of the Lord was like devouring fire on the top of the mount, in the sight of the children of Israel," and which was, in fact, the Shechinah or Divine Feminine. Therefore he said, "There will I meet with the children of Israel, and the tabernacle will be sanctified with my glory;"[2] for the tabernacle was to contain the ark, over which this cloud of glory brooded, between the wings of the cherubim, and from which issued the divine instructions; and so we are told that when the tabernacle was finished, "a cloud 'covered the tent of the congregation, and the glory of the 'Lord filled the tabernacle. And Moses was not able to enter 'into the tent of the congregation, because the cloud abode 'thereon, and the glory of the Lord filled the tabernacle."[3]

Thus was typified that grander tabernacle which has yet to be erected in the hearts of those who have recovered the lost bisexual image: and this is the great consummation predicted by the seer, when he said that God "shall dwell with them; and they shall be His people, and God Himself shall be with them, and be their God."

That this blessed consummation will be the result of the death of Christ, receives a remarkable confirmation in an event

---

[1] Exodus xxiv. 16, 17.   [2] Exodus xxix. 43.   [3] Exodus xl. 34.

which, we are told, occurred on that occasion. It will be remembered that the ark was hidden from the public by a veil, within which only the high priest was allowed to enter; the mystery of the Divine Feminine, which brooded between the cherubim, was thus shrouded. In the second temple, though the original ark was no longer there, the veil still concealed from view the Holy of Holies, which was the sanctuary of the hidden mystery. But at the moment of Christ's death, we are told, the veil of the temple was rent in twain from the top to the bottom. In other words, that act made a breach in the outer covering, and a way was made into the Holy of Holies by which man might henceforth have access to the mystery it had concealed. The words "Holy of Holies" contain another still more esoteric sense which I am not permitted here to explain.

The writer now gives a picture, in glowing and poetic language, of the happiness resulting from the constant presence of God with man, and follows it with a description of the descent of the Bride, the Lamb's wife, typified under the symbol of a bridal city—the New Jerusalem—of which we are told that there was "No temple therein: for the Lord God 'Almighty and the Lamb are the temple of it. And the city 'had no need of the sun, neither of the moon, to shine in it: 'for the glory of the Lord did lighten it, and the Lamb is the 'light thereof. And the nations of them which are saved shall 'walk in the light of it." All these allusions to glory and light refer to the Divine Feminine principle, with which the world has then become endowed through the descent of the Bride. The blessed consequences of this descent are still further developed in the last chapter, where "the pure river of water 'of life, clear as crystal, proceeding out of the throne of God 'and of the Lamb," with "the tree of life, on either side of it, 'whose leaves are for the healing of the nations," need no interpretation.

The story of the race has thus been narrated, in the form of the Word contained in the Bible, from its Alpha to its Omega. It has been shown how it was an emanation from a previous world; how what is called "evil" entered into that world through will-perversion; how evolution could only progress under mixed conditions in consequence; how man was generated by respirative emanation; how he differed as to his atomic substance from the animal, vegetable, and mineral nature by which he was surrounded; how, by atomic affinity with the fallen race of the previous world, he was exposed to their attacks; how his atomic elements underwent changes in consequence, and the Divine Feminine receded from him, while the Divine Masculine took an unnatural and debased form; how his conception of the Deity suffered in consequence; how, under the influence of the infernal masculine and degraded feminine, he fell still further; how the bisexual principle became at last absolutely severed, until he lost consciousness that it had ever existed; how, in consequence of the changes he was undergoing, and the constant attacks to which he was subjected from the Siddim, great portions of the world and of the race upon it were submerged; how a remnant remained to preserve the truth; how it was necessary to veil the truth from the common herd, for fear of its profanation; how it existed in some form or other in the most ancient sacred books of all religions; how it was finally confided to the guardianship of a special race; how, nevertheless, a means existed for preparing man to receive it, and to comprehend and invoke its potency; how that means was a human being, born under appropriate conditions, who should voluntarily allow himself to be put to death, because only thus could he distribute the elements of the Divine Feminine here, and so connect the visible part of our universe by an atomic sympneumatic chain with that which is invisible; how these two, being atomically interlocked, form only one universe, constantly acting and reacting upon one another; how, ever since the first coming of Christ, the sympneumatic processes have been developing both in the visible and invisible worlds; how that development has now reached a stage which has enabled this revelation to be made; how the agency of the forces which they contain, offer the only means of purification for the world from the infernal lust-principle, which has poisoned the springs of its life; how those springs will be purified by the efforts of that portion of humanity which is prepared to give itself up to the work; how, finally, it is only through the co-operation of those of our own race, who have passed into the upper invisible region of our universe, acting under the direction and control of Christ, that this great end can be achieved, which will have for its final result not merely the salvation of our own visible world—not merely that of the lower portion of it which is invisible—but, in the far-distant future, of that still lower world which is the fallen portion of the universe from which we sprang, which is the origin of what we call evil, but which is sustained, nevertheless, by the divine vitality, and bears concealed in its darkest recesses the imprisoned elements of bisexual life, with their latent germs of perfect good and perfect purity.

This is the glorious mission of humanity, "and the pneuma and the bride say, Come."

I cannot close the message, with the delivery of which I felt myself charged, without expressing my sense of the imperfections I labour under as a medium of transmission for the truths which I have endeavoured to convey in these pages.

I have explained in the earlier chapters how entirely the form of such a work is dependent on the idiosyncrasies, the training, and the natural gifts of the person intrusted with its expression, and I am painfully aware of my own deficiency as an instrument for putting into suitable language, the pregnant ideas which have forced themselves upon my consciousness.

Until I was six-and-thirty years of age my mind was wholly absorbed by the pleasures and ambitions of a thoroughly worldly life, and I carefully suppressed an undercurrent of thought which occasionally reminded me that I was not put into the world to gratify my own tastes. At that period, under a pressure that was at the time irresistible, I felt myself compelled, much against my natural inclination, to abandon the life I had hitherto been leading, some account of which I have given in a book which I have recently published,[1] and to devote myself to the investigation of those more hidden laws of nature, which, I felt

[1] Episodes in a Life of Adventure; or, Moss from a Rolling Stone. William Blackwood & Sons.

convinced, concealed divine truths that had as yet been hidden from man. There is no more finality in the knowledge of sacred things than in any other kind of wisdom; but I looked in vain for religious progress in any quarter. The great moral impetus given to the world nearly nineteen hundred years ago soon expended itself, in so far as its practical bearing upon outward daily life was concerned; and since then, the gleams of truth shed upon the problems which vex humanity have been few and fitful.

In the endeavour to throw such light as I have been vouchsafed upon them, a previous scientific or theological training would have enabled me to utilise knowledge which I do not now possess, in further illustration of the subject. This, however, I will leave the men of science and theologians to do for themselves, while I avail myself of this opportunity to assure them, that if I have felt constrained to speak severely of the prejudice and intolerance which characterise both schools of thought, I have not done so from any sentiment of disrespect to the men themselves, feeling convinced that no better men could be found than among agnostic professors and Trinitarian priests; no thanks, however, to the dogmas either of their science or their theology.

I have availed myself of the kind services of a friend who once belonged to the latter category, but who is now able, from his own personal experience, to write from the sympneumatic standpoint, and to confirm by Biblical quotation and illustration the statements made in this book; but I am impressed to inform my readers that this is only the unfolding of the outer covering of the mystery. The real mystery, for which they are not yet prepared, lies within.

This outer covering makes no claim to infallibility, but it does claim to be experimentally tested, and not merely intellectually judged; for the rational faculty of man is too strained and warped by exclusive development, to the sacrifice of his moral evolution, to be of any value in estimating results which have been arrived at by moral, and not by intellectual, effort.

Above all, it is not for the purpose of adding to the number of religious sects which are now existing, that this message has been delivered, but rather for the purpose of preparing the minds of men—whatever be their religious or philosophic opinions — for one which is to follow it, and of urging them to enter upon a more severe and searching process of self-discipline than any Church can impose, for it does not hold out salvation as a reward, nor offer the ægis of a Church as a shelter and support.

Popular theology and popular science will alike prove broken reeds to trust to in the days which are approaching.

APPENDIX I.

APPENDIX I.

I APPEND here some extracts from the Book of the Lesser Holy Assembly (Mather's 'Kabbalah Unveiled,' chapters viii. and xxii.) They will probably be found too mystical for the ordinary reader; but they, together with many other passages in the Kabbalah bearing on the same subject, possess great value and importance, as showing the profound knowledge which existed from a very early period, among a mystical sect of Jews, of the nature of the Divine Feminine, or Pneuma; of the proceeding "Word," or Son; and of the Bride, or Sympneuma—for the Bride of the Son is His Sympneuma, and the two conjoined are the type of all human Sympneumata, whereby we are united through Christ the Son and His Bride, to the Great Father and Mother, the Infinite Two-in-One.

"(As to the sacred name, IHVH.[1]) I, *Yod*, is included in this Chokmah, Wisdom; H, *He*, is Aima, and is called Binah, Understanding; VH, *Vau*, *He*, are those two children who are produced from Aima, the Mother.

"Also we have learned that the name Binah comprehendeth all things. For in Her is I, *Yod*, which is associated with Aima, or the letter H, *He*, and together they produce BN, *Ben*, the Son; and this is the word Binah, Father and Mother, who are I, *Yod*, and H, *He*—with whom are interwoven the letters B, *Beth*, and N, *Nun*, which are *Ben;* and thus far regarding Binah.

"Also She is called Thebunah, the Special Intelligence. Wherefore is She sometimes Thebunah, and not Binah?

"Assuredly Thebunah is She called at that time in which Her two children appear, the Son and the Daughter, Ben Va-Bath, who are *Vau*, *He;* and at that time She is called Thebunah.

[1] (Jehovah.) For the methods of interpretation of alphabetical symbolisms, the reader is referred to Mr Mather's Introduction to the 'Kabbalah Unveiled.'

"For all things are comprehended in those letters, Vau, He, which are Ben Va-Bath, Son and Daughter. . . .

"In the Book of Rav Hamenuna the Elder, it is said that Solomon revealeth the primal conformation (that is, the Mother), when he saith, Cant. i. 15, 'Behold, thou art fair, my love;'[1] wherefore he followeth it out himself.

"And he calleth the second conformation the Bride, which is called the Inferior Woman.

"And there are some who apply both these names (those namely of Love and Bride) to this Inferior Woman, but these are not so.

"For the first H, *He* (of IHVH), is not called the Bride; but the last H, *He*, is called the Bride at certain times, on account of many symbolic reasons.

"For many are the times when the Male is not associated with Her, but is separated from Her.

"Concerning this period, it is said (Lev. xviii. 19), 'Also thou shalt not approach unto a woman in the separation of her uncleanness.'

"But when the female hath been purified, and the male desireth to be united unto her, then is she called the Bride—the Bride properly so called.[2]

"But as to that which pertaineth to the Mother, then the benevolence of them both is not taken away to all eternity.

"Together they (Chokmah and Binah, IH) go forth, together they are at rest; the one ceaseth not from the other, and the one is never taken away from the other.

"And therefore it is written (Gen. ii. 10), 'And a river went forth out of Eden.' Properly speaking, it goeth forth, and never faileth.

"As it is written (Isa. lviii. 11), 'And like a fountain of waters, whose waters fail not.'

"And therefore is She called 'My Love,' since from the grace of kindred association they rest in perfect unity.

"But the other is called the Bride—for when the Male cometh, that He may consort with Her, then is She the Bride; for She, properly speaking, cometh forth as the Bride.

"And therefore doth Solomon expound these two forms of the Woman; and concerning the first form, indeed, he worketh hiddenly, seeing it is hidden.

"But the second form is more fully explained, seeing it is not so hidden as the other.

"But at the end all his praise pertaineth unto Her who is supernal, as it is written, Cant. vi. 9: 'She is the only one of Her mother; She is the choice one of Her that bare Her.'

"And since this mother, Aima, is crowned with the crown of the Bride, and the grace of the letter I, *Yod*, ceaseth not from Her for ever,

---

[1] This affords an illustration of the esoteric meaning attached to certain portions of sacred literature by the Jewish mystics.

[2] This separation symbolises the alienation of humanity, or the earthly bride—also called the Church—because of its uncleanness, from the Divine Spouse.

hence unto Her arbitration is committed all the liberty of those inferior, and all the liberty of all things, and all the liberty of sinners, so that all things may be purified.

"As it is written, Lev. xvi. 30, 'Since in that day he shall atone for you';[1] also it is written, Lev. xxv. 10, 'And ye shall hallow the fiftieth year.' This year is *Yobel*.'

"What is *Yobel?* as it is written, Jer. xvii. 8, '*Va-el-Yobel*, and spreadeth out her roots by the river.' Therefore that river, which ever goeth forth, and floweth, and goeth forth, and faileth not.[2]

"It is written, Prov. ii. 3, 'If thou wilt call Binah the Mother, and will give thy voice unto Thebunah.'[3]

"Seeing it is said, 'If thou wilt call Binah Mother, why is Thebunah added?'

"Assuredly, according as I have said, all things are supernal truth; Binah is higher than Thebunah. For in the word Binah are shown Father, Mother, and Son; since by the letters IH, Father and Mother are denoted, and the letters BN, denoting the Son, are amalgamated with them.

"Thebunah is the whole completion of the children, since it containeth the letters BN *Ben*, BTH *Bath*, and VH *Vau He;* by which are denoted the Son and Daughter.

"Yet AB VAM, *Ab Ve-Am*, the Father and Mother, are not found, save BAIMA, *Be-Aima*, in the Mother, for the venerable Aima broodeth over them, neither is she uncovered.

"Whence it cometh that that which embraceth the two children is called Thebunah, and that which embraceth the Father, the Mother, and the Son, is called Binah.

"And when all things are comprehended, they are comprehended therein, and are called by that name of Father, Mother, and Son.

"And these are Chokmah, Wisdom, Father; Binah, Understanding, Mother; and Däath, Knowledge (the Son).

"Since that Son assumeth the symbols of His Father and Mother

---

[1] The arcanum contained in this passage is, in fact, the mystery of Christ's mission to earth. While the conjugal union of the Son and the Bride is subject to interruption in consequence of the pollution by which humanity has become tainted, the grace of Yod, the Infinite Father, ceaseth not from Aima, the Infinite Mother—in other words, their conjugal union remains ever complete. And it is through the Infinite Mother, "to whose arbitration has been committed the liberty of all things, that all things may be purified," that means have been provided for the redemption and purification of humanity through the operation of the Son, "since in that day he shall atone" for us—this atonement consisting in the incarnation in Christ of those elements of the Divine Feminine through the supernal Son and Daughter, or Bride, which could only be distributed throughout nature by His death; and thus, through the combined operation of the Pneuma and Sympneuma, indissolubly uniting us to the Infinite Father and Mother, Two-in-One.

[2] This river that "floweth, and goeth forth, and faileth not," is the infinite love of Aima, or, when She signifies Understanding, Binah.

[3] According to the English version, "Yea, if thou criest after knowledge, and liftest up thy voice for understanding."

and is called Däath, Knowledge, since He is the testimony of them both.[1]

"And that Son is called the first-born, as it is written, Exod. iv. 22, 'Israel is my first-born Son.'

"And since He is called first-born, therefore it implieth dual offspring."[2]

Although there are many other allusions to this subject, which are deeply interesting, I will only quote part of one other chapter, in the arcana of which may be discovered, by those who carefully study it, the extreme sanctity with which sex-conjunction was invested from the earliest times, as symbolised in the construction of the Jewish Temple. It also found expression in the earliest religions, in Phallic worship, and in those rites and mysteries which were soon so profaned, that the infinitely pure and sacred source to which they owed their origin became choked with pollution, and finally ceased to flow; for the earth was unfit to receive the touch of the Divine Feminine. To protect it from still further prostitution, all consciousness thereof was withdrawn from the minds of men, until nature should receive a fresh discharge of purifying elements through a human organism specially prepared for the purpose. The time has once more arrived when those who are inspired with that courage which a passionate love for humanity can alone impart, may once more approach, with uncovered feet, that holy ground; for it is only in the mystic temple reared by the operation of the Divine Masculine and Feminine principles in the human breast, that the new worship can be inaugurated, and those potencies invoked, which shall redeem and purify the race. It is thus alone that, after her separation because of her uncleanliness, the Bride can be fitted for the arms of the Bridegroom, whose return is predicted in Holy Writ, and for whom those who love Him are eagerly watching.

Chapter xxii. of the Book of the Lesser Holy Assembly, "Concerning the remaining members of the Son, or the Lesser Countenance":—

"734. The Male is extended in right and left, through the inheritance which He receiveth (*i.e., from Chokmah and Binah*).

"735. But whensoever the colours are mingled together then is He called Tiphereth, and the whole body is formed into a tree (*the Autz Ha-Chaiim, or Tree of Life*), great and strong, and fair and beautiful. Dan. iv. 11.[3]

---

[1] Hence He is "The Word."

[2] The dual offspring is humanity, when it has become bisexual through sympneumatic union; and Israel, in this connection, typifies Christ.

[3] The Tree of Life is the bisexual body.

"736. 'The beasts of the field had shadow under it, and the fowls of the heaven dwelt in the boughs thereof, and all flesh was fed on it.'

"737. His arms were right and left. In the right is Chesed and Life; in the left is Geburah and Death.

"738. Through Däath (Knowledge) are his inner parts formed, and they fill the Assemblies and Conclaves as we have said.

"739. For thus is it written, 'And through Däath shall the Conclaves be filled.'

"740. Afterwards is His body extended into two thighs, et intra hæc continentur duo renes, duo testiculi masculini.

"741. Omne enim oleum, et dignitas, et vis masculi e toto corpore in istis congregatur; nam omnes exercitus, qui prodeunt ab iis, omnes prodeunt et morantur in orificio membri genitalis.

"742. And therefore are they called Tzabaoth, the Armies; and they are Netzach (*Victory*), and Hod (*Glory*). For Tiphereth is Tetragrammaton,[1] but Netzach and Hod are the armies; hence cometh that name Tetragrammaton Tzabaoth.[2]

"743. Membrum masculi est extremitas totius corporis, et vocatur Yesod, fundamentum, et hic est gradus ille qui mitigat fœminam. For every desire of the Male is towards the Female.

"744. Per hoc fundamentum ille ingreditur in fœminam; in locum qui vocatur Tzion et Jerusalem. Nam hic est locus tegendus fœminæ, et in uxore vocatur uterus.

"745. And hence is Tetragrammaton Tzabaoth called Yesod,[3] the Foundation. Also it is written, Ps. cxxxii. 13—'Since Tetragrammaton hath chosen Tzion to be a habitation for Himself; He hath desired Her.'

"746. When Matronitha, the mother, is separated and conjoined with the King face to face in the excellence of the Sabbath, all things become one body.

"747. And when the Holy One—blessed be He!—sitteth on His throne, and all things are called the Complete Name, the Holy Name. Blessed be His Name for ever, and unto the ages of the ages!

"748. All these words have I kept back unto this day, which is crowned by them for the world to come. And now herein are they manifested. O blessed be my portion!

"749. When this Mother is conjoined with the King, all the worlds receive blessing, and the universe is found to be in joy.

"750. Like as the Male (the Son) existeth from the Triad *Kether* (the Crown), *Chokmah* (Wisdom), *and Binah* (Understanding), and His beginning is with the Triad, in this same manner are all things disposed, and the end of the whole body is thus; also the Mother (*Inferior*), receiveth not the blessing except in the Syntagma of the Triad, and these paths are Netzach, Hod, and Yesod.

---

[1] Tetragrammaton is Jehovah—that word being too holy to be pronounced.
[2] The Lord of Hosts.
[3] Yesod is the Lord; Tzabaoth, composed of Hod and Netzach, are The Hosts; hence we obtain the full internal significance of the expression, "The Lord of Hosts."

"751. And She is mitigated, and receiveth blessing in that place which is called the Holy of Holies below.

"752. As it is written, Ps. cxxxii. 13—'Since there Tetragrammaton giveth His blessing.' For there are two paths; that which is above, and that which is below.

"753. Hence there is permission granted unto none to enter therein, save unto the High Priest, who entereth from the side of Chesed, in order that none other might enter into that supernal place save that which is called Chesed.

"754. And He entereth into the Holy of Holies, and the Bride is mitigated, and the Holy of Holies receiveth blessing in the place which is called Tzion.

"755. But Tzion and Jerusalem are two paths, one denoting Mercy and the other Justice.

"756. For concerning Tzion it is written, Isa. i. 27—'Through Meshephat, Judgment, it is redeemed.' And concerning Jerusalem, it is written, *ibid.*, 21—'Justice, Tzedek, abideth in Her,' as we have before explained.

"757. And every desire of the Male is toward the Female. But thus are these called, because hence proceed blessings for all the worlds, and all things receive blessing.

"758. This place is called Holy, and all the holinesses of the Male enter therein through that path of which we have spoken.

"759. But they all come from the supernal head of the Male skull, from that portion of the supernal brain wherein they reside.

"760. And this blessing floweth down through all the members of the body, even unto those which are called Tzabaoth, the Armies.

"761. And all that which floweth down throughout the whole body is congregated therein, and therefore are they called Tzabaoth, the Armies; because all the armies of the superiors and inferiors go forth therefrom.

"762. And that which floweth down into that place where it is congregated and which is emitted through that most holy Yesod, Foundation, is entirely white, and, therefore, is called Chesed.

"763. Thence Chesed entereth into the Holy of Holies; as it is written, Ps. cxxxiii. 3—'For there Tetragrammaton commanded the blessing, even life for evermore.'"

These were the last words which Rabbi Simeon Ben Yochai, whom Kabbalists believe to have been the writer of a great portion of the Kabbalah, ever spoke. The scribe to whom he was dictating, Rabbi Abba, said, "Scarcely could the Holy Light-bearer (Rabbi Simeon) finish the word 'Life' before his words ceased altogether. But I was writing them down, and thought there would still be more for me to write, but I heard nothing." The scribe then proceeds to describe the phenomena which attended his death—"And a voice was heard (saying), Come ye, and assemble together, and enter into the nuptials of Rabbi Simeon.

Isa. lvii., 'Let him enter in with peace, and let them rest in their chambers.'" From this it is clear that even in that early day holy men, who were versed in the mysteries, looked forward to that sympneumatic union after death by which they should be completed as to their personalities. And Rabbi Simeon brings this out still more clearly on a previous occasion when he says :—

"And those words have hereunto been concealed, therefore have I feared to reveal the same, but now they are revealed.

"And I reveal them in the presence of the most Holy Ancient King; for not for mine own glory, nor for the glory of my father's house, do I this; but I do this that I may not enter ashamed into His palaces.

"Henceforth I only see that He, God the Most Holy—may He be blessed!—and all those truly just men who are here found can all consent (hereunto) with me.

"For I see that all can rejoice in these my nuptials, and that they all can be admitted unto my nuptials in that world. Blessed be my portion!"

APPENDIX II.

BY

A CLERGYMAN OF THE CHURCH OF ENGLAND

CONTENTS OF APPENDIX II.

NOTE		PAGE
	Preface,	403
A.	On Angelic Ministry, or Spiritual Agency,	405
B.	On Inspiration,	407
C.	On the Nature of God,	411
D.	On the Miracles of Christ,	414
E.	On True Theology,	418
F.	On the Purification of the Human Organism,	421
G.	On the term "Forgiveness of Sins,"	425
H.	On the Dogma of the Atonement,	428
I.	On Implicit Obedience to the Dictates of Conscience,	431
J.	On Love,	433
K.	On the word "Power," as used in the English New Testament,	437
L.	On the Physical Relation of Present Pain to Future Joy,	439
M.	On the Future Life,	442
N.	On the Hidden Meaning of Scripture,	444
O.	On Spiritual Experiences,	445
P.	On the Word "Shaddai,"	447
Q.	On the Atomic Affinity between Christ and True Christians,	453
R.	On the Dogma of the Trinity,	457
S.	On the word "Pneuma,"	463
T.	On the Restoration of True Christianity,	470
	Postscript,	472

APPENDIX II.

PREFACE TO THE NOTES IN THE APPENDIX.

The following notes are the result of a simple and honest search after the truth of God.

The writer, in the course of a somewhat long and varied experience as a priest of the Church of England, had for some time been conscious of a growing uneasiness in his mind as to the present condition of Christianity. He had met, in the course of his ministry, with many evidences of a widespread sense of dissatisfaction at the results hitherto achieved by the dogmas and organisations of the Churches and sects of Christendom.

Nor, so far as his powers of investigation went, did he find it otherwise as regards the effects produced by the other great religions of the world. As to the practical daily life of the human race, the world at this moment is scarcely better than if all its religions had never existed. Evil passions of every kind were never more rampant than they are at present: misery, pain, sickness, and death, devastate humanity with their terrible scourges, as powerfully now as in any age of man's fallen history. In a word, the regeneration of the human race, from sin and its consequences, seems to be as far as ever from its accomplishment.

To any one who truly loves God and his fellow-creatures, this condition of things must appear inexpressibly sad; and to none more so than to honest and candid priests and ministers of religion, who should be the first to welcome any unprejudiced and intelligent attempt to investigate the causes of past failure, and to discover the secret of future success. In order that such an attempt should be made under fitting conditions, it was necessary to divest one's self, for the time, of all preconceived notions,—to remove one's self entirely from the sphere of past duties and associations, and, in the childlike spirit of open receptivity and humble trust, to give one's self up to the guidance of the Spirit of God.

Such has been the simple aim of the writer, who lays no claim whatever to any infallible inspiration, who is conscious of the imperfection of his work, and who neither desires nor expects any of his readers to accept his dictum on any of the subjects treated of, without due investigation and conviction of its truth. All he asks is that his readers will approach the task in the same candid spirit as that which he has endeavoured to maintain for himself; and that they will give him credit for no other motive than that of seeking to discover the truth of God.

He would suggest that these notes can only be profitably studied by those who will be content to take their Bibles and undergo the labour of examining the various passages referred to one by one; for a mere cursory reading of this appendix will do no good whatever.

One other word of personal explanation may, perhaps, be permitted. The writer has at present withheld his name; not because he is ashamed of his efforts in the cause of truth, nor because he is afraid of any results to himself that might attend the publication of it; but for entirely independent reasons, which the reader will doubtless accept as satisfactory when he learns that they meet with the approval of so fearless and straightforward a writer as Mr Oliphant. If at any future time he feels that the cause will be aided by the divulgence of his name, he will no longer keep it concealed.

Meanwhile, to remove all occasion for cavil, he wishes to state that he is at present deriving no personal pecuniary benefit from any ecclesiastical organisation, nor is it his purpose ever to do so again in the future.

M.A. Cantab.

NOTE A.

ON ANGELIC MINISTRY, OR SPIRITUAL AGENCY.

Chapter i. page 21.

"*The unseen world teems with intelligences, whose action upon this one is very direct.*"

One would imagine that this proposition was self-evident to any student of, and believer in, the Bible; and we should scarcely think it worth while to support it by passages from Holy Writ, were it not that the majority of professing Christians deny altogether, in the present day, the action of unseen intelligences and sensible manifestations of their power; though these manifestations are constantly occurring in Bible history, and have, moreover, of late, forced themselves upon public notice by phenomena so remarkable that societies have been formed to investigate them.

The Book of Genesis contains at least twenty-two distinct intimations of this truth (xv. 10-17; xvi. 7-13; xvii. 1-22; xviii. xix. 1-22; xx. 3-7; xxi. 17-19; xxii. 1-18; xxiv. 7; xxvi. 24; xxviii. 12-17; xxxi. 11; xxxi. 24; xxxii. 1, 2; xxxii. 24-32; xxxv. 1; xxxv. 9; xxxvii. 5-11; xl. 5-19; xli. 1-36; xlvi. 2-5; xlviii. 16).

In the Book of Exodus we find six passages which can only be explained by the action of unseen intelligences on the wills or persons of the human beings affected (vii. 13; ix. 12; x. 20; xi. 10; xii. 27-29; xxiii. 20-23).

In Leviticus there are three statements as to those who have "familiar spirits" (xix. 31; xx. 6; xx. 27).

The Book of Numbers records explicitly the direct interference of an angel with Balaam (xxii. 22, &c.)

Deuteronomy speaks again of familiar spirits (xviii. 11).

In Joshua we find the "captain of the Lord's host" appearing to the leader of the Israelites (v. 13-15).

Judges records the appearances of angels to Gideon and Manoah (vi. 11-21; xiii. 3-22).

The 1st Book of Samuel has several notable instances of the action of spiritual intelligences on man (iii. 4-18; xvi. 14-23; xix. 9; xxviii. 3, 7, 13).

In the 2d Book of Samuel it is directly stated that it was an angel, a personal, intelligent, unseen being, that wrought the pestilence in the land of Israel during the reign of David (xxiv. 16, &c.).

Elijah and Micaiah, in the 1st Book of Kings, remind us of

the active interference of the unseen world in the affairs of this earth (xix.; xxii.)

Remarkable instances of the same truth are found in the 2d Book of Kings, especially in the case of Elisha at Dothan, and Sennacherib before Jerusalem (i. 10, 12; ii. 11; vi. 16, 17; xix. 35; xxi. 6; xxiii. 24).

Both the Books of Chronicles contain similar intimations (1st Chron. x. 13; 2d Chron. xxxiii. 6).

Two distinct accounts of the same action are recorded in the Book of Job (i. 6-12; ii. 1-7; iv. 12-17).

The Psalms are full of sentiments expressing a belief in this truth (viii. 5; xxxiv. 7; xxxv. 5, 6; lxviii. 17; lxxviii. 49; xci. 11, 12; civ. 4, &c.)

Ecclesiastes alludes to the same idea (v. 6).

Isaiah dwells frequently and forcibly upon it (vi. 1-9; viii. 19; xi. 2; xix. 3; xxix. 4; xlvii. 9, &c.)

Daniel bears out the same truth (iii. 25; v. 5, 6, 24-28; vi. 22).

Zechariah records a notable account of the action of an angel and Satan with regard to the high priest (i. 9, &c.; iii.)

We have thus deduced at least seventy-two separate instances—amongst others, from the Old Testament—testifying beyond contradiction to the active influence and interference exerted by the intelligences of the unseen world upon humanity.

The New Testament simply teems with passages absolutely irreconcilable with any theory which excludes the doctrine of invisible intelligences.

The following passages may be studied with interest in proof of this:—

Matt. i. 20, 24; ii. 12, 13, 19; iii. 17; iv. 1-11; viii. 8-13, 16, 28-34; ix. 32-34; x. 1, 8; xii. 22-28, 43-45; xv. 21-28; xvii. 18; xviii. 10; xxvi. 53; xxvii. 19; xxviii. 2-7.

Mark i. 13, 23-27, 32-34, 39; iii. 15, 22-30; v. 1-20; vi. 7, 13; vii. 24-30; ix. 17-29, 38; xvi. 5, 9, 17.

Luke i. 11-20, 26-38; ii. 9-14; iv. 1-13, 33-37, 41; vi. 18; viii. 27-38; ix. 1, 38-42, 49, 50; xi. 14-26; xxii. 31, 43; xxiv. 4.

John v. 4; xx. 12.

Acts v. 16, 19, 20; viii. 7; ix. 3-8; x. 3-7; xii. 7-11; xvi. 18; xix. 12-16; xxvii. 23.

1 Cor. iv. 9; vi. 3; xi. 10; xii. 10.

Gal. iii. 19.

Heb. i. 14; ii. 2; xii. 22; xiii. 2.

1 Pet. i. 12.

1 John iv. 1.

The Book of Revelation is so full of the subject that it is impossible to note down all the passages.

But enough has been quoted to show that the Bible at any rate teaches unequivocally the intimate connection between the visible and invisible portions of the universe of God, and their mutual interaction the one upon the other.

NOTE B.

ON INSPIRATION.

Chapter i. page 25.

"*Certainly others should shrink from asserting, as many do assert, not merely that these prophets and apostles speak with the divine voice, but that it has been personally revealed to them that they did so; for it must always come to this, either in the first or second degree, and that every word written was suggested literally by God.*"

It is evident that St Paul himself was conscious of different degrees of "inspiration" at different times; and that, therefore, he himself did not consider his epistles, nor expect them to be considered, as universally divinely inspired, in the sense that every statement contained therein was to be accepted as coming directly and infallibly from God Himself.

Every one of his epistles commences with the distinct announcement that it is *he, Paul*, that is about to write; and not once does he state, or even hint, in the preliminary announcements, that what is about to be written must be taken as coming from God, or held in any other light than an ordinary letter from an earnest and experienced missionary to a friend or body of friends, living in some locality where he has already ministered.

Now and then, indeed, he seems to feel more powerfully than usual a divine influx or afflatus; and on such occasions he makes use of expressions intimating that this is the case.

Sometimes, on the other hand, he is conscious of writing with little or no influx; and on such occasions he speaks diffidently, and seems to indicate that he desires his remarks to be taken for what they are worth. On the whole, his letters are manifestly those of a deeply earnest, truth-seeking, religious man, who thoroughly believes in all that he says, and who expects that his communications will be received by his correspondents with the respect and attention due to one who has been the human instrument of their conversion to the faith, and who is held in esteem and confidence by them for his learning, piety, and nearness to God.

We might go further, and say that, undoubtedly, St Paul wrote under considerable internal influx; but he himself would have been the first to repudiate any claim to infallible inspiration.

This will be apparent, if we take his epistles separately, and freeing them from the false glamour of superstition with which the Church has invested them, read them as we would any other letters written, under similar circumstances, by a missionary to his flock. Thus studied, they will be found to reveal themselves in a light far more beautiful, because more real and genuine, than they have ever appeared before; and in proportion as the false superhuman fades from our view, the lovely charm of the true humanity contained in those marvellous compositions, tempered by the varying shades of internal influx, will be the more clearly realised and appreciated by us.

Nor need any one fear lest this realisation should diminish the value and authority of those writings; for a true conception must carry with it more power of conviction than that which is false.

By way of illustration as to the foregoing remarks, let us take his letter to his Christian friends at Rome, commonly called "The Epistle to the Romans."

After the introductory personal greeting and ministerial blessing, the writer tells his friends how deep is the interest which he takes in their welfare, how pleased he is to hear that they continue firm in their faith, how earnestly he prays for them, and how anxiously he longs to pay them another visit, as soon as the way is made clear for him to do so.—See Rom. i. 8-13.

All this is evidently purely "human," and as such Paul himself regards it. He "thanks God"; he "calls God to witness" of the truth of what he says as to his feelings; he places himself on a level with those to whom he writes, speaking of "the mutual faith both of you and me." Passing on from mere personal matters, he discusses certain points of doctrine and conduct connected with the new religion; and the tone which he employs is just such as we should expect from one writing a letter of serious importance to new converts, who were still in doubt upon many matters of faith and practice. And though he clearly feels very deeply upon the subjects himself, and endeavours to impress his views most earnestly upon his readers, there is no sign throughout that he is conscious of any further inspiration than that accorded to one whose single aim is the truth, and who, by piety and self-sacrifice, has become more than ordinarily open to spiritual impressions, and thus more than ordinarily enabled to distinguish between a true and a false afflatus.

So much, indeed, does his own personality mingle itself with his writings, that, in the very midst of his arguments on certain points of doctrine, he pauses to take his friends into his confidence as to the spiritual conflict through which he himself has passed.

See chap. vii. 9-25. At other times, again, he uses such expressions as the following: "I am persuaded," &c. (viii. 38, 39); "I say the truth in Christ, I lie not, my conscience also bearing me witness" (ix. 1); "My heart's desire and prayer to God for Israel is, that they might be saved" (x. 1); "We that are strong ought to bear the infirmities of the weak, and not to please ourselves" (xv. 1); "I myself am persuaded of you, my brethren, that ye are full of goodness" (xv. 14);—all tending to show how manifestly it was Paul's feelings, Paul's belief, Paul's sympathies, Paul's personality, that were expressing themselves in this epistle.

The very strongest forms of speech that he makes use of are these: "I say, through the grace given unto me" (xii. 3); "I know, and am persuaded by the Lord Jesus" (xiv. 14); "I have written the more boldly unto you in some sort, because of the grace that is given to me of God" (xv. 15); but even in these he claims no infallible inspiration for himself, and in the last passage he explains what he means by "the grace given" unto him—namely, that he "should be the minister of Jesus Christ to the Gentiles."

He concludes his letter by repeating his desire to pay them a personal visit; and remarks that, as he hopes before long to make a trip to Spain, it is very possible that he may be able to take Rome *en route*. He explains his inability to visit them at the present time, owing to his being obliged to take some money to Jerusalem, which had been subscribed for the relief of the poor Christians in that city by the inhabitants of Macedonia and Greece; but he assures them that when he has accomplished that task, he will start as soon as possible for Spain.

A long series of kind regards and messages of friendship and affection to several persons, whom he mentions by name, winds up the letter; and it is absurd to suppose that when Paul penned these private greetings, he could have imagined it likely, or even possible, that his letter could have been considered by future generations as the infallible dictum of the Almighty, or, as it is styled, "the Word of God."

We have selected the Epistle to the Romans, simply because it is placed the first in order of St Paul's Epistles in the Bible; but a careful and candid study of all or any of the others will give very similar results.

The following passages we have noted, as those in which St Paul most strongly suggests his consciousness of writing under an internal guidance.

1. "Now we have received, not the spirit of the world, but the spirit which is of God; that we might know the things that are freely given to us of God. Which things also we speak, not in words taught by human wisdom, but in words taught by a holy

influx; putting influxes together, and comparing them one with another" (1 Cor. ii. 12, 13). See Note S, p. 463, on the "Pneuma."

2. "We have the mind of Christ" (1 Cor. ii. 16).

3. "I command, yet not I, but the Lord" (1 Cor. vii. 10).

4. "I have received of the Lord, that which also I delivered unto you" (1 Cor. xi. 23).

5. "The things that I write unto you are the commandments of the Lord" (1 Cor. xiv. 37).

6. "I delivered unto you first of all that which I also received" (1 Cor. xv. 3).

7. "I certify you, brethren, that the gospel which was preached of me is not after man. For I neither received it of man, neither was I taught it, but through a revelation of Jesus Christ" (Gal. i. 11, 12).

8. "If ye have heard of the dispensation of the grace of God which is given me to you-ward, how that by revelation He made known unto me the mystery . . . which in other ages was not made known unto the sons of men, as it is now revealed unto His holy apostles and prophets in spirit" (Eph. iii. 3, 5).

9. "This we say unto you by the word of the Lord" (1 Thess. iv. 15).

On these passages, we have to remark that 1, 2, 7, and 8 clearly refer to his whole ministry, and assert no infallible inspiration for his writings, and that 3, 4, 5, 6, and 9 allude to Christ's own sayings, as recorded in the gospels, and related by those who heard them. (See Matt. v. 32; xix. 6, 9; Mark x. 11, 12; Luke xvi. 18; Matt. xxvi. 26; Mark xiv. 22; Luke xxii. 19; Matt. xvi. 28; Mark ix. 1; Luke ix. 27, &c.)

On the other hand, in the following passages, St Paul is evidently conscious of writing on his own responsibility, and without internal guidance.

1. "I speak this by permission, and not of commandment" (1 Cor. vii. 6).

2. "To the rest speak I, not the Lord" (1 Cor. vii. 12).

3. "Concerning virgins I have no commandment of the Lord; yet I give my judgment to be faithful as one that hath obtained mercy of the Lord. I suppose therefore," &c. (1 Cor. vii. 25).

4. "If any man seem to be contentious, we have no such custom, neither the churches of God" (1 Cor. xi. 16).

N.B.—St Paul has been here giving certain directions; and in case any objections might be raised to his dictum, he appeals for his authority to the custom of the churches. Had he considered his dictum infallibly inspired, he would have based his appeal upon that inspiration.

5. "We believe, and therefore speak" (2 Cor. iv. 13).

6. "I speak not by commandment" (2 Cor. viii. 8).
7. "Herein I give my advice" (2 Cor. viii. 10).
8. "That which I speak, I speak it not after the Lord, but as it were foolishly" (2 Cor. xi. 17).
9. "I speak foolishly" (2 Cor. xi. 21).
10. "I speak as a fool" (2 Cor. xi. 23).
11. "I speak after the manner of men" (Gal. iii. 15).
12. "I Paul say unto you" (Gal. v. 2).
13. "I count not myself to have apprehended" (Philip. iii. 13).

Finally, he sometimes confesses plainly that he is himself in doubt as to whether he is writing under internal influx or no.

Thus, to give one passage by way of example in 1 Cor. vii. 40, he says: "She is more blessed if she remain thus, according to my opinion; and I think that I have also a divine influx on the matter." See Note S. on the "Pneuma."

It is to be hoped that these few considerations will assist towards removing the epistles or letters of St Paul from the false platform on which they have been placed by ecclesiastical tradition, and presenting them in their true and genuine character.

If this be so, a great step will be gained towards a due appreciation of the entire Bible.

NOTE C.

ON THE NATURE OF GOD.

Chapter ii. page 38.

"*Matter is illimitable. In other words, it is infinite and eternal; and as we cannot conceive of the Deity being outside of what is infinite and eternal, He also must be in this sense material.*"

He who ventures to assert that God is in any sense material, runs the risk of being branded by the Church as a heretic and materialist; the latter term having been invented to describe a believer in what, according to the Church's view, is a heinous and fatal error. And yet it is maintained with equal vehemence by the Church, that there is no particle of matter in which God is not; though at the same time she repudiates the idea of being pantheistic in doctrine.

There seems here to be a somewhat strange inconsistency which is very difficult of reconciliation.

Moreover, the Nicene Creed asserts that God the Son is "of one substance with the Father;" and the 1st Article declares that "in unity of this Godhead there be three Persons of one substance." If substance is not matter, there is no meaning in words.

That the Bible teaches the universality of God in matter is evident from the following passages amongst many others :—
"Whither shall I go from Thy Spirit? or whither shall I flee from Thy presence? If I ascend up into heaven, Thou art there: if I make my bed in hell, behold, Thou art there. If I take the wings of the morning, and dwell in the uttermost parts of the sea, even there shall Thy hand lead me, and Thy right hand shall hold me" (Ps. cxxxix. 7-10).

"Do not I fill heaven and earth? saith the Lord" (Jer. xxiii. 24).

"In Him we live, and move, and have our being" (Acts xvii. 28).

"*In Him* were all things created, in the heavens, and upon the earth, things visible and things invisible, whether thrones, or dominions, or principalities, or powers; all things have been created through Him, and unto Him; and He is before all things, *and in Him all things consist*" (Col. i. 17, Revised Version).

The last three passages clearly indicate that God is material, in the true sense of the word; but the Church has fallen into a confusion of ideas on the subject, owing to the imperfect notion of "matter" which has hitherto existed in it. That term having been confined to the portion of matter which is susceptible to our present senses; or, in other words, to the "gross matter" resulting from the Fall, and therefore essentially connected with sin. The instinctive sentiment of the human breast has naturally revolted against the connection of Deity with matter, understanding thereby a connection between the Sinless and the sin-stained.

But when once we realise that the gross substance apparent to our senses is merely an accretion over all that is true and pure of matter, the difficulty at once disappears, and it becomes a consistent and sublime belief that God is in matter and matter in God, coexistent and inseparable; or, in other words, that God is, in the highest sense, a material Being.

This, in the words of Mr Claude G. Montefiore, M.A., in a paper lately read before the Jews' College Literary Society, "brings us close to the central problem in the philosophy of religion. That problem is to determine the relation of the Deity to nature and to man. Religious thought and religious feeling are both continually desiring two qualities in the Godhead, the combination of which inharmonious unity is always of exceeding difficulty. According as one quality or another is more rigorously insisted on, the character of the entire philosophy which maintains it is determined. . . . Exclusive stress upon the one quality leads to deism, upon the other to pantheism. The problem of all theistic religions is to find the higher unity which shall combine and satisfy the truths for mind and heart, which deism and pantheism alike contain."

In other words, the two qualities in the Godhead, required by the instincts of the human heart, are "distance" and "nearness."

The infinite majesty of One who dwells "in the high and holy place," in the light "which no man can approach unto," tends to remove God far above all nature, and to foster the sense of His immateriality, thus leading to the idea of deism; whilst, on the other hand, the conviction of His omnipotence, and the inner consciousness of a universal need of His unfailing succour, love, and support, tend to bring Him down from His exalted position, and to engender the lower aspect of pantheism.

Both these phases of the conception of the Deity are, in themselves, true; but each depends, for its truth, upon its due and proportionate combination with the other.

It is, to use a homely illustration, like the proportionate combination of oxygen and hydrogen in water.

Take the right proportions of these two gases, combine them chemically together, and water is the result.

Take too great or too small a quantity of either component, and the combination will be spoiled.

So with the component aspects of the nature of God.

Combine them in their due proportions, and the true nature of God will result. Take either in excess, and a false God appears.

Further, to make the illustration complete, as in the one case, so in the other, the difficulty to be solved is how to combine the component parts, even when you have them in their due proportions.

In chemistry, the problem is solved by an electric current; in theology, by the right conception of "matter."

It is the limited idea of gross, sin-polluted matter, which creates deism on the one hand, and pantheism on the other.

Conceive of matter as infinite, eternal, illimitable; divest it of its debased accretion; and the infinite, eternal, illimitable God stands forth, material in the truest and highest sense,— neither the God of the deist nor that of the pantheist, but a compound of both, with being, substance, and qualities as essentially different from either as the being, substance, and quality of water differ from those of oxygen or hydrogen.

NOTE D.

ON THE MIRACLES OF CHRIST.

Chapter ii. page 40.

"*This force it is which, passing through the organism of the operator into the hypnotised patient, controls his will, and inspires his words and acts; and in order to do this, it has to penetrate the atoms of the ordinary matter which compose the fleshly particles of the visible frames of both.*"

Here we have an explanation of miracles, as related in the Bible and elsewhere; and we can see at once how it was that Christ had such miraculous powers of healing. For owing to the special circumstances connected with His birth, and the perfect constitution of His human nature, the outer covering of fleshly matter, apparent to the senses of others, was so infinitely fine and rarefied that the "material force" penetrating the atoms of His visible frame was able to work its way out of Him, into the patient operated upon, with such little let and hindrance, that its effects were virtually instantaneous, and, as it seemed, preternaturally powerful.

A remarkable confirmation of this view is supplied by a careful study of the various modes of dealing with different cases which Christ employed, and the degrees of ease and difficulty which He experienced in achieving the desired results. For evidently the operation of the "material force" would depend not merely on Christ's own atomic nature, which was constant in all cases, but also on the atomic constitution of the fleshly particles of the patients operated upon. Some would be more receptive than others to the influence of the "material force"; while in some cases the density of the fleshly particles would be such that the force would be unable to penetrate them.

This receptivity to the "material force" Christ designates by the term "faith"; and so we find that on two separate occasions, at least, He was unable to perform any miracles, or mighty works, simply, as we are told, because of the "want of faith" exhibited by the people of the place. Thus, in Matt. xiii. 58, we read, "He did not many mighty works there, because of their unbelief;" and in Mark vi. 5, "He *could* there do no mighty work, save that He laid His hands upon a few sick folk and healed them. And He marvelled because of their unbelief."

Setting aside those who were thus impervious to the material force which issued from Christ, we find three different degrees of receptivity, or "faith," in the patients operated upon; and

Christ's miracles of healing may therefore be divided into three classes, corresponding to these three degrees.

In the first, or densest class, are included those cases where bodily contact between Christ and the patient were necessary.

In the second class, are included those cases where, without actual bodily contact, Christ's will acted on the will of the patient, whose "faith" was tested by an obedience to an order.

In the third or highest class, are included those cases where the "faith," or receptivity, was so powerful that the "material force" was able to pass from Christ's organism into that of the patient by a simple effort of Christ's will acting upon the patient's organism, no test of "faith" being required.

We will give a few examples of each class.

1. Those where actual bodily contact was necessary.

"There came a leper and worshipped Him, saying, Lord, if Thou wilt, Thou canst make me clean. And Jesus put forth His hand, and touched him, saying, I will, be thou clean. And immediately his leprosy was cleansed" (Matt. viii. 2, 3). See also Mark i. 40, 41; Luke v. 12, 13.

"He took her by the hand, and the maid arose" (Matt. ix. 25). See also Mark v. 41; Luke viii. 54.

"They bring unto Him one that was deaf, and had an impediment in his speech; and they beseech Him to put His hand upon him. And He took him aside from the multitude, and put His fingers into his ears, and He spit, and touched his tongue; and, looking up to heaven, He sighed, and saith unto him, Ephphatha, that is, Be opened. And straightway his ears were opened, and the string of his tongue was loosed, and he spake plain" (Mark vii. 32-34).

"Jesus took him by the hand, and lifted him up; and he arose" (Mark ix. 27).

N.B.—In none of the instances in this class is any mention made of the "faith" of the patient as an active influential factor in the operation of the miracle.

2. Those whose "faith" was tested prior to the resulting effect of the action of Christ's will upon theirs.

"Then saith He to the sick of the palsy, Arise, take up thy bed, and go unto thine house. And he arose, and departed to his house" (Matt. ix. 6, 7). See also Mark ii. 10-12; Luke v. 24, 25.

"Then saith He to the man, Stretch forth thy hand. And he stretched it forth; and it was restored whole, like as the other" (Matt. xii. 13).

"And when He saw them, he said unto them, Go show yourselves to the priests. And it came to pass, that, as they went, they were cleansed" (Luke xvii. 14).

"Jesus said unto him, Go thy way; thy son liveth. And the

man believed the word that Jesus had said unto him; and he went his way" (John iv. 50).

N.B.—In the cases of this class, we find the faith of the patients or supplicants generally mentioned as special factors in the healing potency.

3. Those whose "faith" was so powerful, that neither bodily contact nor test was required by Christ.

Of this class, the following are among the most illustrious examples:—

The Roman centurion at Capernaum (Matt. viii. 5-13). See also Luke vii. 1-10.

The Syrophœnician woman of Canaan (Matt. xv. 21-28). See also Mark vii. 24-30.

The woman with the issue of blood (Matt. ix. 20-22). See also Mark v. 25-24; Luke viii. 43-48.

Blind Bartimeus at the gate of Jericho (Mark x. 46-52). See also Luke xviii. 35-43.

N.B.—In each case of this class, Christ distinctly avers that the "faith" of the applicants was the principal operating cause of the healing potency. "Thy faith hath saved thee;" "Thy faith hath made thee whole;" "According to thy faith, so be it done unto thee," &c.

This point is very important, and we will therefore make it as clear as possible. When Christ has to put forth physical energy Himself, and place Himself in bodily contact with the subject operated upon, no mention whatever is made of the faith of the patients. When the effects are produced by co-operation between the wills of Christ and the patient, such co-operation being tested by obedience to an order, the faith of the latter is stated to have had its influence, more or less, on the results produced. And when no physical contact, or test of submission of will, is necessary, the faith is said to have actually effected the cure.

Three other classes of miracles, besides those of healing, demand our passing notice.

(*a.*) Those effected on the powers of nature.
(*b.*) The casting out of devils.
(*c.*) The raising of the dead.

(*a.*) Those miracles which were effected over the powers of nature, may be stated as follows:—

Changing water into wine (John ii. 1-11).

Stilling the tempest (Matt. viii. 23-27; Mark iv. 37-41; Luke viii. 23-25).

Walking on the sea (Matt. xiv. 25; John vi. 19-21).

Feeding the multitudes (Matt. xiv. 15-21; Mark vi. 35-44; Luke ix. 12-17; John vi. 5-14; Matt. xv. 32-38; Mark viii. 1-9).

Miraculous draughts of fishes (Luke v. 4-11; John xxi. 3-8).

Withering the fig-tree (Matt. xxi. 17-22; Mark xi. 12-14).

It is only when we realise the intimate connection which exists between all the parts of creation, and especially between those parts popularly but erroneously distinguished as matter and mind, that we can understand how easily the " material force " operating through Christ's organism, being perfect and sublime as it was, could produce results upon the atomic particles and the forces of nature, which would appear miraculously astounding to an ordinary mind.

(*b.*) In the detailed accounts of the various instances of ejection of evil spirits, we can trace clearly and conclusively the existence and operation of the "material force," or δύναμις τοῦ πνεύματος, through the organism of Christ; and a wonderful glimpse is revealed to us of the reality of the invisible world of spirits, as well as of the close affinity and interaction between the seen and unseen portions of our universe.

See Matt. viii. 38-34; xvii. 18; Mark i. 23-27, 33, 34; v. 1-20; ix. 17-29; Luke iv. 33-37, 41; ix. 38-42.

(*c.*) The consideration of the close proximity to this earth of those who have but lately departed from the flesh, taken in conjunction with the infinitely refined atomic constitution of Christ, removes all difficulty in the way of comprehending those three miracles which have always been considered the most stupendous displays of His supernatural power—namely, the restoring to life of Jairus's daughter, the widow's son at Nain, and Lazarus of Bethany.

It has been too much the habit of the apologists of Christianity to assume that there is no middle course between asserting the absolutely supernatural character of Christ's miracles, and the denying them altogether. Thus, in their ardent anxiety to uphold the evidences of the truth of their religion, they have been driven to take their stand on an untenable position, because their view of Christ's so-called miracles has been one opposed to the rational instincts of the human mind.

So far from being supernatural, or from contravening the law and order of the universe, Christ's wonderful works are the natural results of the contact between His person, atomically constructed as it was, and the atomic constitutions of the persons and things with whom He dealt.

The miraculous, or supernatural, wonder would have been, if these forces coming into contact had not produced the results which followed.

NOTE E.

ON TRUE THEOLOGY.

Chapter ii. p. 42.

"*It is by an effort of his affections, and not by one of his brain, that he can fit this key to the lock of knowledge.*"

When the writer of this note passed his "Little-go" examination as an undergraduate at Cambridge, the best paper on Paley's 'Evidences of Christianity' was done by a Jew named Numa Hartog, who was afterwards Senior Wrangler. Of this the writer was himself informed by the Examiner who set the papers. The intellectual faculties of the Jew enabled him to grasp the arguments logically; but this had no effect upon his affectional emotions or on his conscience, for he remained as steadfast a Jew as ever.

We have quoted this instance, as an example of the truth so frequently insisted upon in the Bible, and yet so strangely ignored in practice by those who profess to regulate their lives by the teaching of the Scriptures—namely, that the knowledge of true religion is to be attained by the heart, and not by the mind, or, in other words, by the affections, instead of the brain.

We have no intention to use this example with a view to showing that the Christian is all right and the Jew all wrong, or *vice versa.* We merely desire to point out how absurd it is to suppose that people are to be converted by mere argumentative evidence.

No amount of intellectual disquisition or controversy will help to elucidate the mysteries of divine wisdom; for, if we are to believe what is written in the Bible, the pursuit of knowledge must be conducted along the pathway of practical heart-affection, and not through the dark and mazy labyrinths of mental metaphysics.

It is the "heart," not the "mind," that is appealed to in the Bible, as necessary to be illumined for the reception of God's truth. Countless passages might be cited in proof of this; we will content ourselves with giving a few.

"Oh that there were such an heart in them, that they would fear me," &c. (Deut. v. 29).

"If thou shalt seek the Lord thy God, thou shalt find Him, if thou seek Him with all thy heart and with all thy soul" (Deut. iv. 29).

"I will give them an heart to know me" (Jer. xxiv. 7).

"I will put my law in their inward parts, and write it in their hearts; and will be their God, and they shall be my people. And they shall teach no more every man his neighbour, and every man his brother, saying, Know the Lord; for they shall all know me, from the least of them unto the greatest of them, saith the Lord" (Jer. xxxi. 33, 34).

"Blessed are the pure in heart: for they shall see God" (Matt. v. 8).

"Be ye of an understanding heart" (Prov. viii. 5).

"Wisdom resteth in the heart of him that hath understanding" (Prov. xiv. 33).

"The wise in heart will receive commandments" (Prov. x. 8).

"With the heart man believeth unto righteousness" (Rom. x. 10).

"The heart of him that hath understanding seeketh knowledge" (Prov. xv. 14).

Again, it is owing to a defect in the *heart*, not the *mind*, that men fail to know and understand God's mysteries, according to the Bible. Thus:—

"A deceived heart hath turned him aside, that he cannot deliver his soul, nor say, Is there not a lie in my right hand?" (Isa. xliv. 20).

"Go, and tell this people, Hear ye indeed, but understand not; and see ye indeed, but perceive not. Make the heart of this people fat, and make their ears heavy, and shut their eyes; lest they see with their eyes, and hear with their ears, and understand with their heart, and convert, and be healed" (Isa. vi. 9, 10).

"O Lord, why hast Thou made us to err from Thy ways, and hardened our heart from Thy fear?" (Isa. lxiii. 17).

"This people hath a revolting and rebellious heart; they are revolted and gone. Neither say they in their heart, Let us now fear the Lord our God. . . . Your iniquities have turned away these things, and your sins have withholden good things from you" (Jer. v. 23, 25).

In like manner, we learn from the Bible how vain and useless is a mere intellectual search after the truth, and how impossible it is to treat religion as if it were a science which could be solved by the investigations and discussions of mere mental inquirers.

"Canst thou by searching find out God? canst thou find out the Almighty unto perfection? It is as high as heaven; what canst thou do? deeper than hell; what canst thou know? The measure thereof is longer than the earth, and broader than the sea" (Job xi. 7-9).

"I beheld all the work of God, that a man cannot find out the work that is done under the sun; because, though a man labour to seek it out, yet he shall not find it; yea farther, though a wise man think to know it, yet shall he not be able to find it" (Eccles. viii. 17).

"Then thought I to understand this, but it was too hard for me; until I went into the sanctuary of God" (Ps. lxxiii. 16, 17).

"Thou hast hid these things from the wise and prudent, and hast revealed them unto babes" (Matt. xi. 25).

"Where is the wise? where is the scribe? where is the disputer of this world? hath not God made foolish the wisdom of this world? For after that in the wisdom of God the world by wisdom knew not God, it pleased God by the simplicity of the thing preached to save them that believe" (1 Cor. i. 20, 21).

"Ye see our calling, brethren, how that not many wise men after the flesh, not many mighty, not many noble, are called; but God hath chosen the simple things of the world to confound the wise" (1 Cor. i. 26, 27).

"The natural man receiveth not the things of the Spirit of God; for they are foolishness unto him; neither can he know them, because they are spiritually discerned" (1 Cor. ii. 14).

Lastly, we are frequently taught in the Bible that it is by following the dictates of our consciences and actually rendering the heart-service of our whole lives and beings to God, not by mere meditation and theorising, nor by discussion and controversy, that we shall be enabled to solve the mysteries of religion, and to gain the highest knowledge of God and of His hidden truth.

"Did not thy father eat and drink, and do judgment and justice, and then it was well with him? He judged the cause of the poor and needy; then it was well with him; was not this to know me? saith the Lord" (Jer. xxii. 16, 17).

"Why do ye not understand my speech? Even because ye cannot hear my word. Ye are of your father the devil, and the lusts of your father ye will to do" (John viii. 43, 44).

"If any man willeth to do His will, he shall know of the doctrine" (John vii. 17).

"He that hath my commandments and keepeth them, he it is that loveth me; and he that loveth me shall be loved of my Father, and I will love him, and will manifest myself unto him" (John xiv. 21).

"Keep that which is committed to thy trust, avoiding profane and vain babblings, and oppositions of science, falsely so called; which some professing have erred concerning the faith" (1 Tim. vi. 20, 21).

"Strive not about words to no profit but to the subverting of the hearers. Study to show thyself approved unto God, a workman that needeth not to be ashamed, holding a straight course in the word of truth. But shun profane and vain babblings, for they will increase unto more ungodliness" (2 Tim. ii. 14-16).

Such are the manifest declarations of Scripture. Yet, in the face of all, we have theology set before us as a science, like geology, biology, or any other "ology"; containing, like them, its long-sounding definitions and dogmatical statements; teeming, like them, with matter of continual controversy, and affording subjects of endless heartburnings and disputes; differing only from them in this respect, however, that it is a "science, falsely so called." For no amount of mental culture or scientific research will of themselves bring the inquirer any nearer to the knowledge of the truth; no collection of dogmas invented by man and profanely palmed off upon God, will avail to enlighten the humble student.

Though our universities may provide their well-paid professors of theology, and though learned disquisitions without number may proceed from their pens, these will but serve to "darken counsel," and hinder the progress of the pursuit of true knowledge; for the river of wisdom flows into the organism of man through the channal of his affections and not of his intellect; and it is in the pure, simple, self-denying love of the godlike heart, not in the abstruse and metaphysical dogmas of churches and creeds, that the truth of God shall be revealed.

There is no one more highly endowed with intellectual knowledge of the mysteries of God, no more profound and learned theologian, than the devil himself.

NOTE F.

ON THE PURIFICATION OF THE HUMAN ORGANISM.

Chapter v. page 86.

"*The first experience of which the man engaged in this attempt becomes conscious is, that he is the arena in which two strongly antagonistic currents come into collision, and that he is frustrated in his attempt to open himself only to that which is pure, by a flood of that which is impure, seeking ingress by the opening which his efforts to receive a greater measure of the pure effected in his organism.*"

It was to this internal conflict of antagonistic currents that St Paul so often alluded when he spoke of the warfare between the "flesh" and the "spirit."

By the "flesh" is signified the impure, inverted, and destructive forces, the influx of which into human nature brought about originally the gross fleshly accretion of human organisms, and the action of which tends to render those organisms even more gross and fleshly; whilst by the "spirit" is meant the pure, elevating, life-giving force entitled the "pneuma," which originally assimilated human nature to the divine, and the renewed influx of which into human organisms tends to restore them to their pristine condition.

These two principles, being antagonistic to each other, cause the agonising struggle which a person experiences in his inner conscience, as soon as he lays himself open to the influence of the "pneuma." In the absence of either of these opposing set of forces, there is no consciousness of a struggle, and in consequence there is peace; but the one is the fatal, lethargic peace of death, described by Christ when He says, "When a strong man armed keepeth his palace, his goods are in peace;" the other is the eternal peace, which comes as a consequence of victory after struggle, and which is characterised as "the peace of God, which passeth all understanding." It was to bring this peace eventually to the human race that Christ was born into the world; hence He was foretold by Isaiah, under the title of the "Prince of Peace"; hence also, at His birth, the angel-host proclaimed "Peace on earth"; and hence again, before His death, He bequeathed this legacy,—"Peace I leave with you, my peace I give unto you; not as the world giveth, give I unto you."

But between these two stages of peace, the false and the true, there must come to every one the period of conflict. Hence, even whilst promising His peace, Christ added, "In the world ye shall have tribulation;" and hence He gave utterance to that apparent paradox,—"Think not that I am come to send peace on earth; I came, not to send peace, but a sword."

That St Paul himself experienced this internal struggle, and that it caused him unutterable agony, is evident from his own confession; "We know that the law is that of pneuma; but I am fleshly, sold under sin. For what I accomplish, I do not know; for I do not practise what I desire; but what I hate, that I do. If then I do that which I do not desire, I assent to the law that it is good. Now then, no longer do *I* accomplish this, but the sin which dwelleth in me. For I know that in me, that is, in my flesh, dwelleth no good: for the will is present with me; but how to accomplish the right, I do not find out. For I do not do good, as I desire to do; but the evil which I do not desire, that I practise. I find then the law that, though I desire to do the right, the evil is present with me. For I sympathise with the law of God according to my inner man; but I see another law in my members conflicting with the law of my mind, and enslaving me to the law of sin which is in my members. A miserable man am I! Who shall free me from this body of death? I thank God through Jesus Christ our Lord. So then, I myself serve the law of God in my mind; but in my flesh, the law of sin." (Rom. vii. 14-25).

Again, the same apostle, in his Epistle to the Galatians, describes the combatants on either side of this internal conflict when he says: "The flesh cherishes desires in opposition to the pneuma, and the pneuma in opposition to the flesh; and these are antagonistic to each other: in order that ye may not do the things which ye may desire" (Gal. v. 17).

That this conflict, though essentially subsurface, affects the whole organism, body, soul, and spirit, is also evident from several passages of Scripture, as well as from practical experience.

Thus it is that all three parts of the human organism are spoken of in conjunction, when, in writing to the Thessalonians, St Paul says: "The God of peace make you holy throughout your whole beings, and may your entire organisms, spirit, soul, and body, be preserved blameless in the presence of our Lord Jesus Christ" (1 Thess. v. 23).

The painful disturbance caused in the organism of one who is opening himself to the higher life, by the conflicting elements of flesh and pneuma, may be appropriately illustrated in the following manner.

The human organism resembles a vessel which has been filled in every part with foul and polluted air. A vessel so filled is purified by two means, which may be termed *positive* and *negative*; or, in other words, *infusive* and *effusive*. That is to say, two channels have to be opened, the one for the expulsion of the foul air, the other for the inlet of the pure. These two channels must be open at the same time, and the twofold process must go on simultaneously. The negative or effusive process is not sufficient of itself, as there would be produced merely a vacuum, which is fatal to life. The positive or infusive process is equally inoperative by itself, as, until the foul air is at least in part expelled, there is no due room for the pure.

For the purposes of purification, it is evident that three things are necessary—

1. The opening of channels for the expulsion of the foul air.
2. The opening of channels for the infusion of the pure.
3. The closing of all channels by which a fresh supply of foul air might gain admission.

If these three precautions are rigidly observed, the vessel will gradually become entirely freed from all pollution, and filled with pure untainted atmosphere.

But meanwhile, during the process of purification, there will be a severe atmospherical disturbance in the vessel. The currents of the inflowing pure air will come into collision with the opposing currents of the outflowing impure.

This disturbance will be all the stronger, if the channels of ingress and egress are in close proximity to each other; whilst, if it should happen that the two were identical, it is evident that the process would be rendered far more difficult, gradual, irregular, and hazardous; and all these drawbacks would be immensely intensified if, in addition, the same channel could become the means of letting in new supplies of foul air.

Yet this is exactly the case with our human organisms. They have become filled with foul and polluted spiritual atmosphere. The Greek word ἁμαρτιά (hamartia), used for "sin" in the New Testament, means "that which vitiates or pollutes;" and the phrase translated "forgiveness of sins," means literally, "expulsion of that which vitiates." See Note G, p. 425.

The pneuma is simply the pure spiritual essence, which must take the place of the "hamartia" when it is being expelled from the human organism.

The expulsion of the "hamartia" and the infusion of the pneuma must go on simultaneously, and be in exact correlation to each other.

This is exactly what Christ meant when He said: "When the unclean spirit is gone out of a man, he walketh through dry places, seeking rest, and findeth none. Then he saith, I will return to my house from whence I came out; and when he is come, he findeth it *empty*, swept, and garnished. Then goeth he, and taketh with himself seven other spirits more wicked than himself, and they enter in and dwell there; and the last state of that man is worse than the first" (Matt. xii. 43-45).

The mistake that Christ wished to guard His disciples against, by this melancholy picture, was the idea of imagining that the expulsion of sins from the human organism would be sufficient, without the corresponding infusion of the pure pneumatic essence to take the place of that which is expelled. Now, inasmuch as the organic channels for the expulsion of the foul nature, are identical with those for the admission of the pure; and inasmuch as, moreover, the self-same channels, unless carefully guarded, can easily be utilised by the evil ones for the injection of new supplies of impurity, it will be at once understood how great must be the disturbance, and consequently the agony, which is caused throughout the entire organism, when these opposing currents come into collision.

It will be seen that the whole process must, from its very nature, be *gradual, painful, irregular,* and *liable to error:* gradual, because the infiltration will go on very slowly, the moral atmosphere becoming little by little purer as the foul is ejected and the pure admitted; painful, because of the violent disturbances within the system, caused by the collision of opposing moral currents; irregular, because, as has been shown, foul currents may be, and often are, admitted by the very channels which are opened for the inlet of the pure, thus contaminating, again and again, the organism which is being purified; and liable to error, because it is often very difficult to distinguish the pure currents from the impure.

But yet, notwithstanding these dangers, drawbacks, and delays, if we are only faithful to our trust,—which is to keep careful watch over our channels, so that the purifying element may be constantly flowing in, the vitiating constantly flowing out, and all things pertaining to the gross elements of our fallen earth-nature prevented from obtaining an entrance,—if we thus co-operate with Christ in His saving work, then by slow, painful, yet sure and certain progress, will our whole beings regain their pristine condition, and contain within them, filling them through and through, and permeating every atom of their organisms, the perfect purity of their biune likeness to the Biune God.

NOTE G.

ON THE TERM "FORGIVENESS OF SINS."

Chapter v. page 89.

"From this it is plain that what is generally termed 'sin,' is, in fact, the outward and visible sign of infestation."

The term "forgiveness of sins," so frequently met with in the English translations of the New Testament, and incorporated into the Creeds as a leading dogma of Christendom, conveys to the general mind an erroneous impression. This is owing chiefly to the false doctrine of vicarious sacrifice, upon which we shall dwell in Note H.

There are three Greek verbs in the New Testament which are translated in our versions "forgive" or "remit." These three verbs are ἀφίημι, ἀποτίθημι, and χαρίζομαι. Now ἀφίημι means simply to "send forth," or to "expel"; ἀποτίθημι, to "put away"; and χαρίζομαι, to "show favour." Not one of the three, except by severely straining its meaning, signifies "pardon through a vicarious sacrifice."

1. The word ἀποτίθημι is only used once, in Acts viii. 22, where the passage, "if perhaps the thought of thine heart may be forgiven thee," ought to be rendered, "if perchance the purpose of thine heart may be put away from thee"—an entirely different meaning.

2. The verb χαρίζομαι occurs merely in the few following passages, where it invariably bears the signification of "show favour," or "oblige": 2 Cor. ii. 7, 10; xii. 13; Eph. iv. 32; Col. ii. 13.

Thus, for example, the well-known text in Eph. iv. 32, rendered

"Be ye kind one to another, tender-hearted, forgiving one another, even as God *for Christ's sake hath forgiven you*," should be, "Be ye kind one to another, tender-hearted, showing favour one to another, even as God, *in Christ, hath shown favour to you.*"

Here is an excellent example of the manner in which the English translation has, to use a common phrase, been "doctored," to suit the dogma of vicarious sacrifice. As it is read in the Authorised Version, the text explicitly states that pardon is obtained by us from God, owing to the sacrifice of Christ on our behalf; whereas St Paul simply averred the great truth that God had shown favour to us in the mission of Christ.

3. The force of ἀφίημι, as we have already said, is to "expel"; and when it is used in regard to the relation of sin to God and man, it invariably means the actual expulsion of sin and its concomitants from man by God,—not the withholding of a just punishment from a guilty criminal, because of the sacrifice of an innocent victim in his stead.

A few examples will show how this simple meaning has been perverted in our English New Testament.

AUTHORISED VERSION.	CORRECT RENDERING.
Matthew ix. 2-7.	
"Jesus, seeing their faith, said unto the sick of the palsy, Son, be of good cheer; thy sins be forgiven thee. And, behold, certain of the scribes said within themselves, This man blasphemeth. "And Jesus, knowing their thoughts, said, Wherefore think ye evil in your hearts? For whether is easier, to say, Thy sins be forgiven thee; or to say, Arise, and walk? But that ye may know that the Son of man hath power on earth to forgive sins, (then saith he to the sick of the palsy,) Arise, take up thy bed, and go unto thy house. And he arose, and departed to his house."	"Jesus, seeing their faith, said to the paralytic, Cheer up, my son; thy sins have been expelled from thee. And, behold, certain of the scribes said amongst themselves, This person blasphemes. "And Jesus, observing their considerations, said, Wherefore do ye consider evil in your hearts? For which of the two is the easier, to say, Thy sins have been expelled from thee; or to say, Arise and walk? In order that ye may know then that the Son of man has authority on earth to expel sins, (then He says to the paralytic,) Arise, take up thy bed, and go away to thy house. And having risen up, he went away to his own house."
Matthew xii. 31.	
"All manner of sin and blasphemy shall be forgiven unto men; but the blasphemy against the Holy Ghost shall not be forgiven unto men. And whosoever speaketh a word against the Son of man, it shall be forgiven him: but whosoever speaketh against the Holy Ghost, it shall not be forgiven him, neither in this world, neither in the world to come."	"Every sin and blasphemy shall be expelled from men; but the blasphemy of the pneuma shall not be expelled from men. And whosoever speaks a speech against the Son of man, it (*i.e.*, the spirit which causes him thus to speak) shall be expelled from him; but whosoever speaks against the pneuma that is holy, it shall not be expelled from him, neither in this present age, nor in the age to come."

APPENDIX II.

AUTHORISED VERSION.	CORRECT RENDERING.

Matthew xxvi. 28.

"This is my blood of the new testament, which is shed for many for the remission of sins."

"This is my blood of the new dispensation, which is being poured out on behalf of many with a view to expulsion of sins."

Mark iv. 12.

"Lest at any time they should be converted, and their sins should be forgiven them."

"Lest they should ever turn, and their sins should be expelled from them."

Luke i. 77.

"To give knowledge of salvation unto His people by the remission of their sins."

"To give knowledge of salvation to His people, in expulsion of their sins."

Luke vii. 47-50.

"Her sins which are many, are forgiven; for she loved much: but to whom little is forgiven the same loveth little. And He said unto her, Thy sins are forgiven. And they that sat at meat with Him, began to say within themselves, Who is this that forgives sins also? And He said to the woman, Thy faith hath saved thee: go in peace."

"Her sins, though many, have been expelled, because she loved much; but the person from whom little is expelled, loveth little. He said, then, to her, Thy sins have been expelled. And His companions began to say amongst themselves, Who is this who expels sins also? And He said to the woman, Thy faith hath saved thee; go in peace."

Luke xxiv. 47.

"That repentance and remission of sins shall be preached in His name."

"That a change of mind and expulsion of sins shall be preached in His name."

John xx. 22, 23.

"He breathed on them, and saith to them, Receive ye the Holy Ghost: whose soever sins ye remit, they are remitted unto them; and whose soever sins ye retain, they are retained."

"He breathed on them, and saith to them: Receive a holy pneuma. Whose soever sins ye expel, they are expelled from them; and whose soever sins ye hold fast, they are held fast."

Acts ii. 38.

"Repent, and be baptised every one of you in the name of Jesus Christ for the remission of sins, and ye shall receive the gift of the Holy Ghost."

"Repent, and let each of you be baptised in the name of Jesus Christ for the expulsion of sins; and ye shall receive the gift of the holy pneuma."

Ephesians i. 7.

"In whom we have redemption through His blood, the forgiveness of sins."

"In whom we have redemption through His blood, the expulsion of transgressions."

Hebrews ix. 22.

"Without shedding of blood is no remission."

"Without shedding of blood expulsion is not generated."

1 *John* i. 9.

"If we confess our sins, He is faithful and just to forgive us our sins, and to cleanse us from all unrighteousness."

"If we admit our sins, He is faithful and just, so that He will expel our sins, and make us pure from all unrighteousness."

Many of these passages, which seem at first to be very obscure and incomprehensible, become perfectly plain and intelligible when we bear in mind that all sin is an infestation, and that when "sins" are spoken of, "infestations" are thereby signified.

We are apt to think of sins, as if they consisted of an aggregation of so many sinful thoughts, words, and deeds; whereas these are merely the outward manifestations of the real sins which infest our nature.

Thus, to use a simple illustration—

A person is afflicted with a disease, say, for example, the small-pox. A quantity of noxious eruptions break out in consequence all over the surface of his body. These are not the disease, but the outward manifestations merely, of the disease which infests the body within.

Expel the disease, and the cause of the eruptions disappears, and with it the eruptions themselves.

So with the infestations of sin. The only true salvation is the expulsion of the evil which infests our natures. Forgiveness, in the accepted use of the word, has not the slightest effect in producing the required expulsion; and therefore forgiveness has nothing to do with salvation.

Christ came to save, not to forgive, nor to effect a reconciliation between man and a vindictive, malicious God, who needed the sacrifice of His Son, before His awful wrath could be appeased. God is Love; and being Love, He has secured to man, through Christ, a means whereby sin and its accompaniments may be actually expelled from human nature. This is "the force of the pneuma," ἡδύναμις τοῦ πνευματος, so frequently spoken of in the New Testament.

NOTE H.

ON THE DOGMA OF THE ATONEMENT.

Chapter v. page 96.

"*A scheme for the salvation of man has been constructed by human invention, as opposed to the spirit of the divinely inspired life of the pure Being whose teaching it records, as it must be revolting to all who have ever felt, however faintly, the ineffable touch of the Great All-Father and All-Mother, thrilling the inner sense by contact with the Word made flesh.*"

The particular dogma here alluded to is one of the fundamental doctrines of so-called Christianity; and in its utter fallacy, together with the insult which it offers to the God of justice and love, is probably to be found one of the main secrets of the failure of the religion to work out the objects for which Christ came.

It is well to state the dogma, which is commonly known as that of "justification by faith," in as plain and simple terms as possible. It is, then, as follows :—

"All the human race, with one solitary exception, having sinned against the laws of God,—have incurred guilt deserving of the severest punishment. These guilty criminals are told that God has visited His full wrath upon the One only innocent man, in order that those who merited chastisement might escape scot-free. But this escape from punishment is made to depend upon whether or no they believe that God has really perpetrated this most gross act of injustice. Those who believe it will not only save themselves from chastisement, but will receive a rich reward; those who do not believe such a thing will be visited with punishments of increased severity."

It will be acknowledged that the doctrine is here fairly and tersely stated.

What does it amount to? We can best understand it by a simple illustration. In a certain school, an offence deserving serious punishment has been committed by every scholar except one. The master, well knowing this to be the case, calls the one obedient boy out of the schoolroom. The rest of the pupils are then addressed by an assistant-master in the following terms: "Boys, you are well aware that you all deserve to be severely punished. I am desired to inform you that, because you are all guilty, your kind, good, just master has taken the one innocent boy out of the room, and has given him a sound flogging in your stead. Those who believe what I have told you, hold up your hands!" Some of the boys, delighted at the prospect of escaping punishment, respond immediately by raising their hands; whilst others, impelled by their sense of justice, reply—'We cannot believe, sir, that our master has acted in so terribly unjust a manner. You must have been mistaken; the boy who is innocent cannot possibly have been punished because we are guilty. We would rather suffer punishment ourselves than accept pardon on those terms.'"

"Very well, then," replies the assistant-master, "as you do not believe what I have told you, and as you are so proud as to refuse pardon on these conditions, come out and be thrashed." So the sneaks, who applaud their master's goodness in saving their backs, even at the expense of an innocent victim, are rewarded with a prize; while the honest-hearted lads, who refuse to give their master credit for gross injustice, are branded with pride, and made to suffer a severe punishment.

We see at once the absurdity of this, and its utter violation of the first principles of rectitude. We see that either the master was guilty of the most flagrant injustice, or else that the statement made by the assistant-master was absolutely and entirely false. In either case, we see what a pernicious effect on the boys themselves the inculcation of such a belief would have; how, trained on such principles, they would inevitably grow up false, self-seeking creatures, with utterly distorted notions of right and wrong.

Nor would the case be altered in the slightest degree, unless indeed it were aggravated, if the innocent boy happened to be the master's own son, or if he voluntarily offered himself to be punished instead of the others. The injustice on the master's part would remain undiminished. And yet the Christian doctrine, as commonly accepted, imputes to God an act from which the mind instinctively rebels in the case of a man.

Now it is to be especially observed that throughout the whole teaching of Christ Himself, there is not one word that sanctions this erroneous dogma, not one hint of His being *punished*, in order that the wrath of God against guilty man may be appeased. He did, indeed, lay great and frequent stress upon the necessity of His death in connection with the accomplishment of His mission, but *never once* in any manner that exhibited that death as a propitiatory sacrifice and offering for sin; though, at the same time, it is not difficult to see how His followers so soon fell into the erroneous view which has tainted Christianity with its baleful influence ever since. Unable to discern the real meaning of Christ's death, and imbued with the Jewish idea of vicarious sacrifice, the early teachers of Christianity concluded that that death must have been in the nature of a propitiatory offering; and thus, as is shown by the writings of Paul, Peter, and John, almost from the very commencement of the history of the religion, the great object of Christ's all-important work was buried in the quagmire of an erroneous dogma, utterly incompatible with the nature of God, and sufficient of itself to account for the failure of Christianity. We have taken great pains to collect all Christ's allusions to His coming death. These may be divided into the following classes:—

1. Statements concerning the *fact* of His approaching passion, death, burial, and resurrection. See Matt. xvi. 21; xvii. 22, 23; xx. 17; xxvi. 2; Mark viii. 31; ix. 31; x. 33; Luke ix. 22; xviii. 31; xxiv. 6, 7; John ii. 19; viii. 28.

2. Statements as to the *voluntary nature* of His death. See John x. 11, 15, 17, 18; xv. 13.

3. Statements as to the *purpose and effect* of His death. See John iii. 14-17; xii. 24, 32; Matt. xx. 28; xxvi. 28; Mark x. 45.

Now if all these passages be studied, it will be found that not one of them can by any possibility be construed into an allusion to a "propitiatory sacrifice," with the exception of the last three, those, namely, from Matt. xx. 28; xxvi. 28; Mark x. 45. In the first and third passages, Christ says, "The Son of man came to give His life a ransom for many;" and in the second passage, "This is my blood of the new testament, which is shed for many for" (or, as the Revised Version more correctly puts it, "*into*") "the remission of sins."

It is true the English words "ransom" and "remission" might imply a propitiatory sacrifice; but if we turn to the original text, we find that the Greek word for "ransom" is λύτρον, which comes from λύω, "to set free"; whilst the Greek for "remission" is ἄφεσις, which comes from ἀφίημι, "to send forth" or "expel." Thus, in the first statement, Christ says that He came to give His life in order to set many free from sin; and in the second statement He says that His blood was shed in order to expel sin from many.

Both these statements are therefore identical, and simply mean that Christ's death was to be necessary for the setting free of sin-bound humanity from the thraldom into which the fall of man brought them. This was, indeed, the exact and literal object and effect of that death, not in the manner and sense so ignorantly imputed by the dogmas of the Church, but in a far more real and efficacious way.

NOTE I.

ON IMPLICIT OBEDIENCE TO THE DICTATES OF CONSCIENCE.

Chapter vi. pages 114, 115.

"*It implies a distinct want of faith, if a man's conscience clearly shows him that he is violating it, not to obey the impulse it suggests at all hazards. God does not act thus directly upon the inmost essence of man's nature, without having provided a satisfaction for the craving after truth, which the uneasiness thus engendered indicates.*"

The Bible is full of evidences of this truth, whether in the way of precept, example, or warning. The absolute necessity of following the dictates of conscience, whether it be to avoid evil or to do good, and of leaving the results to God, however improbable it may appear, humanly speaking, that a favourable issue can follow this implicit obedience, is the lesson which we are thus taught.

We will take these points in order.

1. *Dictates of conscience to avoid evil.*

The Scriptural precepts on this point are so numerous, that it is impossible to quote them all; we will, however, state one or two of the most emphatic.

"There hath no temptation taken you, but such as man can bear; but God is faithful, who will not suffer you to be tempted above that ye are able; but will with the temptation make also the way of escape, that ye may be able to endure it" (1 Cor. x. 13).

"The Lord knoweth how to deliver the godly out of temptation" (2 Pet. ii. 9).

"In that He Himself hath suffered being tempted, He is able to succour them that are tempted" (Heb. ii. 18).

Balaam, Saul, the disobedient prophet of Bethel, David, Judas, and Pilate, are all sad cases of warning against the fatal results of disobeying the voice of conscience when it would dissuade from the commission of evil.

On the other hand, we have many notable examples of the blessings which result from obeying the warnings of conscience.

Joseph, when tempted by Potiphar's wife; Shadrach, Meshach, and Abed-nego, who preferred the horrors of the fiery furnace to violating their instincts of rectitude; Daniel, Stephen, and the first apostles of Christianity, all bear testimony to the same great truth.

2. *Dictates of conscience to perform active good.*

Abraham, when obeying in faith the order to sacrifice his only son; Joshua, when leading his army for seven days around the walls of Jericho; the widow of Sarepta, when sharing with Elijah what appeared to be her last earthly meal; Naaman, when bathing in the Jordan for the cure of his leprosy; Simon the fisherman, when casting his nets in the lake of Galilee after a night of fruitless toil;—these and very many other cases all tend to convince us that, even from the lowest point of all—namely, the benefit resulting to one's self—the best and wisest course invariably is to obey immediately the suggestions of conscience, and to do what it dictates, may the consequences of so doing appear ever so futile or hazardous.

Perhaps the most noteworthy incident inculcating this lesson, is that of the three holy women who went on Easter morning to anoint the dead body of Christ.

Their sacred instincts and loving devotion impelled them to undertake this task; they started therefore on their mission, but on the way a difficulty, apparently insurmountable, suggested itself to them. A huge stone had been placed against the mouth of the tomb, and it would be utterly impossible for them to remove it. "And they said amongst themselves, Who shall roll us away the stone from the door of the sepulchre?" (Mark xvi. 3). But their sense of duty would not allow them to be deterred by this obstacle. They would not meet trouble half-way; they would go straight on and leave the issue in God's hands. The consequence was that, at the very place and time when they expected to meet with the greatest difficulty, they found the difficulty had disappeared. "And when they looked, they saw that the stone was rolled away." And their faithful obedience to the voice of their conscience was rewarded by the announcement of the angel at the tomb, "He is not here; He is risen."

So will it always be if we implicitly follow the impulse suggested by the voice of God within us. The clouds which seem so black for us will melt away into golden light, and when we have passed through them, we shall look back in wonder that they had seemed to us beforehand so impenetrable.

NOTE J.

ON LOVE.

Chapter viii. page 133.

"When we reflect upon the bigotries, the hatred, the persecution, and the intolerance which have characterised all Churches that have taken as their chief corner-stone the teaching of Christ, which was pure love and nothing else, we can only account for the people who profess to be animated by this love, and who manifest it by a hate which has provoked bloody wars, as having become insane."

It is important and instructive to note that one, and one only, test was given by Christ, by which His true Church was to be distinguished. This test was no formula of doctrine, no dogma nor creed, no compliance with any form of ritual or worship, but plain, simple, practical love. He does not say, "If you are to be my disciples, you must believe in the doctrine of justification by faith, or in that of the Trinity, or in the dogma of the infallibility of any person or body of persons, or in this, that, or the other shibboleth, theory, or whim, invented by human ingenuity or perverseness,— but, "By this shall all men know that ye are my disciples, if ye have love one to another" (John xiii. 35).

Nor is this the teaching of one isolated passage,—it is the keynote of Christianity. It will be well, in order really to show that this is so, to gather together the most significant allusions, in the New Testament, to *love*, as the groundwork and test of Christ's religion. Thus, in the first place, we have Christ's own declarations on the subject, frequently and emphatically repeated.

" I say to you, Love your enemies, bless them that curse you, do good to them that hate you, and pray for them which despitefully use you, and persecute you; that ye may be the children of your Father which is in heaven" (Matt. v. 44, 45).

"Thou shalt love thy neighbour as thyself" (Matt. xix. 19).

"Thou shalt love the Lord thy God with all thy heart, and with all thy soul, and with all thy mind. This is the first and great commandment: and the second is like unto it, Thou shalt love thy neighbour as thyself. *On these two commandments hang all the law and the prophets*" (Matt. xxii. 37-40). See also Mark xii. 30-31; Luke x. 27.

"A new commandment I give unto you. That ye love one another; as I have loved you, that ye also love one another. By this shall all men know that ye are my disciples, if ye have love one to another" (John xiii. 34, 35).

"This is my commandment, That ye love one another, as I have loved you" (John xv. 12).

"These things I command you, that ye love one another" (John xv. 17).

"Holy Father, keep through Thine own name those whom Thou hast given me, that they may be one, as we are" (John xvii. 11).

"That the love wherewith Thou hast loved me may be in them, and I in them" (John xvii. 26).

Thus the whole teaching of Christ was "love," pure and simple. How little even His immediate followers understood of the simplicity of this religion of their Master, may be gathered from the fact that in the book of the Acts of the Apostles, the subject of love, *nay, the very word itself*, is not once to be found from the beginning to the end. Instead thereof, the book is a melancholy record of quarrels, disputes, and controversies, even amongst the apostles themselves, over matters of dogma, and other concerns of comparatively second-rate importance.

St Paul, however, appears to have grasped somewhat of the overwhelming necessity of making this a subject of primary consideration, at any rate during the latter part of his ministry, when his proselytising zeal had been tempered by age and experience, and his heart opened to the love of Christ, by his self-sacrificing fidelity and nearness of touch to his Saviour.

Thus the following, amongst others, are passages from his epistles, breathing the pure and Christian spirit of love.

"Let love be without dissimulation. Be kindly affectioned one to another with brotherly love; in honour preferring one another" (Rom. xii. 9, 10).

"If there be any other commandment, it is briefly comprehended in this saying, namely, Thou shalt love thy neighbour as thyself" (Rom. xiii. 9).

"Love worketh no ill to his neighbour; therefore love is the fulfilling of the law" (Rom. xiii. 10).

"In all things approving ourselves as the ministers of God, . . . in pureness, in knowledge, in long-suffering, in kindness, in a holy spirit, in love unfeigned" (2 Cor. vi. 4-6).

"All law is fulfilled in one word, even in this; Thou shalt love thy neighbour as thyself" (Gal. v. 14).

"The fruit of the Spirit is love, joy, peace, long-suffering, gentleness, goodness, faith, meekness, temperance" (Gal. v. 22, 23).

"That ye, being rooted and grounded in love, may be able to comprehend with all saints what is the breadth, and length, and depth, and height, and to know the love of Christ, which passeth knowledge, that ye may be filled with all the fulness of God" (Eph. iii. 17-19).

"Forbearing one another in love" (Eph. iv. 2).

"Walk in love, as Christ also loved us" (Eph. v. 2).

"This I pray, that your love may abound yet more and more in knowledge, and in all judgment" (Philip. i. 9).

"Above all these things put on charity (*i.e.*, love), which is the bond of perfectness" (Col. iii. 14).

We have reserved till the end that most beautiful of all the Apostle Paul's writings—namely, his picture of love, in the thirteenth chapter of his First Epistle to the Corinthians.

St James says: "If ye fulfil the royal law according to the Scripture, Thou shalt love thy neighbour as thyself, thou shalt do well" (James ii. 8).

"Above all things," says St Peter, "have fervent charity among yourselves; for charity shall cover the multitude of sins" (1 Peter iv. 8).

And again: "Add to your faith virtue; and to virtue knowledge; and to knowledge temperance; and to temperance patience; and to patience godliness; and to godliness brotherly kindness; and to brotherly kindness charity" (2 Peter i. 5-7). Thus placing charity, or love, in the highest or most important place.

But it is, after all, in the writing of St John, the disciple of love, that the sublime truth is most clearly stated.

"He that saith he is in the light, and hateth his brother, is in darkness even until now; he that loveth his brother abideth in the light" (1 John ii. 9, 10).

"In this the children of God are manifest, and the children of the devil; whosoever doeth not righteousness is not of God, neither he that loveth not his brother. For this is the message that ye heard from the beginning, that we should love one another" (1 John iii. 10, 11).

"We know that we have passed from death unto life, because

we love the brethren. He that loveth not his brother abideth in death" (1 John iii. 14).

"Let us not love in word, neither in tongue, but in deed and in truth" (1 John iii. 18).

"This is His commandment, that ye should believe on the name of His Son Jesus Christ, and love one another, as He gave us commandment" (1 John iii. 23).

"Beloved, let us love one another; for love is of God: and every one that loveth is born of God, and knoweth God. He that loveth not knoweth not God; for God is love" (1 John iv. 7, 8).

"Beloved, if God so loved us, we ought also to love one another. If we love one another, God dwelleth in us, and His love is perfected in us" (1 John iv. 11, 12).

"God is love; and he that dwelleth in love dwelleth in God, and God in him. Herein is our love made perfect, that we may have boldness in the day of judgment: because as He is, so are we in this world. There is no fear in love, but perfect love casteth out fear: because fear hath torment. He that feareth is not made perfect in love. We love Him, because He first loved us. If a man say, I love God, and hateth his brother, he is a liar: for he that loveth not his brother whom he hath seen, how can he love God whom he hath not seen? And this commandment have we from Him, That he who loveth God love his brother also" (1 John iv. 16-21).

It might, perhaps, be thought that we were fighting a shadow, in bringing so many texts of Scripture to bear upon what is acknowledged, "in word and in tongue," to be a fundamental law of Christianity, were it not for the lamentable fact that it is not also acknowledged to be so "in deed and in truth."

There is not one single Church of Christendom at this moment, nor one single sect or party within any of these Churches, wherein the law of love is not wantonly violated, and the commandment of the Lord made of none effect, through the traditions of selfishness, intolerance, uncharitableness, narrow-minded bigotry, and fanatical superstition. Thus, like the dog in the fable, whilst intent on the shadow, they have lost the substance of Christ's religion; and nowhere now can be seen the marks of unity and brotherly affection which drew from the heathen of old the exclamation of wonder and respect, "See how these Christians love one another!"

NOTE K.

ON THE WORD "POWER," AS USED IN THE ENGLISH NEW TESTAMENT.

Chapter x. page 161.

"*This divine force is constantly alluded to in the New Testament; but the word δύναμις is usually rendered 'power' by the translators, and its real meaning, which is 'force,' is thus weakened.*"

The looseness and want of strict accuracy, in regard to certain words and expressions, by the English translators of the Bible, is really most astounding and inexcusable.

This can scarcely be attributable to ignorance, nor would we ascribe it to wilful perversion; and it must therefore be set down either to carelessness about details, or, as is the most probable, to the blinding effects of preconceived theories and dogmatic prejudice.

This remark applies, perhaps, more especially to those who were responsible for what is commonly known as the "Authorised Version"; though the compilers of the "Revised" Edition are by no means free from the same charge.

We shall deal further on with one evidence of this, in the treatment of the Greek word "πνεῦμα," in its several applications.—See Note S, p. 463. We will here give another example, illustrative of our observations.

The word "power" is to be found 145 times in the New Testament (Authorised Version):—

In seventy-six cases, as the translation of δύναμις;
In fifty-six cases, as the translation of ἐξουσία;
In five cases, as the translation of κράτος;
In one case each, as the translation of ἀρχή, ἰσχύς, μεγαλειότης, and τὸ δυνατόν, respectively.

In the remaining four instances—namely, Rev. vi. 4, xi. 3, xiii. 15, xvi. 8—the word "power" is inserted in the English, without any corresponding word in the Greek, though the sense does not at all necessitate its insertion.

In the Revised Version, it has been omitted in every instance, to the great improvement of the passages concerned.

If, now, we examine the various Greek words which have been indiscriminately translated as "power," we shall find a very essential difference in their respective significations.

The import of "δύναμις," as the word implies, is "dynamical power," which is best rendered "force," or "a force," as the sense of the passage may require.

That of "ἐξουσία" is "vested power," in the sense of "authority" or "sway."

That of "κράτος" is "physical power," best rendered "strength."
That of "ἀρχή" is simply "magistracy."
That of "ἰσχύς" is from "ἴς," the same as the Latin "vis," and may therefore be rendered "might."
That of "μεγαλειότης" is, as the Revised Version correctly has it, "majesty."
And "τὸ δύνατον," which is the neuter substantival form of the adjective δύνατος, "able," is equivalent to the English word "potency."

In many of the 141 passages in which these words occur, the meaning will be rendered much more simple and explicit if we read, instead of "power," the word corresponding to the Greek text, as given above; whilst in all the cases it will be well, for the sake of accuracy and distinction, that the reader should make the required substitution.

For this purpose we now proceed to enumerate the different references, after which we will quote at length some of the passages which are more importantly affected.

1. Where "power" = "δύναμις" = "force," or a "force": Matt. xxii. 29; xxiv. 29, 30; xxvi. 64. Mark ix. 1; xii. 24; xiii. 25, 26; xiv. 62. Luke i. 17, 35; iv. 14, 36; v. 17; ix. 1; xxi. 26, 27; xxii. 69; xxiv. 49. Acts i. 8; iii. 12; iv. 7, 33; vi. 8; viii. 10; x. 38. Rom. i. 4, 16, 20; viii. 38; ix. 17; xv. 13, 19; xvi. 25. 1 Cor. i. 18, 24; ii. 4, 5; iv. 19, 20; vi. 14; xv. 24, 43. 2 Cor. iv. 7; vi. 7; viii. 3; xii. 9; xiii. 4. Eph. i. 19, 21; iii. 7, 20. Philip. iii. 10. Col. i. 11. 1 Thess. i. 5. 2 Thess. i. 11; ii. 9. 2 Tim. i. 7, 8; iii. 5. Heb. i. 3; vi. 5; vii. 16. 1 Peter i. 5; iii. 22. 2 Peter i. 3, 16; ii. 11. Rev. iv. 11; v. 12; vii. 12; xi. 17; xii. 10; xiii. 2; xv. 8; xix. 1.

2. Where "power" = ἐξουσία = "authority," or "sway": Matt. ix. 6, 8; x. 1; xxviii. 18. Mark ii. 10; iii. 15. Luke iv. 6, 32; v. 24; x. 19; xii. 5, 11; xxii. 53. John i. 12; x. 18; xvii. 2; xix. 10, 11. Acts i. 7; v. 4; viii. 19; xxvi. 18. Rom. ix. 21; xiii. 1, 2. 1 Cor. vi. 12; vii. 4, 37; ix. 4, 12, 18; xi. 10. 2 Cor. xiii. 10. Eph. ii. 2; iii. 10; vi. 12. Col. i. 13, 16; ii. 10, 15. 2 Thess. iii. 9. Tit. iii. 1. Jude 25. Rev. ii. 26; vi. 8; ix. 3, 10; xiii. 4, 5, 7, 12; xiv. 18; xvi. 9; xvii. 12; xviii. 1; xx. 6.

3. Where "power" = "κράτος" = "strength": Eph. i. 19; vi. 10. 1 Tim. vi. 16. Heb. ii. 14. Rev. v. 13.

4. Where "power" = "ἀρχή" = "magistracy": Luke xx. 20.

5. Where "power" = "ἰσχύς" = "might": 2 Thess. i. 9.

6. Where "power" = "μεγαλειότης" = "majesty": Luke ix. 43.

7. Where "power" = "τὸ δύνατον" = "potency": Rom. ix. 22.

We will now quote a few passages for the sake of illustrating the observations given above.

Matt. xxviii. 18 : " All sway in heaven and on earth has been given to me."

Luke i. 17 : " He shall proceed in his presence under Elijah's pneuma and force."

Luke xx. 20 : " So that they might deliver him up to the magistracy and authority of the governor."

Luke xxiv. 49 : " Remain in the city of Jerusalem, until ye shall be endued with a force from on high."

Acts i. 7, 8 : " It is not for you to know times or seasons, which the Father hath settled of His own authority. But ye shall receive a force, when the holy pneuma has come upon you."

Rom. xv. 18, 19 : " Those things which Christ hath accomplished through me, to make the Gentiles hearken, by word and deed, by means of a force of signs and wonders, a force of a holy pneuma."

1 Cor. i. 18 : " The logos which is of the cross is to those who are being lost folly ; but to us who are being saved it is a force of God."

1 Cor. ii. 4, 5 : " Not in persuasive words of human wisdom, but in personal experience of pneuma and force; in order that your faith might not depend upon human wisdom, but upon divine force."

Eph. iii. 20 : " Who has a force to accomplish exceeding abundantly above all which we ask or imagine, according to the force which energises in us."

Philip. iii. 10 : " That I may know Him, and the force of His resurrection."

2 Tim. iii. 5 : " Having an outward form of religion, but having rejected the force thereof."

NOTE L.

ON THE PHYSICAL RELATION OF PRESENT PAIN TO FUTURE JOY.

Chapter x. page 169.

" *Every pain-atom, whether it be moral or physical pain, becomes a joy-atom when it has done its work of purification here, and passes upwards, like incense, to that bright atmosphere, where it condenses into a joy-atom, and forms a piece of substantial happiness, waiting to be entered into by the one who felt the agony of it on earth, and who, instead of rebelling then, cherished it as a priceless gift from God.*"

The natural and inseparable connection between pain-atoms, patiently endured and rightly utilised on earth, and joy-atoms in the bright hereafter, is a frequent theme in the Bible. But though most readers of the Bible understand and believe that sorrow here below is the prelude to joy hereafter above, few apparently comprehend the truth that *the one actually produces the other;* that is to say, not that joy in heaven will be simply a *reward* for patient endurance of sorrow on earth, but that it is its *offspring,* the former being actually the same substance as the latter, as literally as the child is of the substance of the mother, or as the full-grown corn is of the substance of the seed.

The following passages are a few of those which speak of the intimate relation between terrestrial sorrow and celestial joy; and some of them, to which we will afterwards draw especial attention, trace very clearly the substantial identity between the two.

"Our light affliction which is for the moment, worketh for us more and more exceedingly an eternal weight of glory; while we look not at the things which are seen, but at the things which are not seen; for the things which are seen are temporal; but the things which are not seen are eternal" (2 Cor. iv. 17, 18).

"Wherein ye greatly rejoice, though now for a little while, if need be, ye have been put to grief in manifold temptations, that the proof of your faith, being more precious than gold that perisheth, though it is proved by fire, might be found unto praise and glory and honour at the revelation of Jesus Christ" (1 Peter i. 6, 7).

"Verily, verily, I say unto you, That ye shall weep and lament, but the world shall rejoice; and ye shall be sorrowful, but your sorrow shall be turned into joy. A woman when she is in travail hath sorrow, because her hour is come; but when she is delivered of the child she remembereth no more the anguish, for the joy that a man is born into the world. And ye therefore now have sorrow; but I will see you again, and your heart shall rejoice, and your joy no one taketh away from you" (John xvi. 20-22).

"They that sow in tears shall reap in joy" (Ps. cxxvi. 5).

"Whatsoever a man soweth, that shall he also reap" (Gal. vi. 7).

"He shall drink of the brook in the way; therefore shall he lift up the head" (Ps. cx. 7).

"They shall come with weeping, and with supplications will I lead them; I will cause them to walk by rivers of waters. And they shall come and sing in the height of Zion, and shall flow together unto the goodness of the Lord, . . . and they shall not sorrow any more at all, . . . for I will turn their mourning into joy, and will comfort them, and make them rejoice out of their sorrow" (Jer. xxxi. 9, 12, 13).

"Count it all joy, my brethren, when ye fall into manifold temptations" (James i. 2).

"We behold Him, who hath been made a little lower than the

angels, even Jesus, because of the suffering of death crowned with glory and honour; that by the grace of God He should taste death for every man. For it became Him, for whom are all things and through whom are all things, in bringing many sons to glory, to make the author of their salvation perfect through sufferings" (Heb. ii. 9, 10).

"If so be that we suffer with Him, that we may be also glorified together" (Rom. viii. 17).

"We know that the whole creation groaneth and travaileth in pain together until now. And not only so, but ourselves also, which have the first-fruits of the Spirit, even we ourselves groan within ourselves, waiting for our adoption, to wit, the redemption of our body" (Rom. viii. 22, 23).

"Weeping may tarry for the night, but joy cometh in the morning" (Ps. xxx. 5).

"Sorrow is turned into joy before Him" (Job xli. 22).

"These are they which came out of great tribulation, and they washed their robes and made them white in the blood of the Lamb. Therefore are they before the throne of God" (Rev. vii. 14).

Now from these passages we see four things:—

1. That there is a necessary relation between present sorrow and future joy.
2. That present sorrow produces future joy (2 Cor. iv. 17, 18; 1 Pet. i. 6, 7; Ps. cx. 7; Heb. ii. 9, 10; Rom. viii. 17; Rev. vii. 14).
3. That present sorrow produces future joy, as a woman produces a child (John xvi. 20-22; Rom. viii. 22, 23).
4. As a seed sown produces the fruit which is reaped (Ps. cxxvi. 5; Gal. vi. 7).

N.B.—In Ps. cxxvi. 5, it is worthy of remark that the words "They that sow in tears shall reap in joy," do not mean that those who shed tears whilst in the act of sowing shall rejoice whilst in the act of reaping; but that those who sow in the substance of tears (*i.e.*, sow tears) shall reap in the substance of joy (*i.e.*, shall reap joy).

From these considerations we see that the Bible teaches us that the joy of the hereafter is formed from the sorrow of the present; for sorrow and joy, like all other emotions, are in very truth material atomic substances.

The process by which the substance of the joy is produced out of the elements of the sorrow is analogous to the physical operations with which we are familiar in the science of chemistry.

The atoms of pain are incapable of transformation into those of joy, except by combination with the moral atoms of patience and faith in the human sufferer. In many cases, sorrow and pain fail to produce the desired results; this is because they enter into combination with the wrong moral elements in the person afflicted. Then discontent, peevishness, and a murmuring spirit of faithlessness mar the work which would otherwise ensue.

When suffering and anguish are met by fortitude and patience, and these ingredients are together submitted to the action of the divine crucible, then, and then only, do they "work together for good," as St Paul so beautifully describes it in Rom. viii. 28, where the Greek word exactly implies the action which takes place in a chemical retort. Then, and then only, does the refining fire remove the dross from human nature; and the atoms of sorrow combine with the atoms of patience, producing the glorious, immortal, unalloyed substance of eternal happiness and joy.

NOTE M.

ON THE FUTURE LIFE.

Chapter x. pages 176, 177.

"It is not possible for those who have passed through it into higher conditions to sink back into it again, for the attraction of goodness, in the midst of which they dwell, is too powerful to admit of their doing so; but it is possible for those who have sunk through it downwards to be drawn up to it again, and so finally saved."

This is simply a matter of attraction and gravitation; only the attraction and gravitation is of moral instead of physical atoms. A body escaping from earth into the upper regions of the unseen world comes within the gravitating influence of that region, and that attraction is powerful enough to resist all counter-gravitation. This was exactly the same case with the lower world till Christ went down there, and by His presence and the atomic elements which He deposited there, weakened the gravitation of the lower world to such an extent, that it is now possible for beings to escape from that region into the higher. This was the purpose of Christ's "descent into hell": "He went to set free those who were bound," —bound, that is, by the force of infernal gravitation; He released the "spirits in prison,"—in the prison, namely, of the attraction of the lower world, from which, till the power of that attraction was weakened by the counteracting element of Christ's biunity, they were utterly unable to escape.

This was what Christ meant by the description which He gives of the portions of the invisible world, in the parable of "Dives and Lazarus." We see there Lazarus "carried by angels into Abraham's bosom,"—a figurative expression for the passing of his pneumatic body into the region of angels and departed saints; we see the rich man in the agony "afar off," in the lower regions of Hades.

Between the two "there is an impassable barrier"; so that it is impossible for the denizens of the one locality to pay a visit to the denizens of the other. This "impassable barrier" is the moral expanse of earth, where the counter-attractions of heaven and hell, —*i.e.*, of the upper and lower invisible regions—meet; neither exercising within that region an attraction so irresistible as to nullify the gravitating force of the other. Outside that region, on either side, the condition of things becomes changed, and no attraction whatever from the lower world can reach the upper, just as, before Christ went down into the lower region, no attraction from the upper could penetrate into it. It was for this reason that Christ, before His death and descent into hell, described the rich man and Lazarus as being in positions so entirely asundered that it was impossible for them to come again into contact.

But that picture no longer holds true. Though Lazarus could now by no possibility descend to Dives, any more than he could before, yet it would now be possible for Dives to ascend to the position which Lazarus occupied.

In this supremely potent work of Christ lies the hope, nay, the certainty, of the final salvation of the whole universe. Had Christ been content to humiliate Himself to death, and pass in His pneumatic body into the invisible regions of earth, and thence upwards into heaven, without descending into hell, there could never have been, for all eternity, any prospect of deliverance of the "spirits in prison."

Now, however, as gradually, under the stronger attraction of the upper spheres, beings pass, one by one, from the lower, so does the celestial gravitation constantly increase, with the addition of each new moral force contained in the pneumatic body of each newcomer; whilst at the same time the gravitating force of the infernals in proportion diminishes; and finally it must become altogether extinct, for all will have passed to the upper regions of bliss.

This is the final salvation; this is the universal redemption of the invisible as well as the visible world, which it was Christ's great mission and work to accomplish.

The "impassable gulf" has been a source of great controversy in the Church; and the erroneous conception of the unseen world, based upon an ignorance of the fact that locality there is simply the result of the moral conditions which create it, has given rise to such doctrines as purgatory, on the one hand, and eternal damnation, on the other, and has resulted in causing people to regard the moment of death as fixing for all eternity the condition of the soul. Once let the truth be realised that the *place* where people are in the unseen world, means simply the *state* in which they are, and all difficulties disappear which have given rise to so many conflicting and erroneous dogmas.

NOTE N.

ON THE HIDDEN MEANING OF SCRIPTURE.

Chapter xi. page 185.

"*The fact that the Bible possesses this inner meaning is indicated both in the Old and New Testaments.*"

The frequent occurrence of such words as "mystery," "parable," "dark sayings," &c., testify to the fact that the Bible recognises a hidden meaning in its records and teaching; which fact it is necessary to bear constantly in mind while perusing or studying its pages. Thus, amongst other statements on the subject in Holy Writ, we find the following:—

"We speak the wisdom of God in a mystery, even the hidden wisdom, which God ordained before the world unto our glory" (1 Cor. ii. 7).

"According to the revelation of the mystery, which was kept secret since the world began, but now is made manifest, and by the scriptures of the prophets, according to the commandment of the everlasting God, made known to all nations for the obedience of faith" (Rom. xvi. 25, 26).

"Having made known to us the mystery of His will" (Eph. i. 9).

"By revelation He made known to me the mystery, which in other ages was not made known to the sons of men, as it is now revealed unto His holy apostles and prophets by the pneuma" (Eph. iii. 5).

"The mystery which has been hid from ages and generations, but is now made manifest to His saints; to whom God would make known what is the riches of the glory of the mystery among the Gentiles, which is Christ in you" (Col. i. 26, 27).

"Holding the mystery of the faith in a pure conscience" (1 Tim. iii. 9).

"Stewards of the mysteries of God" (1 Cor. iv. 1).

"I will incline mine ear to a parable: I will open my dark sayings upon the harp" (Ps. xlix. 4).

"I will open my mouth in a parable: I will utter dark sayings of old" (Ps. lxxviii. 2).

"The words of the wise and their dark sayings" (Prov. i. 6).

"Son of man, speak a parable unto the house of Israel" (Ezek. xvii. 2).

"Utter a parable unto the rebellious house, and say unto them, Thus saith the Lord God" (Ezek. xxiv. 3).

"Go, and tell this people, Hear ye indeed, but understand not; and see ye indeed, but perceive not. Make the heart of this people fat, and their ears heavy, and shut their eyes; lest they see with their eyes, and hear with their ears, and understand with their heart, and convert and be healed" (Isa. vi. 9, 10).

"They say of me, Doth he not speak parables?" (Ezek. xx. 49).

"I have declared the former things from the beginning; and they went out of my mouth, and I showed them; . . . I have even from the beginning declared it unto thee; . . . thou hast heard, see all this; and will not ye declare it? I have showed thee new things from this time, even hidden things, and thou didst not know them; . . . yea, thou heardest not; yea, thou knewest not; yea, from that time thine ear was not opened" (Isa. xlviii. 3, 5, 6, 8).

"He revealeth the deep and secret things" (Dan. ii. 22).

"In all his epistles, speaking to them of these things; in which are some things hard to be understood, which they that are unlearned and unstable wrest, as they do also the Scriptures, unto their own destruction" (2 Pet. iii. 16).

"Now we see through a glass darkly; but then face to face: now I know in part; but then I shall know even as I am known" (1 Cor. xiii. 12).

NOTE O.

ON SPIRITUAL EXPERIENCES.

Chapter xi. page 192.

"I appeal to the testimony of others, because, thank God, the number of those who are physically as well as morally conscious of this increasing respiratory sensitiveness, is daily augmenting."

The notion of spiritual influences actually affecting the physical respiration may, perhaps, appear to many people fantastic; yet this is a matter of constant experience to those who have entered on the sympneumatic life. The writer himself could scarcely have credited the physical results produced by spiritual causes, if he had not actually experienced them frequently and powerfully himself, and witnessed them in others.

This respiratory motion is entirely distinct from cataleptic and hysteric convulsions; and yet at times it shakes the whole frame from head to foot with quivering, vibratory currents; whilst at others it produces a sensation of intense difficulty of breathing, at times amounting almost to suffocation.

On two separate occasions the writer has been able to detect the exact position of an obscure malady in another person solely by the magnetic vibrations produced in his entire organism, as soon as his fingers have touched the seat of the disease.

In one instance it was an affection of the kidneys; in another, a tension of the nerves at the base of the spine.

In each case, the writer, passing his hand quietly and gradually down the back of the patient, and exercising at the same time all the powers of his will-force to surrender himself to the guidance of the pneuma, has felt nothing until he has come in contact with the spot overlying the source of the complaint. Immediately he has touched the place, he has felt a powerful current entering his organism, through the tips of the fingers, which were pressed upon the patient. This current has passed up his arm and through his whole frame, and at the same time the peculiar respiratory motion spoken of has visibly taken possession of him. Directly his hand has been removed from the patient, the vibratory currents have ceased. This same phenomenon has occurred every time he has treated the patient thus, and in both cases the patient derived immediate and sensible benefit from every succession of the treatment; being ultimately completely cured after a few days, notwithstanding the fact that, in the case of the affection of the kidneys, a doctor who had been previously consulted by the patient declared that it was impossible for him to recover, except after an illness of long duration.

The writer himself does not attempt to explain the facts; he merely states them as they occurred, acknowledging, at the same time, that he was entirely unconscious of possessing in himself any healing faculty, and that he was throughout distinctly a passive instrument for the transmission of the vital currents. He can only account for the results by the unseen action of higher potencies.

The respiratory motion above described is probably analogous to that which affected Christ whilst curing the deaf and dumb patient in the district of Decapolis. St Mark, who relates the circumstance, expressly mentions that Christ "put His fingers into his ears," and "touched his tongue," and "looking up to heaven, *He sighed*." That which was mistaken for "sighing" was doubtless the outward manifestation of the pneuma, imparting healing potencies through the organism of Christ; for the pneumatic respiration is generally accompanied by a heaving in the throat, best described as a succession of strong sighs.

See Postscript, p. 472.

NOTE P.

ON THE WORD "SHADDAI."

Chapter xvii. page 279.

"It is worthy of note that on the occasion of this covenant we, for the first time, find the word 'Shaddai' used as a name for the Almighty,—a word of the deepest and holiest import, for in its internal meaning it signifies the Divine Feminine."

One of the most remarkable words in the Hebrew Bible is the word שד, *Shad*, with its various derivatives and cognate expressions. A clear understanding of their import will remove much that is obscure, and will throw a wonderful light on the hidden meaning of Scripture.

It must be borne in mind that in the Hebrew language, as in all the oriental languages of antiquity, the forms of words have a deep signification, and that all words compounded of the same root-letters have a kindred meaning.

Furthermore, inasmuch as vowel-points are a later addition to the language, and have nothing to do with root-formations, the vowels may be disregarded in tracing the ramifications of cognate words.

The triliteral root from which שד, *Shad*, comes, is שדה, *Shadah* = "to suckle."

Hence שד comes to mean "the female breast"; and the two-fold ideas of *femininity* and *nourishment* are introduced.

Thus שדה, *Shiddah* = a lady, a mistress, a wife, or a princess;
    שדה, *Sh'dah* = a fountain;
    שדה, *Sadeh* ⎫
  or שדי, *Sadai* ⎬ = a field.

The fountain and the field are, as it were, the "breasts" of the earth; for out of them are produced the nourishment which "Mother Earth" affords to her children.

From the idea of *nourishment* follows that of *support* or *preservation*. Hence that aspect of God which represents Him as the "Almighty Preserver" or "Nourisher of Life," designates Him under the title of שדי, *Shaddai*, which is, consequently, invariably translated as "the Almighty" in the Bible.

This rendering, however, gives but a very faint and unworthy idea of the real meaning of שדי, *Shaddai*.

The name was first revealed to Abram, according to Sacred Writ (Gen. xvii. 1), and afterwards to Jacob (Gen. xxxv. 11), at a special period in the life of each of these patriarchs, and at the moment when they were solemnly informed that they and their seed were to be the depositaries of the arcana of God's mysterious truth.

Hence it was in strict accordance with the gravity and mystery of this revelation, that the title under which the Deity was then revealed should be one of the holiest and most mystic import. Therefore it is that in this word שדי is contained nothing short of the hidden declaration of the eternal Divine Feminine. The "י," the first letter of the sacred and mystic name "יהוה"—commonly but erroneously pronounced Jehovah — designates the divinity; the "שד" declares the femininity.

But this great central truth, which mankind had lost, had to be concealed from general understanding until the fulness of time for its revelation should come; and one curious result of this concealment has been that the word שדי, though indicating the femininity of God, has been handed down to the Jewish nation as a *masculine* Hebrew word.

None the less, however, is it true that, wheresoever in the Hebrew Bible the word שדי occurs, it is, when rightly understood, to be applied to the Divine Feminine.

The translators of the Bible, being ignorant of this hidden aspect of the Deity, have naturally overlooked this truth; and hence they only realised the import of "Shaddai" as "the Almighty" Preserver, when they ought in reality to have regarded it as "the life-nourishing maternity of God."

The word שדי occurs in the following passages in the Old Testament, which we would earnestly recommend our readers to study carefully and separately, remembering that they should substitute for "the Almighty," the words "the Divine Feminine":—

Gen. xvii. 1; xxviii. 3; xxxv. 11; xliii. 14; xlviii. 3; xlix. 25. Exod. vi. 3. Num. xxiv. 4. Ruth i. 20, 21. Job v. 17; vi. 4, 14; viii. 3, 5; xi. 7; xiii. 3; xv. 25; xxi. 15, 20; xxii. 3, 17, 23, 25, 26; xxiii. 16; xxiv. 1; xxvii. 2, 10, 11, 13; xxix. 5; xxxi. 2, 35; xxxii. 8; xxxiii. 4; xxxiv. 10, 12; xxxv. 13; xxxvii. 23; xl. 2. Ps. lxviii. 14; xci. 1. Isa. xiii. 6. Ezek. i. 24. Joel i. 15.

Of these forty-six passages, it will be noticed that no fewer than thirty-one occur in the Book of Job, rightly considered by many as the most mysterious book in the Old Testament. Indeed, so long as the truth of the Divine Feminine remained concealed, it was impossible to understand the Book of Job; for, as we shall see presently, the connection between the two is so intimate that the latter might be appropriately termed, "A Hymn to El Shaddai, the Maternity of God."

Before entering upon this subject, however, it is necessary to consider some further modifications of the root שדה, *Shadah*.

It is a well-known rule of Semitic philology that similar consonants may be interchanged, one with another, this interchange effecting certain regular modulations in sense. Thus, sibilants may be interchanged with sibilants, dentals with dentals, gutturals with gutturals, and so forth.

Now, in the case of שׁד, we have a soft sibilant שׁ, *sh*, and a soft dental ד, *d*.

Corresponding to שׁ, *sh*, we have two hard sibilants, שׂ, and ס, both equivalent to the English *s*.

Corresponding to ד, *d*, we have also two hard dentals ט, and ת, rendered by the English *t*, the latter being sometimes modified into ת, *th*.

These sibilants and dentals may be consequently interchanged with each other, the conversion of the soft consonant into the corresponding hard having just this simple but important effect,—it *inverts* the sense, either partly or wholly, according as to whether one or both of the consonants is changed.

Thus, whereas שׁד, *Shad*, and its derivatives, composed of the soft sibilant and the soft dental, represent the true Divine feminine principle, the compounds of the corresponding hard sibilant and hard dental represent the false—that is, the entire inversion of the true; whilst the compounds of the hard sibilant with the soft dental represent a partial inversion, or a corruption of the original true principle.

A remarkable illustration of this rule is afforded by the word שׁדה, *Shiddah*, and its corresponding word שׂטה, *Sittah*.

{ שׁדה, *Shiddah* = a wife.
{ שׂטה, *Sittah* = a wife *who has become unfaithful*.

Again, שׁדי, *Shaddai*, represents the source from which man in his original perfect bisexual nature drew his nourishment, when he was after God's own image, and was formed entirely of the material of God.

שׂדי, *Sadai*, "a field," represents the source from which man in his fallen nature draws his nourishment, now that he is formed externally of the material of the earth.

Since man has only partially lost the image of God, and only partially draws the nourishment for his organism from the "breast of the earth," only one of the original letters (שׁ) is changed, the other (ד) remaining the same.

But though in the sacred shrine of man's inmost being there still lingers a spark of his original divine reflection, yet the *consciousness* of the feminine principle in the Deity became for the time entirely lost to mankind by the agency of the inverted male principle, as is described in Genesis under the story of the murder of Abel by Cain. Hence, when the first offspring of the new method of generation appeared, his name was called שׂת, *Seth*, to indicate the total inversion of the true principle " שׁד, *Shad*."

So, moreover, those beings of the lower invisible universe, who had assumed to themselves fictitious imitations of the qualities of the Godhead, and who belonged to the fallen portion of that former humanity who are entitled in the Bible "sons of God"—this term sometimes referring to the lower, though generally to the upper or unfallen, beings of the primal universe—are designated under the form of שׁדים, *Siddim*, this being simply the plural form of שׂד, *Sad*, the partial inversion of the true שׂד, *Shad*.

These "Siddim" are the beings referred to in Gen. vi. 2, when we are told that "the sons of God saw the daughters of men that they were fair; and they took them wives of all that they chose."

This nefarious and unnatural sexual intercourse between the Siddim and the daughters of men resulted in a progeny which are called in the Bible "Nephilim," erroneously translated "giants" in the Authorised Version of Gen. vi. 4, but correctly rendered in the Revised Edition. The word נפלים, *Nephilim*, is the plural of נפל, *Nephil*, which signifies primarily, as the Authorised Version translates it in Job iii. 16, and Ps. lviii. 8, "an untimely birth." Hence it comes to mean "an offspring born out of the ordinary course of nature," such as the progeny of "the sons of God," and "the daughters of men." These Nephilim were thus what we term "monstrosities," or "monsters"; and hence, probably, the term "giants." It was doubtless the existence of these *Nephilim* upon the earth which gave rise to the ancient mythological legends of demi-gods, demi-mortals, centaurs, titans, satyrs, fauns, &c.

The disastrous results of the illicit intercourse between the denizens of the fallen primal universe and those of this world, culminated in a tremendous social, moral, and physical cataclysm, which is represented in the Bible under the story of the Flood. It would appear that after this convulsion the intercourse between the two worlds was interrupted for a time; but after a while the Siddim, who in later times have been known under the names of "Incubi" and "Succubi," again infested the earth; and one region at least became the scene of the most abominable illicit traffic between them and human beings. The region thus infested, and in consequence visited by another cataclysm which utterly destroyed it, was called, from the practices of which it was the theatre, the "Vale of Siddim" (Gen. xiv. 8, 10); and the principal town in it, and the one most notorious for the criminal intercourse, was characterised by a name of identical import, and has ever since been a byword for the basest of unnatural crimes. This town was סדם, Sodom.

Captain Conder, R.E., in his 'Handbook to the Bible,' p. 240, remarks significantly, "The name Siddim has always been a puzzle to scholars." In the Kabbalah, however, this contact between the

Siddim and the world is mentioned. See Mather's 'Kabbalah Unveiled,' page 249.[1]

One consequence has been that the particular sin of which the inhabitants of Sodom and Gomorrah were guilty has been entirely misunderstood; and if we bear in mind who these Siddim were, it is easy to understand the behaviour of the men of Sodom towards the two "angels" who visited Lot, as recorded in the 19th chapter of Genesis. The crowning feature of their sin in this respect was due to the fact that these "angels" were denizens of the upper invisible primal universe, and the men of Sodom wished to treat them as if they had belonged to the lower.

Such were the Siddim, fallen, degraded creatures, who assumed fictitious imitations of "Shaddai"; though, at the same time, they do not represent the absolute and total inversion, as is seen by the form of their name, in which only one of the two letters of שד is changed.

The complete inversion, the diametrically antagonistic principle, is formed by changing both the letters into their corresponding hard sounds; and doing this we get שט, *set*, the "backslider," or "the wicked one"; which, amplified, becomes שטן, *Satan!* Hence Satan signifies also "adversary," because the word represents the great antagonistic principle to Shaddai.

The way has now been cleared to a comprehensive understanding of many of those very mysterious passages of Scripture, where Satan is prominently brought forward, especially in that book to which particular allusion has already been made above—that is to say, the Book of Job.

Herein is described, in the mystic language of oriental poetry, the contest for the ascendancy over man between the true and the false principles, represented respectively by Shaddai and Satan.

As Shaddai is the maternal giver and preserver of life, so Satan, the antagonist, is the destroyer. Hence through the agency of Satan, the cattle, the asses, the flocks, the camels, the servants, and the children of Job are destroyed; and Job himself is afflicted with suffering only just short of death. The patriarch is tempted to ascribe to Shaddai the action of Satan, and to impugn the true nature of God.

The various phases through which the conflict passes occupy the greater part of the book, and are disguised under the form of arguments and conversations with personal friends.

The three friends of Job who, under the pretence of sympathy,

---

[1] Since the above was written, the writer has come across the following passage in M. Renan's 'Histoire du Peuple d'Israel,' which affords a remarkable independent corroboration of his account of the Vale of Siddim: "Le nom de Siddim qu'aurait porté l'ancienne vallée est peut-être une fausse prononciation pour Sédim, 'la vallée des démons.'"—P. 116, Note 4.

only aggravate his grief by their words, and who, with their pious hypocritical speeches, goad him on by their insinuations to rebellion against Shaddai, are really the emissaries of Satan in disguise, and represent the threefold weapons of Satan's attacks—"the lust of the flesh, the lust of the eye, and the pride of life" (see 1st John ii. 16).

Eliphaz the Temanite represents "riches, the pride of life," the word "Eliphaz" signifying "God of riches." Bildad the Shuhite represents "the lust of the flesh"; "Bildad" being the same as "Bel-shad," or the "Breast of Bel," the false god of fleshly appetite. Zophar the Naamathite represents "the lust of the eyes"; the word "Zophar," with the appellation Naamathite, signifying together "sensual loveliness."

Thus we have here a poetical representation of a mode of attack made upon Job by Satan, exactly analogous to those which he made upon Eve and upon Christ.

When Eve was tempted by Satan, the forbidden fruit was represented to her under a threefold aspect, as "good for food," "pleasant to the eyes," and "a thing to be desired to make one wise": "good for food," the "lust of the flesh"; "pleasant to the eyes," the "lust of the eyes"; "a thing to be desired to make one wise," the "pride of life."

When Christ was tempted by Satan, the same mode of attack was used: "Command these stones that they be made bread," the "lust of the flesh"; "He showed Him all the kingdoms of the world and the glory of them," the "lust of the eyes"; "Cast Thyself down from the temple, for He shall give His angels charge over Thee," &c, the "pride of life."

The significance of this threefold method of attack by Satan lies in the fact that these are the very temptations specially directed against the true principles of Shaddai.

The Divine Feminine is the giver and supporter of life and all its necessaries. From Shaddai, man in his first pure existence drew all his *food*, all his *pleasure*, all his *satisfaction of life*. From the same maternal divinity, man, in his regenerated condition, will again draw the same essential supplies.

All sin and all disease and misery arise from the fact that man has, through the agency of Satan, been seduced into drawing these supplies from an inverted source, and has thus fallen under the combined temptations of lust, covetousness, and pride, the "lust of the flesh," the "lust of the eyes," and "the pride of life"; choosing, as it were, for his companions and advisers Bildad, Zophar, and Eliphaz the Temanite.

This is the hidden meaning of the Book of Job, before closing our notice of which, we must draw attention to the personality of "Elihu, the son of Barachel the Buzite, of the kindred of Ram."

This mysterious personage, belonging to the family of *Ram*,—the most ancient world-reformer of whom history speaks, and certainly one of the most renowned, living probably more than eight thousand years ago,—comes upon the scene in the Book of Job as an impartial censor, alike of the patriarch himself, as of his three companions. His name "Elihu," is the same in import as "Elijah," and his mission is "in the spirit of Elijah," to prepare the way for the revelation of Shaddai.

Hence we find the name "Shaddai" occurring several times in the course of his speeches; and even when it is not actually mentioned, the whole of his observations bear manifest allusions to the sublime truth of the bisexual unity of God.

So when the revelation came at length, when God addressed Job from out of the whirlwind, the patriarch was ready to recognise the revelation, and to humble himself in the presence of Shaddai.

"Jehovah answered Job, and said, Shall he that cavilleth contend with Shaddai? And Job answered Jehovah, and said, Behold, I am of small account; what shall I answer Thee? I lay my hand upon my mouth" (Job xl. 2-4).

Thus Job emerges safely from his trying ordeal; Satan is frustrated, and Shaddai victorious; the consequence being that "the latter end of Job was blessed more than the beginning," and through the fostering care of Shaddai he received children, servants, camels, oxen, asses, and flocks, far exceeding in numbers those whom he had originally lost.

A glorious prophetic picture this of the final triumph of Shaddai over Satan for the possession of humanity—a triumph which may still be undoubtedly far distant, but which a multitude of signs, scarcely to be mistaken, and a general concurrence of undefined anticipations, are leading many sober and thoughtful minds—whether rightly or wrongly, none can tell—to regard as "near, even at the doors."

NOTE Q.

ON THE ATOMIC AFFINITY BETWEEN CHRIST AND TRUE CHRISTIANS.

Chapter xviii. pages 305, 306.

"*He needed to be born into the earth through a natural woman, and to die, and be lifted up from it, because He could only thus acquire an atomic construction which would enable Him to come into close affinity with man, and so draw all men unto Him. There is no other being in that world, constituted as to His organic ele-*

ments with reference to ours as He is; and hence He is our Saviour, to whom alone we must cling, and through whom alone we can draw the vital currents which will impart the potency necessary for the salvation of the race."

All Churches of Christendom profess to believe that "union with Christ" is a fundamental necessity for salvation. But in most cases this "union with Christ" is a vague and indefinite idea, consisting of a shadowy, unsubstantial attitude of the mind and intellect towards the Founder of the religion, which is called by its possessors "faith." This mental conception is, in reality, entirely different from true faith: and hence it exercises but very little, if any, influence upon their daily life.

The "union with Christ," to be a means of salvation, must be an actual, tangible, concrete union; in other words, it must be "atomic."

This Christ Himself clearly indicated in the illustrations which He employed, when He wished to describe the relations which were to exist between Himself and those who were to be saved by Him.

This is also to be found in more than one of the Pauline epistles.

Two of the commonest illustrations will serve to explain this truth:—

I. A *tree*.

"As the branch cannot bear fruit of itself," said Christ, "except it remain in the vine; so neither can ye, except ye remain in me."

"I am the vine, ye are the branches. He that remaineth in me, and I in him, the same beareth much fruit; for apart from me ye can do nothing" (John xv. 4, 5).

It is to be noted in this passage that the Authorised Version has a very misleading phrase, when it says, "without me ye can do nothing."

The expression "without me" is, in the Greek, χωρὶς ἐμοῦ, which means "outside of me"—*i.e.*, "cut off from me," or, as the Revised Version puts it, "apart from me."

Thus Christ meant to say that true life was inseparable from actual union with Him.

Now let us consider what constitutes a living tree.

A tree is an organism. That is to say, a tree does not consist of a quantity of different pieces of wood, scattered about or heaped together, with a branch here and a bough there; but a tree has all its several parts organically connected together; and each part maintains its life and health by virtue of its being in organic union with the trunk and root. Thus, through this union, the smallest leaf and the remotest bough draws from the root and stem the vital currents which impart the potency necessary for its life and vigour. So long as no organic obstacle occurs to check the flow of the vital current, the leaf, bough, branch, and every portion of the tree maintains its health. Directly the flow of the vital current becomes impeded from any cause, the limb affected loses its vigour and becomes diseased. Once severed from the main stock, the organic union is lost, and the limb can bring forth no fruit, and from that moment begins to die.

The analogy between this organism and the organic union with Christ and those who are to be saved by Him, is very exact.

Christ is the root and stem, and salvation for the human race consists in their being severally and individually brought into atomic union with Him, as is effected by the ingrafting of a bough upon a tree. This St Paul expresses when he says, "If the root be holy, so are the branches. And if some of the branches be broken off, and thou, being a wild olive tree, wert grafted in among them, and with them partakest of the root and fatness of the olive tree; boast not against the branches. But if thou boast, thou bearest not the root, but the root thee. . . . For if thou wert cut out of the olive tree which is wild by nature, and wert grafted contrary to nature into a good olive tree; how much more shall they, which be the natural branches, be grafted into their own olive tree?" (Rom. xi. 16, 17, 18, 24.)

From this analogy of a tree, we see two things of great importance:—

1. No mere attitude of the mind to Jesus, such as feeling a conviction of His power and goodness, or such as commonly goes by the name of "faith," is sufficient to bring a person into saving union with Christ. Nor will any amount of personal excellence of character effect that object. There must be an actual atomic affinity.

A bough may be admirably suited for bearing fruit, if grafted on to a certain tree, but it does not become a part of that tree, nor can it draw any vital current from the root of that tree, until it has been organically united to it by the process of ingrafting. It may actually be bearing fruit as the branch of another living tree, and the fruit may be apparently as good outwardly, but it will not be a fruit of "the tree" which has the particular root, until it has been grafted into atomic union with it.

So it is with Christ's salvation. Until a person has been brought into actual organic union with Christ, that person cannot draw his vital currents from Christ; or in other words, cannot be made a partaker of the "holy pneuma" which flows from Christ into the organism of those who are thus in atomic affinity with Him.

2. *It is not necessary for this atomic union that there should be atomic contact.*

As we have seen, every particle of a living tree is in actual atomic union with the root, though not in actual atomic contact.

A tree may be sixty feet high, for instance, and yet the topmost bough draws all its vital currents from the root as fully and truly as if it were in close proximity to it.

So a human being can draw from Christ the full force of his necessary vital currents, but these currents may pass through many intermediaries between the act of issuing from Christ and the act of entering the human organism.

The intermediaries no more separate Christ from the human being in atomic union with Him and them, than the main trunk and side branches separate the leaf from the root. Indeed, the leaf which is situated on the topmost bough could not live if actually in contact with the root, for it would have become dislocated from its proper sphere of existence.

This important feature connected with the affinity between Christ and man will be even more clearly understood if we consider the second great illustration used in the New Testament.

II. A *body*.

"As the body is one, and hath many members, and all the members of that one body, being many, are one body: so also is Christ" (1 Cor. xii. 12).

"Ye are the body of Christ, and members in particular" (1 Cor. xii. 27).

Now it must be patent to every one that a body is a concrete organism. It does not consist of a head here, a couple of arms there, a couple of legs in another place, and so on; or of different limbs conglomerated together without any organic connection. Every portion of the body is in atomic union with the head, and draws the vital currents necessary for its life and strength from the head, by virtue of the spiritual essence which permeates the whole. Impede the healthy flow of this vital current, and the member affected becomes diseased. Sever a member from the body, and it is immediately dead.

And as in the case of the tree, so of the body, atomic union does not imply atomic contact. The foot is in atomic union with the head, and the hand with the eye, and yet they are not in atomic contact. Moreover, each occupies its proper sphere, and draws its full vital current in proportion as it is content to keep its place and discharge its own functions.

"If the foot shall say, Because I am not the hand, I am not of the body; is it therefore not of the body? . . . If the whole body were an eye, where were the hearing? If the whole body were hearing, where were the smelling? But now hath God set the members every one of them in the body, as it hath pleased Him. ... And the eye cannot say unto the hand, I have no need of thee; nor again the head to the feet, I have no need of you" (1 Cor. xii. 15, 17, 18, 21).

Thus organically united to Christ, as the branch to the vine, or as the limb to the body, and drawing all our vital force from the inpouring of the pneuma which flows forth from Christ as the pervading sap or the permeating spirit, we shall in time "come into the unity of the faith, and the knowledge of the Son of God, unto a perfect man, unto the measure of the stature of the fulness of Christ," and "grow up into Him in all things, which is the head, even Christ; from whom the whole body, fitly joined together and compacted by that which every joint supplieth, according to the effectual measure of the working of every part, maketh increase of the body unto the edifying of itself in love" (Eph. iv. 13, 16).

NOTE R.

ON THE DOGMA OF THE TRINITY.

Chapter xx. page 326.

"*The two dogmas of the Churches of Christendom that operate most powerfully against the descent of the Divine Feminine, which now seeks to impart its purifying and regenerating influence to the 'Bride, the Lamb's wife,' are the atonement, as popularly understood, and the Trinity.*"

The doctrine of the Trinity has become so essentially fundamental and integral a dogma of Christendom, that it will probably be a very difficult task to make people realise that it is, after all, a dogma purely of human invention, and one, moreover, of by no means the most ancient date of Christianity. Another difficulty in the way of dealing with the subject arises from the fact that, in consequence of the action of the ecclesiastical authorities for many centuries with regard to the dogma, and owing to the influence of the anathemas in the Athanasian Creed, it is, in the minds of vast numbers of pious and well-meaning people, an act of sacrilegious profanation, even to discuss the merits of the doctrine at all.

The objurgations of ecclesiastics, and the anathemas of creeds, will not, however, deter for a single moment the honest inquirer after the truth. The most hallowed sanctuary of the shrine of Christendom, the most cherished dogma of the popular faith, must be explored and examined on its own merits; and on its own merits it must stand or fall.

In order to arrive at a just estimate as to the authority and validity of the doctrine of the Trinity, it will be necessary to take a very brief survey of its history, and of the events which led to its formal incorporation into the authorised dogmas of the religion of Christendom. In this we shall endeavour to observe the very strictest truth and impartiality, and without inclining either to the one side or to the other, to present the actual state of affairs to the reader, so far as it is possible to learn them from a careful study of the best authorities, at this distant period of time.

Scarcely had the Church been set afloat by the apostles, before it began to be split up into parties and sects, each clinging to their own favourite modifications of thought and creed. These ultimately arranged themselves into what may be considered under three classes — (1) Judaising Christians, (2) Gnostic Christians, and (3) Platonic Christians. Of the two former, it will be sufficient here to observe, that Judaic Christianity may be said to have virtually terminated with the destruction of Jerusalem and the dispersion of the Jews; whilst Gnostic Christianity, after having maintained an active influence on the religion for the first four centuries, was suffered to die away, much to the detriment in many respects of true Christianity; for with its disappearance there passed away most of the arcana that contained the hidden meaning of the nature and work of Christ.

Platonic Christianity arose and flourished principally in the Church of Alexandria. As Christianity spread over Egypt, it embraced amongst its converts many of the philosophers of the school of Plato, the headquarters of which were at that time at Alexandria. Thus the Christianity of the Church of Africa became impregnated with ideas and doctrines borrowed from two independent sources—the philosophy of Plato, and the immemorial traditions of Egyptian theology. The tendency of the Platonistic influence was to invent and discuss transcendental theories, based upon the teaching of the renowned Greek sage; arguments were constantly arising upon the relations between the Father and the Son.

Meanwhile the essentially Egyptian notion of Trinities gradually incorporated itself into the metaphysical investigations of these Platonic Christians. For thousands of ages the Egyptian system of theology had represented the divine object of worship under varied personified attributes; and all these personified attributes were arranged in various trinities, in which the third member invariably "proceeded from the other two." Thus from Amun and Maut proceeded Khonso, from Osiris and Isis proceeded Horus, from Neph and Saté proceeded Anouki,—and so on.

During the third century of the Christian era, moreover, Plotinus, an Egyptian who had adopted the tenets of the Platonic school, assiduously taught at Alexandria a Trinity in accordance with the Platonic idea.

From this it will be seen how easily the notion of a Christian Trinity might be evolved by these Egyptian and Platonic adherents of the religion out of Christ's injunction to His disciples—"Go ye into all nations, baptising them into the name of the Father, and the Son, and the Holy Spirit,"—as well as from other passages in the New Testament.

But in order that there should be no mistake as to Scriptural authority, a spurious verse was deliberately forged and inserted into the Epistle of St John, affirming, "There are three that bear witness in heaven, the Father, the Word, and the Holy Ghost, and these three are one."

The doctrine of the Christian Trinity, then, was thus first conceived and fostered in the Church of Alexandria, which had become the metropolis of the eastern portion of Christendom, as Rome was of the western. Whilst the Alexandrian Church was thus engaged in formulating dogmas, discussing theories, and wrangling over theological controversies, the Western Church was occupied in a very different manner, and was struggling to acquire the temporal supremacy of the Roman world. Through innumerable trials, hindrances, and persecutions, but aided, on the other hand, by a combination of circumstances which it would be out of the question to discuss in a brief note like the present, the Christian organisation had gradually forced itself into a position of such importance that it was impossible for the Roman emperors to ignore it. By the close of the third century there was not a town or village in the Roman empire, and scarcely a legion in the Roman army, in which Christian organisations did not exist. It was the danger threatened to the imperial system by this state of things that brought about the terrible Diocletian persecution at the beginning of the fourth century. This persecution only served to fan the flame of the religion, and to increase the power which the Christian organisation was so rapidly acquiring. The consequence was that, after the death of Diocletian, when the empire was divided into two portions, eastern and western, over which two rival aspirants to the imperial throne assumed command, the Christians practically held the balance of power in their hands. Licinius, who was reigning over the eastern portion, was not astute enough to grasp this fact, and thinking to crush out the religion, he feebly attempted to revive the persecution of the Christians. But meanwhile there arose above the political horizon a shrewd, uncompromising, keen-sighted, but unscrupulous soldier, who was destined to exercise an overwhelming influence for evil as well as good upon the whole condition of Christianity. He measured with consummate accuracy the proportions of the Christian strength of the empire; and he saw that if he allied himself to the Christian party, he would probably be able to establish himself firmly, and without a rival, upon the throne of the whole Roman empire. He therefore determined openly to proclaim himself on the side of the Christians. He announced that he had been favoured with a miraculous vision; and marshalling his army under the banner of the cross, he advanced to the conquest of the empire. The events of war crowned his enterprise with success; he became established on the imperial throne as the first Christian Roman emperor, and his name has been handed down to posterity as that of Constantine the Great. Having completely routed his rival, he transferred the seat of empire to Byzantium, and called the city, after himself, by the name of Constantinople. The ecclesiastical historians have thrown a glamour of sanctity over the memory of Constantine; but the verdict of the impartial biographer is by no means of a favourable nature. His profession of Christianity was entirely dictated by motives of personal ambition; and though he was obliged to be true outwardly to those who had placed him in power, and who maintained him on his throne, he never conformed to the ceremonial rites of the Church until the close of a life characterised by much firmness, bravery, and foresight, but stained by acts of diabolical cruelty and murder, and by effeminate self-indulgence.

We have dwelt somewhat at length upon the career of Constantine, for to him the Church is mainly indebted for the Nicene Creed, and for the incorporation of the dogma of the Trinity into its authorised Articles of Faith.

Soon after he had become established upon the throne, a tempest broke out amongst his Christian subjects and supporters, which threatened to jeopardise his imperial position. The bishopric of Alexandria had become vacant, and there were two rival aspirants to the see. One was named Arius, the other Alexander. Both had a considerable number of supporters, but Alexander was appointed bishop. Thereupon he was vehemently accused of heresy by the partisans of Arius, and the latter in return was visited by an anathema. The points in dispute hinged upon the different philosophical aspects regarding the position of the Son in the new Trinitarian doctrine, which, as we have seen, had come to the front in the Church of Alexandria. From a theological controversy the quarrel threatened to assume the proportions of a political disturbance, and Constantine felt it imperatively necessary to interfere, and to put an end to the tumult. He therefore, having first ascertained the relative strength of the two parties in the Christian Church, determined to put down the weaker side, which consisted

APPENDIX II. 461

of the adherents of Arius ; and *having himself decreed beforehand how everything was to be settled*, he called together a general council of the Christian Church. This is the true historical account of the origin of the "Council of Nice," which was so called because it was held at the town of Nicæa, in Asia Minor. At this Council, held 325 A.D., the doctrine of the Trinity was first authoritatively put forward as a dogma of the Church, and the creed issued which has ever since been known by the name of the "Nicene Creed." The emperor enforced the decision of the Council by civil authority; he caused letters to be issued denouncing Arius, and threatening his followers with death.

Thus we see that for more than three hundred years the doctrine of the Trinity was unheard of as a necessary article of faith. The apostles and their followers had no conception of such a dogma ; and in all probability it would have entirely died away, like many other theories and doctrines which were broached, fought over, and abandoned during those earlier centuries of Christendom, if it had not been for the decisive action taken by the pseudo-Christian Roman emperor, Constantine.

Such being the case, the dogma can by no possibility be regarded as having a divinely inspired origin; and we are therefore free to discuss it as unreservedly as any other theory or idea that has ever been put forth by man in any age, or in any religion of the world.

So regarded, the doctrine must fall to the ground at once, for it is based on an utter absence of common-sense. The very attempts which have been made to explain it have only served to reveal more clearly how utterly opposed to reason it is ; and the climax of metaphysical nonsense was reached in the composition of the Athanasian Creed, which itself was not written, according to the latest modern authorities, till some three hundred years after the death of Athanasius, and was fraudulently palmed upon that great champion of Trinitarianism in order to invest it with the greater authority. It is not too much to say that scarcely a single follower of Christianity, lay or clerical, would venture in the present day to acknowledge his adhesion to that marvellous document, or would attempt to uphold the dogma of the Trinity, if it were not for the almost universal idea, founded as we have seen upon absolutely false premisses, that the doctrine itself, as well as the creed which endeavours to enunciate it, have a divinely inspired authority.

It is only fair that we should, before we close this note, state the principal passages of Scripture which are relied on by the Church in support of the doctrine.

We have already mentioned the baptismal form, "In the name of the Father, and of the Son, and of the Holy Spirit" (Matt.

xxviii. 19); and, as has been shown by Mr Oliphant, this clearly indicates God, humanity, and the uniting pneuma.

The passages out of St John's Gospel (14th, 15th, and 16th chapters) have also been fully treated of in the body of the book; and we will here merely remark that the Greek word παράκλητος has been quite erroneously translated "comforter," meaning literally "one called in to another's aid," and best rendered by the word "helper."

The doctrine of the Trinity is generally supposed to be indicated in the wording of St Paul's benediction to the Corinthians: "The grace of the Lord Jesus Christ, and the love of God, and the communion of the Holy Ghost, be with you all" (2 Cor. xiii. 14).

But here, again, the words have been adapted to the doctrine, not the doctrine asserted by the words, which are best translated thus: "The saving influence of the Lord Jesus Christ, and the love of God, and the common sharing of the holy pneuma, be with you all."

It was the most natural thing in the world for St Paul to pray that his disciples and friends might experience the saving influence of Christ, the love of God, and the sharing of the pneuma, these three things being all essentially bound up with human salvation; and yet they by no means necessarily imply the dogma of the Trinity.

Another text often quoted in support of the doctrine is "Holy, holy, holy, Lord God Almighty, which was, and is, and is to come" (Rev. iv. 8).

The word "Almighty" is the Greek παντοκράτωρ, which is taken from the Septuagint, where it is erroneously employed as a translation of שַׁדַּי, *Shaddai* (see *e.g.*, Job xxii. 17, 25; xxxii. 8; xxxiii. 4, &c., &c., in the Septuagint).

"Lord" is "Jehovah," יהוה, the import of which word is "male and female, two-in-one."

"God" is "El" (male principle of the Deity).

Hence the tersandus, "Holy, holy, holy, Lord God Almighty," is really "Holy, holy, holy, Jehovah El Shaddai"; that is, "Holy Jehovah, holy El, holy Shaddai"; or "Holy is God, in His divine biunity; holy is God, in His divine masculinity; holy is God, in His divine femininity."

These are really the only passages which even appear to favour the doctrine of the Trinity; and we have shown how consistent they are with entirely different constructions.

On the other hand, if the dogma had been true, it would have been one of such vital and fundamental importance, that Scriptural writers like, for instance, St Paul and St John, if they had known and believed in it, could hardly have failed to have stated and expounded it, in language that could not be misunderstood.

But as we have already pointed out, the doctrine was not invented until long after their decease.

The sooner Christendom realises its fallacy, and expunges it from her creeds, the better for herself and for the cause of truth.

NOTE S.

ON THE WORD "PNEUMA."

Chapter xx. page 327.

"*There is no possible excuse for the word πνεῦμα being sometimes translated 'spirit,' sometimes 'wind,' and sometimes 'ghost.'*"

The word πνεῦμα, "pneuma," occurs in the Greek Testament 305 times.

1. In 90 passages alone without definite article or qualifying epithet; when it means simply "pneuma," or "a pneuma."
2. In 49 passages without definite article, but with the qualifying epithet ἅγιον, "hagion"; when it means "holy pneuma," or "a holy pneuma."
3. In 127 passages with definite article, but without qualifying epithet; when it means "the pneuma," or "my," "his," "her," &c., "pneuma," as the context requires.
4. In 12 passages with both the definite article and qualifying epithet ἅγιον; when it means "the holy pneuma."
5. In 27 passages, in the more emphatic form, τὸ πνεῦμα τὸ ἅγιον; when it means "the pneuma which is holy."

As it is very important to distinguish between these various cases, we earnestly recommend the reader to examine in his English Bible each separate passage, and to note accordingly. For this purpose we will give the different passages under their several headings.

1. "Pneuma," or "a pneuma": Matt. x. 1; xii. 28; xxii. 43. Mark i. 23; iii. 30; v. 2; vii. 25; ix. 17. Luke i. 17, 80; ii. 40; iv. 18; ix. 55; xi. 26; xiii. 11; xxiv. 37, 39. John iii. 5, 6; iv. 23, 24. Acts v. 16; viii. 7; xvi. 16; xxiii. 8, 9. Rom. i. 4; ii. 29; vii. 6; viii. 1, 9, 14, 15; xi. 8. 1 Cor. ii. 4, 13; v. 3; vi. 17; vii. 34, 40; xii. 3, 13; xiv. 2, 32; xv. 45. 2 Cor. iii. 3, 6; vii. 1; xi. 4. Gal. iii. 3; iv. 29; v. 5, 16, 18, 25; vi. 1. Eph. ii. 18, 22; iv. 4; v. 18; vi. 18. Philip. i. 27; ii. 1; iii. 3. Col. i. 8. 2 Thess. ii. 2, 13. 1 Tim. iii. 16. 2 Tim. i. 7. Heb. i. 14; iv. 12; ix. 14; xii. 23. James ii. 26. 1 Peter i. 2; iii. 4, 18; iv. 6. 1 John iv. 1, 2, 3. Jude 19. Rev. i. 10; iv. 2; xi. 11; xvi. 13, 14; xvii. 3; xviii. 2; xxi. 10.

2. "Holy pneuma," or "a holy pneuma": Matt. i. 18, 20; iii. 11. Mark i. 8; xii. 36. Luke i. 15, 35, 41, 67; ii. 25; iii. 16; iv. 1; xi. 13. John i. 33; vii. 39; xx. 22. Acts i. 2, 5; ii. 4; iv. 8; vi. 3, 5; vii. 55; viii. 15, 17, 19; ix. 17; x. 38; xi. 16, 24; xiii. 9, 52; xix. 2. Rom. v. 5; ix. 1; xiv. 17; xv. 13. 1 Cor. xii. 3. 2 Cor. vi. 6. Eph. iii. 5. 1 Thess. i. 5, 6. 2 Tim. i. 14. Titus iii. 5. Heb. ii. 4; vi. 4. 1 Peter i. 12. 2 Peter i. 21. Jude 20.

3. "The pneuma," "my pneuma," "his pneuma," &c.: Matt. iii. 16; iv. 1; v. 3; viii. 16; xii. 18, 31; xxvi. 41. Mark i. 10, 12, 27; iii. 11; v. 8, 13; vi. 7; viii. 12; ix. 20, 25. Luke i. 47; ii. 27; iv. 14, 36; viii. 29, 55; ix. 42; x. 20, 21; xi. 24; xxiii. 46. John i. 32; iii. 6, 34; vi. 63; vii. 39; xi. 33; xiii. 21; xiv. 17; xv. 26; xvi. 13. Acts vi. 10; vii. 59; viii. 29; x. 19; xi. 12, 28; xvi. 7; xvii. 16; xviii. 25; xx. 22; xxi. 4. Rom. i. 9; viii. 2, 4, 10, 11, 16, 23, 26, 27; xii. 11; xv. 30. 1 Cor. ii. 10, 11, 12, 14; iii. 16; v. 3, 4, 5; vi. 11, 20; xii. 4, 8, 10; xiv. 14, 15, 16; xvi. 18. 2 Cor. i. 22; ii. 13; iii. 8, 17; iv. 13; v. 5; vii. 13; xii. 18. Gal. iii. 2, 5, 14; iv. 6; v. 17, 22; vi. 8, 18. Eph. ii. 2; iii. 16; iv. 3, 23; vi. 17. Philip. i. 19. Col. ii. 5. 1 Thess. v. 19, 23. 2 Thess. ii. 8. 1 Tim. iv. 1. 2 Tim. iv. 22. Philem. 25. Heb. xii. 9. James iv. 5. 1 Peter i. 11; iii. 19; iv. 14. 1 John iii. 24; iv. 1, 2, 6; v. 6, 8. Rev. ii. 7, 11, 17, 29; iii. 6, 13, 22; xiv. 13; xix. 10; xxii. 17.

4. "The holy pneuma": Matt. xxviii. 19. Luke xii. 10, 12. Acts i. 8; ii. 33, 38; ix. 31; x. 45; xv. 28; xvi. 6. 1 Cor. vi. 19. 2 Cor. xiii. 14.

5. "The pneuma which is holy": Matt. xii. 32. Mark iii. 29; xiii. 11. Luke ii. 26; iii. 22. Acts i. 16; v. 3, 32; vii. 51; viii. 18; x. 47; xi. 15; xiii. 2, 4; xv. 8; xix. 6; xx. 23, 28; xxi. 11; xxviii. 25. Eph. i. 13; iv. 30. 1 Thess. iv. 8. Heb. iii. 7; ix. 8; x. 15.

Now a considerable amount of confusion and vagueness has arisen in many of the above-named passages for want of a clear understanding of the meanings of the word πνεῦμα, "pneuma," as applicable to each individual passage.

This confusion has been vastly intensified by the unwarrantable use which the English translators and divines have made of the term "Holy Ghost." The word "Ghost," indeed, in its biblical sense, has become so inextricably interwoven with a dogma, and is so unnecessarily interpolated in the place of "pneuma" or "spirit," for the purpose of supporting that dogma, that it would be impossible to exhibit with sufficient clearness the original meaning of the different passages, if we continued to use that term. We therefore recommend our readers, once and for ever, to expunge from their vocabulary the expression "Holy Ghost."

The pneuma spoken of in the New Testament invariably signifies either the divine source from which all life, inspiration, and consciousness of sympneumatic influx originally proceeds, or else the emanation which proceeds, or has proceeded, from that divine source.

In other words, it signifies either (1) the Divine Feminine itself; (2) those created beings who have originally emanated from the Divine Feminine; or (3) the influence which proceeds from the Divine Feminine, and infuses itself into those created beings.

Now these created beings may be classified under four heads: (1) the bisexual beings of the primal universe; (2) the beings of the upper invisible portion of our own universe; (3) the beings of the lower invisible portion of our universe; (4) the inner and most sacred portion of man's own nature, commonly called his "spirit."

We may therefore divide the signification of the New Testament $\pi\nu\epsilon\hat{\upsilon}\mu\alpha$ into the following six classes:—

1. The Divine Feminine.
2. A bisexual sympneumatic being of the primal universe.
3. A being of the upper invisible portion of our present universe.
4. A being of the lower invisible portion.
5. The pneuma or spirit of a human being in the visible world.
6. The influence, or afflatus, which is infused into man's inner consciousness from a higher external source, and which is commonly called "inspiration" or "influx."

We say "from a higher external source," because, although this sympneumatic inspiration or influx proceeds, in the first instance, from the Deity, it descends through Christ to man's inner consciousness by the channels of intervening grades of created beings, from the highest rank of sympneumatic creatures of the primal universe, down to the invisible spirits of our upper spheres who immediately touch the inner pneuma of man.

It being our desire to make this most important subject thoroughly clear to our readers, we will once again take the 305 passages above quoted, and subdivide them into the six classes, named according to the signification to be attached to $\pi\nu\epsilon\hat{\upsilon}\mu\alpha$ in each case.

I. Where $\pi\nu\epsilon\hat{\upsilon}\mu\alpha$ refers to the Divine Feminine: Matt. iii. 16; xii. 18, 31, 32; xxviii. 19. Mark i. 10; iii. 29; xiii. 11. Luke iii. 22; xii. 10, 12. John i. 33; iii. 6, 8, 34; iv. 24; vii. 39; xiv. 17; xv. 26; xvi. 13. Acts i. 8, 16; ii. 33, 38; v. 3, 32; vii. 51; ix. 31; x. 38, 45, 47; xv. 8, 28; xx. 28. Rom. viii. 2, 11, 16, 23; xv. 30. 1 Cor. ii. 11, 13, 14; iii. 16; xii. 4.

2 Cor. i. 22; iii. 17; v. 5. Gal. iii. 14; v. 22. Eph. i. 13; iv. 30; vi. 17. Philip. iii. 3. 1 Thess. iv. 8. Heb. x. 15. Jas. iv. 5. 1 John v. 6. Rev. xxii. 17.

II. Where πνεῦμα refers to a bisexual sympneumatic being of the primal universe, the denizens of which are known under various names, such as angels, archangels, seraphim, spirits, &c.: Matt. i. 18, 20. Luke i. 15, 17, 35. Rom. i. 4; viii. 26. Gal. iv. 29. Heb. i. 14; xii. 9.

III. Where πνεῦμα refers to a being of the upper invisible portion of our universe: Luke xxiv. 37, 39. Acts xxiii. 8, 9. Heb. i. 14; xii. 9, 23.

IV. Where πνεῦμα refers to a being of the lower invisible portion of our universe: Matt. viii. 16; x. 1. Mark i. 23, 27; iii. 11, 30; v. 2, 8, 13; vi. 7; vii. 25; ix. 17, 20, 25. Luke iv. 36; viii. 29; ix. 42; x. 20; xi. 24, 26; xiii. 11. Acts v. 16; viii. 7; xvi. 16. Eph. ii. 2. 1 Peter iii. 19. Rev. xvi. 13, 14; xviii. 2.

V. Where πνεῦμα refers to the inner spirit of a human being living on the visible earth: Matt. v. 3; xxvi. 41. Mark viii. 12. Luke i. 47, 80; ii. 40; viii. 55; x. 21; xxiii. 46. John iv. 23, 24; vi. 63; xi. 33; xiii. 21. Acts vii. 59; xvii. 16; xviii. 25. Rom. i. 9; vii. 6; viii. 10, 11, 13, 16; xii. 11. 1 Cor. ii. 11, 13, 14; v. 3, 4, 5; vi. 17, 20; vii. 34; xiv. 2, 14, 15, 16; xv. 45; xvi. 18. 2 Cor. ii. 13; iv. 13; vii. 1, 13. Gal. v. 5, 16, 17, 22; vi. 1, 8, 18. Eph. ii. 22; iv. 3, 4, 23; vi. 18. Philip. i. 27; iii. 3. Col. i. 8; ii. 5. 1 Thess. v. 23. 2 Thess. ii. 2, 13. 1 Tim. iii. 16. 2 Tim. iv. 22. Philem. 25. Heb. iv. 12; xii. 9. James ii. 26. 1 Peter iii. 4, 18; iv. 6. Jude 19, 20.

VI. Where πνεῦμα refers to the influx, or afflatus, infused into man's inner consciousness from a higher external source, and which always partakes of the Divine Feminine character: Matt. iii. 11; iv. 1; xii. 28; xxii. 43. Mark i. 8, 12; xii. 36. Luke i. 41, 67; ii. 25, 26, 27; iii. 16; iv. 1, 14, 18; ix. 55; xi. 13. John iii. 5, 6; vi. 63; xx. 22. Acts i. 2, 5; ii. 4; iv. 8; vi. 3, 5, 10; vii. 55; viii. 15, 17, 18, 19, 29; ix. 17; x. 19; xi. 12, 15, 16, 24, 28; xiii. 2, 4, 9, 52; xvi. 6, 7; xix. 2, 6; xx. 22, 23; xxi. 4, 11; xxviii. 25. Rom. ii. 29; v. 5; viii. 4, 5, 9, 14, 15; ix. 1; xi. 8; xiv. 17; xv. 13. 1 Cor. ii. 4, 10, 12; vi. 11, 19; vii. 40; xii. 3, 7, 8, 10, 13; xiv. 1, 32. 2 Cor. iii. 3, 6, 8; iv. 13; xi. 4; xiii. 14. Gal. iii. 2, 3, 5; iv. 6; v. 18, 25. Eph. ii. 18; iii. 5, 16; v. 18. Philip. i. 19; ii. 1. 1 Thess. i. 5, 6; v. 19. 2 Thess. ii. 8. 1 Tim. iv. 1. 2 Tim. i. 7, 14. Titus iii. 5. Heb. ii. 4; iii. 7; vi. 4; ix. 8, 14. 1 Peter i. 2, 11, 12; iv. 14. 2 Peter i. 21. 1 John iii. 24; iv. 1, 2, 3. Rev. i. 10; ii. 7, 11, 17, 29; iii. 6, 13, 22; iv. 2; xi. 11; xiv. 13; xvii. 3; xix. 10; xxi. 10.

This note would not be complete without some extracts *in extenso* from the New Testament, where the passages have become especially obscured, owing to an incorrect rendering of the original into English.

We will therefore ask the reader to pay particular attention to the following passages, which we have endeavoured to render with strict accuracy. They should be compared with the Authorised Version, as well as with the Revised, for the sake of a clear apprehension of their true meaning as distinguished from that which dogma has assigned to them.

Matt. xii. 28: "If I cast out the demons by a divine influx, then the kingdom of God has overtaken you."

Luke i. 35: "A holy pneuma shall come upon thee, and a force of a very high being shall overshadow thee; wherefore also the offspring, being holy, shall be called a son of God."

Luke ii. 25: "And a divine influx was upon him; and it had been revealed to him by the divine influx, that he should not see death, before he had seen the Lord's Christ. And he came under the influx into the temple."

Luke ix. 54, 55: "And when His disciples James and John saw this, they said, Lord, wilt thou that we command fire to come down from heaven and consume them, as Elijah did? But He turned, and rebuked them, and said, Ye know not under what kind of an influx ye are."

The meaning of Christ here was, that the influx which prompted the suggestion of His two disciples was of an infernal nature, instead of being, as they imagined, from a high and holy source.

Luke xi. 13: "How much more shall your heavenly Father give a divine influx to them that seek Him?"

John iii. 5-8: "Verily, verily, I say unto you, Unless a man has been born of water and pneuma, he cannot enter into the kingdom of God. That which has been born of the flesh is flesh; and that which has been born of the pneuma is pneuma. Do not be surprised, that I said to you, You must be born from above. The pneuma operates wherever it wills; and you hear its voice, but do not know whence it comes, and whither it leads; thus is every one who has been born of the pneuma."

This very important passage has been entirely misunderstood, and grave errors of doctrine have been founded upon it, owing to several gross inaccuracies in the Authorised Translation.

In the first place, ἄνωθεν, as every Greek scholar knows, simply means "from above"—*i.e.*, from a higher source; and it is palpably erroneous to translate it "again." Thus "you must be born again," is really "you must be born from above."

Secondly, the word translated "Spirit" in one place, "spirit" in another, and "wind" in another, is all one word; and that one word is πνεῦμα, "pneuma." The word πνεώ, translated "blow," is really "breathe"; or, since it is from the same root as πνεῦμα, means the operation of the pneuma, which in outward manifestation is after the nature of breathing.

Again, φωνή, translated "sound," signifies more properly "voice"; and lastly, ὑπάγει, rendered "goeth," is really "leads."

Thus the meaning of Christ's explanation to Nicodemus is this. There are certain conditions on which a human being must enter before he can become partaker of the salvation which Christ came to bring. The entrance on these conditions he calls a birth; and he describes it as "a birth from above," or "a birth into the pneuma." He says that the analogy is very exact between the ordinary fleshly birth into the flesh, and the pneumatic birth into the pneuma. He then goes on to describe the sensational experiences which will follow the birth into pneumatic life. He says that the pneuma operates according to its will; that when it breathes into a person, that person becomes distinctly conscious of its presence, feels its motions, and hears its voice within him, prompting him with its suggestions. He cannot tell from whence this presence, this motion, this suggesting voice, comes; nor does he at all know to what it will lead him, if he follows its promptings. All he knows is, that there it is,—that the suggestion is distinctly pneumatic "from above," and that he must instantly and implicitly obey it.

"Thus is every one who has been born of the pneuma," says Christ; or, in other words, "This will be found to be the experience of all who shall have entered into sympneumatic conditions."

It will be the universal testimony of all who have already entered upon these conditions, or who shall enter upon them in the future, that Christ's description to Nicodemus was accurate and exact in every particular.

Nor can His description be adequately explained in any other way.

It was doubtless the want of this pneumatic experience on the part of our translators which led them to imagine that Christ, when describing to Nicodemus the action of the pneuma, was intending to introduce a popular illustration from the phenomenon of the wind, as an analogy of some vague spiritual process to which it is difficult to see how the illustration applies. See Postscript at the end of the Appendix.

John xx. 22: "He breathed upon them, and saith to them, Receive a holy influx."

Acts ii. 4: "They were all filled with a holy influx." The term ἅγιον, "holy," so often used in connection with pneuma, when it is equivalent to influx, is employed to designate the source from whence it comes, as well as the quality of which it partakes; in order to distinguish it from the unholy or unclean influx which comes from the lower invisible world.

Acts viii. 17-19: "They laid their hands on them, and they received a holy influx. Now Simon, having observed that the influx which was holy was imparted through the imposition of the hands of the apostles, offered them money, saying, Give me also this authority, that upon whomsoever I may lay my hands, he may receive a holy influx."

Acts x. 38: "Jesus, who was from Nazareth, whom God anointed with a holy pneuma and with a force."

Acts xix. 2, 6: "Having found certain disciples, he said to them, Did you, on accepting the faith, receive a holy influx? And they said to him, Nay, not even did we hear if there be such a thing as a holy influx. . . . And Paul having laid his hands on them, the influx which was holy came upon them, and they spake with tongues, and expounded."

1 Cor. ii. 13: "Which things also we speak, not in words taught by human wisdom, but in words taught by pneumatic influx; putting pneumatic influxes together, and comparing them one with another."

St Paul here distinctly disclaims for the teacher of Christ's religion the mere intellectual knowledge which is drawn from human sources of wisdom, and asserts for him an internal afflatus and direction; though, at the same time, he admits the necessity and importance of correcting the human liability to mistake by comparing different influxes, or, as expressed elsewhere in the New Testament, by "trying the influxes, whether they be of God." It is so easy and common for the evil ones to simulate a divine influx, that it is necessary to be constantly on the watch so as to detect and avoid a false afflatus.

1 Cor. vii. 40: "She is more blessed, if she remain thus, in my opinion; and I think that I have also a divine influx on the matter."

1 Cor. xv. 44, 45: "There is a psychic body, and there is a pneumatic body. Thus also it has been written: The first man Adam reached as far as a living psyche, the last Adam as far as a life-giving pneuma."

Gal. iii. 3: "Having entered upon the life of the pneuma, will ye end in going back to the life of the flesh?"

Gal. v. 16, 18: "Go about under the influence of the pneuma, that ye may not perform the desire of the flesh. For the flesh cherishes desires in opposition to the pneuma, and the pneuma in opposition to the flesh; and these are antagonistic to each other, in order that ye may not do those things which ye may naturally desire. But if ye be guided by the pneuma, ye are above earthly law."

That is, the promptings of the pneuma will render you independent of earthly law, since you will be obedient to the higher divine law of the pneuma.

1 Thess. v. 19 : "Do not stifle the influx of the pneuma."

That is, when you feel the promptings of the pneumatic voice within you, beware of hesitating or refusing to obey its impulse.

Heb. vi. 4-6 : "As regards those who have been once thoroughly enlightened, and who have experienced the gift which is from above, and have been made partakers of the divine pneuma, and have consciously felt a helpful voice from God, and the forces of an age yet to come, and have fallen away, it is impossible to raise them up anew again to a change of mind, since they are crucifying afresh to themselves the Son of God, and putting Him to an open shame."

2 Pet. i. 21 : "Not by a man's own impulse was a prophecy ever framed; but holy men of God spake under the influx of a holy pneuma."

Jude 19 : "These are they who banish themselves, being psychic, having no pneuma."

What the apostle here means is, that since the pneuma is the seat of immortal life, those who entirely devote themselves to an existence no deeper than that of the psyche, practically extinguish within themselves the pneuma, and so cut themselves off from the higher life of immortality.

This, however, can only be as regards the conscious continuity of individual existence; the pneuma is of the essence of the Deity, and therefore is, in its essential principle, immortal, and can never perish.

NOTE T.

ON THE RESTORATION OF TRUE CHRISTIANITY.

Chapter xxii. page 372.

"*It was the unfaithfulness of the early Christian Church which healed the deadly wound.*"

The impulse which led to the reformation of Christendom three hundred years ago, was undoubtedly a good and true one. The abominations, which had resulted from the utter inversion of true Christianity throughout the entire pale of Christendom, had become so flagrant and outrageous, that the only wonder is that men should have endured it so long.

The great fault of the Reformation, however, and that which rendered its efforts practically futile, was, that those who sought thus to restore the Church to purity did not probe the evil deep enough, or trace the stream to its very source. They merely went back to the fourth century; they ought to have gone back to Christ. Whilst striving, therefore, to clear away the corrupting accretions which had defiled the truth, they left untouched the essence of the pollution. Thus, cherishing such fundamental errors as the dogma of the Trinity, the doctrine of propitiatory sacrifice, the infallible inspiration of the Bible, and so forth, they failed altogether in restoring to mankind the true religion which Christ came to bring.

They removed, it is true, a great deal of the overlying mud, but they did not bring to light the "pearl of great price" which remained buried beneath the accretion.

That great work has been reserved for the present generation; and with its reappearance we may hope for the restitution of Christ's saving power.

It may be well to point out here that, unlike the later creeds, the original record of Christian faith, contained in what is known as "The Apostles' Creed," may still be held as teaching nothing which is not, if rightly understood, absolutely and entirely true. It has been divided by the Church for purposes of dogma into three separate sections; but as originally written it was in a single paragraph.

"I believe in God the Father Almighty, Maker of heaven and earth" (that is, "I believe in God, the Father-Mother"). Almighty is always equivalent to Shaddai, the Divine Feminine, "Maker of the invisible and visible worlds, and in Jesus Christ His only Son" (that is, the only biune man), "who was conceived of a holy pneuma, born of the Virgin Mary, suffered under Pontius Pilate, was crucified dead and buried; He descended into hell" (*i.e.*, went down into the lower region of the invisible world); "the third day He rose again from the dead" (*i.e.*, to sow the seed of His pneumatic body on earth); "He ascended into heaven" (*i.e.*, into the upper region of the invisible world); "He sitteth at the right hand of God the Father-Mother" (*i.e.*, He is exalted above all as being the express image of the biune God); "from thence He shall come again at the end of the age, to judge the quick and the dead" (*i.e.*, to separate between, or to bring about the crisis, as the Greek word translated "judge" means, between the quick —*i.e.*, those who accept the quickening pneuma,—and the dead— *i.e.*, those who reject it). "I believe in the holy pneuma; the holy universal ecclesia" (*i.e.*, the holy gathering together, as *ecclesia* means, of those who accept Him from universal mankind); "the common sharing of saints" (*i.e.*, in the pneuma); "the resurrection of the body" (*i.e.*, the pneumatic body); "and the life everlasting. Amen."

To every one of these statements we give in our hearty and loyal allegiance; and to the truths therein set forth we confidently look for the regeneration of the human race.

POSTSCRIPT.

Since writing the above notes, an incident has occurred in the writer's experience, which it appears to him incumbent to relate, inasmuch as it illustrates the action of the "pneuma," as described in Note S, page 463, *apropos* of Christ's explanation to Nicodemus. At the same time, it affords another practical instance of the respiratory sensitiveness described in Note O, page 445.

On Friday, December 16, 1887, the writer was asked to visit two poor persons living next door to each other, both of whom were seriously ill. The one case was that of a woman, about sixty years of age, who had been confined to her bed for ten days, quite unable to move, and suffering severely from acute pain at the base of the spine and in the loins. The other was that of a man, sixty-five years old, who had a sharp attack of bronchitis. Having applied the ordinary natural remedies to suit each case, the writer returned home. About 5 A.M. on the following morning he was awakened from sleep by a sensation of the respiratory motion, which he has learnt to recognise distinctly as a sympneumatic descent. Opening himself to the voice of the pneuma, he became aware of the intimation that he was to rise at once and visit the two patients. What was to be the object of his visit he did not know; but the command was clear, and he immediately followed it. On entering the woman's house, he found her in much the same state as on the previous day, and still unable to move through pain. He told her that he felt he had been divinely sent to assist her cure, and she must implicitly obey whatever he ordered her to do. He then passed his left hand gently down her back, at the same time taking her right hand in his. As soon as he touched the small of the back, he felt the strange vibratory motion affecting his whole system, and his inner consciousness became impressed with the conviction that he was to tell her to get up immediately and walk about. Accordingly, he did so; and at once, to her own astonishment and that of the other persons present, she rose from the ground, on which she had been lying, and guided by his right hand, which still retained its hold of hers, she walked up and down the room several times without the slightest effort or sensation of pain. She declared herself feeling quite well, and expressed a desire to go to work. However, he advised her to keep quiet and warm, and not to be surprised if the pain returned in a measure again.

He then went to the house of the other patient, quite prepared to do the same for him if the indications of the pneuma directed him. No sooner, however, had he taken his hand than he felt all influx leave him, and he knew that this case was not one in which he was intended to act spiritually. He was therefore obliged to content himself with administering ordinary injunctions, and offering words of sympathy and encouragement.

The next day—Sunday, December 18—he visited both patients. He found the woman lying on the ground as before, and she had had a slight, but only slight, return of her former pain. This time she rose without his assistance when he ordered her to do so; and after walking about the room for a little while, she again felt relieved entirely.

The man was evidently much worse, and again the writer could feel no influx to aid him. The following day, Monday the 19th, the woman was perfectly well and about her ordinary work; and the man was dead.

THE END.

PRINTED BY WILLIAM BLACKWOOD AND SONS.

www.ingramcontent.com/pod-product-compliance
Lightning Source LLC
Chambersburg PA
CBHW051231300426
44114CB00011B/697